Minorities within Minorities

Equality, Rights and Diversity

Edited by

Avigail Eisenberg and Jeff Spinner-Halev

CAMBRIDGE
UNIVERSITY PRESS

PUBLISHED BY THE PRESS SYNDICATE OF THE UNIVERSITY OF CAMBRIDGE
The Pitt Building, Trumpington Street, Cambridge, United Kingdom

CAMBRIDGE UNIVERSITY PRESS
The Edinburgh Building, Cambridge, CB2 2RU, UK
40 West 20th Street, New York, NY 10011–4211, USA
477 Williamstown Road, Port Melbourne, VIC 3207, Australia
Ruiz de Alarcón 13, 28014 Madrid, Spain
Dock House, The Waterfront, Cape Town 8001, South Africa

http://www.cambridge.org

First published 2005

Printed in the United Kingdom at the University Press, Cambridge

Typeface Plantin 10/12 pt.   *System* LATEX 2$_\varepsilon$ [TB]

A catalogue record for this book is available from the British Library

Library of Congress Cataloguing-in-Publication data
Minorities within minorities: equality, rights, and diversity / edited by
Avigail Eisenberg and Jeff Spinner-Halev.
      p.   cm.
Includes bibliographical references and index.
ISBN 0 521 84314 6 – ISBN 0 521 60394 3 (pbk.)
1. Multiculturalism.   2. Minorities.   3. Minorities – Civil rights.   4. Social
groups.   5. Social conflict.   6. Equality.   I. Eisenberg, Avigail I., 1962–
II. Spinner-Halev, Jeff.

HM1271.M456   2004
323.1 – dc22   2004048199

ISBN 0 521 84314 6 hardback
ISBN 0 521 60394 3 paperback

As this book manuscript was being prepared, Susan Moller Okin tragically passed away. Susan was a pioneering feminist political theorist whose landmark books taught her colleagues and many students to think differently about political theory. We will miss her.

Contents

Notes on contributors

VEIT BADER is a Professor of Social and Political Philosophy and of Sociology at the University of Amsterdam. He is the author of several books and many articles on equality, citizenship and pluralism. He is currently finishing a book on *Religious Diversity and Associative Democracy*.

MONIQUE DEVEAUX is an Associate Professor of Political Science at William College. Most recently, she is author of *Cultural Pluralism and Dilemmas of Justice* (Cornell, 2000).

AVIGAIL EISENBERG is an Associate Professor of Political Science at the University of Victoria in Canada. She is author of *Reconstructing Political Pluralism* (SUNY, 1995), co-editor of *Painting the Maple: Essays on Race, Gender and the Construction of Canada* (UBC, 1998) as well as several articles on accommodating multinationalism and multiculturalism in liberal states.

CINDY HOLDER is Assistant Professor of Philosophy at the University of Victoria. She is the author of several articles on group rights, the most recent of which is a co-authored piece entitled "Indigenous Rights and Multicultural Citizenship" in the *Human Rights Quarterly (2002)*.

JACOB T. LEVY is Assistant Professor of Political Science at the University of Chicago. He is the author of *The Multiculturalism of Fear* (Oxford, 2000) and a number of articles and chapters on multiculturalism and nationalism, the rights of indigenous peoples, language rights and related topics. He is currently writing on the tension between rationalist and pluralist conceptions of liberalism, and associated topics in the history of liberal and constitutionalist thought. His work on the chapter in this volume was partially supported with an Earhart Foundation Fellowship.

GURPREET MAHAJAN is Professor of Political Science at Jawaharlal Nehru University. She has edited and written several volumes on multiculturalism, including *Identities & Rights: Aspects of Liberal Democracy in India* (Oxford, 1998) and *The Multicultural Path: Issues of Diversity and Discrimination in Democracy* (Sage, 2002).

MARGARET MOORE is Associate Professor in the Political Studies Department at Queen's University (Canada). She is the author of *Foundations of Liberalism* (Oxford, 1993) and *The Ethics of Nationalism* (Oxford, 2001).

SUSAN MOLLER OKIN was Professor of Political Science and Marta Sutton Weeks Professor of Ethics in Society at Stanford University. She was the author of *Is Multiculturalism Bad for Women?* (Princeton, 1999), *Women in Western Political Thought* (Princeton, 1979) and *Justice, Gender and the Family* (Basic Books, 1989).

ALAN PATTEN is Associate Professor of Political Science at McGill University. He is author of *Hegel's Idea of Freedom* (Oxford, 1999) and co-editor of *Political Theory and Language Rights* (Oxford, 2003) and has also written several articles on multinationalism and multilingualism.

ANNE PHILLIPS is Professor of Gender Theory in the Gender Institute and Department of Government at the London School of Economics. Among her many books are *Engendering Democracy* (Polity Press, 1991), *The Politics of Presence* (Oxford, 1995) and *Which Equalities Matter?* (Polity, 1999).

ROB REICH is Assistant Professor of Political Science and Ethics in Society at Stanford University. He is the author of *Bridging Liberalism and Multiculturalism in American Education* (Chicago, 2002).

OONAGH REITMAN is a research fellow in the Gender Institute at the London School of Economics. Her research centers on law and public administration in culturally diverse societies, focusing on the interplay between state law and the informal and transnational regulatory practices of some minorities, particularly in the context of divorce. She is completing a manuscript entitled *Regulating Identity: Divorce, Diaspora Style*.

JEFF SPINNER-HALEV is the Schlesinger Professor of Political Science at the University of Nebraska. He is the author of *The Boundaries of Citizenship: Race, Ethnicity and Nationality in the Liberal State* and *Surviving Diversity: Religion and Democratic Citizenship*. He has been a Laurance S. Rockefeller Visiting Fellow at the Center for Human Values at Princeton University, and a Lady Davis Fellow and a Fellow at the Institute for Advanced Studies at the Hebrew University of Jerusalem.

LUCAS SWAINE is Assistant Professor and Rockefeller Scholar in the Department of Government at Dartmouth College. He was previously the Gifford Research Fellow at the University of St. Andrews in Scotland. He has published articles in such journals as *Ethics* and *History of Political Thought*, and currently is working on a book on liberalism, theocracy and liberty of conscience.

DANIEL WEINSTOCK holds a Canada Research Chair in Ethics and Political Philosophy at the Université de Montréal. He has published numerous articles on issues such as deliberative democracy, minority rights, and constitutionalism in divided societies. His present writing projects deal with issues such as the constraints on democratic deliberation in times of war, the ethical foundations of language policy in multilingual societies, and the political philosophy of the family.

MELISSA WILLIAMS is Associate Professor of Political Science at the University of Toronto. She is author of *Voice, Trust and Memory: Marginalized Groups and the Failings of Liberal Representation* (Princeton, 1998). She is Editor of *NOMOS, the Yearbook of the American Society for Political Legal Philosophy*, and was co-editor of *Identity, Rights, and Constitutional Transformation* (Ashgate, 1999).

Acknowledgements

We are grateful to the Department of Political Science and the Human Rights and Human Diversity Program at the University of Nebraska for providing funding for a conference on Minorities within Minorities in October 2002. We would also like to acknowledge the helpful advice that James Bohman, Idil Boran, Suzanne Dovi, Geoffrey Brahm Levey and Jacob Levy gave to several conference participants in their role as discussants.

We wish to thank the Social Sciences and Humanities Research Council of Canada for providing resources that helped in the preparation of the manuscript. We are grateful to Colin Macleod for his advice on this project and on the preparation of the manuscript. We are also grateful to Theresa Gerritsen for her excellent research assistance in preparing the manuscript. Two anonymous reviewers for Cambridge University Press provided helpful suggestions on how to revise the text for the better, and John Haslam of Cambridge University Press was unfailing in his good advice and encouragement.

We thank the University of Chicago Press for granting permission to reprint a revised version of chapter 3 from Rob Reich's book *Bridging Liberalism and Multiculturalism in American Education* (Chicago: University of Chicago Press, 2002).

We thank Sage Publications for granting permission to reprint a revised version of Monique Deveaux, "A Deliberative Approach to Conflicts of Culture," *Political Theory*, vol. 31, no. 6, December 2003, pp. 780–807.

We thank Lucas Swaine for granting permission to reprint "A Liberalism of Conscience," *Journal of Political Philosophy*, vol. 11, no. 4, December 2003, pp. 369–91.

Introduction

Avigail Eisenberg and Jeff Spinner-Halev

Groups have had a role in liberalism since its inception. John Locke argued that churches ought to be voluntary associations, with members freely choosing to join or leave. Tocqueville celebrated the associations he found in America, contending that they were a crucial site where citizens learn democratic virtues. James Madison argued that factions were an important element in maintaining democratic freedom. The existence of factions, along with the protection of freedom of association, ensured that no enduring majority would dominate over any minority because, in order to advance their interests, factions constantly form and re-form alliances with other factions. As Robert Dahl put it some years later, democratic governance was a matter, not of majority rule, but of "minorities rule" (Dahl 1956: 132). The groups celebrated by these classical liberals are open-ended: people presumably join or leave them as they please.

In contrast, ascriptive groups – groups whose membership is not open-ended, such as racial, ethnic, and sometimes national groups – were traditionally not a focal point of liberal thinking until the late 1980s. At that time, the attraction of communitarian thinking, the increased political activism in the United States of religious conservatives, and the rise of nationalism in Eastern Europe after the fall of the Berlin wall in 1989, all contributed to an increased interest in the role that ascriptive groups play in liberal theory and practice. Since then, political theorists have become increasingly interested in a whole range of groups, in the group-based nature of society, in the status of groups rights, and in the sorts of rights groups should be granted.

Both the success of groups at attaining autonomy and the more recent attention directed at the justness of their claims, often in the name of freedom or the protection of their identity, have given rise to a crucial question: what happens to individuals or minorities within protected minorities who find that their community discriminates against them? Traditional family law systems often discriminate against women. Indigenous groups have been criticized for discriminating against women and, in some cases, Christians. Religious groups, too, have been accused of discriminating against women and homosexuals and mistreating children. Many groups prize group obedience and loyalty over independent thinking and thereby have been accused of damaging individual autonomy in a way that jeopardizes the ability of some members, particularly children, to choose the sort of life they want to lead. These issues – the issues raised by minorities within minorities – are the focus of this volume. To what extent should minorities be shielded from majority laws whose aim is to protect individual rights, but whose effect is also to interfere with practices, values and traditions which are integral to minority communities? To what extent and under what circumstances should the liberal state accommodate minority groups which discriminate or appear to mistreat some of their own members? Under what circumstances ought the state to interfere in the internal affairs of a protected minority group when such discrimination takes place? And does it make a difference that some of these minorities have been oppressed by state interference in the past?

These are new issues for political theorists, but in practice most countries have accommodated cultural and religious minorities for decades or even centuries. Many indigenous peoples around the world enjoy limited forms of self-government. Some formerly colonized peoples have systems of compulsory religious or tribal family law that apply only to their communities. Religious minorities often enjoy special rights that exempt them from general laws. National and linguistic minorities sometimes also enjoy special rights that assist them in maintaining their language or culture to protect them from the pressures of assimilation. For other groups, the protections offered by the right to freedom of association, which is guaranteed by most liberal constitutions, is sufficient to ensure their accommodation.

The reasons that have motivated countries to institute minority accommodation vary significantly. In some places, minority accommodation is based on historical arrangements, such as the accommodation of linguistic minorities in Belgium and Canada. Sometimes, group rights are recognized in an effort to correct past injustices, as in recent arguments for the expansion of the rights of indigenous peoples. Other times, identity claims are at work: Catalonia and Scotland have each made arguments for more autonomy as a means to help preserve their identity. Economic concerns can also be at play. In British Columbia, for example, the majority's motivation to negotiate indigenous land claims is driven partly by the need to address investor uncertainty about the costs of development in the absence of settled treaties. Colonialism has also left its mark on group rights. As Susan Okin points out in her essay in this volume, the British codified and institutionalized traditional family law systems within their colonies partly as a means to have a freer hand in westernizing contract law – the law they really cared about. Once these colonies became free states, they often kept these laws out of a need to keep peace, since minorities often cling to their family laws as a safeguard against assimilation into the larger culture. And sometimes accommodation is the result of extending to communities of new immigrants, or immigrants whose freedoms were previously restricted, such as Sikhs or Muslims, the established values of tolerance and individual rights which have been enjoyed by the mainstream within the state. Extending rights to these new groups has given rise to new and unanticipated challenges to the traditional liberal concepts of freedom of association and freedom of religion.

Many minority groups have also become more assertive in demanding autonomy or state assistance to preserve their identity. Ignoring these demands all too easily leads to violence and instability. This was made especially apparent in the last thirty years, when the rise of ethno-national conflict, following the collapse of the Soviet Union, led to concerted efforts, within and between nation states, to renew or reinvent legal and political arrangements for accommodating ethnic and national minorities. As is often the case, attempts to solve problems in one part of the world spark demands in other parts to revisit arrangements for the accommodation of minorities and to recognize new groups claiming minority rights. These demands have led to redrawing national boundaries, such as that between the Czech Republic and Slovakia, or, after considerable bloodshed, in the Balkans. It has led to rethinking and reframing the purposes of federalism in Canada, in Belgium and in Spain. It has required that numerous countries revisit the meaning of freedom of religion and, in this context, review the extent to which their public institutions can or ought to accommodate religious minorities. It has also required that numerous states rethink and revise their legal and political relations to indigenous peoples and develop a means of accommodating forms of internal self-determination.

As minority groups have become more vocal in demanding some form of accommodation, political theorists have increasingly taken an interest in issues raised by both voluntary and ascriptive minority groups. Yet few have paid much attention to the problem of minorities within minorities. This might seem surprising since the nature and limits of minority accommodation have been the focus of so much attention, especially in liberal political thought. But for the most part, efforts to develop reasons why political relations between mainstream majorities and minorities ought to be renegotiated tend to present contending interests as though they are uncontroversial within the groups that hold them. The issue of minorities within minorities is left unaddressed.

Perhaps nowhere is this made more evident than in the scholarship which viewed the problem in terms of "individual vs. collective rights" and which focused, for the most part, on whether minorities were threatened by the individualism of the liberal majority (Glazer 1983; Kymlicka 1995: ch. 3). One consequence of viewing the problem as a competition between fundamental values of the majority and minority communities is that the complex relations within minority groups were largely ignored. Instead, most arguments either took for granted the fact that individual rights were culturally alien to minority groups by focusing on groups for whom this assumption seemed to fit, such as indigenous peoples (see e.g. Svensson 1979; Turpel 1989–90), or argued that individual rights were a means by which the solidarity of minorities was easily sabotaged (see e.g. Kukathas 1992a; McDonald 1991; Sandel 1990), as was typical of many discussions of insular minorities such as the Amish, Hutterites or Doukabours.[1] In both ways, the putative cultural gulf between liberal and illiberal groups tended to obfuscate the complex politics and pluralism of interests within minority communities.

Multicultural theories of citizenship offer another set of principles and options to consider in relation to why and how minorities ought to be accommodated, which are more complex than the simple "individual vs. collective rights" formula. But for the most part these theories also do not tackle the questions related to minorities within minorities. At best, multiculturalists focus on whether measures for group-based accommodation could justifiably violate individual rights. For example, Will Kymlicka argues that strong group-based protections should not be secured at the price of violating rights fundamental to individual well-being. According to Kymlicka, the aim of multicultural citizenship and minority rights is to provide groups with *external protections* and not to protect minorities in imposing *internal restrictions* on their members (1995: ch. 3). This distinction is helpful in highlighting the fact that often at stake in protecting minority rights is the internal relations within minority groups; protecting minorities from mainstream influences (external protections) potentially has the effect of altering relations internal to the community.

While the distinction between external protections and internal restrictions raises the issue of minorities within minorities, it provides limited

---

[1] For example, most discussions in political theory of the Amish focus on the famous case of *Wisconsin* v. *Yoder* which is helpful mainly in highlighting the zero-sum nature of individual and collective interests. See, in particular, the treatment of this case in Arneson and Shapiro 1996 and Sandel 1990. Another good example of a similar phenomenon is *Hofer v Hofer* which involves the communal property ownership in Hutterite communities in Canada. The case is employed mainly in discussions that seek to highlight the "individual versus collective rights" dilemma of minority–majority values. See Janzen 1990 and Kymlicka 1995: 158–63.

practical guidance. Partly this is because Kymlicka is unwilling to argue that the state must restrict national minorities which seek to impose internal restrictions on their members; he merely suggests that these groups should not impose internal restrictions, a suggestion with which he hopes they agree.[2] Beyond this issue of imposition, it is also the case that external protections and internal restrictions cannot be so easily separated. The external protections that minority groups seek are valuable because they allow minorities more power to direct their own affairs, and this usually includes interpreting and imposing traditions and practices on their members – sometimes practices that are oppressive and discriminatory against some of their members. If minority groups were indeed prohibited from imposing internal restrictions on the rights of their members, then drawn into question would be their community rules and practices about membership, governance and participation, marriage and divorce, the distribution of property, and the education of children, all of which are areas of social life over which minorities want some control and protection from the *external* influence of mainstream practices.

The themes

This volume brings together essays about minorities within minorities from key contributors to the debates about multiculturalism in Canada, the United States, Europe and India. The aim of the collection is to address conflicting demands that arise in relation to minorities within minorities. As the contributions to this volume show, there are many different types of minorities, including religious, national, indigenous linguistic, racial and ethnic minorities, and many different types of "minorities within," including women, children, gay men and lesbians, religious dissenters and linguistic minorities within minorities. The sorts of conflicts examined here also implicate different historical, economic and other contextual considerations, some of which are directly relevant to the sort of resolutions that appear to be attractive or acceptable in any given case. The conflict of minorities within minorities poses particularly taxing problems for political theorists. While no contribution to this volume sets out directly to address the potential gulf between theory and practice, many of the essays indirectly address this tension by discussing case studies and showing how political principles and values work in practice to resolve or exacerbate conflicts. The aim, then, is not to find a definitive resolution to all such conflicts, but to explain the ways in

[2] For a trenchant criticism of the division between internal and external restrictions, see Kukathas 2003: ch. 6.

which such conflicts have arisen in a variety of settings and the resources that liberal and democratic theory contain to help resolve these conflicts.

The essays differ in how they view the main problem, in the considerations they view as central to resolving conflicts that involve minorities within minorities, and in the main values of democratic and liberal governance through which they have chosen to explore the conflict. The main themes that inform these essays are toleration, equality, individual autonomy, self-determination and democracy.

Toleration

John Locke, John Milton and other early liberals invoked toleration partly as a means to guide the ways in which different communities can coexist peacefully and justly. People were killing each other over religion and one solution was to persuade people to tolerate religious differences. Yet, many recent liberals have not put toleration at the center stage of liberalism. Amy Gutmann argues that it is individual autonomy, not tolerance, that has primacy in relation to the education of children from insular groups (Gutmann 1995). Eamonn Callan argues that autonomy should be a key aspect of education in liberal democracy (Callan 1997). Steve Macedo agrees, and argues that autonomy is a key liberal virtue (Macedo 1990; 2000). Kymlicka argues that tolerance is dependent on autonomy; although groups should be tolerated, these groups ought to respect the individual autonomy of their members (Kymlicka 1995: 155).

Melissa Williams argues in this volume that, while the ideals of individual autonomy, equality and peace can all lead to tolerance, they all flag limits to toleration as well. Autonomy means allowing people to live as they like. But when people decide to live together in a certain way, their way of life may in fact undermine the autonomy of some members within their group. The same is true for equality: equality may require that minorities be protected from assimilation, but protected groups may seek to undermine the equality of their members. Williams argues that many contemporary liberal theorists, following the logic of equality and freedom, are led down the path of interference in minorities. Without claiming that interference is always wrong, Williams urges us to remember the importance of peace. Groups may jealously guard their practices, and fight any attempts to change them. So the question, Williams suggests, is how do we balance the values of autonomy, equality and peace when we apply toleration to minority groups?

According to Lucas Swaine, liberal states have little balance in their approach to dealing with many conservative religious groups (what he calls theocratic communities) and are too apt to interfere in the internal affairs of these groups. Liberal states make few attempts to provide insular minorities with good reasons why these minorities ought to follow the dictates of the state. In fact, Swaine argues, these groups often suspect that the liberal state's aim is to undermine groups that seem too radical or too autonomous. Liberalism has retreated, Swaine suggests, from religious tolerance to interference. Since many theocratic communities think that the liberal state wants to interfere in their affairs without good reasons and respectful dialogue, it is hardly surprising that liberalism and liberal institutions appear to them to be purely ideological and that their decisions appear to be based on fiat rather than any form of moral or political consensus. One of the disastrous results of this "failure of liberalism," according to Swaine, is to strengthen the resolve of theocratic minorities against the state and broaden among minority groups the sense that the liberal state is biased and acts illegitimately towards them.

Equality

One way to interpret equality in relation to cultural diversity is to suggest that minority accommodation allows minority groups to receive the kind of cultural support that majority groups receive "free" (Deveaux 2000a; Kymlicka 1995; Parekh 2000; Shachar 2001; Young 1990). Most states conduct their business in a particular language, and thereby privilege speakers of that language. A particular group's religious holidays are often the ones celebrated as official state holidays, which is more convenient for those who follow that religion. If the state conducts most of its business in the dominant language, then, some argue, equality requires that the state support minority languages. If the state has historically supported Christian schools, then equality requires that it support Muslim and Jewish schools as well. Indeed, some theorists argue that all or most cultural groups deserve some state support (Margalit and Halbertal 1994; Young 1990), or deserve some sort of state recognition and respect (Deveaux 2000a; Taylor 1992; Parekh 2000).

A predictable consequence of accommodating cultural and religious minorities in the name of equality is that in some groups vulnerable members, such as women, children, nonconformists and dissenters will be made worse off when their communities are accommodated by the state.[3] Accommodation is supposed to empower minority communities. Yet the success of this accommodation sometimes makes it more difficult for vulnerable members to use the power of liberal institutions and the influence

---

[3] This is what Ayelet Shachar calls "the paradox of multicultural accommodation." See Shachar 2000a.

of mainstream culture to change the oppressive and discriminatory traditions and practices of their communities. Therefore, as accommodation strategies have successfully developed and been put into effect by political leaders, the issue of minorities within minorities has come to the forefront of political and philosophical debates about minority accommodation and has raised some basic questions that go to the heart of how we understand principles of equality, autonomy and justice.

It is surprising how few theorists anticipated this problem (some important exceptions include Phillips 1995 and Green 1995). It was brought to the fore in the late 1990s in a series of essays by Susan Okin and also by Ayelet Shachar, in which both posed one of the most central questions raised by minorities within minorities, which is how the protection of cultural minority rights potentially has an impact on women (Okin 1998; Okin 1999a; Okin 2002; Shachar 1998a; Shachar 1999; Shachar 2000a; Shachar 2001). Multicultural theories attempt to address one form of inequality, namely cultural inequality, but in doing so they undermine the prospects of addressing other forms, such as sexual inequality. The problem of minorities within minorities, on this reading, is a problem of "equality of what?" How ought cultural and sexual equality to be prioritized when they conflict? Getting the answer right is not easy: Okin has been criticized for being too cavalier about the preservation of cultural groups (Perez 2002; Shachar 2001; Spinner-Halev 2001; Herr 2004), while Shachar has been criticized for being too attentive to group preservation (Spinner-Halev 2001), and her solutions are criticized as impracticable or ineffective.[4]

Religious and cultural minorities often seek the right to manage their own affairs with respect to membership in their communities by controlling the customs, traditions and practices around marriage and divorce. Most cultural and religious communities have practices, traditions and customs that treat women differently from men, often by depriving women of access to resources or generally treating them unfairly. It is easy to find agreement amongst feminists that women ought to be treated equally and that sexist practices ought to be reformed. But this tells us very little about how to pursue such reforms within minority communities or whether the goal of such reforms should differ depending on the cultural or religious community in which they are pursued.

Susan Okin's chapter points out the complexity of the tensions between cultural identity, equality and individual autonomy. Okin suggests that the state can either force groups to become liberal, or it can allow groups to

---

[4] Shachar's proposal for how to combine sex equality and group preservation is also criticized in this volume by Okin, Reitman and Levy.

decide upon their rules themselves in some kind of democratic fashion. Which is the best alternative depends on whether the group is oppressed or not. Okin favors the democratic route for oppressed groups, but notes that this still means state involvement in the group's affairs. She favors a liberal response to non-oppressed groups. She does not suggest that illiberal groups be made to liberalize, but she thinks that they should neither have any legal force over their members nor receive any kind of state benefit, like tax-exempt status.

Examining the case of India in some detail, Gurpreet Mahajan is skeptical that groups will reform on their own, but she is also reluctant to endorse direct state intervention in groups, particularly those that are oppressed. Mahajan argues that if the state changes the internal rules of an oppressed group, like indigenous peoples or Indian Muslims, this intervention will be viewed as another form of oppression or imperialism. She also argues that it is not enough to wait for internal reform. Even if all Muslims could vote on their personal laws, there is no reason to think that liberal laws would be endorsed. The heavily religious cast of the society, along with the enmity between the majority and minority, make internal liberal reform unlikely. Mahajan argues that for internal reform to succeed, women within the group need to be organized, external pressure from the international community or community members outside the polity can be helpful, and, most important, the state and its cultural majority must not mark out the minority as the quintessential other.

Anne Phillips argues that the tensions many see between equality and multiculturalism are overblown and that many policies made in the name of multiculturalism can simply be described as matters of equality: if the majority group gets a certain kind of good, like funding for religious schools, then minority groups ought to get the same. To frame an issue as a matter of multiculturalism does not add much to our understanding of it and sometimes leads us to think that problems require far more elaborate solutions than, in fact, they do. Nor is it helpful to think about culture and gender as if they generate competing claims to equality since gender exists within culture, never as separate from it. As Phillips shows by examining three examples of such conflicts, the complexities in resolving conflicts that find minority women disadvantaged by their cultural communities lie mainly in understanding the relevant historical contexts and pragmatic concerns, not in searching for some deep disagreement over matters of high principle. Often at issue, she claims, are the reactions of different groups to proposed policies, or policies that are misguided in the first place. If these issues could be examined in calmer political moments, they would be more readily resolved.

Equality is also the central value involved when the discussion turns to language and cultural rights. Linguistic minorities enjoy linguistic protection in a variety of jurisdictions in the world and these protections usually mean that the minority's language exists as the official language in a particular province or region of the country. But attempts to protect minority languages may well disadvantage a linguistic minority that lives within its midst. For example, in Quebec and Catalonia, such protective policies have imposed controversial restrictions on the language of education and the language in which public signs may be written. The protection of French in Quebec from the dominance of English in North America partly entails restricting the use of English in Quebec by restricting the language in which one can educate one's own children and advertise one's business. The same is true in Catalonia, where Spanish is restricted so that Catalan can be protected. As Alan Patten shows, the point of such strict policies is to ensure that the linguistic minority is able to maintain or create a critical mass of speakers large enough to ensure that all opportunities necessary for a viable society are available in the minority language. Without the critical mass, schools in the minority language become unviable, industries lose the incentive to cater to minority language speakers, and employers look to hire dominant language speakers. Therefore any efforts to extend protections to linguistic minorities within minorities depends on sustaining this critical mass of speakers and thus ensuring that people have a full range of opportunities open to them in society.

Individual autonomy

Liberals have traditionally assumed that most groups are voluntary associations. Yet the nature and meaning of community began to loom large in the 1980s, as some political theorists charged liberalism with being too individualistic (Avineri and De-Shalit 1992; Mason 2000; Mulhall and Swift 1996). People's membership in religious groups was characterized by Michael Sandel, for example, in terms of conscience, and not in the liberal language of choice. (Sandel 1996: ch. 3). People follow the dictates of their religion, Sandel charged, not because they choose to do so, but because they are obliged to do so. Communitarians generally charged liberalism with underplaying the importance of community in people's lives. Yet the problem of internal minorities rarely if ever entered the discussions between liberalism and communitarianism even though the focus of these theories was the extent to which individuals are constituted by their community membership and obligations.

The degree to which community membership is voluntary, however, is crucial to the discussion of minorities within minorities. At one end of this debate is Chandran Kukathas, who argues that all groups – religious, national, racial, etc. – should be considered voluntary associations which people are able to enter and leave as they please. If people enjoy freedom of movement, then according to Kukathas, the state should do nothing about a group's internal practices, even if they are oppressive, physically harmful or discriminatory (Kukathas 2003).

Jeff Spinner-Halev takes a more a moderate position in this volume, arguing against both Kukathas and those liberals who argue for interference in groups with illiberal practices. The main thing the liberal state must do, Spinner-Halev argues, is to ensure that each group adheres to minimal educational and health standards, to ensure that people can leave the group if they wish. Spinner-Halev and Jacob Levy, in his article about sexual orientation and exit, argue that for freedom of association to mean something, individuals must have the liberty to join illiberal communities or choose not to leave them. Levy emphasizes the tragic dilemma to which liberalism can lead: people's sexual orientation may lead them to become outsiders in groups they love or very much feel a part of. Yet if liberty is to be meaningful, the liberal state must protect the freedom of religious communities to govern their community life according to their religious beliefs. Doing so might entail organizing themselves in ways that conflict with public and liberal values. Some communities will institute rules that are illiberal, sexist, racist or classist if they are free to do so. As long as the liberal state protects freedom of association, we should expect some associations to be illiberal.

Both Daniel Weinstock and Oonagh Reitman argue that accounts like Spinner-Halev's and Levy's greatly underestimate how difficult it actually is to leave a group, since people's psychological attachment to a group that they were raised in may be quite intense. Reitman suggests that the focus on exit is misplaced and will do too little to help the women who are treated unjustly within their groups. Indeed, Reitman contends that a focus on exit may even make matters worse for them since few women will choose exit because the costs of doing so are so high. Yet the official existence of exit will then mean that the state will not pressure the group to act justly towards its members. Weinstock argues that people do not choose their religious attachments like they treat their chess club membership and therefore cannot exit easily. He argues that many groups are resistant to change because they are small and fearful that some changes are the first step towards assimilation. Therefore, the solution to oppression within minority communities, according to Weinstock, is to put the burden on the majority community, to insist that it create a public sphere where the minority does not feel beleaguered and, in appropriate cases, to require that it set up institutions through which apologies can be developed for past injustices. Rob Reich also raises related issues, but with children in mind: if religious communities educate their children in their own religious values, will these children really be able to choose to leave when they are adults, or will their autonomy be so truncated by their education that they will see no choice but to remain in the group?

Self-determination

The problem of state interference in the besieged and threatened community is nowhere more evident than in cases which involve formerly colonized peoples including indigenous peoples. Recently, political theorists have taken an active and direct interest in indigenous peoples and their distinctive status and claims (Ivison 2002; Ivison, Patton and Sanders 2000; Levy 2000; Siame 2000). Unlike most religious or ethnic minorities, which seek accommodation and tolerance within the nation state, indigenous peoples claim the right to self-determination. Their claims have been acknowledged, albeit in limited ways, in the constitutional laws of numerous states including Canada, the United States, Australia, several Latin American and African states as well as in the protocols, conventions and declarations of the United Nations. The right to self-determination, even an internal and *sui generis* form of self-determination, entails the strongest type of minority claim against interference from the state. The principle of self-determination is unlike the commitment to cultural and religious accommodation precisely in that self-determining communities have jurisdiction to apply their own interpretation to how governance ought to work in their territory and how conflicts which arise ought to be adjudicated.

One of the concerns that often arises in relation to the well-being of minorities within minorities that seek self-determination is that some of these communities have a record of sexual discriminatory practices, persecution of religious minorities, intolerance towards homosexuals, and other rights violations. While this sort of historical record is also held by all liberal-democratic states, it is often used as a political justification to mobilize opposition to further recognition of a group's claim to self-determination. This sort of conflict is exacerbated by the position sometimes taken by formerly colonized peoples that sexual equality and individuals' rights are "Western constructs" to be viewed with suspicion and rejected as part of an effort to reject colonialism and reclaim indigeneity (Narayan 1998).

Avigail Eisenberg argues that one solution to this first problem is to abandon a rights-based way of resolving conflicts that involve minorities within minorities because rights are viewed as too closely tied to the regimes responsible for colonial and indigenous oppression. Conflicts may be better resolved by refocusing political and legal debate on the values that rights are instrumental to protecting. According to Eisenberg these values often include claims by groups for the protection of their identity. And often these claims are met by counter-claims, advanced by individuals and other groups, which often also involve the need to protect an aspect of their identity. According to Eisenberg, liberal institutions should be able to address these claims as matters of identity in a fair and systematic manner, and avoid translating them back into the language of rights where they do not comfortably fit in the first place.

But this sort of solution, which recasts conflicts in terms that non-liberal communities can accept, may also beg a larger question, namely whether self-determination provides a fundamental justification for non-interference. Margaret Moore argues that if indigenous peoples are unjustly ruled by the societies that colonized them, then the question is not whether indigenous peoples have the legitimate authority to treat their members as they choose, but rather, on what basis does a colonizing government have any authority to impose its values on indigenous peoples and to require that conflicts internal to indigenous communities be resolved through legal and political systems dominated by non-indigenous peoples?

Cindy Holder agrees that indigenous peoples should not be treated like other minorities. Working through the Draft UN Declaration on the Rights of Indigenous Peoples, Holder argues that the right to self-determination, commonly thought of as a group right, is also a basic human right. Self-determination need not mean what is commonly understood as sovereignty, however. Instead, Holder questions the current theory of sovereignty, where the state purportedly has uniform jurisdiction over all its members. She argues that, in practice, state authority is not located in one place but dispersed amongst several authorities; indigenous peoples, for example, often have some authority over their members. International law often recognizes sovereignty only in the state, which Holder argues should be changed. By recognizing the right to self-determination and multiple political authorities, Holder argues, indigenous people will receive the respect they deserve.

Democracy

The resources of democratic theory are at least as broad as (and usually overlap) the resources of liberalism in addressing the contending claims of individuals and groups. Many scholars argue that legitimate democratic outcomes are reliant on the right rules being in place to govern democratic discussion (Gutmann and Thompson 1996; Bohman 2000; Chambers

1998). Others, however, worry that the vulnerable position of minorities within minorities will simply be reaffirmed in any democracy in which the majority rules. Democratic discussion and decision-making, even when governed by specific rules of argument which require, for instance, that arguments follow logical steps of reasoning, are civil and ordered, and aim towards a common good, will, nonetheless, favor members of some groups, who argue in these preferred ways, over others (Sanders 1997; Young 2000: chs. 2–3). Often, the powerful and the powerless do not understand each other, even when they use the same words to communicate (Levinson 2003).

However, some contemporary democratic theorists argue that democracy can be quite helpful to minority groups. Scholars who advocate a form of "associative democracy," like Veit Bader, in his contribution to this volume, argue that the resources of democracy are far richer than at first appears to be the case. Bader points out that most communities are interdependent and not insular; and, of those that are insular, their insularity is easily exaggerated. In most cases, minority communities are pluralistic both in the sense that their members have associative ties outside the community and in the sense that the minority itself is reliant on resources, such as public funding and tax concessions, from the broader public. Insofar as communities are interdependent, they can keep each other in check, much as pluralist theorists of democracy argued that they would. Pluralists argue that different aspects of the individual's life and identity are fulfilled and developed within each of the different associations to which she belongs and in this sense individuals are deeply embedded in their associations and communities. But no association or community dominates the individual within a pluralist vision in the sense that none engages her entire identity. In this sense, she is autonomous of each (Eisenberg 1995). Bader explores the ways in which a democracy that is founded on the values of pluralist association establishes a flexible and fair system of governance. Moreover, it is a system that may provide the best protections for minorities and for minorities within minorities using the familiar mechanisms of democratic engagement combined with freedom of association to balance the power of groups and their individual members.

Monique Deveaux provides another reason why democracy's resources should not be so quickly dismissed. She argues that because most communities are reliant on some form of democratic legitimacy and even where they are not so reliant, they can be convinced to employ fair methods of deliberation in order to sort out for themselves internal conflicts rather than have external measures imposed on them. Advocates of democratic deliberation usually want to expand dialogue in existing political institutions, but Deveaux argues that we ought to consider expanding our understanding of where dialogue takes place. What Deveaux is after is not merely more dialogue between the majority and a minority, but to encourage more deliberation between different factions within minority groups, factions which often have different views and interests. Deveaux argues that the reigning models of democratic deliberation place too much emphasis on the interlocutors giving normative reasons for their views; instead, she argues, deliberation should lay bare people's interests so they can better negotiate about them. Deveaux uses an example from South Africa, where members of traditional tribes were brought together to discuss what laws should be enacted to regulate customary marriage. This example of a process of deliberation that brought together the different groups within traditional South African communities resulted in reforms that were generally accepted by all, though not all the reforms are ideal from a liberal point of view.

Part I

Toleration

1   Tolerable liberalism

Melissa S. Williams

Justice, peace and toleration

"No justice, no peace!" The social movement slogan seeks attention for its cause with an outstretched arm that ends in a clenched fist. On one level, we can read it as a sociological prediction: where groups are chronically frustrated in their quest for fair treatment, they will turn to social disruption or even to violence in order to press their claim. Doing justice is the best way to secure peace. On another level, we can read it as a threat that if those in power ignore the group's claims there will be a price to pay. If successful, this strategy will always leave in doubt whether concessions were gained out of regard for justice or for the sake of peace. However valid the phrase may be as a prediction, as a policy for social justice advocates it is a risky venture.

In liberal societies, the slogan has at least as much appeal when it is turned on its head: "No peace, no justice!" Like the first version, this one reads as both an empirical claim and a policy. In its guise as empirical claim it expresses the idea, traceable to Hobbes, that justice can be secure only where there is a stable political authority that has the power to secure it.[1] As a policy, it expresses a refusal to consider claims of justice from

Earlier drafts of this paper were presented at the Department of Philosophy, Queen's University, Kingston, Ontario, the Dutch Research School in Ethics at the Free University of Amsterdam, and the Political Philosophy Colloquium at Princeton University and the University of Chicago. I thank the participants in those forums for their very constructive (and critical) comments. I am especially grateful to Veit Bader, Suzanne Dovi, Rainer Forst, Elisabetta Galeotti, Annabelle Lever, Geoffrey Brahm Levey, Jacob Levy, Benjamin Moerman, Sawitri Saharso, Ayelet Shachar, Odile Verhaar, David Welch and the editors for detailed and thoughtful comments on earlier drafts of this essay. No doubt these thoughtful readers will still find much to disagree with in this essay, though I have attempted to address concerns they raised. Finally, I wish to thank Nancy Rosenblum and Yael Tamir for conversations that set me thinking about justice, peace and religious toleration some years back.

[1] "Where there is not common Power, there is no Law: where no Law, no Injustice . . . Justice, and Injustice . . . are Qualities, that relate to men in Society, not in Solitude. It is consequent also to the same condition, that there be no Propriety, no Dominion, no

19

those who are threatening social order, as in the statement that "we will not negotiate with terrorists." First we secure the peace, and then we will work for justice. But this leaves open the question of what sacrifices of justice – what suspensions of rights, what delays of reform – may be made in the name of peace.

The tensions between the claims of peace and the claims of justice run deep in liberalism. In this essay, I examine the interplay between justice and peace in the liberal theory and practice of toleration, in judgements about what forms of diversity we can live with and what forms must be suppressed.

Such a project is complicated by the fact that each of the three terms central to the analysis – justice, peace and toleration – admits of a multiplicity of meanings. Justice is at once the most ambiguous and the most tractable of these broad concepts. For although justice has had a different meaning in every age and every regime, my subject here is liberalism. And despite differences among liberal accounts of justice, they all begin from the dual premise of individual freedom and individual equality. So in this essay I will disaggregate the concept of justice by examining the place of both freedom and equality in arguments concerning toleration.

Toleration is a concept that can be construed expansively or restrictively. On a restrictive reading of the concept, it encompasses only those actions that forbear from suppressing a doctrine or a practice despite the agent's strong disapproval. This narrow reading of toleration also limits it to the case where the agent has the *power* to suppress but chooses not to. Those who have no option but put up with noxious practices may be long-suffering but (on this reading of the concept) are not tolerant.[2] We might call this restrictive interpretation "negative toleration" both because of the element of disapprobation and because it proscribes state interference with individuals and associations.

On an expansive reading of toleration, it encompasses every case where people who have different moral commitments and ways of life nonetheless manage to live together in peace. To this must be added: they coexist peacefully without domination; this is not the peace of the gulag. In contrast to the narrow reading of the concept, the expansive reading says nothing about whether different groups regard their diversity as regrettable or as a cause for celebration. As Michael Walzer (1997) details in his recent book *On Toleration*, an expansive reading of the concept shows us that humans have devised a number of different political and

---

Mine and *Thine* distinct; but onely that to be every mans, that he can get; and for so long as he can keep it" (Hobbes 1991: ch. 13, p. 90)

[2] Examples of the restrictive reading of toleration include Mendus 1989: 8–9; Newey 1999.

institutional arrangements to sustain peaceful coexistence among diverse human beings.[3] These arrangements range from the hands-off approach that neutralist liberal states prescribe to the millet system of the Ottoman Empire; from sovereignty as an instrument for peaceful international society to group-specific rights and consociational democracy.

It would take a long digression from my central purposes in this essay to discuss the relative strengths and weaknesses of restrictive vs. expansive readings of the concept of toleration. For my purposes here, then, I will stipulate a moderately expansive interpretation of toleration, one that encompasses both negative toleration (state non-interference) and positive acts to accommodate minority religions and cultures (e.g. exemptions from laws that disproportionately burden a minority religion).

Peace, too, admits of a range of meanings, some narrower (and negative) and some broader (or positive). Indeed, a visit to the *Oxford English Dictionary*'s main entries under "peace" leads us down a path that begins from the negative and ends at a positive definition of peace.[4] The first entry defines peace purely negatively, i.e. in terms of the opposite, war: "Freedom from, or cessation of, war or hostilities; that condition of a nation or community in which it is not at war with another." The violent conflict of armed forces is what is at issue here. The second definition is a bit looser: "Freedom from civil commotion and disorder; public order and security." Here, again, peace is defined in terms of an opposite, but the opposite in question is of a less virulent type than in the first definition. It is not necessarily *violent* conflict involving the *force of arms* that threatens peace, but "commotion" which could take a non-violent form. The third definition further broadens this positive definition by extending the meaning of peace beyond the sphere of civil order to encompass other spheres of life: "Freedom from disturbance or perturbation . . . quiet, tranquillity, undisturbed state. Also emphasized as *peace and quiet(ness)*." With the fourth definition we begin to move from the negative to a positive rendering of peace. Although it, too, begins with the opposite by defining peace as "Freedom from quarrels or dissension between individuals," it continues in a positive vein: "a state of friendliness; concord; amity." The idea of peace thus encompasses every social state between outright war between enemies and perfect social harmony among friends.

I do not stipulate a particular definition of peace for the purposes of this essay, because the very variability of its meanings is a key feature

---

[3] Walzer delineates five conceptually distinct "regimes" of toleration: multinational empires, international society, consociations, nation-states and immigrant societies (Walzer 1997: ch. 2).
[4] Oxford English Dictionary Online, s.v. "peace" http://dictionary.oed.com (accessed 28 January 2004).

of liberal judgements about what to tolerate and what to suppress. The good of peace is clearly tightly linked to the good of stability that sometimes preoccupies liberals; there are moments at which the two goods are indistinguishable from one another. But the principal point to notice here is that the various meanings of peace stand on a continuum that lacks clear stopping points between one definition and the next. One might say, indeed, that when we employ the concept of peace in practical judgements about what to tolerate, we step onto a slippery slope that may incline in one direction or the other, towards peace-as-the-absence-of-war or towards peace-as-social-concord. And once we recognize that both justice and peace figure into our practical judgements about toleration, it becomes clear that we face a *political* choice whether to tilt that slope in one direction or the other. Such, in any case, is the conclusion of this inquiry.

The essay proceeds towards that conclusion in several stages. In Part II, I will argue that freedom (often read as individual autonomy), equality and peace are among the most potent and lasting foundations of the liberal theory of toleration. All of them provide reasons in support of toleration, but each also provides clear limits to toleration. But as I have already suggested, these principles do not always lead to the same practical judgement about what a liberal society should tolerate and what it should suppress (supposing, of course, that we have a choice between these options). So I also consider in this section what priority rules liberal theory offers for ordering these principles, and show that it establishes a clear hierarchy in the weight these different kinds of reasons should carry in our moral deliberations: first freedom, then equality, and then, and only at the margin, peace.

Part III of the essay turns from liberal theory to liberal practice as manifested most in Anglo-American jurisprudence concerning religious and cultural minorities. Here, again, I explore the interaction among freedom, equality and peace-based arguments concerning toleration to see whether they conform to the priority rules liberal theory sets out. What I find is that despite the marginalization of peace-based considerations in the liberal theory of toleration, in practice such considerations creep in constantly to temper the judgements that freedom or equality would dictate.

In the following section I consider what the implications of this liberal practice should be for liberal theory. Should we conclude simply that we are hypocrites? Or has liberal theory done an injustice to the moral relevance of peace by insisting on pressing it to the margins of moral judgement in a manner that is at odds with human moral psychology? Having argued for the second option, I conclude the essay with a consideration of the implications of this analysis for a renewed liberal practice of toleration, and present a defense of a practice of "presumptive accommodation."

The reader might justly ask at this point: What is the relevance of the interplay of discourses of peace, freedom and equality in the theory and practice of toleration to the problem of "minorities within minorities" on which this volume is focused? Quite a bit, I hope the reader will agree in the end. For the inclination to temper our interest in justice with our interest in peace – or vice versa – often results in an unprincipled rejection or accommodation of the claims of religious and cultural minorities. Sometimes we exaggerate the vulnerability of internal minorities or groups; sometimes we give their vulnerability insufficient moral weight. By paying close attention to the psychological forces at play in these judgements, especially the force of our own *fearfulness*, we provide ourselves with a shield against our unprincipled inclinations. The practice of presumptive accommodation aims at a principled resolution of the tensions between peace and justice in our judgements about toleration, and perforce a principled response to the problem of internal minorities.

The spirit of Judith Shklar is a constant companion in this enquiry, which affirms her strong view that liberals have good reason to "fear a society of fearful people" (Shklar 1989: 29). In the wake of the events of 11 September 2001, we are living in a very fearful time. Fear clouds our moral and political judgement and inclines us to sacrifice our moral commitments for the sake of security. The detention without legal charge of "enemy combatants" in Guantanamo and of "suspected terrorists" in the United States and Canada; the deportation of persons with suspected links (however tenuous) to terrorists or terrorist activities to countries that torture prisoners;[5] the detention and questioning of foreign students in the United States (Schemo 2003: A11); an intensive program to call legal immigrants into federal immigration offices for questioning and fingerprinting:[6] these are only a sampling of the ways in which basic civil liberties have been weakened in the wake of 11 September. We may well question whether history will vindicate these fear-inspired moral and legal

[5] Maher Arar, a Canadian citizen of Syrian origin, was detained by United States immigration officials during his transit through John F. Kennedy International Airport. Without consulting Canadian consular officials, US officials deported him to Syria, where he was subjected to interrogation under torture for ten months. For a chronology and overview of the news reporting on Arar's case, see http://www.cbc.ca/news/background/arar/ (accessed 3 December 2003).
[6] The Department of Homeland Security's special registration requirements apply to all male immigrants aged sixteen or older from twenty-five designated countries (mostly Middle Eastern countries). These requirements are posted at: http://uscis.gov/graphics/shared/lawenfor/specialreg/index.htm (accessed 2 December 2003). Acknowledging that the program has yielded little by way of security-related information, the Homeland Security Department has recently announced its discontinuation. Some 85,000–150,000 immigrants reported for registration since its inception. See "Immigration Registration Requirements Eased," *Washington Times*, 1 December 2003, available at http://washingtontimes.com/upi-breaking/20031201-021143-5478r.htm (accessed 3 December 2003).

compromises. More often than not, the burdens of fearful times fall most heavily on minorities; and when minority groups feel especially vulnerable to external forces, the voices of dissent within them may fall silent. Muslims in Canada and the United States report a mixed reaction from non-Muslim citizens to their visible presence in North America: while the number of attacks on Muslims and the incidence of discrimination against them has increased, many non-Muslims have also expressed sympathy and support.[7] Yet racial profiling and the selective government monitoring of foreigners (and especially Muslims) have gained a new respectability in the public mind and a new prominence in state practice.[8] We are walking a fine line, and history teaches us that it is especially in times like these we must guard against our inclination to overstate the limits of both liberty and toleration.[9]

The discourses of freedom, equality and peace as foundations of liberal toleration

Freedom

Of the three grounds of toleration and group recognition, the argument from individual freedom or autonomy is the most widely accepted among liberals, and has the strongest hold on us. Its paradigm begins with the early arguments for religious toleration: that salvation is not gained

---

[7] For an overview of the consequences of 11 September for Muslim minorities within Canada, see Abu-Laban 2002.

[8] Daniel Pipes is a prominent example of such new respectability. In August 2003, Pipes was appointed by President George W. Bush to the United States Peace Institute during a Senate recess (normally such appointments require Senate approval). Defending the selective scrutiny of Muslims (including US citizens) by state authorities, Pipes writes: "There is no escaping the unfortunate fact that Muslim government employees in law enforcement, the military and the diplomatic corps need to be watched for connections to terrorism, as do Muslim chaplains in prisons and the armed forces. Muslim visitors and immigrants must undergo additional background checks. Mosques require a scrutiny beyond that applied to churches and temples" (Pipes 2003). Racial profiling at the US–Canadian border was especially intense for several months, when US authorities were selectively screening and questioning Canadian citizens born in Arab countries. Canadian Prime Minister Jean Chrétien protested against this practice and issued a travel advisory to such citizens that they should avoid travel to the United States. In response, the US government pledged to cease the practice. See Dunfield 2002.

[9] Thus my project here has important affinities with the work of Jacob Levy, who also follows Shklar in articulating his conception of a "multiculturalism of fear." Against a multiculturalism that celebrates identity as a good in itself, he argues for "a political theory of multiculturalism which . . . focuses on mitigating the *recurrent dangers* such as state violence toward ethnic minorities, inter-ethnic warfare, and intra-communal attacks on those who try to alter or leave their cultural communities" (Levy 2000: 12–13; emphasis added).

through the mere profession of faith in true doctrine, but only through actual faith, through the voluntary affirmation of true belief. No souls are gained for the Church through forced conformity to orthodox practice; they can only be won through voluntary conversion as a consequence of persuasion or revelation. There is therefore no appropriate role for political authorities in the enforcement of religious doctrine.

This argument is a logical and historical precursor to the Kantian formulation of autonomy: that our dignity as moral beings consists in our capacity to act according to principles that are consistent with our nature as free and equal rational beings. A respect for the moral dignity of the person requires that she be left free to choose the principles of her action, even though that freedom leaves open the possibility of error. As beings capable of moral autonomy, whose highest interest (including our interest in salvation) consists in our exercising that capacity correctly, in making the right moral choices about the course our lives shall take, we also have a profound interest in being free to revise our judgements and beliefs about our good. We need to be free to change the course our lives have taken should it turn out that we have fallen into the error to which our capacity for autonomy leaves us vulnerable. These arguments broaden the claim for toleration beyond religious toleration to a toleration of a diversity of both religious and non-religious understandings of the human good, by focusing attention on the importance of individuals' freedom to choose and to change the ends towards which their lives are aimed.[10]

The autonomy-based argument for toleration generates strong moral reasons for making social space for those with whom we disagree; historically it has been the most powerful and persuasive foundation for liberal toleration. As many commentators have noticed, it is strongly allied to fallibilism, if not skepticism. The insufficiency of human understanding to place the fundamental questions of religion and morality beyond dispute plays at least two roles in liberal thought. It leads us to respect the moral agency of those with whom we disagree as capable of moral reasoning even if we believe their reasoning has led them to the wrong conclusions. But it also means that because these questions are the most important for beings who aspire to lead moral lives, we have a strong stake in keeping our minds open to a revision of our moral and religious judgements. Both of these consequences of fallibilism are strong supports to the attitudes and institutions of religious toleration.

Recent developments in liberal theory have further expanded the autonomy-based argument for religious toleration to encompass forms of special recognition for ethno-cultural minorities, of which the most

[10] For a helpful overview of some of these arguments, see Kymlicka 1989a: 9–13.

prominent is Will Kymlicka's (1989a, 1995). A concern for autonomy should lead liberals to go beyond *laissez faire* toleration to embrace special protections for minority cultures, he argues, because we can meaningfully exercise our capacity for free choice only within the context of a secure system of social meanings, i.e. within a stable culture. To the extent that minority cultures are threatened with dissolution, members of these cultures lack that secure context, and so may be deprived of the prerequisites for autonomous choice (Kymlicka 1995: 126–30).[11]

But the autonomy argument also provides strong reasons to limit the scope of toleration. Within its framework of toleration, no group that fails to respect the autonomy of its own members, or deprives them of the prerequisites of the kind of critical reflection that constitute autonomous judgement, can justly claim to be tolerated, let alone accommodated, within a liberal society. As Rob Reich argues in his contribution to this volume, children's interest in developing their capacities for autonomous thought and for functioning in the broader society may sometimes count against the claims of cultural or religious communities to state non-interference in their systems of education. Cultural groups that deny their members' rights of religious freedom or dissent are similarly worrisome, as several contributors emphasize. Without autonomy-based limits on toleration and accommodation, liberal societies risk becoming – to borrow Leslie Green's powerful phrase – "a mosaic of tyrannies; colorful, perhaps, but hardly free"(1994: 116).

Equality

The second general variety of argument for toleration and group accommodation is grounded in the principle of equality more strongly than that for freedom or autonomy. In recent literature, the paradigm for accepting minority practices is that of the historically oppressed group that requires forms of group recognition or group rights in order to overcome relations of domination and oppression. The goal here is equal membership in a shared political or legal order (whether a constitutional order of the modern state, or the legal order governing the relations between self-governing national minorities in Kymlicka's sense and the larger constitutional regimes in which they are situated). Certainly it is a requirement of public policy in any democratic society that no law should single out a group for discriminatory treatment. Yet even policies that are facially neutral may sometimes impose disproportionate burdens on some religious

---

[11] See Kymlicka 1995: 126–30, for a summary of his main arguments.

or cultural groups. In these cases, a purely negative conception of toleration – a policy of benign neglect or of *laissez faire* – will not be sufficient to secure equality before the law. Where no overriding public purpose can justify the disproportionate impact of public policy on a particular group, an egalitarian defense of toleration requires that we go beyond passive acceptance of a group to take positive action to accommodate its practices. Treating individuals as equals may require giving direct recognition to the groups to which they belong, for to apply a universal standard sometimes imposes the norms and practices of the dominant groups upon oppressed groups and simply requires the latter to conform to the ways of the former.[12]

It is worth noting that the equality argument is a relatively recent addition to the arguments for toleration; it appears in the jurisprudence concerning religious freedom only in the twentieth century, and has been developed as a principled argument within political philosophy only in the last decade or so.[13] Indeed, it is the equality argument that does the real work in transforming toleration from a negative practice (non-interference) to a positive program of accommodation. Although some theoretical treatments of toleration have emphasized the conceptual difference between the toleration of diversity and its positive affirmation, as a practical matter the equality argument blurs this boundary. It is perhaps because the equality argument has taken hold in the popular mind that the negative connotations of toleration – to suffer what we disapprove – no longer attach to the concept as securely as they used to. If toleration no longer requires that we simply restrain ourselves from actively suppressing a group or a practice, but now requires that we change our own rules and practices to accommodate another, it is more difficult psychologically (though not impossible) to maintain the attitude of condescension that many have seen as a central paradox of toleration (see, e.g. Scanlon 1996: 226–39).

Like the autonomy arguments, a concern for equality presents both an argument for and a limit to toleration. Most commonly, we see equality functioning as a limit to toleration and accommodation in cases involving internal minorities or vulnerable groups. If accommodating a religious or cultural minority empowers that community to impose patriarchal hierarchies upon their female members, or to deny rights of equal membership to religious dissenters or cultural nonconformists, then there is a strong tension between the principle of individual equality and the practice

---

[12] For examples of the equality-based argument for group accommodation, see, e.g., Kymlicka 1995: 108–15; Young 1990; Williams 1995.
[13] Lord Scarman labels it "the new tolerance" in Scarman 1987.

of group accommodation.[14] These equality-based concerns, together
with the autonomy-based concerns noted above, constitute the problem that Ayelet Shachar helpfully labels "the paradox of multicultural
vulnerability": "the ironic fact that individuals inside the group can be
injured by the very reforms that are designed to promote their status
as group members in the accommodating, multicultural state" (Shachar
2001: 3).

Peace

The third discourse that pervades contemporary debates over the scope
and limits of toleration is grounded in the value of peace. The received
wisdom about the historical origins of liberal toleration locates the practice of toleration neither in autonomy nor in equality but, indeed, in a
concern for peace. Following the Reformation, the story goes, Protestants and Catholics alternately sought the security of their own religion's
control of the state apparatus through the policy of intolerance. They
paid the costs of the violent suppression of religion over and over, until
finally they happened upon toleration as an alternative. As Michael Walzer
sums it up, the form of toleration that emerges out of the religious wars
of the sixteenth and seventeenth centuries "is simply a resigned acceptance of difference for the sake of peace. People kill one another for years
and years, and then, mercifully, exhaustion sets in, and we call this toleration" (Walzer 1997: 10). But other readings of the history of liberal
toleration see this not as the substance but only as the beginning of toleration. For John Rawls, the toleration that begins as a peace treaty is
soon reconceived as a remarkable discovery: that stability can actually be
better served through tolerating than through suppressing one's religious
opponents.[15]

How does a concern for peace yield a practice of toleration? The psychological calculus of toleration owes a great deal to Hobbes, who used
the same logic to justify the power of an absolute sovereign: when combatants can perceive that they lack the power to dominate others, or that

---

[14] This concern is the central thrust of Susan Okin's critique of multiculturalism in Okin
1999a.

[15] "[T]he success of liberal constitutionalism came as a discovery of a new social possibility: the possibility of a reasonably harmonious and stable pluralist society. Before the
successful and peaceful practice of toleration in societies with liberal institutions there
was no way of knowing of that possibility. It is more natural to believe, as the centuries-
long practice of intolerance appeared to confirm, that social unity and concord requires
agreement on a general and comprehensive religious, philosophical, or moral doctrine.
Intolerance was accepted as a condition of social order and stability" (Rawls 1993:
xxvii).

their efforts to do so will lead them into an endless cycle of revenge, they may judge that they have more to gain from laying down their arms than from continuing the battle. Even for those who have the upper hand, the use of this power to suppress religious opponents may be very imprudent, as it will arouse a sense of righteous anger and encourage efforts at subversion. Indeed, in one passage in the first *Letter Concerning Toleration* Locke even goes so far as to suggest that the magistrate's failure to treat religious groups even-handedly is the sole cause of conspiracies against the state by religious minorities:

[T]here is *only one thing* which gathers people into seditious commotions, and that is oppression. . . .

Take away the partiality that is used toward them in matters of common right, change the laws, take away the penalties unto which they are subjected, and all things will immediately become safe and peaceable; nay, those that are averse to the religion of the magistrate will think themselves so much the more bound to maintain the peace of the commonwealth as their condition is better in that place than elsewhere; and *all the several separate congregations, like so many guardians of the public peace*, will watch one another, that nothing may be innovated or changed in the form of the government, because they can hope for nothing better than what they already enjoy – that is, an equal condition with their fellow subjects under a just and moderate government. (Locke [1689] 1955: 54–5; emphasis added)

The desire to attain peace leads to a prudential agreement to lay down arms, which is the original form of the practice of toleration. But once peace is established, the practice of toleration helps to secure it by making possible a system of government that the governed can acknowledge as equitable and legitimate. Since all benefit from the peace so secured, all have an interest in maintaining the regime of toleration that makes it possible. It is precisely this story that Rawls retells in his account of how a *modus vivendi* can become transformed into a constitutional consensus, and later into an overlapping consensus (Rawls 1993: 158–68).

In this formulation, peace is not an end in itself, but is an instrumental good: we require a stable and peaceful order as a precondition of our freedom to pursue all of the other human goods we may seek. These goods include the good of salvation, whose pursuit may require only our inner conformity to the principles of faith but is certainly aided by our freedom to perform their outward expression as well. But other goods – the pursuit of scientific knowledge, the development of the arts, and economic prosperity – likewise depend on peace as their precondition. Again, to this extent the peace-based argument for toleration owes a great deal to Hobbes, despite the fact that he is not often cited as a theorist of toleration.

Like the autonomy and equality arguments for toleration, the peace-based argument for toleration has a self-limiting logic. If peace is the end that toleration serves, and is a legitimate interest of all governments, then governments should not extend the practice of toleration so far as to embrace religious factions that would, if they could, take political power into their own hands and use it to suppress other groups. In a less optimistic mood than the one I just quoted, Locke is very clear that the claim to toleration belongs only to those who have no designs on state power. For similar reasons, groups who believe they owe a greater loyalty to a foreign government than to their own (as Locke emphasized in the case of Muslims and (implicitly) Catholics) have no claim to toleration (Rawls 1993: 51).

Let us suppose, following Rawls's story, that a regime of toleration has been established and civil order prevails. We can see from the brief reflections above that a concern for peace presents political actors with a choice between two mutually exclusive strategies towards groups that stand on the margins of the political community. Where a group threatens disorder through its aspirations to political power, political actors have an interest in – and a justification for – acting to suppress the group. Alternatively, political agents can act to secure the peaceful co-operation of a marginal group by pursuing a policy of strict equity or even of generous accommodation, which may weaken the group's inclination to oppose the regime and strengthen whatever bonds of attachment the group may feel towards the regime.

Both approaches to alien groups flow directly from a desire to secure the peace, and both are present in liberal thinking about toleration at least since Locke. The first is the path of fear, and the second is the path of hope. The difficulty is that in cases where a group's loyalty to the regime is uncertain but not proven to be hostile, the choice between them becomes a dilemma. A move to suppress, if it stops short of eradicating the group altogether, will give the group's members ample cause for more energetic efforts of resistance, and so may jeopardize the future peace of the regime even if, in the short term, it secures it. But a move to accommodate the group, if it might truly harbor designs hostile to the regime, seems like an act of foolish generosity. Thus the strategy of accommodation is made more difficult and less likely by the fact that it invites a different sort of fearfulness, and fearfulness inclines actors to the strategy of suppression.

In democratic societies these alternatives take on a further significance. Let's begin from the supposition that the strength of a democratic political order depends on a sense of shared citizenship among its members. If so, the strategy of suppressing a marginal group carries especially high costs: not only does it kindle a livelier spirit of opposition, but it also makes it more difficult to forge bonds of shared membership in a single political community. The more groups feel alienated by the practices of the state, the weaker the sense of political community they share with the majority that put that state into power.[16]

On the other hand, many critics of group recognition have argued that a strategy of toleration or accommodation will also weaken political community by creating enclaves of citizens who do not affirm liberal principles and who do not feel a sense of shared membership with other citizens. Again, considering this possibility generates anxiety that the regime is too generous, and this anxiety about future disorder or disloyalty justifies measures to suppress group claims to accommodation (see, e.g., Schlesinger Jr. 1992).

Disconnected discourses

We have seen that all three discourses of toleration can cut both ways when it comes to the question whether to tolerate a particular practice. My purpose in the preceding section has not been to offer judgements about which of these arguments is the most convincing, but simply to point out some distinct discourses of toleration at work in contemporary debates over religious toleration and cultural accommodation.

What has not been so clear from the foregoing account is the extent to which, in the philosophical literature on liberal toleration, there is a clear hierarchy among these discourses. As I have argued, taken together the autonomy and equality arguments define the claims of justice in the sphere of toleration, and are sharply distinguished from considerations of peace. Whereas these claims define the *moral* dimensions of toleration, the concern for peace reflects a *merely prudential* ground of toleration.[17] Autonomy is the most commonly expressed and is generally treated as the weightiest argument for toleration; many philosophical treatments of toleration neglect to discuss equality as an element of the justice of toleration (see, e.g., Raz 1988: 155–75), and those who do tend to treat it as subordinate to autonomy in the hierarchy of moral values.[18]

---

[16] See Macedo 2000: 207: "A rigid insistence on the sanctity of exceptionless rules may reflect nothing more than bureaucratic convenience. To unfairly marginalize even unreasonable people is to fan their alienation and resentment, to encourage their disaffection with our political system."

[17] See, e.g., Mendus 1987, where she distinguishes "rational," "moral" and "prudential" grounds of toleration. As she notes (11), "The argument from prudence justifies toleration by reference to considerations of public order, and thereby suggests that where tolerance will not foster good order in society, it should be abandoned."

[18] This is mostly implicit in Will Kymlicka's work; it is explicit in Geoffrey Brahm Levey's work. For the latter, see esp. Levey 1997.

Even more striking is the degree to which recent discussions of toleration in the context of multiculturalism have tended to separate out justice
arguments from peace arguments altogether. Those who are concerned
about the justice of group recognition and accommodation tend to reason
from the principles of autonomy and equality to reach judgements about
what is required in a particular case. As Chandran Kukathas nicely sums
it up: "We establish the limits of tolerance in principle and then whether
or not particular practices are consistent with them, and thus determine
whether or not to intervene in traditional societies or minority groups
by providing state subsidies, disincentives, or penalties for particular
practices" (1997: 71).[19]

This logic is perfectly sensible if, following Rawls, we consider the right
as prior to the good or, following Dworkin, we consider justice claims as
trumps. If these orderings of value are correct, then they do prescribe a
clear structure for the processes of moral reasoning we should follow in
reaching judgements about what to tolerate. We begin with the two pil-
lars of liberal justice, freedom and equality, and reason from them about
whether a particular minority practice is consonant with them. If it is,
then we ought to permit it; if not, we should feel justified in discouraging
it or, in appropriate circumstances, suppressing it. This is the logic that
Will Kymlicka follows in his discussion of non-liberal minorities (1995:
163–72), that Martha Nussbaum follows in her discussion of clitoridectomy (1999: ch. 4), and that Susan Okin follows in her discussion of
multicultural accommodation for patriarchal cultures (1999a: 7–24).

This is by no means to dismiss these thoughtful and important moral
reflections on what are currently among the hardest questions in moral
and political philosophy. Again, it is not my purpose here to take issue with
the substantive judgements these thinkers reach about the consonance
of a particular group or practice with a commitment to autonomy and
equality. Nor do I want to disavow these principles themselves. Rather,
my purpose here is simply to notice that those thinkers who are currently
engaged in the justice discourses about toleration are by and large not
engaged with the peace discourse. Or to the extent that they are, they
affirm a strong hierarchy between reasons from justice and reasons from
peace, and tend to be dismissive of the latter as "merely prudential"
considerations that do not have a direct bearing on our moral judgement
per se. The difficult work, this approach supposes, consists in knowing
what we ought to do as a matter of justice. If the claims of justice must be
tempered by pragmatic concerns about social stability, this is something

---

[19] Kukathas goes on to argue for a regime of toleration which gives much less scope to the
principles of autonomy and equality than I would defend.

that must be dealt with in context and is not susceptible to philosophical analysis.[20]

Conversely, those who proceed within the peace discourse to grapple with the challenges of multiculturalism tend not to engage with the justice discourses. As I have suggested above, peace-based critiques of group recognition focus on the threat of instability that (they argue) quickly ensues. One species of these critiques may be summed up as the threat of "balkanization".[21] The logic of "balkanization" arguments runs roughly as follows: The recognition of one group's claim will lead other groups to make claims on their own behalf. Before long, the floodgates have been opened and there are more demands on the political system than it can bear. Meanwhile, it encourages individuals to identify themselves with the interests of their group rather than with the public interest, fueling group insularity and weakening the bonds of citizenship. The specter of anarchy or "system overload" thus looms over every group claim for recognition. Since peace and stability are elemental components of the public good, the normative conclusion follows syllogistically: peace is a good; group claims threaten peace; therefore group claims are a public evil.[22]

Nowhere does the justice or injustice of a particular group's claims enter into this process of reasoning. It proceeds directly from the evil of instability to the prescription of non-recognition, without pausing to consider whether the price of peace – the refusal to recognize potentially just claims – is too high. What we have here, I think, is an intrusion of the moral reasoning of exigency into the realm of normal political conflict. The doctrines of exigency – of emergency powers – provide that in matters of self-preservation other considerations of morality are temporarily suspended. But whereas that doctrine supposes that under normal circumstances justice claims will take precedence over other political aims, the "balkanization" arguments crowd out justice claims for the sake of a civil peace even where the threats to peace are of the vaguest and most speculative variety.

Let's shift our focus from theoretical discussions of the limits to toleration back to our practical judgements about those limits. What we find

---

[20] I should note here that Rawls is a very important exception to this tendency, as he has always been concerned to reconcile the claims of justice with the claims of peace and stability. Indeed, that impulse underlies the whole project of *Political Liberalism*. The problem is that he copes with the claims of peace by wishing away the sources of conflict rather than by offering a strategy for weighing peace against justice in a principled way.

[21] I discuss "balkanization" arguments in greater detail in Williams 1998.

[22] For examples of such arguments, see *City of Richmond v. J. A. Croson Co* 1989: 505 (accepting minority claims would "open the door to competing claims for 'remedial relief' for every disadvantaged group"); Glazer 1978: 30–1; Glazer 1981: 22; Glazer 1983: 227–9, 284). Glazer's position on group-specific remedies for inequality has shifted in recent years. See Glazer 1997.

is that in practice we do not tend to divide justice arguments and peace arguments so neatly from one another; most of our practical judgements about the tolerability of minority practices are suffused with all three concerns: autonomy, equality and peace. Rather than following a strict priority among these goods, we usually give some consideration to each, weighing them off against one another. Consider, for example, the case of the Amish in the United States or the Hutterites in Canada. As liberal theorists have recently argued very persuasively, viewed from the standpoint of autonomy these communities have little claim to accommodation. Some impose restrictions on their members that make it difficult for them to leave. They may also attempt to shield their children from exposure to mainstream culture that would lead them to understand that they have an exit option, or to be equipped with the skills that would enable them to exercise that option.[23] Yet by and large both the US and Canada have chosen to accommodate these groups. It is not the case that *no* plausible equality or autonomy arguments can be marshaled on behalf of accommodation, but in the final analysis these arguments are not what carry the day. Rather, we tend to judge that, despite the compromises with autonomy and equality that we have to make in order to do so, we can *afford* to accommodate these groups because they do not threaten stability. They are small, insular, and not only make few demands on the state but also eschew political power for themselves (Macedo 2000: 207). Their way of life is very difficult to follow, so it is unlikely that other groups will use their example as the basis of extensive accommodations for themselves (Spinner 1994: 107). Consequently there is little reason to fear that granting their claims will lead to an unmanageable torrent of claims by other groups.[24] It doesn't hurt their case that we tend to find them charming. In short, we can afford to tolerate them, and this has weight in our decisions whether to tolerate what stands independently of our principled commitments to equality and autonomy.

If in the case of the Amish and Hutterites we are generous to a fault, it is more common that when we weigh peace more heavily than justice, we do so at the expense of a minority. One of the clearest cases of this in the twentieth century was the detention of persons of Japanese descent in both the United States and Canada. Because there was some evidence

---

[23] See, e.g., Gutmann 1987: 29; Kymlicka 1995: 161–3. See also Spinner-Halev 2000: 50, for an argument that it is nigh impossible for such religious communities to insulate themselves – and their children – from the surrounding society altogether.

[24] In *Wisconsin v. Yoder*, for example, a US Supreme Court case involving a partial exemption from public schooling requirements for Amish children, the Court's opinion notes that the Amish made a "convincing showing" for their case, "one that probably few other religious groups or sects could make" (*Wisconsin v. Yoder* 1972: 236).

of political subversion and espionage among a small group of Japanese-Americans, the military judged that it had to detain the lot. In such cases, we judge that we cannot afford to tolerate a group, quite irrespective of the question of whether there are good autonomy-based or equality-based reasons for suppressing them. As the US Supreme Court put it in the infamous *Korematsu* case, "It was because we could not reject the finding of the military authorities that it was impossible to bring about an immediate segregation of the disloyal from the loyal that we sustained the validity of the curfew order as applying to the whole group" (*Korematsu v. United States* 1944: 219).

The tendency to give peace and stability priority over autonomy is apparent in more recent decisions as well. Most notorious in recent years is the 1990 case of *Employment Division of Oregon v. Smith*, where the Supreme Court considered the constitutionality of a state decision to deny unemployment compensation to two Native American employees who were fired from their state jobs for using peyote. The two men were members of the Native American Church, whose religious practices include the sacramental use of peyote. Oregon law makes the use of peyote illegal, and has no exception for religious uses of the drug. There were clear autonomy and equality issues at stake in the case, as indeed the Court majority did not deny. The autonomy concerns embedded in Free Exercise cases are self-evident, and the equality concerns were brought out by Justice O'Connor's concurring opinion: "[T]he essence of a free exercise claim is relief from a burden imposed by government on religious practices or beliefs, whether the burden is imposed directly . . . or indirectly through laws that, in effect, *make abandonment of one's own religion or conformity to the religious beliefs of others the price of an equal place in the civil community*" (*Employment Division v. Smith* 1990: 898; emphasis added). But Justice Scalia's opinion for the Court overrode these concerns by rousing the specter of civil disorder: "If the 'compelling interest' test is to be applied at all . . . it must be applied across the board, to all actions thought to be religiously commanded . . . *Any society adopting such a system would be courting anarchy*, but that danger increases in direct proportion to the society's diversity of religious beliefs, and its determination to coerce or suppress none of them" (*Employment Division v. Smith* 1990: 886; emphasis added).

While I share the widespread judgement that the *Smith* decision was ethically indefensible, my concern here is not just to point out that liberal democratic practice is hypocritical or morally feeble. It is true enough that we – members of liberal democratic constitutional societies – often fail to live up to our own moral commitments. But the lesson I would draw from these examples is rather that we should pay closer attention to the role that concerns about peace and stability play in our judgements about minority practices. If we do so, I think we will find something more interesting than hypocrisy: that our prejudgements about the nature of a group and whether it poses a threat to liberal principles or to political stability have an independent force in shaping our judgements about whether to tolerate their presence or their practices. Toleration may be stretched or truncated depending on our sympathies or fears towards particular groups.[25] As a consequence, our judgements-in-context about what we can afford to tolerate are often different from our judgements-in-retrospect about what we should have tolerated. If we distrust a group's loyalty to the liberal regime, or worry about the spread of its illiberal doctrines, we have a tendency to overstate the threat to stability that its presence poses. Moreover, once we have reached a judgement that a particular group identity is incompatible with liberal commitments, we direct our gaze towards the group and its practices, and tend to be especially chary of its claims to accommodation. The consequence is that we often measure their practices against the standards of autonomy and equality with much closer scrutiny than we apply to practices within majority religions and cultures.[26]

Giving peace its due

I have argued that in our theoretical treatments of toleration, we tend to seal off questions of justice and questions of peace as if they involved entirely separate processes of reasoning and brought entirely different sets of reasons to bear on the scope and limits of toleration. In our practical judgements, we do weigh the claims of justice and the claims of peace against one another all the time – but we generally fail to acknowledge that this is what we are doing, except at the limit, i.e. in cases of exigency. Moreover, even when we do acknowledge it, the balance we strike among these values is seldom principled. This is not surprising insofar as these judgements are often pervaded by fear. As Hobbes taught us so well, fear is an emotion that shapes our reasoning more powerfully than any other, and knows no natural limit. Our sense of security depends upon protecting ourselves not only from "clear and present dangers" but also from those vaguer and more distant dangers that lurk around the corner or down the road.

In both theory and practice, toleration contains a plurality of goods or values; making the right choices about what to tolerate requires achieving

---

[25] I owe this formulation to Nancy Rosenblum.
[26] For some examples, see Carens and Williams 1998.

the right balance among those goods. If the most important goods in question are those of justice and of peace, then how ought we to understand toleration as a balance between these values, keeping in mind the tendencies to excessive fearfulness that tend to take over when we focus on peace? How can we discover the right balance? Let us begin with a thought experiment. We have seen that current liberal theory gives priority in moral reasoning to the claims of justice, and considers the claims of peace as a secondary concern, if at all. How would questions of toleration look different if we were to reverse this order – as indeed we often do in practice, though in unprincipled ways – and give priority to peace?

The first thing that becomes apparent if we do this is something I pointed out earlier: that a concern with peace confronts us with two mutually irreconcilable choices. The first consists in taking seriously the threat to stability from subversive and anti-liberal groups, and being willing to place restrictions on those groups so as to limit the damage they do to liberal institutions. But as we have seen, once we head down this path there is no natural limit to its logic, and it functions to anger and alienate those who are its targets, making it more difficult to establish the relations of trust that are the precondition for shared citizenship.[27]

The second strategy consists in promoting peace by accommodating minorities, and hence giving them reason to believe that their interests are tied in with those of the regime. When peace is the motive, we look for those forms of living-together that are mutually acceptable, and are willing to accept the proposition that compromise has an appropriate place in our decision-making. The search for mutually acceptable arrangements does not presuppose that one or the other group's practices will prevail. Perhaps the solution that will be acceptable to both sides will be a moderated form of one group's practice; perhaps it will be a combination of both groups' practices; or perhaps the solution will be found in an entirely new practice. In the quest for peaceful accommodation none of this is prejudged.

Peace-seeking, by itself, does not yield any *a priori* choice between suppression and toleration. There may indeed be circumstances in which the security of a liberal democratic regime is genuinely threatened by non-liberal groups, and in those circumstances there may be no choice but to restrict the groups' actions.[28] But as a general matter, it seems fair to say

---

[27] Here I bracket the following consideration: that if resolving conflicts over non-liberal practices requires the real or threatened use of force, there are good reasons for thinking that that, by itself, is a departure from the principle of peace. Of course, this would not be the Hobbesian view of peace, which is perfectly consonant with (indeed depends upon) the threat of coercion.

[28] Yael Tamir argues that some ultra-right religious groups pose such a threat in Israel, and should be restricted (Tamir 2000).

that the fearfulness that leads to suppression generates the wrong balance between the claims of peace and the claims of justice, and overprivileges the former. It is for this reason that liberals have good reason "to fear fear itself," as the late Judith Shklar emphasized in her distinctive version of liberalism.

The choice of toleration requires several virtues. We must have self-restraint, to be sure. But we also need courage, the ability to reject our impulses to fearfulness and to take the risk of trusting even those who are very different from ourselves. When toleration entails more than just passive acceptance, when it entails some positive accommodation, it also requires a willingness to view minority practices from the minority's perspective, and to take seriously their reasons for wishing to maintain those practices. This activity requires the further virtues of open-mindedness and a capacity for generous listening. So understood, toleration is by no means an easy affair.

Now let us consider extending our experiment a step further. Let us give priority not just to peace, but to its second path, the path of toleration and accommodation, and see how it affects our approach to non-liberal practices. This is not to say that we should give peace absolute ethical priority; to do that would be to counsel peace at all costs, which cannot be a moral doctrine. Instead, I propose giving toleration *deliberative* priority in our moral reasoning. We might call such a practice "presumptive accommodation": when confronted with a minority practice that appears to conflict with liberal principles, we might ask first what would be necessary to accommodate the group, and only then to subject the results of that enquiry to the tests of autonomy and equality. This approach to practical reasoning stands in clear contrast to the process that currently prevails, which involves measuring the practice against the standards of equality and autonomy first, and then asking whether or not it should be suppressed.

Such an approach to toleration would have a number of advantages. First, it might generate more constructive forms of engagement between majority and minority cultures. The prevailing liberal formula requires little discussion between liberals and cultural minorities; it tends to presume that liberals comprehend the significance of minority practices for equality and autonomy, and justifies liberals in suppressing practices which they find violate those principles. There is little need for a direct encounter between liberals and minorities at all, and indeed much of the literature that follows this formula does not delve very deeply into the lived experience of the minorities it proposes to regulate. This has the effect of leaving religious and cultural minorities feeling as if they have been silenced, as if their own experiences cannot provide a credible basis for ethical judgement. It also closes off the possibility that minority cultures' own interpretations of their practices as equality- and freedom-enhancing might persuade liberals to different moral judgements.[29] A practice of presumptive accommodation would, at the least, make it more likely that minorities would feel that their self-understandings had been recognized and acknowledged by others, which is a critical first step towards the mutual trust that is necessary for a strong democratic culture.

Second, giving deliberative priority to accommodation would help us to avoid the danger of the moral double standard. Well-meaning liberals are frequently charged with holding cultural minorities to much stricter standards of autonomy and equality than those to which they hold themselves.[30] By asking first what we would have to do to accommodate a group, and only then subjecting the result to the standards of autonomy and equality, we might find that accommodation would not require any more serious compromise with those commitments than we already countenance with respect to majority practices.[31] In some cases, this may lead us to go ahead and refuse accommodation, but also to insist on the

---

[29] Some of the cultural practices that liberal feminists condemn as oppressive to women are celebrated by feminists within those cultures as emancipatory. Some Muslim feminists, for example, argue that the practice of *hijab* (wearing modest dress and covering the hair) liberates them from the sexualizing "male gaze," and hence enhances their ability to function as equal participants in the workplace and in society. See, e.g., Bullock 2002; Al-Hibri 1999. A deliberative engagement between liberal feminists and Muslim feminists might incline the former to be more accepting of *hijab* as a form of feminist practice, and to be more supportive of efforts to eliminate the workplace discrimination that women who choose to wear *hijab* sometimes confront. For a report on recent cases of *hijab*-related employment discrimination in the United States, see Nimer 2001.

[30] One example is the over-discussed topic of female circumcision, which in its milder forms is no more damaging to the health or sexual function of women than is the male circumcision that is universally permitted in Western democracies. In its mildest form, female circumcision involves no more than a pinprick that draws blood. See, e.g., Tamir 1996; Carens and Williams 1998. For an updated discussion, see also Carens 2000: ch. 6. A deliberative engagement between liberals and members of cultural communities whose traditions include female circumcision might make those communities more accepting of mild forms of the practice as an alternative to the extremely harmful forms (excision and infibulation), and of medical supervision to ensure that the milder practice is carried out in sanitary conditions. Alternatively, such an engagement might lead liberals to the conclusion that if female circumcision should be banned, so should male circumcision. If female circumcision should be banned even for adult women, perhaps we should also ban the many forms of cosmetic surgery (breast implant surgery, rib removal surgery and the like) that are arguably just as harmful to women's health. For a discussion of the latter, see Morgan 1991.

[31] On this point I part company with Martha Nussbaum when she argues that we should not insist that we rid our own culture of oppressive practices before criticizing them in others. See Nussbaum 1999: 121–2. Where the degree of oppression elsewhere is severe, I agree that we ought not to restrain ourselves from resisting it; but if there are practices in our own society that are as severe, we might do well to focus our energies there first, as much to establish our moral credibility as anything else. But when we're discussing minority practices *within* our own societies, the question of the moral double standard sharpens into a question of equality before the law; holding minorities to a stronger standard of justice than we do ourselves, itself becomes a form of unequal treatment.

revision of majority practices. In others, it may lead us to accept accommodation and, in doing so, accept that a strict adherence to justice is not
always the most morally compelling course.

It is not the case that presumptive accommodation would reliably lead
to a liberalization of minority cultures, to a greater appreciation of the
goods of toleration or a stronger affirmation of egalitarianism. There
would certainly be some cases in which accommodation would mean
giving support to anti-liberal groups. Certainly I am not arguing that there
should be no limits on those supports. But I do think that, in general, a
liberal society is better off making space for them than trying to suppress
them, that we do better to stare down our fear of others rather than risk
the needless suppression of those who disagree with us.

Giving deliberative priority to peace-as-social-concord is likely to lead
to a more creative liberalism. It may indeed aid us in understanding that
liberal democracy is more capacious than we often assume, and admits of
advancing aspirations to freedom and equality in many different, context-
dependent ways.[32] It would, I wager, generate a more humane and less
doctrinaire liberalism – in short: a tolerable liberalism.

---

[32] For a thorough account of contextualism in political theory, see Carens 2000.

2   A liberalism of conscience

Lucas Swaine

Quae tibi laeta videntur dum loqueris, fieri tristia posse puta.[1]

Ovid, *Ex Ponto*, 4.3.57–8

Despite their steps forward with respect to toleration, stability and legitimacy, the liberal democracies of the new millennium have inherited unresolved and what appear to be ultimately irresolvable religious differences. The world's great democracies contain within them a wide variety of comprehensive doctrines, religious and otherwise. Not all of these doctrines derive from a Christian fount: democracies are increasingly multicultural places, featuring wide racial and ethnic diversity, and legions of religious communities representing every major religious tradition. The condition of permanence attached to this array of comprehensive doctrines prompts some writers to suggest, quite rightly, that there is a "fact of pluralism as such," in the sense that pluralism of this kind exists at present and is not likely to disappear at any time in the foreseeable future (Rawls 1996: 36–8). As John Rawls remarks, notwithstanding the efforts of those who have toiled in vain to unite, coalesce or eradicate religious doctrines, "the fact of religious division remains" (1996: xxvi).

Religious divisions in contemporary liberal societies are not only permanent and profound; they also exist between liberal and non- or anti-liberal religious devotees. For among the people who support the array of doctrines that simple pluralism implies are theocrats, those persons who

An earlier version of this chapter was presented at the 2002 American Political Science Association Annual Meeting, and published in the *Journal of Political Philosophy*, Vol. 11 (2003). I thank Christopher Eisgruber and Jeff Spinner-Halev, respectively, for excellent commentaries. For further instructive and insightful remarks, I wish to acknowledge David Archard, Veit Bader, James Bohman, Avigail Eisenberg, David Estlund, William Galston, John Gray, John Haldane, James Bernard Murphy, Susan Moller Okin, Rob Reich, Oonagh Reitman, Nancy Rosenblum, Kay Lehman Schlozman, John Skorupski, Walter Sinnott-Armstrong, John Tomasi, Jeremy Waldron, and Alan Wolfe. I thank also the editors of the *Journal of Political Philosophy*, and four of their referees, for providing detailed, propitious comments and suggestions.

[1] "Consider that those things which seem to you to be joys have power, while you speak, to change to sorrows."

affirm theocratic conceptions of the good. In this chapter, I shall undertake to describe the legacy of theocracy in modern constitutional democracies, by identifying and classifying two main forms of theocratic allegiance in free societies. I shall then distinguish a particularly troubling series of prudential and moral problems that theocrats raise for liberal government. I will explain exactly why the problems of theocracy are both philosophically and politically serious, and propose that those problems put the legitimacy of liberal government and institutions at risk both at home and abroad.

I shall argue that despite the important gains won by liberal societies, the achievements of liberal political philosophy have amounted to disappointment with regard to the legacy of theocracy. In particular, I will contend that liberals have failed properly to provide reasons for theocrats to affirm liberalism, faltered in identifying grounds on which to govern theocrats, where appropriate, and neglected to devise a well-formed schema for treating theocrats ensconced in liberal democracies. While these failures are serious, I shall propose that they do not ring the changes for liberalism. I will close by providing suggestions on how liberals can speak to the challenges of theocrats and theocratic minorities, combat the legacy of religious discord, and revivify the liberal project for the future.

Theocratic minorities in liberal democracies

The term "theocracy" comes from the ancient Greek word *theokratia*, a term coined by the Jewish historian Josephus Flavius *circa* AD 100. In *Against Apion*, the work in which the term first appears, Josephus proposes that the best government is a theocracy, the government under which the Jews were meant to live. The theocrat "[places] all sovereignty and authority in the hands of God," rather than locating sovereignty in multiple gods, the populace or elsewhere (Josephus 1976: 359, 389–97). Theocrats do not favor popular rule, Josephus contends: the theocrat embraces a Mosaic code that envelops "the whole conduct . . . of life," since nothing ought to be left "to the discretion and caprice of the individual" (1976: 355, 363). As a form of government, theocracy frequently recurs in polities both ancient and modern, in preindustrial societies, and in religious communities outside of the Western tradition. Theocracy also has a richly filigreed history in the West: the English Puritans promptly set up theocratic governance once they reached America, living according to strict, religious regulations and punishing severely dissenters and undesirables.

I should like to follow Josephus here, and characterize theocracy as a mode of governance in which persons endeavor to live according to a conception of the good that is strict, non-liberal and comprehensive in its range of teachings.[2] Theocratic conceptions of the good, on this understanding, are impermissive with respect to the range of life practices to which those conceptions apply. Theocratic conceptions are also comprehensive, ranging across nearly all facets of life, covering personal associations, familial structures, institutional arrangements, practices of ritual and worship, ideals of character and the like (Rawls 1996). A theocratic conception of the good is other-regarding in its strictness and its thoroughness, furthermore, looking to regulate the lives of a community of persons, and not only focusing upon the life-plans of he who holds such a conception.[3] The group of persons to whom a theocratic conception of the good applies may be a small assemblage of devout believers, or it may be the whole of humanity that lies within the regulative vision of the theocrat's conception, if the doctrine is strongly in favor of proselytizing.

Theocrats in modern liberal democracies divide naturally into two different kinds; I focus here upon the American example, but this classification and the argument I shall provide have a wider application. The first kind of theocrat I shall call *ambitious*. Ambitious theocrats are enthusiastic participants in democratic life, engaging in public discourse and political affairs with a view to supplanting liberal institutions with strict, religious government. Religious extremists and elements of the religious right in America are exponents of ambitious religious conceptions of the good, as are members of Nation of Islam and other Muslims who, in the words of Martin Luther King, Jr., "have lost faith in America . . . [and] absolutely repudiated Christianity" (King 1963: 70; cf. DeCaro 1998: chs. 4, 12). Ambitious theocrats are *politically* ambitious, promoting their doctrines fervently and in earnest, and using a variety of means to try to topple the liberal establishment and the debased values that they believe its institutions enshrine. It is no secret that Western democracies have a healthy contingent of ambitious theocrats, since those religious adherents regularly are active and vocal across a broad spectrum of public matters.[4] They are a symptom of democracy's discontent, one could say, concerned with the loss of self-government, the collapse of public morality and the erosion of community (Sandel 1996: 3).

---

[2] Cf. Rawls 1993: 12–15, 174–6ff.; cf. also Rawls 1999a: 40, noting that peoples of constitutional democracies have no comprehensive doctrine of the good. Theocratic communities could be said to have comprehensive religious doctrines, but it is only the constitutive members of those communities *per se* who properly hold conceptions of the good.

[3] Edmund Morgan reminds us that the Puritans endeavored to live a "smooth, honest, civil life," and tried to "force everyone within their power to do likewise"; see Morgan 1966: 2.

[4] See, e.g., Schaefer 1999, who emphasizes the social and theological diversity of both evangelical and fundamentalist Christians.

The second kind of theocrat may properly be called *retiring*. Unlike their ambitious counterpart, these theocrats withdraw from everyday affairs; they are reluctant to participate in political or other public matters, working to live instead in small communities where they may practice their religion in seclusion. In America, examples of such communities include Old Order Amish settlements, the Satmar Hasidim of the Village of Kiryas Joel, Native Indians from the Western Pueblos of New Mexico, extant polygamous Mormon communities, and the former City of Rajneeshpuram in Oregon. Each of these groups strives or has striven to form and maintain their communities in seclusion from outside life, withdrawn into their own villages, settlements or territories for the purposes of their religious practice (see Lee 1996: chs. 2, 5, 6).

Theocratic communities are non-liberal, not inasmuch as they all reject liberty, equality or religious neutrality in the same fashion, or equally, but in the sense that they undertake strictly to maintain the tenor of their religious communities by discouraging or forbidding outright such practices as individual free expression, freedom of association, etc. Both retiring and ambitious theocrats are theocratic by degree: some are more hostile to liberal values than others, and not all theocrats are dedicated to replacing governing liberal institutions with strict religious laws and authorities. For instance, some retiring theocrats, such as the Amish, have neither the desire to wield the sword of secular authority, nor the will to use corporal or more extreme forms of punishment against their members; others are not so tame. Furthermore, leaders of theocratic communities within liberal democracies are legally forbidden from coercing dissenters severely, they are unable to stop those who wish to exit their communities from so doing, and their authority over outsiders is very limited. Yet despite these restrictions, theocratic communities continue to manifest themselves in liberal democracies, representing religious traditions and ways of life stemming from each of a variety of religious doctrines.

Discord in the public realm

With this brief characterization of theocracy in hand, and with the distinction between ambitious and retiring theocrats in place, consider two notable species of problems that ambitious theocrats cause for liberal government. First, ambitious theocrats create a problem of *political discordance* with the controversial and at times incendiary policy proposals that they advance in public. By "political discordance" I mean to identify strife or variance produced in public arenas, respecting views on policy issues and other matters of debate and public concern. Ambitious theocrats demand, *inter alia*, a strong fusion of church and state; the reintroduction, vigorous promotion and strict enforcement of religious values in public life; censorship of irreligious speech (see Oldfield 1996: 58); legal sanctions against minority faiths;[5] the legal prohibition of abortion (Oldfield 1996: 60; cf. Reed 1996: 192, 273); and the penalization or criminalization of homosexuality (see Utter and Storey 1995: 87–9; Oldfield 1996: 60; Reed 1996: ch. 8). The latter two demands in this list are not made exclusively by theocrats, since less extreme religious devotees join the chorus of disapproval on abortion and homosexuality, as do some secular parties. Nor are all of these demands common to theocrats, strictly speaking: the particular content of the theocrat's appeals depends upon the doctrine to which he adheres. Some theocrats do not take serious objection to the practice of abortion, for instance, while others do. But strong proposals of these kinds are often incorporated in theocrats' belief systems, and I identify them here so as to help to distinguish the landscape of theocratic views.

A second species of problems that ambitious theocrats create for liberal government is what I shall call one of *participatory discordance*, respecting the *way* in which theocrats participate in public affairs. Ambitious theocrats make demands based on religious reasons that they offer in support of some particular course of public action. The ambitious theocrat's demands often threaten and anger various sectors of the populace, with proposals grating strongly against liberal values, public opinion, and accepted or received views. Further, ambitious theocrats at times ignore the concerns of their secular cohort, or contend that their religious reasons trump secular interests, or flatly propose that secular concerns are not worth considering at all. This is a well-known political problem; but it is not only a political issue. For beneath the participatory discordance there lurks a knotty philosophical puzzle. Whether religious reasons should count as admissible in public debate is a hotly disputed matter philosophically; and it is an issue itself associated with political discord, since theocrats complain frequently about their disenfranchisement and disillusionment with liberal government and politics, where their reasons are said to be politically inadmissible or their political proposals are defeated (cf. Diamond 1998: 76–80).

Do retiring theocrats cause problems for liberal government? Although they live withdrawn from participatory society, retiring theocrats'

---

[5] Members of Nation of Islam, for instance, have spoken out strongly against Catholicism and supported a variety of sanctions against Jews; see DeCaro 1998: 131–2; cf. Lee 1996: 80–3, 103–4, 109–12. See also *ADL Fact-Finding Report* 1995. Cf. Gates 1998: 18–51. Nation of Islam has published an account of the slave trade that vilifies Jews; it is entitled *The Secret Relationship Between Blacks and Jews* (1991). See Lieb 1998: 216–18.

uncommon practices and convictions spark firestorms of controversy, igniting disagreement over the validity of their lifestyles and the extent to which government ought to tolerate their ways of life. For retiring theocrats do not fit well with the liberal democratic frameworks that surround them, and their communities prove to be very difficult to handle under existing political and legal structures. This is an important way in which retiring theocrats differ from their ambitious counterpart: the retiring theocrat dwells in a community that is itself a source of political discordance. Four of the five retiring American theocratic communities mentioned above have been prodded to defend their practices all the way up to the United States Supreme Court. The Amish were forced to defend themselves against numerous challenges to their educational practices;[6] the Pueblo Indians were taken to task over their criteria for tribal membership;[7] Mormon polygamists were forbidden from living in uncommon family units;[8] and members of Kiryas Joel found that the Supreme Court deemed state law to be unconstitutional, where that law had created a special school district corresponding to the territory of their religious village.[9] The City of Rajneeshpuram disintegrated before any case could be made to the Supreme Court, but there was no shortage of controversy over that community's incorporation as a city. The state of Oregon successfully attacked the legality of the incorporation of the City of Rajneeshpuram, on the grounds that the action violated the Establishment Clause of the United States Constitution, and Article I of the Oregon Constitution as well (see Sanders 1985: 710, 712–24).

Now, it should be plain that the mere fact that theocrats cause political or participatory discordance does not suffice to show that there is any cause for alarm. That is to say, the kinds of controversy that theocrats create do not obviously give liberals or other citizens reason to take theocratic issues especially seriously. For a number of participatory groups and individuals make extreme demands in the public realm, or they participate in public debate in what one might call unreasonable ways, and those individuals and groups could be said to merit equal or greater concern. Furthermore, communities other than theocratic ones cause serious controversy too: private or residential associations are good examples here, as they have excited debate and litigation in recent years; Nancy Rosenblum's work in this area is especially illuminating.[10] Theocrats seem to

---

[6] *Wisconsin v. Yoder*, 406 US 205 (1972).
[7] *Santa Clara Pueblo v. Martinez*, 436 US 49 (1978).
[8] *Reynolds v. United States*, 98 US 145 (1878).
[9] *Board of Education of Kiryas Joel School District v. Grumet*, 114 S.Ct. 2481 (1994).
[10] See Rosenblum 1998: ch. 4. See also "The Rule of Law in Residential Associations," *Harvard Law Review*, 99 (1985): 472–90.

be just one problematic category of citizens among many others; what, if anything, is special or exigent about them and their concerns?

Four prudential problems of theocracy

Here I shall identify four prudential problems raised by theocrats, as well as the accompanying reasons that there are for liberals and other citizens to take special notice of them. First, both ambitious and retiring theocrats clearly have a sense of deep disaffection with the governments of free societies, cultivated in their belief that liberal institutions do not respect them, their concerns or their ways of life. Ambitious theocrats frequently propose that secular government disenfranchises them, and for retiring theocratic communities the sentiment is similar.[11] Unlike other groups with a sense of disenfranchisement, however, theocrats oppose not simply particular policies or laws, or the actions of particular arms or offices of government; nor do they complain merely about existing exclusion with respect to policy-making or legal procedure. Rather, the theocrat's disaffection runs much deeper, reaching down to the very sea floor of liberalism and liberal governance itself. For the theocrat's dissent is not localized within a general consensus on liberal principles, but is based instead on the very rejection of liberal values. This fact helps to illuminate a prudential reason for taking theocrats seriously. Since their objections to liberalism and its standing institutions are so fundamental, and since theocrats remain motivated to struggle to foster and maintain their religious practices, theocrats are a persistent source of public grief in liberal polities.

Second, the modern liberal state is strong, but some theocrats have shown a willingness to fight openly against it and its citizens nonetheless. The example of Rajneeshpuram in Oregon is a case in point: thirty-four of the group's leaders were charged with a variety of state and federal crimes, including attempted murder, assault, arson, burglary, racketeering, electronic eavesdropping and criminal conspiracy (see Manuto 1992: 26–7; Callister, Long and Zaitz 1985). The Sons of Freedom, a branch of Doukabors in western Canada, are another case in point. Beginning in the early twentieth century, homestead laws, census takings and public schooling for Doukhobor children enraged the Sons of Freedom. They bombed schoolhouses and burned or otherwise wrecked power plants, bridges and rail lines (see McLaren and Coward 1999: ch. 8). The Sons of Freedom protested against legal interference by destroying all of their

[11] For accounts to this effect, see Macedo 1995a; see also works by Stephen L. Carter 1993, 1998, 2000.

own property as well, forsaking even their clothing, and showed their loathing of liberal laws, values and institutions by walking through the countryside, solemnly and *en masse*, completely naked. Not all theocrats are prepared to act in illegal or violent ways, of course: the Amish are resolute and unyielding pacifists, refusing under any circumstances to use force even to protect themselves physically. But theocrats are marked by a preparedness to defend their religion against attack, and in cases of perceived interference they have a propensity to strike out violently; and while not only theocrats stand prepared to use violence to fight for their communities and their ways of life, this propensity distinguishes theocrats generally as posing a greater prudential risk than most dissenting parties in liberal democracies. Here there is a second prudential reason to take theocrats seriously: a failure to do so can result in illegal activities or attacks from theocratic quarters, in cases where religious devotees have some quarrel with liberal institutions, and where they believe that violence or other criminal activity is justified.

Third, where government's severe actions against retiring theocrats enjoy no sound, publicly accessible justification, its conduct may excite militant responses from extremist groups sympathetic to the theocrats' plight. The events consequent to the siege and assault on the reclusive Branch Davidians at Waco, Texas, in 1993, are a good example of how such phenomena can and have occurred in the recent past. Militant groups in America were outraged by the federal government's handling of the Waco affair. It was government's unprincipled and ham-handed treatment of the Branch Davidians which catalyzed strikes from militant groups, assaults which included the dreadful Oklahoma City bombing of 19 April 1995. The imminent danger of attack from militia groups was not unforeseen either: six months prior to the Oklahoma City bombing, a report published by the Anti-Defamation League of B'nai B'rith warned that extremist American militia groups were dangerous and looking for suitable provocation for combat.[12] And the peril remains; for militant and other extremist groups continue to view the maltreatment of theocrats as indicative of the moral bankruptcy of liberal government, reacting where government is seen to ride roughshod over retiring theocratic

---

[12] See *ADL Fact-Finding Report* (1994). See also Schwartz 1996: 255–61. Whether militia or other militant groups would have attacked government if the Waco affair were handled differently is, of course, difficult to determine. However, it is worth noting that American extremists claim that the Waco incident has motivated them against government, and continue to perform terrorist acts on 19 April, the anniversary of the final day of the Waco siege. See " 'No Sympathy' for Dead Children, McVeigh Says," *New York Times*, 29 March 2001; see also Michel and Herbeck 2001.

communities.[13] In this, there is a third prudential reason to take theocrats especially seriously: where government mishandles theocrats, it risks attacks from extremist third parties within the body politic, against its own citizens and institutions. This is a grave concern that will remain as long as government has no principled, morally sound policy by which to treat theocrats. John Locke showed prescience in this regard, where he foretold, in *A Letter Concerning Toleration*, that there will be no peace so long as perceptions of religious persecution are found (1689: 56).

Fourth, and finally, with government activity of the sort displayed at Waco, liberal polities may unwittingly cultivate a broad sense of the illegitimacy of liberal government, one that expands well beyond theocratic and extremist spheres. For people in democracies such as America have not taken well to recent terrorist attacks against their own institutions and fellow citizens. They naturally wonder why those assaults occurred, even questioning what value there is in a regime that does not effectively prevent such grave dangers from taking form. It is true that the terrible violence of September 2001 seems to have galvanized citizen support for American government and institutions, contrary to the intended effects of the zealous assaults. However, further attacks could critically damage citizens' sense of the legitimacy of liberal government, and affect their behavior in turn.

Is there any empirical evidence to support such a dark contention? Despite the weak connection between feelings of trust in government and voter turnout (see Abramson 1983; Teixeira 1992), there is evidence to suggest that the most cynical are more politically engaged than are average citizens (Parry, Moyser and Day 1992). There is also reason to believe, as the study from *Voice and Equality* seems to show, that the decline in voting in America has not meant a decrease in political activism (Verba, Schlozman and Brady 1995; see also Putnam 2002). It seems therefore plausible to suppose that a strong sense of alienation or a widespread perception of illegitimacy could mobilize citizens at least to throw out officeholders and to seek institutional redress, if not to take more extreme political action (see Citrin and Green 1986). To this one could add an auxiliary point on the obverse: Pippa Norris has argued that data from the 1995–7 World Values Study indicate that the perception of legitimacy in government contributes to voluntary compliance with the law, although strengthening civil liberties may be even more important in securing such compliance, at least in burgeoning democracies (Norris 1999: 264–5).

[13] Militia groups normally are principally concerned with other issues than religious liberty, such as government encroachment on Second Amendment rights, but they are nonetheless excitable over government invasion of religious communities.

So the fourth prudential concern is that an absence of a sense of legitimacy could contribute significantly to an undesirable form of citizen mobilization. Under a direr scenario, one might witness disaffection moving from theocratic and militant pockets into the body politic, plaguing common citizen and tame religious believer alike. Here one must be chary, since it is important not to overestimate the extent to which the continuing maltreatment of theocrats, coupled with attacks from extremist groups, could fuel a disastrous legitimation crisis. However, there is some reason to think that a serious crisis in confidence in liberal government could ignite, sparked by perceptions of its lack of legitimacy, if the problems of theocracy are left to grow unchecked.

Four moral failures of liberalism

The prudential problems pertaining to theocrats are serious enough to warrant careful and direct attention on the part of liberals and liberal government. But how will these problems auspiciously be addressed? The best effort to assuage the combativeness and public grief that theocrats bring to bear, and the prospects of a legitimation crisis, cannot simply be an exercise of public management on the part of liberal government. For liberal theory and liberal government each bear some responsibility for the prudential problems that I have outlined, and it will only be through a sustained treatment of a series of *moral* shortcomings in liberalism that these prudential problems will be stabilized and resolved. It is not my purpose to lay blame here, and certainly I shall not suggest that liberal government is blameworthy for the recent terrorist attacks against its citizens and institutions. However, four moral shortcomings of liberalism have contributed to the prudential dangers that I have distinguished here, as well as being serious failures in their own right.

The first moral failure of liberalism is this: liberal government lacks a well-devised and justifiable schema for treating theocrats dwelling in liberal democracies, one that is able to handle theocrats' contributions to public debate, and which is capable of treating theocratic communities properly under law. The lack of a standard of that kind places government in the awkward position of being at times unable to justify its laws and its procedures to its citizens. Furthermore, the missing standard permits government to commit injustices against religious devotees in cases where, for instance, government organizes ambitious theocrats' concerns out of public debate without cause (see Bachrach and Baratz 1962, 1963; see also Lukes 1974), or where government violates people's moral right to religious free exercise by impacting religious communities with excessive entanglements and by making their religious practice very nearly impossible. I have addressed this issue at some length elsewhere (see Swaine 2001), but it bears mention here since liberal government's current practice of handling theocratic communities is a clear case of moral failure on its part.

The second moral problem is that liberal government should, but does not, have proper and identifiable grounds in hand for governing theocrats *simpliciter*. This issue is distinct from the question of whether liberals have devised a schema by which to handle theocrats in an appropriate manner; it is in fact analytically prior. Here the concern applies not merely to how government treats theocrats, but, more fundamentally, to whether liberal government has any right to govern them at all.

I should like to expand upon this concern briefly here; for the thought needs some elaboration. Why would one entertain the idea that liberal government might *not* have a right to govern its theocratic citizens? Consider first the kind of value conflict that obtains between theocrats and liberals. Like other religious practitioners, the theocrat holds firm to his belief in otherworldly powers and ends, such that disabusing him of the notion that such ends exist and are valuable would be very difficult indeed. But more pointedly, theocrats' conceptions of the good seem as though they may be fundamentally different and discordant with respect to those conceptions of other citizens, bringing forth a conflict of commitments and values for which no rational solution is available (see Berlin 1969; Griffin 1986: 31–4, 64–8; Larmore 1996: 158–63; Lukes 1989; MacIntyre 1984: ch. 6; Williams 1977: ch. 5; see also Rawls 1996: 54–9). It could be the case that liberal and theocratic values are incommensurable, in the sense that they are not equal values, nor is one set of values superior to the other.[14] Why is this important? To the minds of some philosophers, this situation of deep value conflict has decided implications for political theory and for the prospects of resolving actual political conflict. Given the fundamental and rationally irresolvable conflict between liberal and theocratic conceptions of the good, they argue, a *modus vivendi* between people is that for which government should aim. John Gray has proposed as much in recent years.[15] The arguments in this regard are not just that there is no way to show people like theocrats the appeal in any Enlightenment or universalist version of liberalism and liberal institutions, but also that there simply is no reason for theocrats to accept liberal values either.

---

[14] Joseph Raz provides the following definition of incommensurability: "*Two valuable options are incommensurable if (1) neither is better than the other, and (2) there is (or could be) another option which is better than one but is not better than the other*"; see Raz 1986: 325. Cf. also Griffin 1986: 77–91ff.; see also generally Chang 1997.

[15] See the work of John Gray 1994, 1998, 2000.

That liberal government enjoys *de facto* rule over theocrats dwelling in liberal democracies is quite clear. Government continually enacts laws which impact on theocrats and their religious practices in numerous ways, regulating and interfering with the affairs of theocratic communities, and at points coercing theocrats outright. However, the fact that liberals have brought theocratic forces partially or even largely under control says nothing of whether they have done so by right. Nor does it indicate that the continuing domination is morally acceptable. The mere fact that some combatant has won a victory over his opponent does not, and never could, justify the triumph in a moral sense. Here one must take note of the fact that theocrats object strenuously and profoundly to liberal values and the impositions of liberal government, proposing that they have good religious reasons for departing from liberal standards. Their reasons, they argue, outweigh the claims and concerns of liberal government. Where liberals provide secular arguments in favor of liberal values and institutions, and in defense of liberal government's right to govern theocrats within liberal polities, theocrats respond that those arguments belie their conclusions. For the theocrat contends that his particular religious dictates override liberal concerns, justify the illiberal treatment of refractory members within his theocratic community, or undercut the supposed right of liberal institutions to govern theocrats. Liberals must think that the grounds on which to govern theocrats have been uncovered at some point; but the problems involved simply with locating grounds with which to justify liberal government's treatment of theocrats are serious indeed. Insofar as liberals have struggled to identify those grounds in a satisfactory way, they have failed to shore up a serious moral shortcoming of liberalism.

Here is a third moral inadequacy. Since liberal government is in the habit of coercing theocrats where they break the law, it would seem that government owes them an explanation as to why it does so. Not just any explanation will do, either. The United States Supreme Court's decision outlawing polygamy, in *Reynolds v. United States* (1878), is a good example of an inadequate explanation for a specific legal restriction on theocrats.[16] In that case, the Mormon George Reynolds was charged with bigamy for having married more than one woman. Reynolds claimed that it was his religious duty to practice polygamy, contending that the practice was enjoined by God and the Bible, circumstances permitting, with his failure or refusal to practice polygamy resulting in damnation (161). In the Court's decision, Chief Justice Waite remarked that polygamy "has always been odious" to the northern and western nations of Europe; the

---

[16] *Reynolds v. United States* 98 US 145 (1878).

English, he noted, have for ages treated polygamy as an "offence against society" (164). To this *argumentum ad antiquitam* he added that marriage is a "most important feature" of social life: marriage is a "sacred obligation" as well as a "civil contract," and so it can rightly be regulated by law (165). Polygamy, on the other hand, edifies and enlivens "the patriarchal principle," fettering members of large polygamous communities in "stationary despotism"; Waite admonished Americans not to neglect the "pure-minded women and . . . innocent children" who suffer under polygamous arrangements (166, 167–8).[17] Whether God might require such suffering among the faithful, Waite did not consider; instead, he moved to *petitio principii*, proposing that there "cannot be a doubt" that, in the absence of constitutional restrictions forbidding it, civil government may legitimately determine whether to allow polygamous or monogamous marriages (166). As to whether Mormon polygamists might be granted an exception to bigamy law, the Court determined that taking such a course of action would be unacceptable: allowing exceptions simply because of religious belief would make religious doctrines superior to the laws of the land, and make each citizen a law unto himself (166).

The point here is not that polygamous arrangements should ultimately be considered desirable, morally unproblematic, or harmless to women and children. Rather, it is that arguments such as those expressed in *Reynolds* simply do not yield an adequate explanation for disallowing polygamy, certainly not in the face of the competing claim that God commands that practice among true believers on pain of damnation for defeat. The arms of liberal government should hand down explanations for policies, procedures and laws that are powerful and well-reasoned, and which go a long way towards justifying the laws liberal institutions use to regulate theocrats and theocratic communities. And one expects that any liberal will agree that such explanations should be forthcoming as well.[18] After all, liberals are supposed to be united against excessive or unlimited government, lawless rule, state oppression and unwarranted interference by state institutions in quotidian affairs. So there is a matter of principle at stake, for the liberal, as well as a question of consistency. But there is even more on the block than this: for if no good explanation can be provided as to why liberal government may rightly govern

---

[17] Waite added that polygamous communities may also disturb people in neighboring vicinities.

[18] Amy Gutmann and Dennis Thompson's conception of deliberative democracy, for example, affirms this view. "At the core of deliberative democracy," they write, "is the idea that citizens and officials must justify any demands for collective action by giving reasons that can be accepted by those who are bound by the action"; see Gutmann and Thompson 2000: 35–6. See also generally Gutmann and Thompson 1996.

theocrats or coerce them where they break the law, then probably liberal government should refrain from so doing. In cases where no compelling reasons to interfere in the lives of citizens can be provided, it is the liberal's contention that government should stand down from its threat of interference, allowing persons to behave as they will, and in the manner in which they are inclined.[19]

Finally, here is the fourth moral failure of liberalism that I shall identify. I have suggested that liberal government owes theocrats an explanation, based on good reasons, as to why government may apply its laws to them, given the deep disagreement that theocrats have with liberal values and government. Those reasons should be reasons that theocrats can accept, reasons that hold for theocrats given their concerns and commitments. This is another point with which one would expect liberals broadly to agree, inasmuch as liberals concur with Rawls that liberal principles of justification must win their support by "addressing each citizen's reason."[20] But here is the problem: not all reasons hold equally well for all people. In stating this claim, I do not mean to dispute the thesis of the universality of reasons; indeed, it seems quite plausible that if something is a reason for one person to act, feel or believe in a certain way, then that reason must hold for another person who is similarly situated (cf. Skorupski 1999: 440, 446–7). Rather, I wish to point out that theocrats and liberals take quite different positions on the nature of otherworldly values and ends, on the content of religious dictates, and on the respective priority of secular and religious values in public life, such that it looks as though theocrats and liberals simply are not similarly situated parties. A series of good secular reasons for accepting liberal government might hold for other secularists; but for those who flatly deny the importance of temporal life, or who give priority to salvation over toleration, secular reasons may not have much bearing. I do not suggest that theocrats are strangers to Reason, reasons or reasoning; quite to the contrary, theocrats begin from different premises than secular liberals do, but they are still receptive to reasons. I am instead proposing that no adequate explanation, based on reasons that are good or acceptable to theocrats, has yet been given to justify liberal government's right to govern theocrats dwelling within

---

[19] Consider, e.g., John Stuart Mill's remarks on this issue: "[The] burthen of proof is supposed to be with those who are against liberty; who contend for any restriction or prohibition . . . [the] *a priori* assumption is in favor of freedom" (Mill 1991: 472). See also Gaus 1990: ch. 8, 1996: ch. 17.

[20] Rawls 1993: 143. Cf. Gutmann and Thompson 2000: 37–8: "The very activity of providing an account that other citizens can be expected to understand as reasonable (even if not right) indicates the willingness of citizens to acknowledge one another's membership in a common democratic enterprise."

liberal polities, despite the liberal's rightful philosophical commitment to the principle that such reasons ought to be supplied as required.

The charge of liberalism: meeting the challenges of theocracy

Each of the four moral failures distinguished above is serious in its own right; and none is offset by liberalism's success in fostering and maintaining societies free from outright religious persecution. For while the toleration of liberal societies is a wonderful development, it does not excuse or balance out the moral shortcomings that liberal theory has displayed. For this reason, it unfortunately seems fair to say that liberals bear some responsibility for the prudential problems mentioned above. Naturally, the extent of an actor's responsibility for a problem is logically independent of that party's ability to address and repair the matter. But in this case, a serious, sustained effort to address and fix the moral shortcomings of liberalism, on the part of liberals and liberal institutions, apart from being an effort worth undertaking for its own sake, could also lead to an improvement in the prudential dangers I have outlined in this chapter.

Here one might object to the idea that liberals need to do more to give ambitious or retiring theocrats an adequate explanation as to why liberal government may apply its laws to them. For liberal theorists have already given justifications and guidelines for various forms and degrees of interference in the affairs of theocrats, the objector may contend. One might admit that reasons for interference declared in various wings of government have been at times inadequate, but insist the offerings of liberal political philosophers are surely better grounded and articulated. That theocrats have not accepted the reasons or justifications that liberals have presented hardly means those reasons and justifications are not powerful or compelling. Indeed, there is only so much that liberal theory can be expected to accomplish with regard to theocrats; so this objection might go.

The problem here is that liberals have been notoriously slack in their failure to address the most challenging claims of theocrats. There is no shortage of liberals who advocate some kind of interference in the lives of theocrats, but practically none has faced the prior question of the right of liberal institutions to intervene. For instance, Amy Gutmann, Meira Levinson, Stephen Macedo and Rob Reich all advocate interference in the affairs of theocratic communities for the sake of education (see Gutmann 1987, 1995, 1996; Levinson 1999; Macedo 1990, 1995a, 2000; Reich 2002). Levinson and Reich plead in favor of interventions and restrictions for the sake of protecting minors within minorities; children are especially vulnerable, they notice, and must be protected by liberal institutions against illiberal practices (Levinson 1999; Reich 2002). Susan Moller Okin has similarly admonished liberal multiculturalists and advocates of group rights for failing to take gender inequality sufficiently seriously (2002: 206; see also 1997: 25–8; 1998).[21] Defenders of group rights or exemptions for cultural or religious groups "are often relatively insensitive to issues of gender," Okin charges (2002: 216). She notes that liberal theorists agree on the centrality of the right of exit for members of minority groups in liberal polities. But when it comes to patriarchal religious communities that "discriminate against or oppress women," Okin maintains, mere formal rights of exit would repeatedly leave women in the "impossible position" of choosing between "total submission [or] total alienation" from their communities (2002: 229).

Okin's reprimand is inadvertently ironic: she rebukes liberals for not having properly considered how women will fare under various schemes for minority rights and exemptions, but her own work omits any serious, scholarly consideration of religious arguments marshaled to defeat claims she advances on the proper treatment of women. That liberal political philosophers should rethink the ways in which their theories might differentially and inequitably impact on women I shall not dispute. But there are prior questions here about the acceptability of liberal government interfering in the affairs of theocrats for the sake of women, for educational designs, or for other liberal purposes such as that of equal citizenship.[22] One needs to have an argument about the appropriateness of intervention in these areas, given theocrats' claims that they have God-given, *ultima facie* reasons to depart from liberal standards. Indeed, the theocrat who stands on those reasons may contend not only that he should be exempted from various liberal policies and laws, but that his religious conception of the good must be imposed upon liberal society broadly, with a severe punishment for failure awaiting in the afterlife. Contemporary liberal arguments such as Okin's provide merely *pro tanto* and insufficient reasons to justify interference in theocratic affairs (cf. Rawls 1996: 386–90); and they give little subjective reason for theocrats to affirm liberalism, since they speak hardly at all to theocrats' most central and pressing concerns. Liberals must give reasons and explanations that can withstand theocratic challenges, if the liberal project is actually to make headway on the prudential and moral problems of theocracy that I have identified. Otherwise, liberal theory will tumble to the floor of philosophy, rolling like a lopped and leering *caput mortuum*.

---

[21] Ayelet Shachar has argued similar points in recent years (Shachar 2001; see also 1998a).
[22] For arguments in favor of interventions for the sake of citizenship, see Callan 1997. See also Macedo 1990.

Nor will one find philosophical solace in liberal constitutional arguments such as those offered by Ronald Dworkin. In *Life's Dominion*, Dworkin (1994: 162–8, *passim*) argues that an appropriate constitutional understanding of religion, in the context of the Free Exercise Clause of the First Amendment, illuminates a ground for abortion rights.[23] Theocrats could agree that the United States Constitution allows, perhaps even enjoins, laws protecting "procreative autonomy" (see Dworkin 1994: 157–9, 162–8, 172–6). But to this they may add that God's commands overrule the Constitution, and as such abortion simply must not be permitted. The same problem holds for Christopher Eisgruber's work on the constitutional value of assimilation: theocrats might grant that the Constitution endorses a series of substantive values which, when fostered appropriately, would dispense with the effective segregation of theocratic communities and assimilate theocrats into a stronger political unity (see Eisgruber 1996: 90–1, 99–103, *passim*, 1994, 2001). But theocrats can claim that God's commands trump those constitutional values; and in the absence of further argumentation to demonstrate the implausibility of such a position, the assimilationist argument sputters and grinds to a halt.

Not even Rawls's promising work on liberal legitimacy and reasonableness suffices to ward off such strikes from theocratic challengers. The Rawlsian liberal does not count persons as unreasonable simply for being religious, or for their mere disagreement over a political conception of justice. Instead, the Rawlsian contends that for persons to be counted as reasonable, they must accept a liberal principle of legitimacy (Rawls 1996: 136–7, 216–17, 393–4, 428–30). But why *should* theocrats affirm a Rawlsian, liberal principle of legitimacy? Indeed, theocrats may not simply refuse to accept such a principle: they can also claim to have good reason to reject fair terms of co-operation or the burdens of judgement, as Rawls delineates them (1996: 15–22, 49–50, 54–8), based on what they understand to be God-given commands on how to speak to others on such crucial issues as abortion, education, protecting rituals of worship or tolerating heretics. Furthermore, with respect to Rawls's list of primary goods, theocrats can and do reject the idea that basic rights and liberties, freedom of movement, free choice of occupation, and income and wealth should count as "basic all-purpose means" to pursue a permissible conception of the good (Rawls 1996: 178–83, 187–90). Theocrats do not make these maneuvers merely to suit some immediate selfish interest: to the contrary, they do so in the larger purposes of trying to save souls,

[23] Dworkin proposes that "the right to procreative autonomy, from which a right of choice about abortion flows, is well grounded in the First Amendment" (1994: 166).

avoiding eternal damnation, or achieving some other otherworldly value, so conceived. For these difficult theocratic challenges, political liberalism requires a more complete and powerful response.

Still, the argument to this point leaves unanswered the question of just what liberals can do to address liberalism's moral shortcomings. One might object that it is quixotic to hold that the conflict between liberal government and theocratic religious devotees could ever be settled. What real hope is there that any solution for the conflict between theocrats and liberals could ever be achieved?

First of all, to assuage the conflict between liberals and theocrats, liberals would do well to scrutinize the values and commitments that theocrats hold in common. For a careful examination of the theocrat's commitments to otherworldly values, and to strict, religious life, holds the potential of bringing to light the reasons there are for theocrats to affirm a liberal order. I do not have space to elaborate the case here, but I propose that reasons for theocrats to affirm a liberal order do indeed exist, and that these reasons theocrats should in fact accept. That is to say, *pace* the complaints of John Gray, Stuart Hampshire (2000) and others who have proclaimed such value conflict to be insuperable by reason, I suspect that the value conflict between theocrats and liberals *is a rationally soluble problem*. For theocrats seem to be committed rationally to normative principles of liberty of conscience, given their common purpose to accept the good, to reject the bad, and to distinguish between the two. This rational commitment has institutional implications for protecting liberty of conscience, implications that could be articulated to speak to theocrats in new and better ways. A fuller treatment of this matter I provide elsewhere;[24] but the point here is that if theocrats are indeed rationally committed to normative principles of liberty of conscience, that commitment could serve to build reasons for them to affirm liberalism. It might even illuminate a path liberals can take to justify the right of liberal institutions to govern theocrats in liberal democracies.

Second, liberals could marshal a complex of related reasons for theocrats to affirm liberalism as part of a larger effort to better relations with theocrats, and to demonstrate the appeal that liberal institutions could hold for them. I expect that those reasons will have three central components. First, the reasons must have a *prudential* component, involving an account of the variety of threats and dangers countries face when ruled under unmitigated theocracy, such as the strong propensity for such

---

[24] I offer rudiments of such an account in Swaine 2003a, 2003b. I provide a more complete treatment in *A Liberalism of Conscience: American Liberalism and Theocratic Communities* (forthcoming, Colombia University Press).

polities to pervert the religiosity they mean to promote. This prudential element could also include an articulation of the benefits of co-operating with liberal regimes, and the disadvantages for non-compliance.[25] Second, reasons for theocrats to affirm liberalism will have to have a *theological* element, speaking to such matters as what one rightly can believe God commands of His followers. This component will be crucial, since without it theocrats will have recourse to the claim that neither secular argumentation, nor a Rawlsian understanding of public reason,[26] overrides the religious dictates that God has given them. Third, the reasons must have a *conciliatory* component, according to which liberal government will need to show its willingness, and its ability, to develop a friendlier disposition even to theocratic religiosity and religious forms. One way to demonstrate this flexibility would be to grant semi-sovereignty to theocratic communities in liberal democracies, provided that those communities meet some general criteria such as respecting basic human rights and rights of exit from communities (see Swaine 2001: 324–38). Another way would be to behave more carefully and respectfully, when it comes to religious practice and polities internationally. For it will be important for liberalism authentically to affirm religiosity, not just to tolerate religion, if there is to be any real advance on the moral and prudential problems I have identified.

Third, along with a careful consideration of theocratic commitments and the reasons there may be for theocrats to affirm a liberal order, a solution to the challenges of theocracy will involve institutional innovation. As a first step here, it will be important to consider a broad range of possible structures of governance for ambitious and retiring theocrats. Without a broad consideration of this kind, it remains premature to conclude, for example, that only a *modus vivendi* between theocrats and liberals is possible, or that liberal government could never rightfully govern theocrats, or that liberal government has no right to apply its laws to theocrats other than that given by the sword. I have suggested above that one piece in this institutional puzzle will be a well-formed schema for handling retiring theocratic communities, as a way of addressing the moral and political problems that those theocrats raise. What is more, I have argued elsewhere that the option of semi-sovereignty for theocratic communities could free retiring theocrats from a range of injustices to which they are currently

[25] Included here could be economic incentives for theocrats internationally, since many (but by no means all) theocratic polities are not only impoverished but arguably are also resentful of liberal democratic wealth.

[26] Rawls distinguishes between public reason and secular reason, where he understands the latter as "reasoning in terms of comprehensive nonreligious doctrines"; see Rawls 1999b: 583, cf. 587–8. Theocrats could object even to public reasons, so construed, if those reasons are not shown to be consistent with or overdetermined by commands of God.

subject, properly respecting their moral right to religious free exercise and enlivening the liberal commitment to religious freedom as well (see Swaine 2001: 324–43). A second step towards solving the institutional components of this puzzle will be to fill in the missing standard for admissible discourse in public reason, and, in particular, to clarify the kinds of religious reasons admissible in public debate. This latter problem has not been handled well, unfortunately, and its presence does liberals and liberal government no favors. For the lack of an adequate, well-reasoned and publicly accessible standard by which to handle religious contributions to public debate has motivated growing numbers of zealots against liberalism and its trademark values and institutions, threatening the very stability and legitimacy of the liberal order.

Current liberal theory has made little effort to try to show the appeal of liberalism to theocrats, perhaps due to the relatively recent belief that liberalism must not only be neutral towards reasonable conceptions of the good, but also justified in terms of secular reasoning alone. This was not the approach of the primogenitors of liberalism, such as Thomas Hobbes or John Locke: those theorists were keen to try to provide a religious ground for their political theories, one that could appeal to a broad range of religious devotees.[27] The extent to which Hobbes or Locke were themselves Christians or authentic believers in the religious arguments they advanced are independent questions. For Hobbes and Locke realized that religious devotees might well only be reached with arguments that speak to their deeply held religious values. And so they engaged religiosity at that level, considering problems in the interpretation of Scripture, arguing that apparent religious differences between Christians are not as great as they may seem, and working to provide a religious justification for the political institutions and frameworks that they advocated. Indeed, theological efforts such as these were once perennial, blooming colorfully in the liberal gardens of John Stuart Mill, Lord Acton, Bernard Bosanquet and Thomas Hill Green.

However, liberals have largely abandoned the attempt to provide reasons for problematic religious devotees to affirm a liberal order. What accounts for liberalism's movement away from Hobbes and Locke in this regard? While this too is a complex and difficult question, one notices that liberal theory currently is marked by the refusal even to engage with philosophical or theological political visions advanced under religious conceptions of the good, especially those visions of the non-liberal or illiberal varieties. A number of liberal theorists now assume, or argue explicitly, that no engagement with theological matters is required for a full-flowered

---

[27] See Hobbes 1991, 1680, 1963. See also Locke 1689, 1999.

liberal theory sufficiently broad to handle the range of persons and conceptions of the good to which it is meant to apply. Jeff Spinner-Halev
reflects that liberals and multiculturalists may simply "have little sympathy for the reasons why people are religious," insofar as many of those
theorists assume that religion is in the end just another obstacle to human
progress (2000: 213; cf. McConnell 2001: 17–24). Along with Spinner-
Halev, Robert Audi and William Galston stand among the handful of
liberals who have considered the value of arguments for more extreme
religious devotees to affirm liberal institutions; their sensitive efforts count
among only a few exceptions to the rule.[28]

Conclusion

Contemporary liberal theorists have done well to build upon the secular
elements of early liberal and proto-liberal arguments, and liberals have
as a result produced some powerful political theories for modern constitutional democracies. However, liberalism's response to one of the most
serious challenges of simple pluralism amounts to a qualified failure. Here
one must give some credit to those critics of liberalism who have voiced
concern that the laws of liberal polities are based on fiat rather than on
consensus or sound moral and political principles (see, e.g., Fish 1999;
Connolly 2000). Some such critics maintain that liberalism proves in
the end to be just another partisan doctrine, one giving priority to more
autonomous conceptions of the good and disadvantaging others, including those conceptions that may not even be inimical to liberalism and
liberal institutions. Other critics have gone so far as to prophesy gloom
and doom for liberal polities, suggesting that liberalism's partisan nature
will be its downfall. I fear that the critics are correct to the extent that they
have noticed that the actual practices of liberal governments often are not
morally justified, and insofar as critics have realized that citizens of liberal
polities could come to see that the ideals of liberty and equality have not
been promoted fairly within their countries. The good news is that none
of it suffices to show that theocrats are in fact correct to deny politically
liberal values. For that matter, the shortcomings do not indicate that no
version of liberalism could properly meet the challenge of handling its
theocratic citizens in an appropriate way, nor is it obvious that liberalism
could hold no appeal for theocrats.

A sustained treatment of the moral failures of liberalism is worth pursuing for moral reasons; but such a treatment also holds the promise of

---

[28] See Audi 1989, 1997, 2000; see also Galston 1995, 2002: 40–2. See Greenawalt 1995
for another fairly sensitive treatment of these matters. See also Larmore 1987: ch. 6,
1996: 30–5, 41–4, 46, 167–9.

attenuating the significant prudential and political problems that I have outlined in this chapter. If in fact there are reasons for theocrats to affirm a liberal order, the communication of those reasons, articulated and voiced in suitable ways,[29] should help to mitigate the prudential problems caused by insurgent theocrats and extremist third parties. After all, theocrats have been inflamed by what they take to be the dearth of reasons for them to affirm liberal institutions and laws, and for a liberal order to apply its laws to them. As such, steps forward of the sort that I have proposed in this chapter could hopefully be of some help; and they could serve to head off the most extreme prudential problem I have identified here, viz., the widespread perception of the illegitimacy of liberal institutions, fostered by the perception of the mistreatment of theocrats and promoted by the ongoing conflict between theocrats and liberal government.

Of course, shoring up the failures of liberalism by providing adequate, accessible and acceptable reasons for theocrats to affirm a liberal order will not solve all of the problems associated with zealotry in the world, nor would it easily harmonize the values and practices of reclusive theocrats with those of other citizens in a well-formed liberal order. It would be unrealistic to hold that the provision of such reasons will suffice to quell all religious discord, if only because new theocratic groups continually burgeon forth in democratic societies as new flora in the simple pluralistic array. Nor do I wish to suggest that it would be desirable or reasonable to expect theocrats and liberals ultimately to converge on a shared conception of the good; conflict and disagreement are an important condition of politics itself, and free societies will never do away entirely with political and participatory discordance. Rather, the point is that theocrats' objections to liberalism appear to be serious and profound, but the conundrum may well not be rationally irresolvable. It is still too early to suggest that the attempt to provide reasons for theocrats to affirm a liberal order can only fail to mitigate the prudential problems associated with the legacy of theocracy in democratic polities.

It is the liberal's charge to face the challenges of theocracy in the spirit of his primogenitors, in order to renew the liberal project. Perhaps now more than ever, liberal theory needs a sound argument as to why theocratic religious practitioners have good reason to affirm liberalism and liberal institutions, based on arguments *for them*, run on premises that theocrats could accept, and which they might even find appealing. To make this argument, liberals will do well to treat the problems of theocracy with public reasons, respectful dialogue and institutional innovation.

---

[29] See Audi 2000: 47–8, 175. For theocrats living in modern democracies, the reasons to affirm liberalism may take a slightly different form than they do for theocrats dwelling in other kinds of polities.

This shall form the heart of a liberalism of conscience. One suspects that the renewal of the liberal project will require this work, despite the aversion to such endeavors in contemporary liberalism. The promise of such efforts is a new dawn for liberalism; the failure to respond will mean not just persistent moral disappointment, but, one fears, possible political disaster.

Part II

Equality

3   Multiculturalism and feminism:
     no simple question, no simple answers

Susan Moller Okin

Most political theorists who have written recently about multiculturalism
and feminism acknowledge that there are quite serious tensions between
them. Since there is a vast range of beliefs and practices both within and
among cultures about the appropriate status and roles of women, it seems
almost inevitable that there should be some conflict between aiming to
support and protect many cultures and aiming to promote the equal dignity of and respect for women. Ayelet Shachar's *Multicultural Jurisdictions:
Cultural Differences and Women's Rights* (2001) is the lengthiest work on the
subject to date. She devotes several chapters to analyzing and explaining
the origins of "the paradox of multicultural vulnerability," as she aptly
calls it, before looking at ways in which it has been addressed within
various, basically liberal regimes and offering thoughtful proposals about
how it might best be addressed. Convinced that the rights and interests of
vulnerable individuals – in particular, individual women, but also others,
such as children and dissenters – can be jeopardized by group rights
and other well-intentioned efforts to accommodate groups, Shachar
writes:

Multicultural accommodation presents a problem . . . when pro-identity group
policies aimed at leveling the playing field between minority communities and the
wider society unwittingly allow systematic maltreatment of individuals within the
accommodated group – an impact which in certain cases is so severe that it can
nullify these individuals' citizenship rights. Under such conditions, well-meaning
accommodation by the state may leave members of minority groups vulnerable
to severe injustice within the group, and may, in effect, work to reinforce some of
the most hierarchical elements of a culture. (Shachar 2001: 2–3)

Others, too, including Jeff Spinner-Halev and Chandran Kukathas,
have published recent papers on tensions between multiculturalism and

This paper was first written as a lecture for presentation at the American Political Science
Association's Annual meetings, Boston, Massachusetts (28 August–1 September 2002)
and at a conference on "Minorities within Minorities" at the University of Nebraska,
Lincoln, Nebraska (4 October–5 October 2002). Thanks to Cass Sunstein, Suzanne Dovi,
Avigail Eisenberg and Jeff Spinner-Halev for helpful comments.

feminism. Spinner-Halev, in "Feminism, Multiculturalism, Oppression, and the State", says that, at least in the case of those groups which Will Kymlicka (1995) has termed "national" minorities, "the feminist critique is surely right that group autonomy can harm women" (Spinner-Halev 2001: 92). Kukathas, in "Is Feminism Bad for Multiculturalism?" agrees that "[t]here is no question that there is a conflict between feminism and multiculturalism," acknowledging that "[they] remain in tension to the extent that there are *any* groups which neglect the interest of women, and which seek accommodation within the polity." In his view, "[t]he issue is, which should prevail when this conflict arises . . .?" (Kukathas 2001: 88) Jacob Levy devotes a section of *The Multiculturalism of Fear*, entitled "Internal Cruelty," almost entirely to problematic cultural practices concerning women and girls (Levy 2000: 51–62). He has no doubt that "feminist voices about multiculturalism have real force and weight" (Levy 2000: 53), and suggests several reasons for feminist concern about cultural group rights.

Most recently, Marilyn Friedman and Monique Deveaux have each addressed the problem of tensions between multicultural group rights and women's equality. Like Shachar, Friedman and Deveaux take substantial steps beyond diagnosing the problem: each proposes how it should be addressed, in the context of liberal states seeking to accommodate minority cultural groups that hold to less liberal norms about women. Friedman, in a chapter on this issue in her new book, *Autonomy, Gender, Politics* (2003), remarks that it is "no surprise" that women and girls are especially affected by "minority cultural practices," in part because "[c]ultural minorities that reside in liberal democratic states featuring powerful capitalist economies may find that the only areas of life in which they can hope to exercise some communal control over their lives and practice their cultural traditions unimpeded are areas commonly treated as matters of 'privacy' by the surrounding liberal society" (179). Friedman responds at some length and with considerable skill to some of the criticisms of my work on the subject (with which she largely agrees); she then presents arguments about how she thinks the problem should be resolved, which I shall discuss below. Monique Deveaux also proposes a solution, in "A Deliberative Approach to Conflicts of Culture" (this volume). Citing Brian Barry's, Will Kymlicka's, Martha Nussbaum's and my contributions to the debate, she writes: "The broad political approach to the challenges posed by non-liberal cultural practices favored by these thinkers is one that endorses liberal but not necessarily *democratic* principles and procedures"(this volume, p. 340). Dissenting from the approach she discerns in these theorists' works, she presents "a democratic, pluralist, and manifestly political approach" to mediating such challenges within liberal democracies, also discussed below.

As the person who stepped into something of a political minefield (some might say, the one who threw a verbal "grenade" into a simmering discussion) by publishing two overlapping articles on multiculturalism and feminism in the late 1990s, I think it is time to revisit the subject (Okin 1998, 1999b; see also Okin 1999a, 2002). Recognition of a conflict or tension, such as I just noted, by no means foretells agreement about either the precise nature of the conflict or what should be done about it. There has been some agreement with and some dissent from my specific diagnosis of the problem, a great deal of criticism of the ways in which I raised and discussed it, and virtually no attention paid to how I suggested it might best be addressed. The third point is odd, since (as I shall explain) the suggestions I made in these initial explorations of the subject are in accord with most of the more developed solutions to the problem put forward since by others. However, my suggestions were briefly stated, by no means rich in specifics or spelled out in detail, and the subsequent, more detailed proposals made by other theorists that are in broad agreement with them deviate from each other quite significantly. Some proposed solutions to the paradox of multicultural vulnerability tend more towards stressing the values of liberalism; some place more emphasis on the importance of arriving at solutions by democratic processes. Whereas some advocate that liberal states require that cultural sub-groups living in their midst adopt liberal norms and non-discriminatory practices regarding their own members, especially and including women, others advocate that the tension between multicultural group rights and women's equality be addressed via democratic processes, which might not lead to liberal solutions. Yet a third approach attempts to combine reliance on liberal values with appeals to democratic procedures.

I shall discuss proposed solutions of the predominantly liberal and the predominantly democratic varieties, below – Friedman's and Deveaux's. But first, I will devote a few pages to the criticism that my work on the topic has invoked and to clarifying my original stance – focusing especially on what I said then about resolving the multiculturalist/feminist dilemma.

Posing a question, positing an answer?

The oddly incomplete and inaccurate readings of my early papers on this topic may have resulted in part from their frankness and their provocative tone. Some have called it arrogant or even "militantly insensitive."[1] In

---

[1] The charge of arrogance is at least implicit in several of the critiques of my title essay in *Is Multiculturalism Bad for Women?* (1999a). "Militant insensitivity" is the term Seyla Benhabib uses before she misrepresents my views about cultures; since she quotes me accurately, however, it is easy to see that her account of what I say is mistaken (Benhabib 2002: 100, 103).

addition, it is clear that my reference to particular situations in which some cultures' "becom[ing] extinct" might not be altogether a bad outcome has immensely displeased and disconcerted numerous, though by no means all readers.[2] But some misunderstandings of the papers seem to be due to my having entitled one version of my argument in the form

[2] In both versions of my argument I stated that, in certain circumstances, it might (or may) be preferable for the women of a relatively patriarchal minority culture if their culture were to "become extinct" as they integrated from it into the majority culture. Although the wording surrounding the phrase was highly qualified, some readers have been very put off by this suggestion – or at least by the way it was phrased. Some seem unfazed by it; Spinner-Halev, for example, quotes from my statement, pointing out that "this is exactly what happens in most immigrant communities" in the United States, and later very reasonably asks the question "[W]hy should group identity be preserved if the group's members object?" (Spinner-Halev 2001: 90, 112). Marilyn Friedman quotes the passage in full, without comment (Friedman 2003: 180). And according to Kukathas's version of multiculturalism: "Groups, or religious or cultural traditions, in the end, have to survive by their own resources . . . [They] do not matter in themselves. They only matter because they are important for the well-being of individuals" (Kukathas 2001: 92). Thus he too seems not to be bothered by my phrase about cultures becoming extinct, though he clearly disagrees with what he reads as my clear prioritization of feminism over multiculturalism. For some other readers, though, the phrase has aroused such negative reactions that they have quite misunderstood the point. Readers like Shachar and Levy do not seem to have been willing to read beyond it, since they entirely ignore my subsequent proposals about how one might start to address some of the tensions between feminism and multiculturalism. Levy quotes only half of the sentence, even though to do so renders it (and consequently, his own sentence) ungrammatical, and obscures my meaning. He responds: "aiming at [cultural extinction] tends to produce interethnic violence and cruelty without much diminishing internal cruelty" (Levy 2000: 52). But I said nothing at all about *aiming* at cultural extinction. And Ayelet Shachar primarily bases on this same sentence (from which she quotes a few phrases) her assertion that I think societies "should completely abolish minority group practices which do not adhere to the state's legal norms, or else they should require these practices to 'transcend' themselves to such an extent that they practically conform to the norms and perceptions of the majority communities" (Shachar 2001: 67). But I said nothing about *abolishing* minority cultures' practices nor about *requiring* them to transcend themselves. What I actually wrote was clearly in the context of whether group rights should be granted to cultural groups living within liberal societies, and it was this:

In the case of a more patriarchal minority culture in the context of a less patriarchal majority culture, no argument can be made on the basis of the enhancement of self-respect or the greater capacity for choice that the female members of the culture have a clear interest in its preservation. While a number of factors would have to be taken into account in assessing the situation, they *may* be much better off, from a liberal point of view, if the culture into which they were born were either gradually to become extinct (as its members became integrated into the surrounding culture) or, preferably, to be encouraged and supported to substantially alter itself so as to reinforce the equality, rather than the inequality, of women – at least to the degree to which this is upheld in the majority culture. Other factors that would need to be taken into account include whether the minority group speaks a different language that requires protection, [or] suffers from prejudices such as racial discrimination. But it would take significant factors weighing in the other direction to counterbalance evidence that a group's culture severely constrained women's choices or otherwise undermined their well-being. (Okin 1998: 680; cf. similar passage in Okin 1999a: 22–3)

of the question: "Is Multiculturalism Bad for Women?" Readers have tended to infer from this, despite considerable textual evidence to the contrary, that I think the question has a simple, affirmative answer.

Even Chandran Kukathas, who in general presents my work accurately, writes that I "pose the question: Is multiculturalism bad for women?" and answer "yes." He follows up with: "Okin's suggestion is that, to the extent that the two are incompatible, so much the worse for multiculturalism" (Kukathas 2001: 85–6). Kukathas is wrong to assume that I answer the question with a simple and unqualified "yes" and, though his second statement is closer to the mark, it doesn't take account of my concern to try to resolve the incompatibility of feminism and multiculturalism so as to minimize the likelihood that societies would be faced with a stark choice between the two. Ayelet Shachar, whose presentation of my work is a great deal less accurate than Kukathas's, derives from the very question posed by my title, "Okin's *assertion* that multiculturalism is *merely* bad for women" (Shachar 2001: 67; emphases added). On the one hand, she writes: "It may well be that Okin is correct in arguing that a basic tension exists between the traditional practices of many minority groups and the basic citizenship rights of women," a problem about which she speaks in the strong terms I quoted earlier (Shachar 2001: 65). On the other hand, despite the extent of her and my agreement about the problem, she critiques me for dividing the world into "us" versus "them," "good" versus "bad," "liberals" versus "non-liberals" and "feminists" versus "multiculturalists"; and she finds the root of all these "clear-cut dichotomies" to be, somehow, "tellingly revealed in the title of [my] article 'Is Multiculturalism Bad for Women?'" (Shachar 2001: 66 and n.15). She depicts me as forcing on women of minority cultures an "ultimatum . . . either your culture or your rights" (Shachar 2001: 114). However, my views and arguments about, and briefly suggested solutions to problems that arise from tensions between feminism and multiculturalism are not only considerably more nuanced than this suggests, but have much in common with Shachar's own, considerably fuller account of the very same problems and suggested solutions. As I have pointed out elsewhere, I consider her feminist analysis of the issues, in particular their history, excellent (Okin 2002: 208). I find her proposed solution to the problem less than persuasive (Okin forthcoming). But I am pleased to acknowledge our agreement that any legitimate liberal model of multiculturalism must "take into account . . . the voices of less powerful group members" – notably, women (quotation from Shachar 2000a: 81; cf. Okin 1998: 683–4).

Although, after something of a struggle, I finally agreed with the editors of the *Boston Review* to call my essay "Is Multiculturalism Bad for

Women?", I had already chosen the far more neutral title of "Feminism and Multiculturalism: Some Tensions" for the longer and more philosophical version of the same argument that was to appear in *Ethics* (Okin 1999a, 1998). I should probably have vetoed the more provocative title, avoiding the impression created even by posing in such a stark and simple form a question that is not only complex but that one cannot answer in any depth without taking account of the particular context in which it is asked. However, I thought it was clear in the text of both versions not only that I consider the answer to be far from simple, but also, and even more importantly, that I do not think the answer is *mine* to spell out in any detail. I conclude both papers by suggesting that those in the best position to answer it, in each specific context, are the women who are at the intersection of the issue – those within whatever minority cultural or religious groups are claiming group rights as necessary to preserve their group values and ways of life. In light of misunderstandings by some of the original commentators, I clarified this further in my simultaneously published response to their comments. But evidently several things are still far from clear.

Thus I would like now, briefly, to clarify my initial position. Then I shall summarize and respond to some solutions proposed in the recent work of those addressing the tensions between feminism and multiculturalism, and spell out further my own suggested solutions, noted only briefly in the original articles. This chapter accordingly has three purposes: to respond to some recent critiques of my early papers on multiculturalism and feminism, explaining where they involve misunderstandings or misrepresentations of the position I argued; to discuss some proposed solutions put forward in the subsequent debate; and finally (benefiting from both the suggestions of other theorists and my reactions to them), to elaborate on my initial suggestions about how to resolve or at least alleviate the tensions.

I argue, near the end of both versions of the paper, first, that those making liberal arguments for group rights should pay special attention to inequalities within the pertinent groups, especially to inequalities between the sexes, which are often less easily discernible, because they are less public than other inequalities (Okin 1999a: 23, 1998: 683–4). And second that, because of this, policies responding to the needs and claims of more patriarchal cultural or religious groups in a less patriarchal liberal context must ensure the participation or adequate representation, in such negotiations, of the less powerful members of such groups, including the women, and especially the younger women (Okin 1999a: 23–4, 1998: 684). I point out that groups' "self-proclaimed leaders – invariably composed mainly of their older and their male members" – cannot be assumed to represent the interests of all of their members (Okin 1999a: 24). I also state explicitly that consideration of any minority groups' rights or other modes of positive reinforcement within liberal states whose majority culture is less patriarchal should take account of other serious factors (such as language differences or racial discrimination) which are likely to weigh in heavily on the side of such support, even as the "patriarchy differential" is likely to weigh in against them. Thus the status and treatment of women within groups should be an important factor, but not the only factor, in negotiation about group rights.

In my response to the commentators on the *Boston Review* essay, which was published with it and their comments in the book, I wrote a further elaboration of this, already aware from some of the comments of the likelihood of being misinterpreted:

The majority has . . . a special responsibility to members of minority groups whose oppression it may promote or exacerbate by granting group rights without careful consideration of intragroup inequalities. . . . Giving credence to such claims of unity [as are put forth by the leaders of most groups] by granting group rights to a nondemocratic community thus amounts to siding with those in power, the privileged against the marginalized, the traditionalists against the reformers, who often portray dissent as disloyalty to the group. (Okin 1999a: 121)

Thus, just as the question is not simple, neither should the answers be. When the question "Is Multiculturalism Bad for Women?" is asked, the context in which it is asked and its particular contingencies are crucial, which is one of the reasons why it is so important that the relevant women be involved in the attempt to design the form of multiculturalism that is most likely to benefit and least likely to harm them.

Just as Ayelet Shachar (2001) misinterprets my diagnosis of the problem, so she simply invents "my" proposals, ignoring what I said. As I mentioned earlier, my work represents, for her, a simplistic "either your culture or your rights . . . ultimatum" to women of minority cultural groups and a diversity-denying "re-universalized citizenship approach" (7, 68, 114, 118, 150). I allow, according to Shachar, that "women may *either* enjoy the full spectrum of their state citizenship rights *or* participate in their minority communities. They cannot have both simultaneously" (68). The position I allegedly take "forces at risk group members into a stand-off between two vital aspects of their lived experience"; it "fails to provide room for women . . . to maintain their cultural identity, if they still hope to be able to utilize their state citizenship rights to transform their historically subordinated intra-group status"; it "imposes a potentially wrenching decision upon those already left vulnerable, while withholding the legal and institutional resources necessary for improving their positions from within their *nomoi* groups" (Shachar 2001: 68; see also 146).

What an odd position this would be for a feminist to take! It bears no relation to my position about what should be done about the tension between feminism and multiculturalism. I have said nothing to suggest that the women of any culture should be presented, by the liberal theorist or the liberal state, with the unpalatable choice of "your culture or your rights." Shachar herself argues that the very point of ensuring the representation of a group's more vulnerable members is to find out (and take into consideration) what is *their* view of their culture, and their status – including the rights they should have – within it, rather than assuming that the view of the group's (often self-appointed or self-perpetuating) "leaders" is the only valid one.[3] As the passages referred to above indicate, this is my reason, too, for insisting on the representation of minority women in any negotiations about group rights. This very important intersecting population, women within a minority culture, can reasonably be expected to have varying interests in and concerns about *both* the status and rights of women within their culture *and* the status and rights of their cultural group within the larger polity. Whether their views are heterogeneous or homogeneous, singular or multiple, *consulting with them* seems essential, in the course of considering whether a relatively patriarchal cultural group should enjoy exemptions, subsidies or other privileges that will – whether directly or indirectly – have differential impacts on the lives of its various members. Thus my reason for specifying that the female members of a relatively patriarchal minority group must be included in discussions is certainly *not* to force them to choose between their culture and their rights. If this is the choice the vulnerable sometimes find thrust upon them, in such contexts, it is far more likely to be because the privileged, male, traditionalist elite within their groups, accustomed

---

[3] Shachar writes, in criticism of the solution to the paradox of multicultural vulnerability she terms "contingent accommodation": "Here . . . there is no necessary positive correlation between the enhancement of the self-governing powers of the accommodated group *vis-à-vis* the state and the improvement of the status of *all* group members. Unless they are granted a formal voice in the original negotiation process, there is little guarantee that the concerns and interest of traditionally vulnerable group members will be heeded or consulted in decisions to split jurisdictions between the two membership communities" (Shachar 2001: 113). My point, exactly. Later, discussing her preferred system of "transformative accommodation," she specifies that the historically disempowered members of *nomoi* groups should have input into decisions regarding the specific sub-matters with regard to which they are most likely to need "option-protection" (129). Compare my statement that "[i]t is therefore of considerable importance that policies that aim to respond to the needs and claims of cultural minority groups take seriously the need for adequate representation of the less powerful members of such groups (Okin 1998: 684; see also my very similar wording in 1999a: 23).

to speaking for all, may question the loyalty of any members who proffer any other perspective – especially a feminist one – on the cultural norms. Whereas Shachar at times seems well aware of the potential abuse constituted by intra-group pressures to be "loyal" on the vulnerable members of *nomoi* groups (Shachar 2001: 96, 108–9, 138–9), it is (quite unaccountably) not them but me she finds guilty of issuing the coercive "your culture or your rights ultimatum". What I proposed, however, is that discussion about group rights should be premised on a good-faith effort to ensure that liberal-multicultural aims do not contribute to unequal intra-group social power that is perpetuated by undemocratic means. It is a position that Shachar herself wholeheartedly proclaims, and develops at great length, as I shall explain below. But in the face of clear textual evidence she does not regard me as either a precursor of her views or an ally in her cause.

In the rest of this essay, I will focus on two recent proposals about how the multicultural/feminist paradox might best be resolved within generally liberal contexts, attempting to assess some of their strengths and weaknesses. With the help and inspiration of the wisdom evident in these proposals, I conclude with some thoughts of my own on the matter.

Marilyn Friedman's autonomy-based approach: leaning towards liberalism

In the final chapter of her recent book on autonomy and gender, entitled *Cultural Minorities and Women's Rights* (2003), Friedman applies her new theory of liberal autonomy to the problem at hand. In this discussion of multicultural group rights claims in liberal states, her primary aim is to find "common ground" between liberalism and the values adhered to by the various cultural minorities, in arriving at a solution to the tensions between group rights claims and the contemporary liberal norm of legal sex equality. By seeking such common ground, she hopes that concerned feminists can avoid the charge of seeking to impose liberal values on non-liberal cultures.[4] Friedman finds much common ground between

---

[4] Friedman responds deftly to those who have critiqued me for presuming the superiority of liberalism over the values of other cultures. She points out that the question that she and I both address, "What should liberal states do when the practices of minority cultural groups within them violate rights generally upheld in the society?", does not assume the superiority of liberal values any more than the same question, if asked about what an Islamic society should do in the case of a cultural minority whose practices were at odds with Islam, would assume the superiority of Islamic values. However, I have stated, and still believe, that liberalism, despite its many failings, usually respects women's (at least, formal) equality more than do most minority cultures that currently seek group rights within liberal societies.

the two sides. She points to Jeffrey Reiman's arguments that the claims
multiculturalists make often depend upon liberal values such as "individual sovereignty" – the capacity to live one's life free of the domination
of others. She cites Uma Narayan's observation that critics of Western
liberalism often appeal to the ideals of equality and rights, just as liberals
do (Friedman 2003: 181). Surely, then, to appeal to these values oneself
but then to deny appeal to them, as liberal and therefore alien values,
by the more vulnerable members of cultural sub-groups, is inconsistent
and hypocritical. Friedman finds the specific common ground she seeks
in the idea of political legitimacy as based on consent. She claims that
this, too, is appealed to by many multiculturalists who defend the sex-
discriminatory practices of cultural or religious groups, by arguing that
"[c]ultural practices that violate women's rights are nevertheless justified
when the women in question want to live under those practices and choose
to do so voluntarily" (182). She herself defends the consent justification
for political legitimacy earlier in the book, and applies it specifically here,
concluding that "[n]o social institution or practice in which people can
violate each other's rights is legitimate unless all significant groups that
have to live under it consent to it" (183). Thus, she argues, it becomes
crucial to solicit the views of any women who have to live under various
cultural group norms and practices that liberal states might allow, such
as personal status (marriage, divorce and custody) laws, or the regulation
of sexuality and reproduction. Do they indeed consent to them?

This solution sounds more democratic than liberal, similar to my own
suggestion that the women of cultural or religious groups need to be
consulted when any group rights are negotiated between such groups
and liberal states. However, as Friedman says, so far she has presented
just "a guideline," "an abstract ideal that could ground an ethical stance
that, in turn, could become the basis of liberal political policy toward
cultural minority practices." She suggests that we need a clear idea of
what constitutes acceptance or consent: Would acceptance by a simple
majority do? Or by some larger number? Should only actual consent
count? Or "is rationally reconstructed hypothetical consent adequate?"
(183).

Friedman's approach as a whole favors liberalism over democracy. This
becomes apparent as she starts to respond to some of these questions. In
particular, it becomes clear that she thinks following the democratic procedure of polling all of the women involved, even if they were unanimous,
is insufficient to legitimate a practice or norm that violated their rights.
In line with the conception of liberal autonomy she has developed earlier
in the book, she says that the women's choices and views are reliable indicators of consent only under three conditions: the women must be "able

to choose among a significant and morally acceptable array of alternatives"; they must be "able to make their choices relatively free of coercion, manipulation, and deception"; and they "must have been able to develop, earlier in life, the capacities needed to reflect on their situations and make decisions about them" (Friedman 2003: 188; also 201). While Friedman acknowledges that such qualities of personal autonomy are not valued or subscribed to by many peoples, and that some actually reject them, she claims that multiculturalist appeals to women's own choices about or preferences for their cultural traditions as justifying those traditions implicitly rely on placing value on the women's autonomy.

Friedman distinguishes between a "content-neutral" conception of autonomy and a "substantive" conception of autonomy and argues (drawing on arguments made earlier in the book) that only the former is required for consent. The substantive autonomy of a choice depends upon the *contents of what is chosen*, requiring that these contents be consistent with the value of autonomy (summarized at Friedman 2003: 190). But the content-neutral autonomy of a choice depends only on its being made under *conditions* of autonomy; therefore one can "content-autonomously" choose to live under conditions that do not permit one to be "substantively autonomous." Friedman concludes that "the consent of women in a minority culture to their own cultural practices that seem to violate their rights provides, on the face of it, a significant degree of justification for the cultural practices in question, so long as that consent is *content-neutrally autonomous*." Thus, a liberal society's respect for the content-neutral autonomy of women participants in culturally sanctioned practices that negatively affect their substantive autonomy gives the society at least one good reason to allow the practices to continue (191). She gives as an example the practice of female genital surgery, if it is chosen by an adult woman who "may wholeheartedly prefer [it] to the alternative of not having the surgery, in accord with her deepest values and concerns, and may have reached that conclusion through careful reflection devoid of undue coercion, or manipulation by others" (190). What this means in practice, as Friedman makes clear, is that liberal societies, in attending to any situation in which women consistently choose to live in ways that violate their rights, must pay attention to such matters as whether they have genuine alternatives, whether their choices are subject to coercion, manipulation or deception, whether they are able in the context of their culture to develop the competency for autonomy, and whether conditions such as extreme poverty, lack of education, malnutrition or abuse undermine such competencies.

What if such autonomy-destroying or undermining factors do prevail? Then, Friedman concludes, there is no justification for the liberal state to continue to allow the individual rights-violating practice(s) of the group of which the women are members. Presumably, its members would be subject to whatever laws of the larger society might apply to the situation, laws from which the cultural minority should be exempt if and only if its female members *had* content-neutral autonomy and consented to such practices.

Wisely, Friedman makes it clear that her conclusions apply not only to the practices of minority groups, but to all practices and norms that violate the rights of individuals (198–9). She also points out that her conclusions are just as appropriate (or more so) for strains of mainstream culture such as southern Baptist culture as for any immigrant or indigenous ethno-cultural group in the US. For "no cultural tradition anywhere is, or should be, exempt from attempts of outsiders to understand or assess the place of women and girls within it – or that of men and boys, for that matter." And, she asks, "why should any group of women have to live under social conditions they have no opportunity to revise or reject?" (199).

I have several concerns about Friedman's solution, thoughtful and thought-provoking as it is. First, in requiring autonomous, liberal subjects to give their consent, in order for rights-violating practices to continue, it addresses only very briefly the not unusual situation in which it is as girls or very young women that the female members are most seriously (and often permanently) affected by their group's rights-violating practices, such as genital cutting or very early marriage. The logic of Friedman's argument seems to suggest clearly that such practices should *not* be allowed, since there is no way that children can be considered to have the qualities necessary for content-neutral autonomy. However, she does not draw this conclusion, instead declaring the problem of children for liberal notions of legitimacy "a continual challenge" (202). Second, Friedman does not answer some of the important questions she raises, such as whether the consent of a bare majority of the women concerned is adequate, whether a super-majority is needed, or whether the consent of every person whose rights are potentially negatively affected by the cultural norm or practice is necessary in order to justify its continuation. Without such specification, how her theory might be applied in practice remains very vague. Third, Friedman's conditions for content-neutral autonomy are so stringent that it seems unlikely that many women (or indeed many men) in any known society could meet them. How many people's socialization places much emphasis on fostering their capacity for autonomy or gives them genuine alternatives for how to plan their lives? How many people are free from manipulative interferences as they make their choices in life (given, to mention even three common factors, parental pressures, religious education and capitalist advertising)? How many people are really capable of reflecting on their cultural practices – or even of knowing which of their practices are "cultural" ones? Given this stringency of Friedman's liberal conception of autonomy, my final concern is that she appears to leave no opportunity for input for those who do *not* meet its standards. Are their voices not to be heard at all? This is where her proposed solution deviates seriously from being democratic, since women who cannot meet its high standard of autonomy appear to be excluded from any deliberations and decisions about their groups' practices that occur. Yet surely women (or other less empowered members) of a cultural or religious group within a liberal state should not have to prove that they can think autonomously about their lives, in order to be entitled to put forth their views about their cultural practices. It is possible, of course, that by applying such a high standard of procedural, content-neutral autonomy, Friedman is really saying that there are almost no circumstances in which liberal states should empower groups to enforce non-liberal norms on their female members. At any rate, I now turn to a proposal that includes a much more substantial element of democracy.

Monique Deveaux's deliberative approach: emphasizing and expanding democracy

Deveaux has recently proposed a demanding but apparently more practicable approach to the problem of reconciling multicultural with feminist aims in a liberal society. She rejects what she calls the *a priori* liberal approaches of others as flawed in at least three ways: they misunderstand the "actual or *lived* form of [cultural] practices," they are likely to lead to outcomes that are both ill-conceived and undemocratic, and may make the conditions of the vulnerable members of the cultural groups more rather than less oppressive (this volume, pp. 341–42).[5] She contends that such imposed liberal solutions do not take account of the inadequacy of formal equality in the face of "deep social and cultural inequalities" (p. 341). She argues instead for a democratic, pluralist, and manifestly political approach to mediating conflicts of culture in liberal democracies, especially those concerning contested gender roles. Mediating disputes between liberal values and traditional cultural practices requires, Deveaux argues, that women members of

---

[5] On this, see also Deveaux's earlier book, *Cultural Pluralism and Dilemmas of Justice* (2000a: especially chapters 5 and 6). As I mentioned above, Deveaux includes me among the "*a priori* liberals." But like her, I advocate consultation with the women of any group with whom the liberal state is negotiating group rights claims that might jeopardize or compromise women's rights.

cultural groups have a "direct say in these matters, through the expansion of sites of democratic contestation and the inclusion of women in formal decision-making processes" (p. 341). Such solutions to conflicts of culture are not only likely to yield more beneficial reforms; they are likely to have greater legitimacy. But as Deveaux makes clear, there is no guarantee that they will lead to liberal, non-discriminatory outcomes.

One of Deveaux's primary reasons for calling for more democracy – and specifically, democratic deliberation of a political kind rather than an idealized discourse-ethical model – is her concern that the *various* voices within a cultural minority are heard, given the likelihood of intra-cultural plurality of views on such matters as the status of women, marriage and divorce, and the regulation of sexuality and reproduction. For this reason, too, she discounts the likelihood of agreements being reached on these important matters, settling instead for the outcomes of bargaining and compromise. She considers that it is preferable to let partial interests surface and be recognized as such in the course of deliberations, rather than to attempt to neutralize them by requiring that all arguments be made in terms of reasons acceptable to all, as some deliberative democratic theorists do. Deveaux stresses that democratic deliberation about contested practices should take the form of a transparent political process, and should aim to accurately describe the lived form of contested cultural practices; moreover it should aim to generate "negotiated political compromises"(p. 347).

Three normative principles of Deveaux's model need to be specified before I summarize her account of a recent case in which she considers it to have been quite nearly approximated: the negotiations in the late 1990s about how to reform the South African customary marriage laws. First, the principle of non-domination or non-coercion: the traditional leaders or elites of cultural groups must not be able to silence dissenters through overt or covert modes of oppression. Second, political equality: the presence of real opportunities for all citizens to participate in the debates and decision-making. Third, the principle of revisability: the aim is not to arrive at a solution of the cultural conflicts for all time. Deliberations and negotiations are likely to need to occur again and again, as attitudes, relations between the majority and the various minority groups, and other aspects of the situation change.

Deveaux illustrates the working of the solution she advocates by examining the attempts in South Africa, leading up to the Customary Marriages Act of 1998, to reconcile two conflicting provisions of the country's recently adopted Constitution. The Constitution, on the one hand, specifies equal individual rights and prohibits discrimination of precisely seventeen different kinds, including racial and sexist. On the other hand, it recognizes the rights of cultural, linguistic and religious groups, including the various systems of customary African law and traditional leadership, which were in many cases both patrilineal (male primogeniture has prevailed) and highly patriarchal.[6] As Deveaux makes clear, while customary law and the right to culture are protected constitutionally only to the extent that they are consistent with the rights guaranteed by the Bill of Rights, including the right to equality, "the relationship between customary law and sex equality in South Africa remains to some extent indeterminate and fraught with political uncertainty" (p. 355). The consultations and hearings that were held in preparation for the Customary Marriages Act are a particularly good (because particularly tough) example of a conflict between feminist and multiculturalist aims. There were clearly two kinds of oppression present that would need, eventually at least, to be overcome. First, apartheid had undoubtedly oppressed the South African peoples and their customary laws. As part of this pattern of oppression, their customary marriages had never been legally recognized, though they were entered into by more than half the Africans who married. But second, the patriarchy of most of the customary laws oppressed women. It was virtually impossible to transcend the two kinds of oppression simultaneously, for if the customary laws were so much transformed at the moment of their recognition as to become non-sexist, they might appear never to have been recognized. The colonial origins of the paradox of multicultural vulnerability are as clear in this instance as in any. (In South Africa, as in so many cases, colonizers enforced their own laws regarding contracts, crimes and other matters they cared about upon the colonized, but permitted them to retain their own laws concerning marriage, divorce, inheritance and other matters of far less interest to them.)

As Deveaux relates, representatives of a wide range of groups were consulted: the traditional leaders' congress, women's groups, legal reform groups, and scholars of both constitutional law and customary law. A wide range of views was heard regarding the advantages and disadvantages of various aspects of customary marriage laws.[7] There was much frank discussion of the actual lived practices of customary marriage, as contrasted

---

[6] In many of the tribal systems, women were until recently treated as legal minors, unable to inherit land, enter into contracts, or initiate divorce. They were also pressured into staying in bad marriages, even if abusive, by the customary practice of *lobolo* or bride price, which had to be repaid by her family if the bride left her marriage (Deveaux, p. 354).

[7] Advocates of women's equality and legal reform opposed primogeniture and women's status as legal minors, but there was little support for the institution of a single civil code of marriage in place of the various customary laws.

with illusions about it, "the more pernicious interests and motivations" were easily exposed, and "the process of deliberation . . . [put] into motion a politics of negotiation and compromise in which the focus was on practical interests, prospective policies and their potential consequences" (p. 357). According to a customary law expert among the participants, the tribal leaders kept "hiding behind the word 'culture' " when making their case against reforms and against a greater social decision-making role for women (p. 356). However, the chiefs were eventually persuaded that reforming the customary marriage laws was less likely to erode their traditional authority than was preserving them as they were.

Hence, as a result of the deliberations and negotiations, partial reform was achieved. Wives now have formally equal status with husbands (the default position is one of community property in marriage, women can now initiate divorce proceedings, parents are equally guardians of their children) and only family courts (not tribal courts) may handle important matters of family law. On the other hand, concessions to the chiefs included the continued recognition of *lobolo*, or bride price, though it is no longer required in order for a customary marriage to be recognized. In addition, polygyny, which many expected to go, was preserved, both because it was seen as an important (though declining in frequency) variant of customary law and for the more practical reason that it was feared that women in *de facto* polygynous marriages would be worse off without it. However, it has been modified, in that a man who seeks to marry a further wife is now required to make a written contract with his existing wife, protecting her financial interests during his life and dividing them equitably upon divorce or his death.

Deveaux argues that the explicitly political deliberative procedure made the power and the interests involved more visible than they would have been otherwise, that the openness of the process brought out both the most forceful complaints against some existing traditions and the reasons other practices were valued, and that reforms were both proposed and dismissed in ways unlikely to have happened otherwise. Though various constituencies were unhappy with aspects of the compromise reached, she notes that they were "seen by most as a fair and legitimate outcome of deliberation and negotiation" (p. 359). In addition, this basically democratic consultative process yielded some results – notably the retention of polygyny and *lobolo*, albeit both modified – that, being sex discriminatory, are not consistent with liberal norms. As Deveaux acknowledges, such open-endedness of outcomes is a necessary part of giving centrality to democratic participatory norms.

I am largely sympathetic with Deveaux's model, and with her endorsement of the South African process, as "meet [ing] the demands of democratic legitimacy and demonstrat[ing] respect for the diverse cultural and religious commitments and attachments of citizens" (p. 360). However, I have doubts about whether the process as it seems to have occurred met two of her three own criteria for the democracy of such processes: non-domination and political equality. However pragmatically necessary it may have been in the South African context in the 1990s to give a role to tribal leaders *as* such leaders or *as* representatives of such leaders, how can this be considered consistent with these two criteria? The chiefs or leaders do not owe their positions to democratic election, yet they seem to have been present in far greater numbers than their proportion of the tribal population would justify on a democratic basis. (Deveaux does not tell us about the numerical representation of the various constituencies – leaders, rank and file members, men, women – in the talks.) Even if the leaders or chiefs were not overrepresented, is it not inevitable that, in a consultative process involving representatives of other categories of tribal members, such as women, or non-elites in general, such leaders would have more than equal power? Even if they were able to be prevented from overtly pressuring other tribal members, the other members were surely unlikely to be able to forget that certain views were being expressed by the leaders, and other views (merely) by the rank and file members of the various African peoples. The very existence of undemocratically chosen leaders as respresentatives in the process poses problems for any democratic solution to the feminist/multiculturalist dilemma. At least, it seems necessary to ensure that they are not represented in the deliberations any more than their own numbers in the population warrant.

In her general discussion of the concept, Deveaux notes, following James Bohman, that political equality requires preventing "extra-political or endogenous forms of influence, such as power, wealth, and pre-existing social inequalities" from having an impact on deliberation and its outcomes (p. 350, quoting Bohman). In addition, she makes the point that, in many cases of cultural claims, problems are inherent because "who can participate in political life is, for many, culturally determined" (p. 351). But in her discussion of the South African deliberations, she makes only passing mention of the fact that at least some of the traditional leaders "steadfastly resisted suggestions that women should enjoy greater decision-making roles in African society"(p. 356). Surely, though, this stated resistance itself must have affected the power dynamic of the process, especially that between the women (whom such leaders could hardly have regarded as their political equals) and the leaders (whom quite probably some of the women saw as "more than equals").

However, this critique of Deveaux's application of her theory tends to confirm rather than to detract from the value of the theory. For, by her own account of the process, if the tribal leaders had not prevailed – as they might not have if they had not had the undue influence of being tribal leaders – it would have been less likely that the sex discriminatory practices of polgyny and *lobolo* would have survived the consultative process to the extent that they did. A *more democratic* process, in which the criteria of non-domination and political equality had modified the numbers and the roles of the tribal leaders, might have yielded significantly *more liberal* results.

I am reminded by Deveaux's requirement of non-domination of two scenes that occur in one of the documentary films that I show my class when discussing issues arising from the universal claims of human rights in the context of diverse cultural practices – most specifically claims for women's equality in the context of traditional (or neo-traditional) cultural groups. The film, entitled *Sister Wife*, is a close examination of polygyny within the neo-traditional culture of the Hebrew Israelites, a community of African-Americans who emigrated to Israel during the 1960s and 1970s (Goldshtain and Kleinman 2000). They live as a tight-knit community in accordance with the customs and norms of archaic Judaism. During an early scene in the film, a woman who has been married for twenty years and is the mother of nine children is asked for her reaction to her husband's imminent second marriage to a woman about the age of his eldest daughter. Interviewed in the company of her husband, the rabbi, and the proposed second wife, the first wife replies that her husband's upcoming marriage will be a challenge for her, but that challenges are good for one's character and she accepts the one she is about to face. She smiles when the camera is directed at her; when it is not she looks extremely depressed. In a subsequent scene, the first wife is filmed in a much more casual setting – sewing the dress of the bride-to-be, in the company of a close friend. They seem almost unaware of the camera. When the first wife's friend asks her what she intends to give the bride, as a tribute or present, she laughs slightly and wryly and replies: "I'll give her *him, on a platter.*"

The question this raises (at least for those of us who think we know from this what she really thinks about her husband's taking on an additional wife) is: How might the deliberative democratic process Deveaux advocates ensure that women's real views about polygyny emerge during the deliberative process? Certainly, they must have the opportunity to talk in freedom from coercion, but what does this require in practice? That anyone hoping to achieve democratic agreement or compromise go around with a tape recorder, hoping to capture the women's candid views, as those of the woman in *Sister Wife* were captured, in a moment of spontaneity? Or are the women members of such a patriarchal cultural group likely to be more frank and less defensive about polygyny when collectively asked about its general practice than each might be when asked about her husband's intention to marry a second wife? When, during an international conference in Singapore in the late 1990s, I asked an Indonesian woman in a traditional version of Muslim attire what she thought about some Western feminists' defense of practices such as polygyny on the grounds that the women involved themselves defend and uphold the practice, she at first couldn't even comprehend my question. But once she did, amazed, she quickly and firmly responded: "No woman likes polygyny." I didn't think to ask her whether, and under what context, Indonesian women would be willing to express these negative views, but the way she stated them implied that such views were hardly kept secret. Perhaps, though, they are views shared, however widely, only among women, and perhaps it might take considerable skill to ensure that they surfaced during negotiations about the claims of cultural or religious minorities.

However daunting the complexities of its implementation, what Deveaux's proposed solution to conflicts involving culture emphasizes is that, during a democratic process that involves bargaining and compromise as well as deliberation about norms, the various views of different sub-groups of the cultural groups are likely eventually to emerge, as are their real reasons for holding such views.

Conclusions

It should be apparent by now that I am greatly indebted to many of the political theorists and philosophers who have recently addressed the multicultural/feminist tension or dilemma. I have also learned much from the critiques made by and the questions asked by many colleagues.[8] Here, I have tried to respond to some of the criticisms. And by attending to and

[8] From Chandran Kukathas, with whom I still disagree about the general priority of multiculturalism over feminism, but with whom I agree to a surprising extent regarding the practical implications of our respective theories, I take seriously the warning that we should be skeptical of the power and interests of states, especially with regard to matters over which they have often ruled at best insensitively, and at worst, very destructively. In response to Jeff Spinner-Halev, whose relevant paper I have said very little about here, I accept and acknowledge a related message: that we theorists discussing multicultural accommodations should never forget that we are almost always discussing religiously or culturally based groups that have been oppressed because of their differences from the more powerful majority. Keeping that oppression at the forefront of our minds is crucial, even as we examine and object to the internally oppressive practices of some groups. By Jacob Levy's work, I am most reminded of the importance of the proverb directed to those in "glass houses": that it is unacceptably hypocritical to find fault with other cultures but not to be ready and willing to criticize one's own at least to the same extent. While I have expended considerable energy critiquing my own culture and its sexist theoretical underpinnings (Okin 1989, 1999b), I can never be reminded too often that, as

commenting on recent solutions to the dilemma proposed by two other theorists, I have tried to clarify my own position about how basically liberal societies might best respond to this problem of tensions between multiculturalism and feminism, or the paradox of multicultural vulnerability. I have been pressed to think about whether I advocate a solution that favors democracy or one that favors liberalism, when the two conflict. To summarize the question: If a liberal state is discussing or negotiating with an internal cultural group, collective rights that seem to reinforce the inequality of the sexes within the group, if the women (including the younger women) of the group have been consulted and adequately represented during the course of the negotiations, and if they have stated in large enough numbers and in clear enough terms that they support their group's illiberal norms and practices that seem oppressive of them, what should the state do?

Democracy seems to require in such a case that the group rights claims not be hindered and, rather, that they be strengthened, by such findings, even though an unintended consequence of granting them is very likely to be continued subordination and denial of equal rights of women within the group. But liberalism, grounded in the equal rights of individuals, would not concur in this outcome; indeed a state that values liberalism above all would have no more need to consult with the women of such a group than it need consult with slaves before it insisted upon their emancipation or with workers before it insisted upon their protection from deadly workplace hazards. Of course, such consultation might well be considered desirable, not only because of the respect it shows to some of the most vulnerable members of the society, but also because it is likely to lead to more contextually wise solutions to the problem – ones that might, because of increased awareness of conflicting interests, be applied with more caution and less speed, or that would be applied more sensitively in different ways in different contexts. But the liberal would

Levy puts it, "there is an easy tendency to see everyone else's cultures as repressive and intolerant, whereas the socialization and norms of our own culture are invisible to us" (Levy 2000: 62). From Shachar I have learned a great deal about the intersections of gender with culture, and about the very difficult position such intersections put women in, sometimes together with children, dissenters or other historically vulnerable members of groups. I find Shachar's connection of this with women's roles in transmitting culture inter-generationally particularly fruitful and of great interest. I have gained insight from her work about some of the ways in which societies have tried to resolve the tensions between claims made on behalf of cultures and religions, and claims for equality or equity, between men and women. One of the most important questions was asked by Dennis Thompson in a Harvard Political Theory seminar in the spring of 2002. Though unfortunately I didn't really understand his question about liberal or democratic solutions until after the event, it has considerably affected the thinking that has gone into this paper.

stress that basic rights – which arguably include, along with the rights to personal freedom and to be able to earn one's living without endangering one's life, the right to basic, legal equality in the most intimate sphere of life – should not be granted or withheld depending on the outcome of democratic procedures. They should be guaranteed for all – even for those who would abjure them for themselves.

As I argued in my "Response" in *Is Multiculturalism Bad for Women?* (1999b), I favor the liberal response in the case of patriarchal religions that can make no good claims of past oppression. I can see no good reason why, for example, the Catholic Church should enjoy privileges such as tax-exempt status, so long as it radically discriminates against women in all of its most important hiring decisions and in the distribution of institutional power. Catholic women's apparent consent to such unequal treatment does not justify the endorsement of it by the liberal state. There is no more reason why liberal states should tolerate such discrimination in groups that benefit in any way from public support than they tolerate racial discrimination from such groups. However, my more considered view, still, at this point, favors democracy over liberalism in the case of cultural or religious groups that have recently suffered, or still suffer, from oppression at the hands of colonial powers or of the larger society. (I say "still," because this was implied by the phrasing of my initial brief insistence that, in negotiations about group rights, the women of the group be consulted.) As numerous contributors to this debate have noted, women members of such groups or communities have many reasons to identify with their culture or religion (as well as with their sex). Thus they should be taken seriously if, when consulted in truly non-intimidating settings, they produce good reasons for preferring to continue aspects of their traditional subordinate status over moving to a status of immediate equality within their group.

Not surprisingly, there are reasons to favor and not to favor both kinds of solution – the liberal and the democratic. But it should be noted that *some* kind of coercion of most traditional *nomoi* groups that seek group rights is involved, whichever value one favors, for such groups tend to be neither liberal nor democratic. Is it worse to force them to be democratic or to be liberal as a cost of acquiring special rights or privileges? It is not at all obvious, but it should be kept in mind that the enforced liberalism would be permanent, whereas the enforced democracy might well be temporary – insisted upon only for the purpose of discovering the views/position of the more vulnerable, normally less empowered, members of the group. The democratic solution has what might well be considered the defect of giving the present generation control over the conditions under which future generations will live. This problem is partly addressed by Deveaux's very reasonable requirement that the issues be (fairly regularly?) revisited. But the democratic solution, by *requiring* attention to the views of the most vulnerable, is also likely to lead to the attention to context and specifics that the liberal solution might neglect. In the South African negotiations discussed by Deveaux, it was by means of consultation with the women of the various South African peoples that their preference for the (at least, temporary) continuation of polygyny was not only discovered but understood. For it was not based on positive support for the institution of polygyny, but on pragmatic, largely economic reasons having to do with the protection of especially vulnerable women and children. While, as accounts of adaptive preferences show, there is no guarantee that a seemingly oppressed sub-group will consider itself oppressed, one is surely more likely to find out about and to understand the actual conditions of what seems to be oppression by consulting the people who seem to be oppressed than by only consulting those who seem to be oppressing them.

Anyone favoring the democratic approach to group rights, however, should face the radical challenge to the larger or "host" society that this solution presents in turn: How can one reasonably expect minority groups to cleave to and to practice democratic ideals if the wider society itself is failing to abide by such ideals? As I thought about this essay, a picture kept repeatedly coming into my mind. It was a picture of the US Congress, as assembled to listen to the State of the Union Address in January 2003: row upon row upon row of white men over the age of fifty, interspersed with the occasional white woman and the even more occasional Black, Latino or Asian man or woman. I further envisaged the following scenario: the self-appointed or otherwise not democratically chosen leaders of cultural or religious groups appear before Congressional committees, in the process of seeking exemptions or rights to practice their cultural norms. They are told by the august committees of our Congress – even more white, male and old in their composition than its general membership – that, in order for their claims to be heard, they must go away and come back with the women and other less powerful people of their groups, who must be directly involved in discussions about such rights and privileges.

Such a demand seems absurd, even though there are a couple of obvious differences between the situations of the two "supposedly representative" sets of leaders. First, the Congress *is* chosen by an electoral process in which all citizens can vote, albeit a process that favors incumbency, money, majority-race status and male career paths to an extreme extent; whereas the leaders of *nomoi* groups are usually not elected at all. Second, the groups are seeking to enforce internal laws and other norms that differ from the wider society's norms and violate some of the rights that their individual members would have if they were not group members. Thus, they might be expected to provide *more* evidence that the group as a whole agrees with the internal norms for which they seek protection. Nevertheless, the challenge that the democratic solution to the multicultural dilemma poses to the wider, supposedly democratic society seems clear enough. To sum it up as my late mother would have done: "Surely democracy for the goose is democracy for the gander?"

4   Can intra-group equality co-exist with cultural diversity? Re-examining multicultural frameworks of accommodation

Gurpreet Mahajan

I

Most societies today are plural and internally diverse but we cannot, by this token alone, say that they are multicultural. The existence of many different cultures does not by itself make a society multicultural. It is only when these diverse cultures exist as equals in the public arena that a democracy can claim to be multicultural. The concern for equality is a constitutive element of multiculturalism. It is therefore not surprising to find that votaries of multiculturalism are particularly attentive to the criticism that multicultural policies and practices promote inter-group equality but remain largely insensitive to demands for intra-group equality.

The first wave of multicultural writing deconstructed the nation-state and challenged the picture of a homogenized political community. Distinguishing between majority and minority communities they had shown that the policies of the state systematically disadvantage minorities in the public arena. The second wave of multicultural writing has extended this analysis by deconstructing the cultural community along with the nation-state. Addressing the anxieties of their liberal and feminist critics these theorists accept that communities are internally differentiated and there exist hierarchies of power and domination within each. Consequently, special rights given to communities may at times be appropriated to empower traditional leadership and to sanction practices that endorse existing inequalities between groups. Recognition of this possibility has triggered some rethinking on multicultural frameworks with a view to ensuring that the concern for equality within the community is accommodated along with the commitment to promoting equality between communities.

Within multiculturalism equality between communities is generally pursued through policies aimed at promoting cultural diversity. The

Paper presented at the Conference on Minorities within Minorities: Equality, Rights and Diversity, University of Nebraska, Lincoln, 4–5 October 2002.

presence of diverse cultures in the public arena signals the absence of cultural homogeneity; at the very least, it restrains the nation-state from pursuing its project of cultural assimilation in a way that necessarily disadvantages minority communities. Cultural diversity is not, however, valued for this reason alone. Charles Taylor (1994), for instance, sees it as a kind of sacred trust. Following Herder he suggests that "all this variety of culture was not a mere accident but was meant to bring about a greater harmony" (Taylor 1994: 72). Will Kymlicka (1989a) and Bhikhu Parekh (1994) maintain that the presence of cultural diversity can serve a practical and critical interest. Exposure to other culturally distinct ways of life stimulates us to reflect upon the limits of our knowledge and the finitude of our existence. It reveals to us different human projects and ways of organizing society, thus creating conditions that prompt a critical self-understanding (Parekh 1994: 207–8) and revision of our inheritances (Kymlicka 1989a: 164–6).

Cultural diversity is here valued for itself. It does not simply mark the absence of cultural homogeneity but is considered to be a collective good in and by itself. Consequently, protecting the existing diversity of cultures and ensuring that minority cultures survive and flourish is also a primary concern of multiculturalism. Votaries of multiculturalism therefore face a difficult challenge: they have to create arrangements that address the issue of intra-group inequality while protecting and promoting diversity. Will Kymlicka had advocated special rights for minorities, in the form of cultural community rights, separate representation and self-government rights, but these were aimed mainly at curbing homogenization and protecting diversity. Should these rights be given to minorities if they are used to sanction values that subordinate marginalized sections of the community? Can these rights be exercised in a way that promotes intra-group equality? These are questions that present themselves to us today and it is these that theorists of multiculturalism have to address.

These issues, of course, arise whenever we extend cultural rights to communities, be it the majority community or the minority communities. However, we are here considering the context of minority communities alone since multiculturalism supports special rights for minorities alone; and these rights are given, at least in part, to ensure that these communities are not unequally treated within the polity. Consequently, it is pertinent in their case to ask whether the rationale that minorities are using within the state to seek special rights is being extended within the community to ensure that minorities within the minority community are also fairly treated. There is a further reason for focusing upon the minority communities. In a liberal democracy the state is commonly entrusted with the responsibility of promoting fair and equal treatment for all. However, multiculturalism links the state with the majority community; the policies of the state are said to reflect the culture of the majority. Hence, the state can justifiably legislate only for the majority community and its interventions in the life of the minorities remain suspect. They lack legitimacy such that even those actions that are aimed at enhancing equality for the vulnerable sections of the community raise the specter of cultural assimilation. Since state-sponsored actions meet with suspicion, and even resistance, the issue remains as to how equality for internal minorities (i.e. minorities within minority communities) may be ensured within a framework of special rights.

In India this is the question that confronts the state, minority communities and women's organizations. Here, in conformity with the multicultural logic, the state merely introduced changes in the Personal Laws of the majority community. Even though the Personal Laws, that govern matters dealing with family, of all communities treat women unequally, changes have only been made in the Hindu Personal Law. No corresponding changes have been introduced in the Personal Laws of the minority communities. Initiative for change has been left with the communities themselves and this has disadvantaged women doubly. On the one hand, the state has abandoned its responsibility to them as citizens and, on the other, cultural communities have been largely inhospitable to their demands for equal treatment. Non-interference in the practices of the minority communities may have been justified in the spirit of multiculturalism but it has not made the struggle for equality for women any easier. Women's groups are also caught in a bind. Noting the unequal status of women within community Personal Laws, they demanded the formulation of a Uniform Civil Code. But, until recently the government in power at the centre was actively affirming the agenda of cultural majoritarianism and advocating the dissolution of community-based Personal Laws. In this situation, they felt that the demand for a Uniform Civil Code may well provide an opportunity to impose the norms of the majority upon the minorities. Hence, they now affirm the importance of retaining the existing framework of plural Personal Laws but find that the minority communities are not always willing to initiate changes to ensure equal treatment for women. It is in this context of the dilemmas posed by multicultural commitments that the issue of minorities within minorities has come to the fore. Needless to say, it is women within the minority communities that have become the focus of debate although it cannot be said that women in the majority Hindu community enjoy equal treatment in all respects.

The issue of equal treatment for internal minorities has become further complicated with the endorsement of the ideal of cultural diversity within multiculturalism. The notion of diversity assumes that the different cultures coexisting are incommensurable. That is, each culture is distinct, with its own unique pattern of internal and external organization. Hence, it must be judged on its own terms, with reference to the values that inform it. Implicit in this view is the assumption that there is no *a priori* or universal vantage-point from which these diverse cultures can be analyzed. We cannot identify any set of practices as egalitarian or liberating in itself. The assessment must come from within the culture. This idea of diversity privileges the voice of the culture and simultaneously puts a question mark against all other voices that come from outside. Since the onus lies entirely with the community it is assumed that if the cultural community continues with its existing practices, which appear to us from our perspective to be unfair to women, the authority of the community cannot be challenged. How do we then expect change to occur, especially since women are among the most vulnerable members of the community and they may not count in community decisions? These are aspects of the multicultural framework that have drawn attention to the plight of minorities within the minority communities.

Before discussing the issue of equal treatment for internal minorities any further it must be mentioned that within each community there exist minorities of many different kinds. In India there are at least four types of internal minorities: language-based groups, caste groups, women and denominations/sects. Within the majority religious community – Hindu – there are Arya Samajis, Brahmos, Sanatanis, followers of RamaKrishna Paramhansa, and the Swaminarayan sect, to name but a few. Each of them has its own theology, deities, modes of worship and ethical codes; and they see themselves as discrete groups. Then there are Hindus whose mother tongue is Hindi, and Hindus who speak Tamil, Telegu or some other Indian language. There are Hindu brahmins and Hindus belonging to "depressed" classes. Similarly, minority communities also have internal minorities. Within the Muslim community there is a fairly sharp distinction between Shias and Sunnis; there are also many other groups with distinct socio-cultural practices, such as Khojas, Bohras, Mers, Meos and Mapillas. Additionally, there are Urdu-speaking Muslims and non-Urdu-speaking Muslims. Women are a subordinated minority in each community. In brief, there is a range of internal minorities, with some seeking recognition of their difference and others desiring equal treatment.

The idea that communities are both stratified and internally diverse has not been sufficiently acknowledged in multiculturalism. Existing systems of stratification yield minorities for whom the crucial issue is equality while minority groups that embody heterogeneity raise demands of diversity. In India, language-based groups as well as sects/denominations within each religious community are markers of internal heterogeneity, and they aspire for some degree of autonomy vis-à-vis the parent community. That is, they plead for freedom to continue with their social and religious practices and, by extension, desire some exemptions from the codified laws of the community as well as its leadership. By comparison, women as a group, like many subordinated castes within the Hindu fold, do not simply seek diversity or freedom to express their difference. Their struggle is against their continued subordination in the community. They seek, in other words, opportunities that might enable them to lead a reasonably dignified life with some protection against conditions that render them destitute and vulnerable to exploitation.

The presence of these diverse kinds of internal minorities reveals that communities are neither homogeneous entities nor self-evidently given wholes. Communities are the product of historical and political construction, and they represent both an affirmation of difference as well as their suppression. In India, for purposes of Personal Law, the Constitution recognizes four religious communities: Hindus, Muslims, Christians and Parsis. Although at the time of framing the Constitution, Sikhs and Buddhists were identified as distinct religious communities and represented on that basis, in matters of family and personal law these communities were eventually included as Hindus. The Parsi community, which does not even find a separate mention in the census and is subsumed under the category of "other communities," was recognized as a separate and distinct religious community with its own Personal Law. Likewise, in the Constituent Assembly a distinction was made between Anglo-Indians and Indian Christians but they were subsequently considered to be part of one religious community. A whole range of fairly heterogeneous communities, like Meos, Memons, Bohras and Khojas, were similarly clubbed together as Muslims. In an analogous manner, language groups have also been subject to constant construction and reconstruction. The 1961 census recorded the existence of 1,652 mother tongues in India. After further consolidating several dialects and languages, the 1981 census registered the existence of 145 languages, of which thirty-five were being spoken by more than one million people. The Constitution of India today recognizes 114 scheduled and non-scheduled languages. Of these eighteen are granted the status of official languages of the state. Minorities, and the majority, have thus been fashioned by effacing some differences and affirming others. The issue of minorities within minorities gains a special significance on account of this process of homogenization and differentiation.

This chapter does not, however, address the issues raised by all these different kinds of internal minorities. It focuses only on internal minorities such as women, who seek equal treatment. In part this is because the issue of internal diversity has to some extent been addressed in India. Groups that resist assimilation into the larger religious community have at times been designated as a "minority" by the Supreme Court. Even though there are several amongst them that are still struggling to claim this status, and others who maintain that the law and practice differ substantially, there is a framework of institutionalized practices within which these issues and demands can be, and have been, dealt with. By comparison, it is the issue of equal treatment for internal minorities such as women that has posed a problem. This is not entirely surprising for claims of diversity are more easily reconcilable with multiculturalism. They can in principle be accommodated by granting facilities and rights analogous to those granted to minorities within the state. For the multicultural framework the real challenge comes from internal minorities who seek equal treatment within a community. It is in their case that we need to ask whether diversity and equality can co-exist.

Theorists of multiculturalism have in recent times addressed this issue by exploring ways in which the claims of vulnerable and subordinated minorities for equal treatment within the community can be accommodated along with the legitimate claims of the minority community for equal treatment within the polity. In the main, three different suggestions have been offered: (i) prescribing the limits of permissible diversity by invoking a historically or politically shared universal; (ii) providing exit options for community members; and (iii) seeking a deliberative consensus within the community. The following pages draw upon the Indian experience to reflect upon these alternatives to see if the concerns of equality raised by marginalized internal minorities can be adequately reconciled with claims for protecting diversity that come from minority communities within these frameworks of multiculturalism.

II

Human beings, it is said, are "culture-producing creatures" (Walzer 1983: 313). They "make and inhabit meaningful worlds" (313). Since we have no way of evaluating these world-views or assessing their worth (Taylor 1994: 72), we do injustice to men and women when we judge their creations by our external standards. Justice, by this reasoning, demands that we respect the various cultural worlds that individuals have created for themselves and which give meaning to their existence. Instead of asking them to conform to some apparently universal norms, every community must have the opportunity of organizing their lives in a way that is "faithful to the shared understanding of the members" (Walzer 1983: 313). The dilemma for multiculturalists is what should be done when a cultural way of life sanctions practices that violate our basic understanding of human dignity and equality. What happens when respect for group difference becomes a mode of suppressing and subordinating vulnerable members of the community? In such circumstances, should we, for the sake of protecting cultural diversity, permit practices like polygamy, *Sati*, child marriage and female circumcision; or allow communities to deny what Shachar calls "at risk individuals" equal opportunities and treatment (2001: 71)? Further, within multiculturalism culturally distinct ways of life are protected on the assumption that there is a consensus in the community on what are collectively valued social goods. However, what happens if these social goods are not collectively shared? What must be done when members disagree about the value of endorsed social goods and contest the desirability of specific norms and practices?

Theorists of multiculturalism have responded to these challenges in different ways. Will Kymlicka, Joseph Carens and Bhikhu Parekh address these issues by attempting to draw the boundaries of "permissible diversity" in liberal democracies (Parekh 1994: 215). Looking at the many cases where interests of individuals and groups conflict with those of the community, they neither accept the autonomy claims that come from the community nor do they unconditionally privilege the individual *vis-à-vis* the community. In lieu of communitarian and liberal modes of reconciling these conflicts they refer to collectively shared norms within the political community. In contemporary liberal democracies, what are designated as "basic" or "fundamental" rights are considered inviolable, and the boundaries of permissible diversity are drawn with reference to this historically and politically defined universal.

It is assumed that no society can tolerate all forms of diversity. While we cannot on the basis of our contemporary sensibilities determine what must be permitted in all societies we can nevertheless do so for those who share our world-view. As historical beings we are constituted by our prejudgements; we cannot simply set aside our *weltanschauung* and become an-other. Instead, "we should try to understand, we should listen respectfully, but we should not *abandon our own commitments for the sake of respecting those of others*" (Carens 2000: 42; emphasis added). Based on this understanding of a situated self, these theorists identify certain historically or politically constructed universals and it is with reference to these that they explore the limits of what may be tolerated in a society.

In a liberal democracy, it is the notion of basic rights that are viewed as collectively affirmed universals. Community cultural practices that do not breach these rights are allowed while those that do are deemed unacceptable. Since the notion of basic rights is somewhat ambiguous, often it is the Constitution and the "operative public values" enshrined in it that are used to draw the boundaries of "permissible diversity" (Parekh 1994: 215–17). The Constitution is seen as a reliable indicator of the values that are collectively cherished by the political community as a whole. According to Bhikhu Parekh, even those who do not believe in the existing public values have to abide by them in the conduct of their affairs, and people who wish to change these norms also have to work within the parameters specified by them.

The idea that not all forms of diversity are acceptable and that practices that violate "core public values" or "basic" rights may not be permitted in a liberal society brings the concern for equality into the discourse of diversity. It suggests that minority communities, while safeguarding their distinctiveness, may nevertheless be expected to ensure that the basic public values are not violated. In this sense the political community may define the boundaries of what is permissible. And, what is perhaps even more significant, it may do so in terms of what liberal democrats define as the basic rights of all, or what the Constitution represents as the shared understanding of the political community. In other words, this mode of multicultural accommodation allows for intervention, however indirect that may be, by an external agency as well as the application of an external criterion for determining what is acceptable. It is by using collective societal norms of what is acceptable that certain kinds of practices are to be disallowed and the concern for equal treatment brought in.

It is, of course, assumed here that the Constitution expresses shared political values and is not therefore "external." Also, that every society has some collectively valued social goods and these, as they are enshrined in the Constitution, can provide the basis of determining what is acceptable. Even if these assumptions are accepted the difficulty is that the Constitution is a complex text. It incorporates shared norms and aspirations but reflects a consensus that is historically specific. Further, it is constructed as much by interpretation and legal commentary as it is by the written and codified document. In India, for instance, the Constitution gave to its citizens the right to profess and practice their religion. Even though formal equality was accepted as the general norm it was mediated by the commitment to protect diversity of religious practices. Since it is religious communities that determine what is a shared religious practice they have used this provision to question state interventions in community Personal Laws. Although the Constitution, in the Chapter on Directive Principles of State Policy, endorsed the need to formulate a gender-just Uniform Civil Code, the right to religious practice has repeatedly been used to argue for the continuation of community Personal Laws, all of which place women in a subordinate position. The "core public norms" have not been able to reconcile the concern of women for equal treatment with that of diversity. In fact, as is often the case, the norms of equality and diversity, as endorsed in the Constitution of India, push in different directions. If the women's movement has used Article 44 of the Constitution to seek equality for women, minority religious communities have used the commitment to diversity to defend their autonomy. Invoking shared public norms and guaranteed basic rights has not assisted the struggle of women within each community for equal treatment in any way.

Contradictions of this kind that we witness in India are not, however, peculiar to it. They surface in much of the recent literature on multiculturalism, including theories which maintain that there are a set of non-negotiable basic rights, such as, the right to political participation, equality for all, freedom of belief, and protection from bodily harm and injury. Joseph Carens (2000) in his book *Culture, Citizenship and Community* argues, for instance, that equality for all, which includes gender equality, and democracy are basic values in all liberal democracies and cannot be compromised.[1] If certain practices violate these basic principles then we need to stand up for our commitments. He invokes these sentiments to argue that practices like female circumcision (genital mutilation), *Sati* (self-immolation by the Hindu widow on the funeral pyre of her husband) and human sacrifice cannot be accepted in a liberal democracy.

In a similar vein, Will Kymlicka argues that liberals cannot just permit violations such as "slavery or genocide or mass tortures and expulsions" (1995: 169). He also accepts that special rights granted to minorities are not instruments that may be used to oppress internal minorities. Yet, both Carens and Kymlicka invoke liberal commitments and basic rights only to prohibit and challenge practices involving extreme degree of violence and explicit bodily harm. The violence and inequality implicit in a whole range of other practices – such as child marriage, triple *talaq* (instant divorce), denial of the right to education and inheritance to a section of the population and refusal to allow religious conversions – do not elicit a similar response. While most of these practices impose severe restrictions upon community members they are not seen as fit cases for intervention by the larger society. Joseph Carens writes:

---

[1] Interpreting and applying this criterion, Carens argues that Quebec may require immigrants to send their children to French language public schools. Since no one is entitled to an education at public expense in the language of their choice (Carens 2000: 129), such legislation, it is said, does not violate any fundamental rights of citizens. But the society cannot claim a right to exclude people from citizenship who live there. The latter would be unacceptable in a modern democratic polity.

different traditions have different views of the proper roles of men and women and the proper relations between them . . . [S]ome religious and moral traditions sharply differentiate the roles of men and women, assigning women to the domestic sphere and limiting their public activities, and emphasizing the authority of husband within the family. Other traditions . . . seek to minimize gender differences, encouraging both females and males to develop their talents and capacities whatever these might be . . . Within broad limits, *a liberal democratic society ought to tolerate these sorts of cultural differences* among groups and thus cultural differences between the sexes when these emerge from a group's inner life . . . *These differences may affect the life-chances of group members . . . but these sorts of consequences are an inevitable by-product of respect for people's religious and cultural commitments* (Carens 2000: 100–1; emphasis added).

Faced with cultural community practices of the same kind, Kymlicka also advises extreme caution for it involves "interference in the internal affairs of a national minority" (1995: 169).Just as we do not interfere in the affairs of another country when it denies political rights to women or other immigrant groups, similarly, he argues, we should be extremely reluctant to intervene in the internal affairs of a national minority. In both cases matters are left by and large in the hands of the minority community. Differences that seriously affect the life-conditions of the members and their capacity to lead a meaningful life where they can make choices and protect themselves against conditions of acute destitution are seen as an "inevitable by-product" of respecting cultural diversity. As a consequence, equal treatment for internal minorities remains a pipe-dream. If we look at the struggles of women in India and elsewhere in the world, we find that they are questioning the unequal access to life opportunities and, by extension, their ability to lead a dignified human existence. Under these circumstances to say that these inequalities are simply differences that arise from a "group's inner life" or that we must respect the autonomy of communities, only legitimizes the status quo. If anything it suggests that justice, defined as affirmation of diversity, may imply in several significant spheres unequal treatment for internal minorities.

Some of these difficulties and contradictions arise because both Carens and Kymlicka accept that the state expresses the culture of the majority community. Consequently they are apprehensive of state interventions on the ground that the norms of the majority culture would be applied to minority community actions. Yet, they are compelled to note that minority communities and their cultural practices may infringe the rights of the vulnerable individuals and groups within the minority community. Hence, they create room for state interventions but, given their understanding of the state, such interventions are limited. The state can intervene in situations that involve direct physical harm, injury and violence against the individual. Hence, this alternative remains caught in a strange paradox: it acknowledges and values cultural differences yet it is reluctant to accommodate all forms of diversity. At another level, the state is equated with the majority and this leaves little room for its involvement in the life of the minority, yet it is empowered to act to affirm what are seen as basic rights and shared values of a political community.

It is contradictions of this nature that the second alternative seeks to address and overcome. Theorists like Chandran Kukathas, who articulate this point of view, respond to the issue of internal heterogeneity and oppressive or inegalitarian community practices by recommending the right of exit for the individual. In advocating the right to exit, these theorists acknowledge that individual members may not share the same set of collective goods, and that a culture may affirm values that do not conform to the values of the dominant majority within the polity. In view of the former, we cannot simply grant cultures rights to perpetuate themselves and protect their difference. At the same time, given the incommensurability of cultures, we cannot give the state or any other external agent the right to intervene in the affairs of the community. If differences are to be respected a culture should not be expected to liberalize and conform to what is regarded by the wider society as an acceptable form of diversity (Kukathas 1992a: 116–22). Consequently, what is advocated is that cultural communities be conceived as associations, such that individuals have a right to enter into them and abide by their norms, if they so desire. Or they may, if they find that way of life unacceptable, dissociate themselves from these communities into which they are born and charter a different life for themselves.

In this framework the choice is left to the individual. No attempt is made in advance to determine which cultural practices are acceptable in a liberal democracy. Instead what is argued is that liberal democracies must be hospitable to differences and they must learn to accommodate and tolerate all forms of diversity. In effect this means that the boundaries of permissible diversity cannot, and indeed must not, be drawn by invoking liberal values, such as the principle of autonomy, free speech or freedom of conscience. If individuals wish to live by old traditions and withdraw their children from public schools or disallow religious conversions or abide by the tenets of their religion, then they must have the freedom to do so. "Liberalizing" the culture cannot be a condition for granting cultural rights to individuals or for determining what may or may not be permitted in a polity (Kukathas 1992a: 122).

The only thing that matters is whether the different cultural forms are imposed or voluntarily chosen. If individuals opt to live by the norms of a cultural community and affirm collective social goods then they must have the opportunity to do so. Equally, if individuals wish to dissociate themselves from the community into which they are born they must have a right to do so and the community should not be in a position to enforce its views on them. Individuals should, in other words, have the right to choose and even more importantly, given the nature of cultural communities, they must have the right to exit.

The right to exit addresses the dilemmas faced by internal minorities by giving moral value and autonomy to the individual. While most theories of multiculturalism value cultural diversity and posit a contradiction between the state which expresses the culture of the majority and the minorities within the polity, this framework places the individual against the state as well as the community. Consequently, it recognizes the oppression engendered by the state as well as the cultural community. While it does not consider cultural community membership to be crucial or even "fundamental" (Kukathas 1992a: 111) in the construction of personal identity, it accepts that individuals "find themselves members of groups or associations which not only influence their conduct but also shape their loyalties and their sense of identity" (110). As such, it acknowledges the importance of group identities and memberships to the life of the individual. Where it departs from other multicultural theories is when it denies cultures the right to perpetuate themselves. In place of valuing cultural diversity as a valued good it argues that collective entities matter only because individuals consider them to be important to their well-being. Individual choices must count: if individuals regard certain ways of life as being valuable to them, they must have the option of associating with them, and *vice-versa*, if they find them oppressive they must have a right to dissociate from them.

This framework of multicultural accommodation overcomes the problems associated with invoking a universal criterion and determining what is or is not acceptable in a given society. However, what needs to be considered is whether the claims of equal treatment that come from vulnerable internal minorities can be adequately addressed by giving individuals a right to opt out of the community. As Ayelet Shachar points out "[M]inority group members such as women who are subject to strict intra-group controls and sanctioned maltreatment are precisely those members who commonly lack the economic stability, cultural 'know-how,' language skills, connections, and self-confidence needed to successfully exit from their minority communities" (Shachar 2001: 69). Lacking the necessary resources to exit from the community is only one of the problems associated with the exit option. An equally important issue is whether exit is really a matter of individual choice. Often individuals may not see themselves as belonging to a particular cultural community; they may not affirm the values and practices of the community in everyday life, and the community too may not have the resources or inclination to enforce conformity. Yet others outside the community may continue to identify them as belonging to that community. A person may not, for instance, wear a turban or offer *namaaz* five times a day, but in the public arena these individuals may be ostracized as Sikhs or Muslims. If individuals are branded and asked to prove their loyalty to the nation-state not because of their beliefs or actions but because of their name and the identity with which they are born, exit is not, and cannot be seen as a matter of individual choice. Indeed it is futile to speak of a right to exit when community identity may be thrust upon the individual from the outside. For the same reason it is naïve to suggest that problems faced by internal minorities can be satisfactorily resolved by giving members the right to exit.

Even though exit is hardly ever a matter of individual choice, one can envisage exit as a form of legal strategy while dealing with vulnerable minorities like women. When exit is given a legal content it can give women a right and a choice not to be governed by the norms of their community if they so desire. They can choose to be governed by community codes or by civil codes formulated by the state, if they feel that the former are oppressive and unfair to them. This is a strategy that has been used in India and is seen as a viable way of accommodating the concerns of diversity with those of intra-group equality. The difficulty, however, is that such strategies ask the individual to choose between community membership and fair treatment, and this is by no means a choice that any individual should be expected to make. If a person's life is to some extent shaped by community affiliations, as Kukathas says it is (1992a: 110), then asking an individual to give up what has in part given meaning to her life places too heavy a price upon her. It is difficulties of this kind that compel us to look for ways in which issues of equal treatment for internal minorities can be addressed within the community itself, without asking the individual to relinquish her identity.

The third alternative attempts just this solution. Based on the understanding that the state reflects the culture of the majority it excludes external interventions in the affairs of the community and at the same time it accepts the value of cultural community identity for the individual. Hence, it does not resolve the issue of equal treatment for internal minorities by giving individuals the right to exit. Advocates of deliberative consensus accept that communities are internally heterogeneous and there may be no consensus on shared collective goods or community practices. Consequently, they argue, in situations where internal differences exist, a community must be "faithful to these disagreements" (Walzer 1983: 313). It must provide institutional channels for the expression of these differences and for the articulation of alternative distributions.

The assumption here is that a community may say that it has its own reasons for doing what it does. However, it cannot say that it has no reasons at all (Chatterjee 1994: 1775). In a democracy it is obligatory that these reasons be discussed and made known to others; and *vice-versa* the reasons that others offer for amending or abandoning a practice must be heard and taken into account while determining collectively valued goods. No community can therefore be exempt from collective deliberation through democratic participation and decision-making processes. It cannot, in the name of difference, deny the necessity of deliberative consensus within a democracy.

The votaries of the deliberative consensus model work with the assumption that collective and democratic methods of decision-making would enable different sections of the community, including those that were previously excluded or marginalized, to express their point of view and be counted. As a consequence, what are affirmed as shared values and collective goods within the community are in fact representative of the collectivity. It is further assumed that open debate and dialogue will enable members to interrogate existing practices, alter their views in the light of normative claims presented by others and arrive at what might be called, following Habermas, a "rationally motivated consensus." Oppressive and inegalitarian structures and community practices would in this process give way to those that are just and fair to the weaker sections.

This framework of multicultural accommodation accepts that cultural community membership is valuable to the self and that cultural diversity enriches society. Hence it respects the autonomy of the community and allows it to determine its own distinctive way of life. Further, instead of relying on the state to initiate reforms, it places the responsibility with the community and suggests procedures that are democratic without appealing to any external norm or authority. The agenda of reforms from within the community thus combines the commitment to protect cultural diversity with the need to ensure fair and equal treatment for minorities within the minority community. Since reforms initiated by the state often meet with hostility and suspicion from the minority community, and principles that are endorsed as universals may reflect the sentiments of the majority within the political community, the idea of accommodating internal minorities democratically through a process of collective deliberation and consensus has won considerable support in recent times. To many it appears to be the most appropriate way of affirming cultural diversity without ossifying the community or privileging existing practices and leadership.

There is no doubt that this framework provides a democratic solution that is also respectful of the multicultural perspective on state, society and the value of cultural diversity. Even though inclusion has rarely, if ever, been enough for dismantling structures of power and oppression, this alternative is favored today by many groups in India and also by multiculturalists elsewhere in the Western world. All of them assume that democratizing the process of decision-making within the community will yield an outcome that is acceptable and fair to all. This is an assumption that needs some justification, particularly since democratization within the polity has not yielded such results in other spheres of social and economic life. It needs also to be noted that this framework rests upon one basic contradiction. It affirms cultural diversity and maintains that different communities endorse different conceptions of the good life. Yet it expects all of them to abide by the same procedures of decision-making. Further, in line with liberal understanding, it assumes that conformity to certain procedures of decision-making is not an imposition. It does not minimize diversity or freedom of the community. Despite this contradiction the "reforms from within" approach has gained fairly wide acceptance in minority communities, state machinery and women's groups in India. Almost all minority communities have initiated internal reforms to address the claims for equal treatment that have come from minorities within, particularly from women within the community. The experience has provided important insights that we may need to consider while searching for adequate ways of accommodating the concerns for intergroup equality with those of intra-group equality.

III

The Constitution of India provided equality before the law for all citizens irrespective of their religion, race, caste, creed, language or gender (Article 15). At the same time, it affirmed the value of cultural diversity. The framers of the constitution recognized that religion was an important marker of individual identity and, given the large presence of the Hindu population, they wished to assure all minority religious communities that they will be equal members of the polity. To this end they gave each community the right to "profess, practice and propagate" their religion (Article 25, clause 1). The right to religious practice has, among other things, been used to uphold Personal Laws of different religious communities, the majority as well as the minorities. Thus, in all matters pertaining to family, from marriage, divorce, separation and custody of children to inheritance and maintenance, it is the plural structure of community laws that governs the individual. At the time of framing the Constitution, several members and women representatives opposed the right to religious practice. RajKumari Amrit Kaur, Hansa Mehta and several other members argued that the right to religious practice might be used to continue with practices that subordinated women and treated them as less than equal. However, despite these objections the Constitution eventually respected cultural diversity and allowed individuals the right to religious practices (Mahajan 1998: 45–50, 79–82). Since it is the community that determines what is or is not considered to be a religious practice, it is the will of the community that prevails. This logic has been applied to community Personal Laws too. The Constitution directed that the state must, over time, formulate a Uniform Civil Code that applies to members of all religious communities and is just to women. However, this was a part of the Directive Principles of State Policy and was non-justiciable. In contrast, religious practice was a fundamental right and it was in extension of this right that individuals were to be governed by the Personal Laws of their community.

The Personal Laws of all communities, the majority as well as the minorities, disadvantaged women. However, even before independence, the government had appointed the Hindu Law Committee to look into the question of reform in Hindu Personal Law. As a consequence of these efforts, in 1956 the Hindu Code Bill was passed by the Parliament, despite considerable opposition from members of the Hindu community, and it did, to some extent, improve the condition of Hindu women. Similar changes were not introduced or initiated in the Personal Laws of the minority communities. Neither the Constitution, the "operative public values" enshrined in that document nor a shared conception of "basic" rights have yielded reforms in the Personal Laws of various minority communities. A notion of "basic" rights enabled the framers to make the task of formulating a uniform civil code a subject of a Directive Principle of State Policy but it has not translated into public policy. The state responded to the concerns of gender justice by legislating the Special Marriage Act in 1954. This gave individuals what might be called exit options. Individuals could choose to be married under this Act and be governed by the law of the state, which was more gender-just than the existing Personal Laws. If they did not make this choice, however, then they would be governed by the Personal Law of their community. The choice was left to the individual. In theory this provided a way of protecting cultural diversity without necessarily justifying or supporting unfair treatment for women. But the existence of this option meant that there was no pressure upon the communities to reform their Personal Laws and make them more fair to women. The fact that the communities were let off the hook and the state dismissed its responsibility towards women as citizens of the polity is significant because this strategy operated with the belief that women can make a choice. Several scholars pointed out that a large number of citizens were not even aware of this option, but that was by no means the major problem. The more serious issue was that women, who are a marginalized minority, with few resources to support their independent existence, were in no position to challenge the existing orthodoxy and make choices about their lives. Since the law suggested that if the choice was not exercised at the time of marriage, then individuals would be governed by the Personal Law of their community, this effectively provided little or no relief to women as a disadvantaged and vulnerable group within the community.

Taking cognizance of this limitation some feminists have suggested the criterion of what has come to be called "reverse optionality." The aim once again is to accommodate the concern for equal treatment for internal minorities with the commitment to cultural diversity by giving members exit options. The critical difference is that the options are being reversed here. Individuals would be governed by the civil law of the state unless they made a choice and opted for religious Personal Laws. The belief is that this might give several individuals, who are uninformed about the choices available to them and the implications of making a certain choice, the benefit of being governed by more just laws. The difficulty that this option presents is that in a society where religion influences individual lives deeply and where secularization of society and religion has not occurred to any significant degree, religious authority and membership are likely to influence actions. Most individuals are probably going to have a religious marriage irrespective of their knowledge of option. Consequently, they will be governed by the Personal Laws of their community. Besides, if religious and cultural identities matter then no one should have to choose between identity and fairness. Even though cultural community membership is not merely a question of adhering to given practices or Personal Laws, it is in rituals and activities surrounding birth, marriage and death that identities are sharply etched. Therefore, even in a secularized society, no one should be called upon to efface their identity at a moment that is so important in their lives, and at which the markers of their identity give expression to their sentiments and meaning to their actions.

It is difficulties of this order that have pushed in the direction of seeking reforms from within the community. The idea that the Personal Laws of each community should treat women fairly fits well with the multicultural framework. It acknowledges the value of cultural identities for the self and the importance of protecting diversity of cultures in a plural society. At the same time, it is sensitive to the fact that the state may be closely associated with the majority; hence its actions may meet with resistance, and even suspicion, from the minority communities. It consequently places the onus upon the community and suggests that democratic methods of decision-making be adopted to develop a deliberative consensus on Personal Laws within the community. In privileging the deliberative model, there is no recourse to any external set of values or authority. A consensus is to be achieved on the basis of the reasonableness of the proposed claims of different parties. It is assumed here that religious leadership will not by itself define community norms; as such, defense for cultural diversity will not translate into support for the status quo.

This alternative has in recent times received considerable support from different quarters. In India some sections of the women's movement have given up the earlier demand of framing an egalitarian uniform civil code and are defending the need to arrive at gender-just community Personal Laws through a process of internal reform. In part this is a response to the current political scenario, where the ruling party actively promoting a Hindu cultural identity for the entire political community is asking for a change in the Personal Laws of minority communities. The target of their campaign is the Muslim minority, and in this context women's groups fear the demand for a code may be appropriated to impose a code that is based on the practices of the majority Hindu community. Consequently, they have distanced themselves from the majoritarian sentiments by asserting that changes should be possible within the plural structure of community Personal Laws. Political considerations aside, there is a growing feeling that cultural diversity may well be accommodated along with the demand for gender equality, and that changes can be, and must be, made within the existing framework. It is from this perspective that reforms from within the community have been recommended and even attempted in each of the recognized religious minorities in the state – Muslims, Christians and Parsis.

Attempts to reform minority Personal Laws from within have been going on for some time now. If we look at the experience of the last two decades or more, we find that this process has yielded three sharply different, if not contrary, results. It is this difference that compels us to reflect more deeply upon frameworks of multicultural accommodation. Of all the minority communities, the Parsis have been most successful in effecting changes in their Personal Laws and making them more fair for women. They have also been most effective in ensuring that these changes receive the formal sanction of the Parliament quickly. However, the most striking feature of these reforms was the complete absence of women. The initiative, Flavia Agnes points out, was taken by a few liberal male members of the community and at no stage was the name of any woman from the community mentioned or associated with the process of change (Agnes 1999: 136). The proposal for reforms was based on the recommendations of the 110th Law Commission and it was this model that the Board of Trustees of the Bombay Parsi Panchayat took up while "modernizing" their Personal Law in the late 1980s. Thus even though these were reforms initiated from within the community, indirect influence of external institutions having some relation to the state apparatuses was present. Hence, the state/community dichotomy did not prevail in the traditional sense. The distinction did exist in a formal sense but the community was not averse to considering different proposals and recommendations. This was possible perhaps because the Parsis did not see the state or its various institutions as being hostile to the community. The state, too, responded in the same spirit and in 1991 a law giving effect to these changes was passed by the Indian Parliament. One cannot help but speculate that changes initiated and supported by the dominant, male members of the community received state endorsement more readily. This becomes evident when we turn to the case of the Christian community.

The Christian community has also been able to reform its Personal Laws. Different sections of the community Personal Law have been amended and endorsed by the Parliament in 2000 and 2001. These amendments, however, have taken more than twenty years.[2] The initiative for change came from the Joint Women's Programme (JWP) and it involved at each stage constant struggle by an organized women's movement within the community as well as the support of those outside. Altering the Christian Personal Law and getting the revised Christian Marriage Bill and Christian Adoption Bill approved in Parliament was by no means an easy task. Since women are not at the forefront of religious ideological production, reforming these laws meant that they had to gain mastery over the scriptures, negotiate with competing schools of thought within the community and effect compromises between contending churches. In addition they had to constantly remind and persuade the state, particularly the Law Ministry, to take necessary action even after a consensus had been reached within the community.

The case of the Muslim community is markedly different from the Parsi as well as the Christian community. Here, despite the efforts of Muslim women, no significant change has been made in the community Personal Law. Even though many members of the community accept that several

---

[2] In the Parsi and Christian community the new amendments have modernized the law and made it more receptive to issues of gender justice. But a number of inegalitarian provisions continue to exist in each case. For instance, the Parsi Personal Law continues to treat women as minors, and hence provides for a trust to be set up with respect to their maintenance allowance. The Christian Marriage Bill also has several unequal provisions. It allows a husband the right to dispose of joint property and the property of his wife; it also allows husbands to claim maintenance from wives and enables both spouses to claim damages from an adultress/adulterer (see Agnes and Gowda 2000).

aspects of the family law disadvantage women, they maintain that the rigidity and inequality that characterize this law are not intrinsic to the Islamic law (see Mahmood 1995: 143–77). It is a contingent effect of the dominance of the *hanafi* tradition. Others argue that the Islamic law permits *ijtihad*, i.e. the application of independent reason to the interpretation and modification of law (Ahmed 2001). In brief, arguments are continually offered to suggest that changes can be made in the Islamic law; that multiple traditions exist which can be invoked to re-establish laws that are fair to women. The ideas that women should be treated as equal and their divorce or death of their husbands should not leave them destitute are accepted, yet no reforms have been successfully made. The community continues to be faced with innumerable cases of wives and children being abandoned, left with no maintenance, and frequently denied *Maher*. Problems are accentuated since literacy among the women in the community is extremely low and fertility rates high compared to women of other minority religious communities.[3]

IV

The multicultural strategy of reforms from within has thus yielded three very different and contrasting results. If we reflect upon this experience three things come to the fore. First, contrary to common belief the inclusion of women in the deliberative process is by no means enough for altering existing community practices and making Personal Laws more just to women. While it is possible to envisage change from within, women have a difficult task before them. They need to build a consensus by getting the co-operation of the male members as well as the religious leadership, which is predominantly male. For this they need the support and backing of organized women's groups. The effort that is required cannot be easily sustained by a few lone voices. Even if the community members are the primary agents, it is essential to create space for the *organized* group voice of women. The presence of the latter can play a critical role in effecting reforms.

Second, external pressures, for instance, those that come from the international community and community members outside the polity, can also act as a positive influence pushing in the direction of reforms in favor of gender-just laws. While these external entities are not directly

---

[3] The literacy rate among women of the Muslim community is 38%; for Christian women it is 76.5%; and for other minorities it is 43.8%. The fertility rate among Muslim women between the ages of 15 and 19 is 5.8%; among Christians it is 2.1%; and among other minorities it is 3.9% (India Human Development Report, 1999 quoted in Hameed 2000: 26, 27).

involved in the process of change, nevertheless the norms endorsed by the community elsewhere do help to sustain the process of reform. At the very least these act as a facilitating condition. Consequently, even while affirming democratic deliberation as the mode of accommodating diversity with equality, one needs to recognize that the internal and the external elements can intersect in many ways. There is no reason to insulate the internal from the external entirely. While the latter must not impose its will upon the former, there is reason, particularly while dealing with issues of intra-group equality, to open oneself to the possibility of a more positive and enabling interaction between internal processes and external influences.

Third, and perhaps most important of all, the success of the reform process depends heavily upon the way in which a community perceives and relates to the state, and assesses its status within the political community. It is interesting to note that the process of change from within was smoother and more efficacious in the case of the Parsi community, a group that does not share the sentiment of being minoritized. While it does see itself as a minority with a distinct cultural identity, one that is not reflected in the culture or civil religion of the polity, nevertheless it is not the quintessential "other," which has a sense of being persecuted and demonized by the nation-state. In contrast, the process of internal change meets with the greatest resistance and the least success in the case of the Muslim community. This community is perceived as the metaphorical "other" and the identity of the majority is increasingly being defined in contradistinction to this community. The Muslim community, too, sees the state as the voice of the majority. For them it is the "hostile other." This negative perception of the state has not only helped to consolidate and privilege the religious identity of the community, it has also made the community more resistant to change, even when the impetus and demand for that change come from within.

What follows from this is that a secure cultural structure is by no means sufficient for inculcating the spirit of revisability. In the book *Liberalism, Community and Culture*, Kymlicka argues that it is "only through having a rich and secure cultural structure that people can become aware, in a vivid way, of the options available to them, and intelligently examine their value" (1989a: 165). When a culture is eroded due to pressures from outside, and not on account of the choice of its members, dependency, escapism and a variety of other associated problems surface. In making this argument Kymlicka stresses the value of cultural membership and, along with it, suggests that it is in a secure cultural context alone that individuals can distance themselves from the beliefs and practices they have inherited. When the culture is under siege or faced with pressures of disintegration it is difficult for individual members to critically interrogate and revise existing frameworks of beliefs or practices. In part at least, it is this understanding of the importance of a secure cultural context that informs Kymlicka's defense of minority rights. There is no doubt that cultural membership is deeply valued by individuals, and their conception of who they are is to some extent shaped by their collective community identity. Yet a secure cultural context, desirable as that might be, is not a sufficient or a crucial condition for reconsidering community norms and opening oneself to the possibility of change. Rather, it is only when the state is not perceived as a hostile entity that communities become less resistant to change and more open to the task of accommodating voices of dissent internally.

When the state is viewed with mistrust, as has happened in the case of the Muslim community in India, protecting and consolidating the community identity becomes the primary concern. This has worked to the advantage of the religious leadership; it has enabled them to resist external interventions as well as expressions of differences within. It is also necessary to add that in India the experience of communal violence has assisted in this process. It has privileged the religious community identity, making it exceedingly difficult for individual members to take up agendas that question the way that identity has been defined in recent times. The elected representatives, who belong to that community, are reluctant to oppose religious community leadership in this situation, fearing that their actions would be interpreted as being anti-community. Similarly, the state, when it wishes to appear sympathetic and fair to the minority community, negotiates with the religious leadership and tries to accept the perspectives that come from that quarter. Writing about the experience of the Joint Women's Programme in reforming the Christian Personal Law, Jyotsana Chatterjee states that in 1992 the Joint Women's Programme with the support of the Church of India finalized the draft legislation indicating the necessary changes. The proposal had previously been through a process of consultation with the Catholic Bishops' Conference, the All India Catholic Union and several other smaller churches. Yet when they approached the prime minister with the draft they were informed that no amendments would be entertained in the present form for some Christian leaders who were consulted by the Government were opposed to any change (2001). Similarly, in the case of the Muslim community the Rajiv Gandhi government, after the judgement in the Shah Bano case, appeased the more orthodox sections of the religious leadership by denying Muslim women the existing option of appealing to the Court as destitute persons. In both cases it is the concern for equal treatment that is voiced by women members that falls by the wayside.

In India the Constitution provides rights to minorities to protect and pursue their distinct way of life. A certain degree of public recognition and space is thus given to minority cultures. Although there is legitimate concern about certain kinds of state interventions and non-recognition of specific languages, the cultural structure of these communities is not under pressure. But the presence of a secure cultural context has not been sufficient for providing the space for what Kymlicka terms "revisability." If we look at cases where changes have been introduced in community laws and where they have been resisted the most, it is striking that when basic rights of citizenship are denied and challenged, resistance to change is the strongest. Communal violence brings home the sense of discrimination by systematically targeting individuals belonging to a community and denying them the most essential rights – namely, the rights to life, liberty and property. It is communities that have been victims of such violence, and whose most basic rights have not been protected, that are most closed to change even when it comes from within the community.

In brief, the point that needs to be underlined is that in the multicultural framework the state is implicated in the culture of the majority community. This undermines its authority to intervene in the affairs of the minority community. It also makes it extremely difficult for the state institutions and the women's organizations to justify any kind of external intervention. This itself empowers the community, making it considerably more autonomous in determining the fate of its internal members. Under the circumstances reforms from within appear to be the only way of accommodating the demands of internal minorities for equal treatment in the community. But the presence of dissenting voices within and a plural cultural tradition does not by itself yield the desired results. Nor does respect for cultural diversity prepare the way for bringing in the concern for equality. The latter takes a back seat when the status of community members as citizens is undermined in the polity. If we are at all to accommodate the concern for equal treatment for internal minorities with the commitment to protect cultural diversity, then making a culture secure by granting it special rights to continue with its distinct way of life remains less than adequate. The basic condition of "revisability" is equal status as a citizen and member of the polity. When minority communities are denied that status then all tactics of multiculturalism fail to accommodate diversity with equality.

5   Dilemmas of gender and culture: the judge, the democrat and the political activist

Anne Phillips

The phrase "minorities within minorities" alerts us to both parallels and potential collision. It suggests a symmetry between groups that have been minoritized by virtue of their race, ethnicity, religion, language or culture, and sub-groups within these, minoritized by virtue of age, sexuality, gender or class. If the disadvantages suffered by the larger minority give rise to legitimate claims, consistency requires us to address further disadvantages that may affect minorities within it: we cannot, in all fairness, say that public authorities should tackle the injustices that attach to one group but feel under no obligation to deal with those that attach to the others. The further implication is that these two concerns may collide. In particular, actions designed to strengthen the position of a cultural or religious minority within the larger society may simultaneously strengthen the power of cultural and religious leaders over dissidents within their group. Women and young people will often bear the brunt of this.

This tension has been the burden of much recent discussion of the relationship between feminism and multiculturalism (e.g. Okin 1998, 1999a, 2002; Deveaux 2000a; Shachar 2001; Spinner-Halev 2001). Multiculturalism takes issue with the monoculturalism that informs much contemporary thought and practice, stresses the diversity of the many cultures that make up contemporary societies, and argues that societies and/or governments should recognize the legitimacy of at least some cultural claims. These have ranged from appeals to the wider society to recognize the validity of a variety of norms and traditions, to calls for legislative exemptions to accommodate what would otherwise be deemed illegal practices, to the devolution of authority to cultural communities in the regulation of marital and familial affairs. Since much of what we understand by culture revolves around the expectations attached to being male and female,

I am grateful to the Nuffield Foundation, which funded the research on which this chapter is based; and to the organisers of the Minorities within Minorities conference for providing such a fruitful context in which to discuss the ideas.

113

the understandings and practices of sexuality, and the conditions under which people marry, have children and divorce, it is evident that some of these claims could have unhappy consequences for women.

Consider polygamous marriages, which are perfectly legal in many parts of the world, but have been prohibited under English law; or marriages involving spouses under the age of sixteen, also legal in a number of jurisdictions (including some states in the USA) but prohibited by English law. One result of this is that immigration officials will refuse entry clearance to second wives or under-age spouses even when one party to the marriage is a UK citizen and the marriage is fully recognized elsewhere. The marital conventions of one culture are thereby imposed on all, and in at least some versions of multiculturalism, this is seen as unfairly disadvantaging members of the cultural minority.[1] Yet addressing this seeming inequity would remove what many women experience as an important protection, legitimating multiple wives for men, and making it easier for parents to pressure young girls into marriage. As Ayelet Shachar (2001: 4) puts it, "well-meaning accommodations aimed at mitigating power inequalities between groups may end up reinforcing power hierarchies within them"; where this happens, "at-risk group members are being asked to shoulder a disproportionate share of the risks of multiculturalism" (2001: 17).

And this problem is likely to intensify, for when cultural groups feel themselves under threat, perhaps precisely because of pressures to assimilate, the first sign of danger may well be an unwelcome assertiveness on the part of women or younger members. One frequent response is to recodify the norms regulating family life in an ever more restrictive way: what Shachar has termed a "reactive culturalism" in the face of rapid social change. Traditions are rediscovered or even created, and practices that have long been contested are restored to a central defining role. The codes regulating gender relations then become bound up with notions of cultural authenticity, and the defence of one's culture becomes in large part the defence of that culture's notions about what it is appropriate for women to do. In this context, otherwise well-intentioned moves towards recognizing the legitimacy of a multiplicity of cultures could encourage public authorities to turn a blind eye to coercive practices that institutionalize women's subordination; strengthen the power

---

[1] In his review of English law, for example, Alex Samuels (1981: 251) argues that "If a person is bona fide polygamous then . . . he ought to be allowed to take a polygamous wife in England provided that he conform to the law of the polygamous group to which he belongs, or abroad, provided that he conforms to the local law. There is no longer any reason, if ever there was, for making English law the personal law of all persons domiciled in England. A personal law based upon personal religion or culture is far more acceptable in a multi-racial society."

of self-styled community leaders – almost always male – who represent a
very partial view of "their" community's most cherished traditions; and
lead to a paralyzed relativism that puts sensitivity to cultural difference
over the rights or needs of women.

The strategies adopted by political theorists for dealing with this
dilemma mostly fall into one of two camps. The first is broadly judicial. It brings to bear a number of principles relating to the rights of the
individual and group, and arranges these in the appropriate hierarchy in
order to generate a solution. Among frequently invoked principles are
the right of nations to self-determination (most commonly employed in
relation to indigenous minorities), the freedom of religion, and the right
of women to be treated equally with men. In much – though by no means
all – of the feminist literature, this last takes priority, and sex equality
then becomes a non-negotiable condition for any practices of multiculturalism. Outside this literature, sex equality tends to drop down the list.
As Susan Moller Okin (2002) has recently noted, liberal theorists commonly rate principles of racial equality above those of religious freedom
or cultural autonomy, but rarely attach comparable weight to the requirements of gender equality.[2] Meanwhile, for some critics, the very idea that
a cultural group might have rights is felt to be highly contentious; and
the "minorities with minorities" dilemma is settled by rejecting the very
notion of minority rights (e.g. in Barry 2001a, 2001b).

The less judicially inclined have looked to democratic deliberation as
the better way of addressing value conflict, arguing that inter-cultural
dialogue can generate a more culturally sensitive agreement on core
principles of justice; or that greater democracy within each community
can redefine values in ways that meet women's equality concerns (e.g.
Gutmann and Thompson 1996; Deveaux 2000a; Benhabib 2002). This
approach takes as its starting point that principles of justice are formed in
particular historical contexts, and cannot therefore be appealed to as the
deus ex machina to settle inter-cultural disputes. It also stresses that the
most deeply held of values still remain open to change, and that seemingly

---

[2] She gives as one example William Galston's support for a Supreme Court judgement
that refused tax-exempt status to Bob Jones University because it forbade its students, on
supposedly religious grounds, from inter-racial dating; and contrasts this with his criticism
of another Supreme Court judgement that ordered the reinstatement of a pregnant school
teacher who had been sacked by her fundamentalist Christian employers. In both cases,
religion had been cited as the justification for discriminatory treatment (the school teacher
was sacked for supposedly religious reasons to do with the undesirability of mothers with
young children working outside the home); Galston is prepared to consider this legitimate
in the second case but not in the first. It seems that when questions of religious freedom
come against questions of racial discrimination, they should be settled in favor of racial
equality; when religion comes up against sexual discrimination, religion wins out.

incompatible value systems can come closer to resolution in the course of discussion and debate. Instead, then, of a judgement handed down via externally generated principles of justice, this approach envisages a dialogic exchange between individuals from different cultural groups. People may embark on this process with an acute sense of what differentiates them, but hopefully will discover significant common ground between their different value systems, and/or come to accept that some aspects of their own value system are harder to defend than they thought. Some versions of this have invoked a plurality of cultural communities represented by relatively uncontested cultural authorities: this seems to be the approach of Bhikhu Parekh (2000), who calls on societies to establish mechanisms for the inter-cultural valuation of disputed practices such as polygamy or female genital mutilation, but tends to envisage the dialogue as carried out by "minority spokesmen." Most of the feminist literature, by contrast, stresses the pluralism within as well as between communities, and argues for mechanisms of empowerment that will enable women within each group to challenge patriarchal definitions of their supposedly shared culture. In both cases, however, the emphasis is on resolution through dialogue rather than adjudication from on high.

The judicial approach has been seen as problematic because it appeals to principles of justice that may themselves be the sedimented norms of a dominant culture. The deliberative approach corrects this, but despite its more encouraging view of value resolution, can still be said to exaggerate the scale of value conflict. One of the central points in this chapter is that political theorists have promoted an overcharged understanding of the "minorities within minorities" dilemma, simultaneously overestimating the value conflicts associated with cultural pluralism and underestimating the political ones. The inflation arises partly because the literature on multiculturalism has developed in close association with a literature on minority rights, which in turn has drawn heavily on the experience of indigenous peoples. As a result of this, it has inclined to the view that there are fundamentally different belief systems and fundamentally opposed principles of justice. The inflation also reflects an occupational hazard for political theorists, who like the experience of grappling with "hard cases," and sometimes make them harder than they are in order to highlight the resolution. In many cases, I argue, there is no deep disagreement: no fundamentally opposed understandings of justice that have to be weighed up or democratically resolved.

What we face, rather, are complex matters of political judgement and strategy that derive their complexity from the specificities of historical context, and the often agonizing gap between the messages we intend to send out and the ones those around us receive. When people make their claims – for sex equality or minority rights or cultural recognition – they intervene on a stage already set by previous interventions, and employ discourses already mobilized to serve what may be very different ends. The history of these discourses forms the inevitable backdrop to political action, and since we cannot just assert, with Humpty Dumpty, that we will make the words mean what *we* choose, this history frames and informs our political choices. Culture, for example, can be deployed in highly opportunistic ways, as in "cultural defences" that represent (usually non-Western) cultures as more accommodating towards rape and murder; and abuses of this kind stoke up much of the opposition to multiculturalism (see Phillips 2003; Chiu 1994; Volpp 1994; Coleman 1996; Kim 1997). The rights of women can also become the rallying cry for projects that have little to do with feminism, as when a discourse of sex equality is employed to justify military intervention in Islamic countries or to represent the backwardness of colonized peoples. The discourse then seems to assume a life of its own, often far detached from its original uses.

We can, of course, say that the meanings others attach to our principles are beside the point: that the task is to determine what is right and just; and that it is no concern of ours if the arguments we derive fuel developments in unwanted directions. But most of those involved in political campaigns remain acutely aware that they are making both normative and strategic judgements, assessing not only what is "right" but what best advances their claims in a given historical context. Many of the dilemmas associated with the "minorities within minorities" conundrum – and more specifically, with the feminism/multiculturalism debates – are best understood in this light, as dilemmas that are political and contextual. They certainly involve normative judgements, but even when solutions are theoretically available that finesse the seeming contradiction between sex equality and cultural attachment, in practice these two may still be counter-posed. The judge and deliberative democrat provide us with two models for addressing dilemmas of gender and culture. But if much of the complexity lies in assessing the impact of particular claims in particular historical contexts, we may have to move beyond these two figures to include the perspective of the political activist.

I approach this in three stages. In the first section, I take issue with the notion of intractable value conflict, arguing that the questions addressed in this collection become more open to (at least theoretical) resolution when framed within a common rubric of equality, and that this enables us to move beyond what might otherwise seem incommensurable claims. The theoretical argument is reinforced by an empirical claim about the modesty of most of the policies practiced under the name of multiculturalism, particularly in the multicultural societies that have been formed by more recent large-scale migration. In the second section, I question the tendency to separate gender from culture. This tendency is most marked when sex equality is set up as a competing value to cultural integrity, and the adjudicator has to decide which one matters most; but it is also at issue under a common rubric of equality, which too readily generates a notion of competing equality claims. In the third section, I briefly consider three illustrations, two much discussed in the literature and a third arising from recent British debates. None of them raises hugely complex questions about justice. In varying degrees, however, they all raise difficult questions of political action, and part of that difficulty is contextual. From the perspective of the judge, the task is to determine which principles of justice to follow. From the perspective of the democrat, this involves a more dialogic process, but still one that should ultimately generate normative agreement. From the perspective of the political activist, the question of what is ethically just cannot be so easily detached from judgements about the effects of one's actions, and where there is reason to think that these will be at odds with the original intentions, it can be an abdication of political responsibility not to take this into account. In my view, it is in this, rather than "deep disagreement," that many of the dilemmas of multiculturalism lie.

Against intractable value conflict

The first point is that the tensions within the politics of minority rights become more amenable to settlement when we take equality as the defining concern. The literature on multiculturalism is not always helpful here, for while cultural diversity claims typically invoke some notion of equality (as in the equal right to respect, or the equal requirement for a meaningful cultural context), the emphasis has often been on the need for recognition. When multiculturalism is theorized primarily as a way of meeting claims for cultural recognition, it can indeed be difficult to address conflicts between a group's right to cultural autonomy or recognition and a sub-group's right to equality. Failing some *a priori* commitment to either sex equality or cultural recognition, there seems no obvious way of resolving the tension.

The problem changes shape, however, if we think of multiculturalism as a way of meeting legitimate equality claims. Multicultural policies are still a pressing objective, necessary to address the unequal treatment of minority cultural groups and the "culture-racism" to which so many are exposed. If, however, the object is to promote equality, then an inequality of women enters on the same terrain. This echoes a similar point made by Jacob Levy (2000), who reconfigures multiculturalism as a way of redressing cruelty and violence, and argues that there would not be the same "moral difficulty" (he acknowledges continuing practical difficulties) in restraining internal practices of cruelty against women if multiculturalism were itself grounded in the need to avoid cruelty. By the same token, there would not be the same moral difficulty in challenging an inegalitarian treatment of women if the whole point of multiculturalism were to challenge the unequal treatment of minority groups. The treatment of women figures more centrally in a discourse of either equality or cruelty than one that revolves around the recognition of cultural groups.

My own position is that egalitarians should be committed to both sex equality and at least some version of multiculturalism. That they should be committed to equality between women and men can probably pass without further comment, though it is worth noting that self-professed egalitarians adopt very different positions on what this equality entails. In the case of multiculturalism, there is not even the initial consensus: there are egalitarians who object to what they see as its social divisiveness and cultural relativism; and pragmatic supporters who see it as a way of pre-empting political friction rather than anything to do with equality *per se*. Many of the difficulties here arise from problematic claims about "cultural equality": problematic both in treating "cultures" as distinct and separate entities, and in the suggestion that all cultural practices are of equal moral worth. If we steer clear, however, of this more dubious terrain, it is possible to establish a pretty strong connection between egalitarianism and at least some version of multiculturalism. In the multiethnic, multireligious, multicultural societies that characterize this age of global migration, the idea that access to resources, occupations or political voice should be conditional on adopting what one (usually historically dominant) group has deemed the appropriate practices and values is self-evidently coercive. It is a form of coercion, moreover, that actively asserts the superiority of one set of cultural beliefs and practices over all others, or – perhaps more commonly – simply fails to notice that these beliefs and practices are imbued with the cultural traditions of a dominant or majority group. Principles of non-discrimination alone suggest that societies need to revisit their legislative codes and administrative practices to determine which of these operates as a means of cultural domination. Principles of political equality additionally suggest that they should address taken-for-granted assumptions about who can speak and in what terms. The impetus towards multiculturalism arises from a perception of indefensible inequalities that have become associated with cultural membership, and a suspicion that numerical majorities have imposed their own cultural values under the guise of what they take to be universal norms. It also arises – and this has become particularly important in recent years – from a perception of the "culture-racism" that increasingly substitutes for the crudities of biological racism, and reframes now discredited notions of biological superiority in a less overtly racist discourse about practices that are "backward" or "foreign."

If equality is the key value underpinning initiatives on multicultural-ism, it will continue to be cause for gloom if policies designed to redress the disadvantages of a cultural minority backfire on the women within it, but hardly an occasion for cross-cultural despair. Indeed, in many ways, the deliberative apparatus proposed by political theorists for dealing with troubled questions of cultural pluralism seems unnecessarily large for the task. Commenting on a *Report on the Future of Multi-Ethnic Britain* – the work of a commission chaired by Bhikhu Parekh, and significantly influ-enced by his vision of inter-cultural dialogue – Brian Barry notes that virtually all the recommendations can be justified by reference to prin-ciples of non-discrimination. There was, in his view, no need to muddy the waters by a dubious accretion of cultural pluralism: "the Report gives hostages to fortune by propounding a theory of multiculturalism as plu-ralism that is almost entirely dispensable as a support for its specific rec-ommendations" (Barry 2001b: 56). Or consider an example Monique Deveaux (2000a) offers of the potentially deep clash of values within cul-turally plural societies: the bid for state funding for Islamic schools in the UK. She presents this as at odds with liberal sensibilities because children educated in such schools would be discouraged from taking up lifestyles at odds with Islam; and proposes inclusive procedures of democratic dia-logue as a way of dealing with these potentially incommensurate moral and social beliefs. Yet this question was largely resolved by reference to principles of equality, for in a country already practicing state funding for religious schools (and funding large numbers of Catholic and Anglican schools), principles of non-discrimination alone required the extension of state-aided status to a wider range of denominations.[3] It was hardly necessary to invoke the additional apparatus of inter-cultural dialogue to reach this conclusion; indeed, it might be argued that making such dia-logue a precondition for policy change constitutes Islam as intrinsically more sexist and coercive than the Christian religions.

---

[3] In belated recognition of this point, the Labour government elected in 1997 extended state-aided status to a number of Hindu, Muslim and Seventh Day Adventist schools. Since state funding comes with conditions, including requirements in relation to the cur-riculum and principles of non-discrimination on the grounds of sex or race, this promises better protection for young people than the relatively unregulated private school sector.

Deep value conflict is more rare than is sometimes suggested, and not much in evidence in most of the policies associated with multiculturalism, which fall largely into the categories of extensions, exemptions and autonomy.[4] Some policies seek to extend to other cultural groups "privileges" previously enjoyed only by members of the majority or dominant culture; the object, in other words, is to redress a previous bias – sometimes deliberate, sometimes just unthinking – and ensure more equitable treatment. Extending a principle of state support for denominational schools to include religions associated with more recent migrants would be one obvious example of this. Other initiatives seek exemptions for members of particular cultural groups from requirements that are legally binding on other citizens, the usual justification being that conformity requires a greater sacrifice of cultural or religious values for some groups than others. The equality at issue is usually the equal freedom to pursue one's religion, though it may also be that, failing the exemption, a cultural group would be discriminated against in its pursuit of employment. (This last was part of the argument in the UK for exempting turban-wearing Sikhs from a requirement to wear safety helmets on building sites.) Exemptions are, on the face of it, more troubling to notions of citizen equality than extending to other groups privileges previously enjoyed only by one – except that most of the current examples relate to relatively innocuous matters of food and dress. While these give a public validity to claims about cultural identity, and could as a result strengthen the power of religious and cultural leaders over dissident members of the cultural group, the immediate implications for gender equality are pretty mild.

Autonomy has been a rarer occurrence, mainly arising as part of a historical settlement with indigenous peoples; under colonial practices of indirect rule; or in countries where potentially hostile communities would actively resist incorporation into a single legislative norm. In these cases, cultural communities retain authority in the regulation of certain aspects of property or family affairs, and citizens may come under different jurisdictions depending on their religious or cultural attachments. This is the category that has been thought to throw up the hardest cases, for the resulting regulations may well put women at a disadvantage in relation to men, thereby raising the prospect of external intervention

[4] Levy (2000: ch. 5) offers a more complex categorization that covers exemptions; assistance to do the things the majority can do unassisted (this includes some of my extensions category); self-government claims; external rules restricting non-members' liberty (as in the Quebec language law); internal rules enforcing members' conformity to cultural prescriptions; recognition/enforcement of traditional legal codes; representation of minorities in government bodies; and symbolic recognition.

to secure more equitable treatment. Yet even here, the disagreement is hardly a matter of deep value conflict, rooted in incommensurable traditions and beliefs, for what is at stake is which group has the power to decide. The arguments are typically conducted in a shared language of self-government: do indigenous minorities, for example, have the right to determine for themselves their own practices in relation to inheritance? Do religious authorities have the right to regulate their own members' marital affairs? Does the larger state have the authority to impose the practices it regards as the best? There is undoubtedly disagreement on such issues, but the substance of the argument is about power.

Gender versus culture: not a matter of competing equality claims

Moving towards a common rubric of equality undercuts some of the more tendentious claims about deep value conflict, and provides a promising guide in situations where the needs of the larger and smaller minority threaten to collide. It is tempting, at this point, to adopt a language of competing equality claims: to say that multiculturalism addresses the inequalities experienced by cultural minorities and feminism the inequalities experienced by women; that both these projects draw on a shared commitment to equality; and that the two concerns must therefore be balanced in circumstances where they appear to collide. Neither, in other words, "trumps" the other, and since both are driven by the same underlying commitment, the promotion of the first must not be at the expense of the second.

The partial truth in this is that both sex equality and multiculturalism are driven by questions of equality, but I argue here that it does not help to set them up as competing equality claims. Such a formulation generates an understanding of gender and culture as two distinct systems; this encourages us to think there is a pristine set of "cultural" claims that then have to be modified by gender concerns. Culture is thereby degendered, and one of the central themes of feminist scholarship over the last twenty years is that when something is degendered, a masculine interpretation usually rushes in to fill the vacuum (e.g. Pateman 1988). If this insight is correct, then setting up culture as a separate system (defining our first minority group), whose claims we subsequently balance by considerations of women's equality (our second minority group), is likely to reinforce precisely those patriarchal interpretations of cultural traditions and values that feminists have been criticizing. This dual systems approach does not, of course, commit us to condoning all these traditions, for we are then supposed to weigh up their claims against the claims of sex equality. But it gives an added authenticity to the more conservative representations of culture – and to that extent, already concedes more than it should.

One of the key challenges for any discussion of culture is to avoid what Uma Narayan (1998, 2000) has termed the "package picture of cultures": the presumption that cultures exist as neatly wrapped packages, sealed off from one another, and identifiable by core values and practices that mark them out from all others. The package picture is highly congenial to cultural spokesmen – usually men – who want to claim particular practices as definitive of their culture; and is all too often adopted by Western liberals whose anxieties about cultural imperialism lead them to exaggerate the "otherness" of cultures they see as different from their own. Yet in a process Narayan terms "selective labelling," certain changes in values and practices are designated as consonant with cultural preservation while others are treated as threatening the entire survival of the culture. (One example she notes is that Indian "culture" now seems to have accommodated the public education of women, yet cultural entrepreneurs continue to raise the specter of cultural betrayal when young women challenge the tradition of arranged marriages.) Culture can also be drafted in to explain behavior that is more accurately described as authoritarian parenting or domestic violence, and this is one of the perennial risks in legal defenses that refer to religious or cultural beliefs to explain or mitigate the defendant's behavior. Feminists have criticized the use of culture in the courts to excuse violence against women,[5] but the point is not just that something called cultural identity has sometimes been allowed to take precedence over ensuring women's equality or safety. In many cases, the claim that an action was culturally driven also does deep disservice to other members of that cultural community, whose beliefs and practices are being misrepresented to explain behavior they would never support (for a fuller discussion of this, see Phillips 2003).

Caution is always necessary in dealing with invocations of culture, for this is a term that lends itself readily to cultural essentialism, cultural reification, and the dissemination of cultural stereotypes. The balancing of "cultural" against "gender" concerns should also be treated with caution, for such an approach encourages us to accept a pristine definition of

---

[5] One much-discussed case is that of Dong-lu Chen, a Chinese immigrant to New York who battered his wife to death with a hammer some weeks after discovering she was having an affair. The judge accepted that Chen was "driven to violence by traditional Chinese values about adultery and loss of manhood," convicted him of second degree manslaughter, and sentenced him to five years' probation: *People v. Chen* (Supreme Court, NY County, 2 December 1988). For two very different readings of this case, see Volpp 1994 and Coleman 1996.

culture, which we only then interrogate by reference to women's equality concerns. Meanwhile, setting up gender as distinct from culture encourages the belief that there is a culture-neutral set of values that provides us with the principles for equality between women and men. And where do we find these? Usually in the dominant, therefore less visible culture, which has become such a taken-for-granted background that its members no longer think of themselves as sharing any particular cultural traditions or beliefs.

The selective invocation of culture leads to an over-culturation of those marked by a minority ethnicity or religion – a tendency to treat their every characteristic or behavior as an expression of their culture – but also to an under-culturation of those associated with the dominant group.[6] The hyper-visibility of culture for one group is then linked to an invisibility of culture for another: "they" have cultural traditions, while I have moral values. Again, the analytic separation of gender from culture makes it harder to avoid this trap. When gender is stripped of its cultural context, the less visible, because dominant, culture rushes in to fill the vacuum, and we then have a culturally informed interpretation of sex equality that presents itself as above all culture. Black feminists used to say of an earlier theorization of gender and race that it gave the impression that all the women were white and all the blacks were male. Similar problems arise when we set up gender and culture as separate concerns.

The further difficulty with the discourse of competing equality claims – and here I return to my central argument – is that this formulation misrepresents what are often political and strategic questions as more fundamental conflicts of justice. Though the notion of competing claims helpfully provides us with a common measure of equality through which to address dilemmas of cultural pluralism, it does so in a way that reinforces the more conservative (because pregendered) representations of minority cultures, and in the process heightens the differences between one culture and another. This exaggerates the dilemmas that arise where the practices of multiculturalism fall into the rather modest categories of extension or exemption, and where there may be relatively few areas of principled disagreement. It also, I think, exaggerates those that arise in countries where there has been a significant devolution of power to

---

[6] I take this point from the work of Leti Volpp, who has carried out comparisons of legal cases in America involving under-age sex or marriage. She shows that these are treated as a problem of "culture" when the individuals involved are immigrants of color, but are rarely regarded as a reflection of American cultural values when the people involved are white. As she puts it, "Behavior that causes discomfort – that we consider 'bad' – is conceptualized only as culturally canonical for cultures assumed to lag behind the United States"(Volpp 2000: 96).

cultural or religious groups. But in defining cultural problems as primarily conflicts of value, the literature also *underestimates* the more contextual political dilemmas. It is in these contextual dilemmas that many of the problems lie.

Political dilemmas

The first example revolves around the conflict that has arisen between recognizing the self-government rights of indigenous minorities and ensuring the equal status of their men and women members. In many parts of the world, Aboriginal peoples were thrust into a quasi-colonial system of native reserves or reservations; these worked as a kind of apartheid, but within their much circumscribed limits, they usually provided Aboriginal communities with some self-government powers. In both Canada and the USA, the membership rules governing these communities have sometimes been overtly sexist, most typically in disenfranchising the women (and their descendants) who married outside the group but not the men who did so. Women have sometimes challenged this by reference to a wider federal or international authority, and have then have found themselves in conflict with the self-government claims of their group.[7] This has been particularly problematic for those who support both claims.

Legislation in Canada in 1985 reversed the membership discrimination, to the dismay of some band councils, who not only felt themselves ill-equipped to provide for those who now applied to be reinstated as full-status Indians, but also regarded the change in membership rules as an illegitimate intervention in internal affairs (Deveaux 2000b). This linked to the larger issue of whether Indian councils should be bound by the sex equality provisions of the 1982 Charter of Rights and Freedoms, which had proved an important instrument for securing women's rights. Matters came to a head in 1992 with the referendum on the Charlottetown Accord. The Accord contained a strong statement recognizing the "inherent right to self-government," and while the precise implications of this were left unclear, it was explicitly stated that self-government would include the power to suspend aspects of the Charter. At this point, two principles seemed on a collision course. The rights of the larger minority could be recognized in the right to self-government; or the rights of the minority within the minority could be recognized through the Charter of

---

[7] The example most discussed in the literature is the *Martinez* case, where a woman member of the Santa Clara Pueblo tribe appealed against the discriminatory family laws that granted tribal membership to the children of men who married outside the group, but not of women (like herself) who did so.

Rights and Freedoms; how were these competing and seemingly irreconcilable claims to be resolved?

As is often the case, this way of posing the issue exaggerates the essential conflict. Deveaux (2000b) has shown that many of the women involved argued *both* for a constitutional recognition of the right to self-government *and* for an assurance that this would not override their federally guaranteed equality rights. Self-government, in their view, did not mean being relieved of all wider obligations in national and international law, and certainly did not mean being relieved of the obligation to treat men and women as equals. And this was not just muddled thinking, or trying to have things both ways, for only a very strict interpretation of sovereignty (of the kind implied by those who view UK membership of the European Union as destroying the sovereignty of the nation state) would see it as at odds with any wider restrictions. Indeed, in a world where international conventions of human rights increasingly set limits to national sovereignty, it seems anachronistic to insist that being "a government" means retaining the authority to determine all aspects of internal affairs. The judicial approach to minority rights thrives on either/or choices that require careful adjudication. In this instance, there was no such stark alternative.

Or rather, there was no such stark alternative in principle, but at the moment of the referendum, this finessing of self-government with sex equality was not the choice on offer. Aboriginal women had to choose between supporting (somewhat unspecified) powers of self-government or insisting on sex equality rights, and if they chose the latter, there was a good chance that the referendum would fail. In the event, this was exactly what occurred. Their leaders, most notably the Native Women's Association of Canada(NWAC), were highly critical of an agreement that had been drawn up without their involvement, and challenged a version of self-government that implied an erosion of women's rights; the Accord was defeated (interestingly, it was rejected by two-thirds of native peoples living on reserves); and the much-publicized division between native women's groups and other Aboriginal leaders was held partly responsible for the defeat.[8]

At a theoretical level, there was no need for this conflict: no reason why self-government could not be combined with an assurance of sex equality rights. But in the political context of the early 1990s – and, of course, the longer historical context of dispossession and denial – there must have

---

[8] As in Deveaux's assessment that the "much-publicized rift between some native women's groups and mainstream Aboriginal bodies . . . may have served to erode support for the Charlottetown Accord" (2000a: 528).

been much agonizing on whether joining battle on the sex equality front was going to undermine initiatives towards fuller self-government; and some people certainly felt that the position adopted by the NWAC bolstered general opposition to any kind of Accord. In her reading of events, Monique Deveaux notes that a later Commission on Aboriginal Peoples recommended increased self-government rights, but now attached to this a much stronger insistence that native communities should not use discretionary powers to suspend women's rights. She suggests, that is, that the First Nations might soon get both self-government *and* sexual equality. A more gloomy reading might say that, in the conflict between the two, substantive self-government had had its day. Let me stress here: I am not at all suggesting that native women should have set aside their equality concerns in order to ensure a smoother passage to self-government. I am just pointing out the difficult choices posed by political context, even when the principles may seem relatively clear.

Similar difficulties arise when denouncing practices of sexual discrimination becomes a vehicle for attacking a minority group. This was a key issue in the Shah Bano case in India, which revolved around the inequitable treatment of women under systems of Personal Law, but became bound up with tensions between the Hindu majority and the Muslim minority. The post-partition settlement in India has retained many of the features of British indirect rule. Instead, that is, of a uniform civil code governing all matters of marriage and succession, four religious communities (Hindu, Muslim, Christian and Parsi) have their own separate systems of Personal Law; while other groups like Buddhist, Sikh and Jain are subsumed under Hindu law; there is also provision for people to opt for a secular code. Though all the Personal Law systems discriminate in some way against women, some are more sexually egalitarian than others. Polygamy is permitted, for example, under the legislation governing Muslim marriages, but was eventually prohibited under the Hindu code; and one recurrent problem for Muslim women is the derisory divorce settlements they have been awarded under the usually very conservative interpretations of Islamic Personal Law.

Up until 1986, their main recourse was to the Criminal Procedure Code, which forbids a man of adequate means to leave close relatives in a state of destitution. Since this code applied to all, a number of Muslim women had successfully appealed to it to establish claims to maintenance on divorce. Shah Bano, unilaterally divorced after forty-three years of marriage, and left with little more than the dowry payment she originally brought to the marriage, took her case to the Supreme Court in 1985, where she was awarded a monthly maintenance payment. But the Chief Justice took the opportunity to single out Muslim men and the Islamic system as almost uniquely unjust to women, and said it was about time India moved to a uniform civil code. Not surprisingly, this was interpreted by Muslim religious leaders as part of a growing pattern of Hindu supremacy. After the very public campaign then waged against the ruling, the Government introduced in 1986 the misleadingly titled Muslim Women's (Protection of Rights On Divorce) Act, which deprived Muslim women – and only Muslim women – of the right to claim maintenance under the Criminal Procedure Code. In one of the saddest aspects of the case, Shah Bano capitulated to what must have been almost unbearable pressure from the leaders of her community, renounced her claims to maintenance, and declared her full support for the operation of Islamic Personal Law.

The Muslim Women's Act seems to me thoroughly indefensible, as does a system of Personal Law that permits the unilateral divorce of a wife of forty-three years and allows her virtually no claim on the family assets. But against the background of the very fraught relations between Hindus and Muslims, and the heavily disadvantaged position of the Muslim minority, it was not just a question of what is right and wrong, but how best to intervene in a context where sex equality issues are employed to promote hatred between different communities. Political context matters, and it has proved hard in the Indian context to detach the case for a uniform civil code from its association with Hindu attacks on the so-called "special privileges" (polygyny, lesser maintenance obligations) of the Muslim minority. As groups jostle to establish their moral superiority, issues relating to sex equality are often harnessed to more devious ends, and those whose own practices bear little scrutiny may still revel in their claim to be better in their treatment of women. The Committee on the Status of Women in India reported in 1975 that despite being banned for Hindus and legal for Muslims, the incidence of polygyny was actually higher among Hindu than Muslim men (5.8 percent of the former, 5.7 percent of the latter); one would never guess at this similarity from some of the denunciations of Islamic law.

Before these events, Indian feminists tended to favor a uniform civil code. Since then, they have been much divided on the issue, but virtually none now argues for state imposition of a uniform civil code; the main options instead being either reform from within of the various Personal Law systems, or a state-sponsored civil code that operates in some way alongside Personal Law (Sunder Rajan 2003: ch. 5; also Pathak and Sunder Rajan 1989). In the immediate aftermath of the Shah Bano controversy, it was still hoped that a uniform civil code could be developed that detached it from association with the Hindu right: if the campaign for a civil code stressed, for example, the severe disadvantages women suffer under all the religious jurisdictions, and rejected any version that simply generalized from the provisions of Hindu personal law. It might in this way be possible to detach the demand from its murky association with Hindu fundamentalism, and prevent "Hindu communalists from using what is essentially a women's rights issue for the purpose of stirring up communal hatred against Muslims and other minorities" (Kishwar 1986: 13). Now even that hope has been largely abandoned.

The positions adopted today are not entirely driven by strategic considerations. As Rajeswari Sunder Rajan notes (2003: ch. 5), there is also concern that the implicit secularism of the mainstream women's movement pays too little attention to the differences among women that derive from their religious identities, and the possibly greater importance of these identities to lower-caste women. But while there is enormous disagreement among feminists on the best way of reforming Personal Law, the fact remains that there is no deep disagreement on substantive issues. For Indian feminists, this is not so much a normative debate as one inextricably embedded in a particular political context. And even when we turn to Martha Nussbaum's discussion – on the face of it framed by a more conventionally judicial opposition between sex equality and religious freedom – we find the issue largely settled by political concerns. Nussbaum (2001) uses the introduction of the Muslim Women's Act to illustrate the conflicts that can arise between the claims of religious freedom and sex equality. She seeks to settle this by establishing that the Act creates rather than prevents religious discrimination (because it denies to Muslim women rights available to women of other faiths); that it weakens rather than strengthens the position of the Muslim minority (because it enables Hindu fundamentalists to present Hinduism as more sexually enlightened than Islam); and she concludes that the actions of the Muslim clerics were "counter-productive as well as unjust" (Nussbaum 2001: 228). But in line with the majority of Indian feminists, she still holds back from arguing for a uniform civil code, for "given the history of Muslims in India, it seems apparent that any abolition of the system of Islamic law would be a grave threat to religious liberty and a statement that Muslims are not fully equal as citizens" (211). The conflict between religious freedom and sex equality is not in the end resolved through a judicial weighing of these two concerns. Nussbaum's conclusions are ultimately driven by political and contextual concerns.

The same complex of political and contextual dilemmas recurs in my third example: recent initiatives in Britain to address the problem of forced marriage, and the difficulties of disentangling these from association with a potentially racist immigration debate. (This is discussed at greater length in Phillips and Dustin 2004.) In South Asian families – Hindu, Sikh and Muslim – parents and sometimes some other family elders have commonly played a role in the selection of marriage partners for their children, often promoting marriages between first cousins or between uncle and niece. The tradition is in decline amongst those living in Britain, and while a majority still consult their parents, most young Hindus and Sikhs now say they make the final decision themselves. Arranged marriages are also declining among those of Pakistani and Bangladeshi origin (95 percent of whom are Muslim), but here a majority even of the under-35s still report that their parents made the decision.[9] The government line is that arranged marriage is an entirely legitimate cultural variation, but there has been growing concern over the up to 1,000 young Asian women who are thought to be forced into marriages each year, and considerable government activity in recent years to tackle this problem.[10]

This is not, on the face of it, an issue that throws up particularly vexed questions of cultural accommodation, for no one is suggesting that the state should defer to some cherished minority custom of forcing young girls into marriages against their will. None of the spokesmen of the South Asian communities claims *forced* – as opposed to *arranged* – marriage as part of their cultural or religious heritage; and no one suggests that laws against rape, child abuse, abduction or false imprisonment should be suspended in deference to "cultural" practice. The difficulty, rather, is that the initiative on forced marriage has become entangled with immigration issues, with the distinction between arranged and forced marriage getting superimposed on a rather different distinction between marrying someone from Britain or overseas.

Some *arranged* marriages involve partners from overseas; and some of the most dramatic examples of *forced* marriage involve young people

---

[9] In the last major survey of ethnic minorities in Britain, the overwhelming majority of older Hindu, Sikh and Muslim respondents reported that their parents had decided their marriage partner. Among those under 35, the one group for whom this remained the majority experience was Muslim women, where 67% still reported a parental decision. The change has been most dramatic among Hindu and Sikh women: 86% of Sikh women over 50 said their parents decided their marriage partner, but only 27% of the under 35s; 74% of Hindu women over 50 reported that their parents made the decision, but only 20% of the under 35s. Interestingly, 41% of the younger Sikh men said their parents still decided; 18% of younger Hindu men; and 49% of younger Muslim men (Modood et al. 1997: 318).

[10] The Home Office established a Working Group on Forced Marriage in 1999; its report, *A Choice by Right*, helped clarify the distinction between arranged and forced marriage. A joint Foreign and Commonwealth Office/Home Office Action Plan was drawn up in 2000 to tackle the overseas dimension; and in 2002 the FCO, Home Office and Association of Chief Police Officers published police guidelines on dealing with cases of forced marriage.

being tricked into traveling to Bangladesh or Pakistan only then to discover that a marriage has been arranged. Whether consensual or coerced, these transcontinental marriages will usually result in the spouse's application for entry to Britain, and for some commentators, the distinction between arranged and forced then becomes irrelevant, for any marriage between a British citizen and a spouse from the Indian sub-continent will be regarded as "bogus," entered into for purposes of migration.[11] There has been a long history in the UK of immigration officials subjecting marriages with spouses from the Indian sub-continent to close and suspicious scrutiny. This practice was indeed officially sanctioned under the now repealed "primary purpose" rule, which gave entry clearance officers the power to decide whether a marriage was entered into primarily for the purpose of migration to the UK. There is no known "primary purpose" case involving two white spouses (Menski 1999); and the rule was widely perceived as a way of restricting the number of black and Asian people entering the country. For many Britons of South Asian origin, the government's new zeal for addressing the incidence of forced marriage looks suspiciously like a back-door attempt to restore this rule. Indeed, when the Foreign and Commonwealth Office sponsored research into perceptions of forced marriage in Britain's Bangladeshi and Pakistani communities, it uncovered widespread suspicion (though primarily among middle-aged and older men) that the government's preoccupation with this issue reflected racist and Islamophobic intentions. "Immigration control was considered to be the authorities' main aim and the research was seen as a veiled assault on arranged marriages" (Samad and Eade 2002: 112). Or as one interviewee put it, "The British immigration [service] is just fed up of granting visa to the spouse of our sons and daughters who are having arranged marriages in Bangladesh. They are trying to stop that" (Samad and Eade: 105).

The (mainly Asian) women's groups that have campaigned to expose the incidence of forced marriage have been more unambiguous in supporting strong public action on this issue, but they, too, have registered concern about the way initiatives to tackle the undoubted harm of forced marriage get caught up in a potentially racist immigration debate. It is troubling, for example, that all the major developments in relation to

---

[11] For example, in this comment by a *Daily Telegraph* journalist: "It is hard for people in this country to avoid suspecting that this (i.e. arranged marriage) is done largely for the purpose of giving the foreigner a British passport and other rights here. But whatever the motive, many new spouses arrive with little or no understanding of life here and little or no knowledge of English or interest in integration. Many of them are very poorly educated, if educated at all" (*Daily Telegraph*, 15 December 2001). The implication is that all such marriages should be stopped.

forced marriage have focused on what is termed the "overseas dimension": these include the creation of a highly effective Community Liaison Unit in the Foreign and Commonwealth Office, which has so far helped to repatriate over 100 young people threatened with forced marriage in Pakistan, Bangladesh or India; but no comparable unit in the Home Office to address the (largely uncharted) incidence of forced marriage between people already settled in the UK. It is also troubling that immigration control figures so prominently among mechanisms for tackling forced marriage. Denmark took the lead here, with an Aliens Consolidation Act in 2002 which prevents people from bringing in overseas spouses or cohabitees when either party to the marriage is under 24[12]; and this has inspired a recent change to immigration regulations in the UK that makes it impossible for citizens under the age of 18 to sponsor the entry of an overseas spouse.[13] The restrictions have been justified as protecting young women from what may be very heavy family pressure to accept a marriage partner from overseas, the presumption being that young people over 18 (in the UK case) or over 24 (in Denmark) will be in a better position to refuse an unwanted marriage. The other obvious effect is to reduce the incidence of transcontinental marriage – regarded by some politicians as delaying the process of assimilation – and keep immigrants out.

This merging of sex equality with immigration issues makes for difficult political terrain, and while Asian women's groups have mostly welcomed the government's belated recognition of the problem of forced marriage, their work on this issue is repeatedly framed by worries about playing into the anti-immigration camp. When, for example, Shamshad Hussain of Keighley Women's Domestic Violence Forum reports the organization's success in helping women already forced into marriage with an unwanted overseas partner to block their new husband's visa application, she notes that, "[i]t is sad that we have to use what we have always viewed as racist legislation to keep these men out."[14] Enabling women to

---

[12] The minimum age before 3 June 2000 had been 18; at that point, new regulations came into force, abolishing the automatic right to family reunification for spouses aged 18–25, and replacing it by a discretionary right that depended, among other things, on establishing that the marriage was "undoubtedly contracted at the resident person's own desire." The Aliens (Consolidation) Act 2002 eased up a bit on age (24 instead of 25), but significantly reduced the scope for discretion.

[13] From 1 April 2003, UK citizens under the age of 18 are not permitted to act as sponsors for the entry of overseas spouses; they can still get married at 16, but if the partner comes from outside the EU, they will have to wait two years before sponsoring his/her entry visa.

[14] Shamshad Hussain of Keighley Women's Domestic Violence Forum, quoted in "Bounty hunters tail runaway brides," *Independent*, 20 July 1998.

escape the threat or reality of a forced marriage remains the overwhelming priority, but when the defense of women's rights threatens to resuscitate the now discredited primary purpose rule, this is inevitably a source of concern.

Those who regard the "minorities within minorities" dilemma as throwing up "hard cases" of value disagreement may object that I have considered the above examples from the perspective of political activists, thus from the perspective of those who already share a similar moral universe, and have already worked out (to their own satisfaction, at least) their stance on the normative concerns. But this is precisely my point. Even when there is no deep disagreement, there are still enormously complex dilemmas; and many of these arise because discourses of women's rights can be deployed to serve such different ends. In each of the above examples, campaigners face dilemmas of political context: they are seeking to ensure that women's equality is not sacrificed to the claims of expediency or traditional culture; but seeking to ensure at the same time that these equality claims are not invoked as part of a project of cultural supremacy or a form of immigration control.

The cases do not, on the whole, illustrate a conflict between the rights of a minority group and the rights of a sub-group within it. Such a formulation presumes in advance that something called "culture" dictates inequality between the sexes, and attributes any incidence of women's subordination to cultural values and traditions. This is a risky assumption: it is not "culture" that dictates the unequal treatment of women, but particular interpretations of cultural tradition, sometimes quite deliberately invoked so as to block women's equality claims. The point, to reiterate, is that the value conflict – between the values of sex equality and the values of particular cultural traditions – is often overstated. It is not that there is a fundamental conflict between two equality claims, or that societies must devise complex adjudication procedures or new practices of democratic deliberation in order to balance these out. The more pressing problem, in many cases, is that sex equality claims are already implicated in other discourses – anti-immigrant, anti-Muslim, anti-indigenous peoples – that egalitarians will want to avoid.

Political theorists tend to get stuck on the normative issues: What principles of justice? What principles of adjudication? How to determine what is right and wrong? The point I have stressed is that many of the (very real) dilemmas signposted by the phrase "minorities within minorities" arise somewhere else in the chain. Often enough, the most pressing issue is how to formulate strong policies for sex equality that do not feed on and feed into cultural stereotypes; and how to reframe discourses of sex equality so as to detach them from projects of cultural or racial superiority. The key problems, to put it another way, may be those that arise from the perspective of the political activist rather than that of the constitutional lawyer, or even the deliberative democrat. In my view, it is these problems of political action that represent the real challenge for those committed to both multiculturalism and sex equality.

6   The rights of internal linguistic minorities

Alan Patten

Considerable attention has been devoted to theorizing the rights of minority cultures in recent years. Political theorists have developed accounts of the normative questions raised by issues of race, immigration, nationalism, indigenous peoples and religion. After a period of neglect, theorists are now starting to turn their attention to the normative issues posed by another form of diversity: linguistic diversity. The past few years have seen the publication of a number of accounts of the implications of normative principles of equality, autonomy and democracy for language policy.[1]

Although normative theorizing about language rights is still in its infancy, it is becoming possible to make out the main positions. The debate over language rights typically pits "nation-builders," who emphasize the goods that can be realized by diffusing a single language and culture throughout the state, against "language maintainers," who stress the value of preserving vulnerable languages and language communities.

The nation-builders are, at best, indifferent to minority language rights, and often argue against them on the grounds that they discourage state-wide linguistic convergence. They may allow a "norm-and-accommodation" regime of language rights that permits certain transitional accommodations for people with limited proficiency in the normal state or "national" language. But they typically oppose "official" language rights – that is, rights that minority-language speakers might enjoy to the public use of their language (e.g. in the delivery of public services, in the public schools, etc.) even when they are perfectly fluent in the majority language that would otherwise be used in public settings.[2]

The language maintainers, by contrast, stress the value for people of having their own language used in public settings. In part, this value

I am grateful to the editors of this volume for their written comments on an earlier draft of the paper and to participants in the October 2002 Conference on Internal Minorities held at the University of Nebraska for their insights and discussion.
[1] See Patten 2001, and Patten and Kymlicka 2003, for overviews of recent work.
[2] For the distinction between "norm-and-accommodation" and "official" language rights regimes, see Patten and Kymlicka 2003.

135

reflects the straightforward fact that, at any given moment, some people will lack fluency in any other language besides their own. If public institutions do not recognize and accommodate their own language, these people will be severely disadvantaged. On its own, this form of argument can only ground a case for norm-and-accommodation rights, however, and so most language maintainers offer further justifications for preserving vulnerable language communities. They stress, for instance, that language is an important part of a person's culture and identity. The health of one's language community is something that people can care about deeply and the opportunity to use their language in certain contexts can be experienced as an indicator of public recognition and respect.

Often overlooked in this debate between nation-builders and language maintainers is the position of internal linguistic minorities. The concept of an "internal linguistic minority," as I shall understand it, has several elements to it. To begin with, it presupposes that the state has a majority language group as well as one or more minority language groups. (From now on, to keep the exposition as uncluttered as possible, I'll generally assume that there is only one relevant minority language.) Second, the minority language group enjoys some degree of territorial concentration in the state in which they are a minority. In particular there is some territorially defined jurisdiction of the state in which they form a majority. Finally, living amidst this group that forms a regionally concentrated national minority (but a local majority) there are also speakers of the language that is in the state-wide majority. It is this last group, that is part of the state-wide majority, but forms a local minority or a minority-within-a-minority, that I will refer to as an internal linguistic minority. Examples of such internal linguistic minorities include English-speakers in Quebec, Spanish-speakers in Catalonia and Dutch-speakers in Wallonie.

This concept of an internal minority could be broadened somewhat in several different directions. For instance, the insistence that an internal minority correspond to a state-wide majority could be weakened to just require that the internal minority correspond to a group that forms a majority in some relevant region elsewhere in the state. With this modification, French-speakers in Flanders, and French-speakers in German-majority Swiss cantons, would count as internal minorities. Or, the emphasis on states could be dropped from the account of internal minorities altogether and replaced with an idea of regions that include several states. On a suitably formulated version of this view, Russian-speaking populations in the Baltic states would count as internal minorities. Of course, the precise contours of the concept of an internal minority are not going to be settled by definitional fiat. Instead, they should be drawn according to the normative questions being pursued and the norms and values that are brought to bear in answering those questions.[3] It will be enough for my purposes in the present chapter to keep to the basic idea of an internal minority outlined in the previous paragraph.

The rights of internal linguistic minorities (RILMs) do not typically show up on the radar screens of either nation-builders or language maintainers. For nation-builders, RILMs are not really an issue because nation-builders do not favor significant accommodations or rights for the national minority in the first place, even where the minority forms a local majority in some region. The aim of language policy for nation-builders is to encourage a state-wide convergence on a common public language. This is usually interpreted to mean that the majority should enjoy rights across the country (including in those places where they form internal minorities) and that the rights accorded to minority languages should be restricted to transitional accommodations for those who lack proficiency in the state-wide majority language. So, for nation-builders, RILMs are largely irrelevant, because they are reluctant to extend the kinds of language rights or accommodations to (state-wide) minorities that would give rise to a call for RILMs.

The attitude of language maintainers to RILMs is more complicated and interesting. For many language maintainers, RILMs are not so much irrelevant as unjustifiable. In part this reflects a dialectical relationship with nation-builders. It is assumed that people who defend RILMs are really nation-builders who want to deny the legitimacy of minority rights altogether. The struggle over RILMs thus becomes a proxy for the larger debate about whether the state will seek to establish a single public language shared by all citizens or whether it will accept and accommodate the more-or-less permanent presence of a state-wide linguistic minority as well.

This attitude towards RILMs does not really get to the heart of the matter, however, since it is open to a defender of RILMs to join language maintainers in rejecting the nation-building perspective. On this view, the proponent of RILMs accepts that linguistic minorities should enjoy official language rights (and not just transitional accommodations). She just thinks that these official language rights should not only be reserved for state-wide linguistic minorities that form a local majority but should be extended to internal linguistic minorities as well.

[3] For instance, it might be proposed that *any* linguistic group that finds itself in the minority on a territory that is dominated by a language group that is itself a national minority should be counted as an internal minority. On this broad view of an internal minority, Cree-speakers in Quebec or Aran-speakers in Catalonia would be considered internal minorities. An advantage of the narrower view stipulated in the text is that it allows us to explore the question of whether it makes any moral difference that the members of a local minority have co-linguists living in another part of the state.

Language maintainers have additional, more theoretically interesting reasons for being skeptical about RILMs, however. In this paper, I want to examine from a variety of points of view one influential anti-RILM argument that I'll term the "territorial imperative" argument. It emphasizes, on the basis of socio-linguistic assumptions, that a language can only be maintained if it has a territory in which it is hegemonic.

In evaluating the territorial imperative argument I will attempt to steer a course between the proposition that a refusal of RILMs is generally legitimate and the proposition that it is never legitimate. More concretely, I will try to identify in a fairly precise way the conditions that have to be present or absent for a refusal of RILMs to be a just and reasonable policy.

A broader theoretical objective of the paper is to lend some support to a thesis that I have been developing in other work (Patten 2001, 2003a). The thesis is that debates about language rights – and about cultural rights more generally – have been overly enthralled by a series of related dichotomies: between "nation-building" and "language maintenance"; between a "politics of universalism" and a "politics of difference" (Taylor 1994); between "liberalism 1" and "liberalism 2" (Walzer 1994); between ideals of "assimilation" and "difference" (Young 1990); between the "common rights of citizenship" and "group-differentiated" or "minority" rights (Kymlicka 1995, 2001); and between "unitary republican citizenship" and "multiculturalism" (Barry 2001a). My claim is that RILMs are sometimes a valid and important part of a defensible regime of language rights, even though neither nation-building nor language-maintenance approaches have much use for them. If this claim is correct, then it is suggestive of a third perspective on linguistic and cultural rights – obscured by all the dichotomies – that is worth identifying and articulating.

The territorial imperative argument

In a widely cited book Jean Laponce (1984) has argued that minority languages are subject to what he terms a "territorial imperative" (see also Van Parijs 2000; Kymlicka 2001: 213). They must establish themselves as the dominant language on some particular territory or else be faced with extinction (Laponce 1984: 1, chs. 5–6, conclusion). For Laponce, the coexistence of two flourishing language communities on the same territory is almost never a stable equilibrium. One language will invariably offer more opportunities, and a higher status, than the other, and it will gradually drive the weaker language into extinction as an ever greater number of people add it to their own, or to their children's, linguistic repertoires and neglect or fail to pass on the weaker language.

The political conclusion Laponce drew from this analysis is a preference for what he termed in a subsequent article "ethnic federalism" (Laponce 1993). The internal boundaries of a multilingual state should be drawn so as to create jurisdictions in which national minorities form local majorities (see also Laponce 1984: 1–2, 139–40, 144; Van Parijs 2000). Within these minority-dominant jurisdictions, the minority language should be the sole official language used in public settings. Although Laponce does not say so, presumably he would permit transitional accommodations (e.g. in courts, hospitals, tax offices, etc.) to be made for internal minorities who lack proficiency in the official language. But beyond this, he implies, RILMs should not be recognized (Laponce 1993: 37). With the minority language dominant in its own territory, people will have little choice but to maintain it as an important part of their language repertoires. A recognition of RILMs, by contrast, would allow people to get around the need to learn the vulnerable minority language. The refusal on the basis of the territorial imperative to recognize RILMs would help, therefore, to secure and maintain the minority language community.

A blunt empirical challenge to the territorial imperative argument might question whether the recognition of RILMs is, in fact, incompatible with the flourishing of the minority language community. The French-language community in Quebec and the Catalan-speaking community in Catalonia seem to be doing fairly well, for example, despite the fact that internal linguistic minorities in each case (i.e. English- and Spanish-speakers respectively) enjoy significant sets of language rights.

These empirical counter-arguments are not, however, accepted by everyone who worries about the health of the minority languages in question. There may be certain indicators that are positive now, it is argued, but the long-term prospects remain bleak. This is mainly because societies such as Quebec and Catalonia have low birth rates coupled with high levels of immigration. Immigrants remain attracted to the state-wide majority languages (English, Spanish) and as their demographic weight grows this attraction will have a broader impact on the health of the minority language. The best way to block or reverse this pattern is to take a tough stance against RILMs. Moreover, in Quebec and Catalonia there is not perfect equality between the majority and minority languages. Certain rights (e.g. relating to the language of public schools) are extended to French and Catalan that are not accorded to English or Spanish. It might be argued that this moderately anti-RILMs stance is partly responsible for the modest successes enjoyed by the French and Catalan languages in those contexts.

Instead of addressing these long-standing empirical disputes, I wish to pursue a different kind of issue raised by the territorial imperative argument, one that may help us, in the end, to approach the empirical issues with a more refined set of questions. The territorial imperative argument defends the conclusion that RILMs should be refused on the territory in which the minority language community forms a local majority. It reaches this conclusion on the basis of two premises:

1. The minority language community would decline or even disappear unless RILMs are refused on the territory in which that community forms a majority ("the empirical conjecture").
2. If there is a trade-off between recognizing RILMs and maintaining the minority language community, priority ought to be given to the latter option ("the priority of language maintenance principle," or "priority principle" for short).

As I just mentioned, much of the controversy over the territorial imperative argument surrounds the empirical conjecture. For the remainder of the chapter, however, I want to bracket this debate and explore, instead, the priority principle. What reason do we have to accept this principle? If we should accept the principle, should we do so in all sorts of empirical contexts or are there particular kinds of situations in which language maintenance should be especially prioritized?

One strategy for defending the priority principle would be to claim that there is little positive reason for thinking that RILMs should be recognized. This strategy shifts the burden of proof over to the defenders of RILMs and challenges them to come up with some argument for why we should be concerned about RILMs in the first place. If they cannot produce such an argument, then it would seem that there is nothing terribly objectionable about a policy of prioritizing language maintenance. A second strategy for defending the principle is to offer some positive account of why it matters that threatened language communities should be maintained. This account need not offer a justification for maintaining language communities that is so powerful that it defeats all possible countervailing considerations. But it would need to offer a justification that is strong enough to defeat any reasons that could be assembled in favor of recognizing RILMs. The analysis to follow will touch on both of these possible strategies.

Laponce, it should be noted, devotes hardly any attention to the normative principle on which his argument depends. In his view, the importance of preserving vulnerable languages and language communities is a "value assumption" that is not amenable to reasoned argument (Laponce 1984: 144). The closest he comes to exploring the priority principle is in a passage where he remarks that language is a "value in itself," in which "the polis has its cement and its soul," rather than a "simple, interchangeable instrument of communication" (144).

In fact, if Laponce's Herderian talk of the polis having a "soul" is glossed in a certain way, then the passage can be read as alluding to two major and often emphasized kinds of interests that people have in connection with language policy: the interest in being able to *communicate* with other members of one's society; and the interest in having one's *identity* recognized and respected. Corresponding to these two sorts of interests, one might try to defend the priority principle by arguing along communication and/or identity lines. The passage cited above suggests that Laponce is likely to be rather dismissive of communication-based arguments. I shall argue, however, that there are resources in both communication-based and identity-based arguments for defending the priority principle but that neither form of argument offers general support of that principle. In some situations we should follow the priority principle; in others we should privilege the recognition of RILMs.

Communication

Communication-based arguments seek to ground claims on behalf of particular language policies and distributions of language rights by appealing to the interests that people have in communicating with others around them. There are several versions of such arguments depending on which area of communication – in which domain of language use – is emphasized. For instance, the argument might stress the interest that people have in being able to communicate with the public officials who offer public services and who interpret and enforce laws and official regulations (the "public access" version). Or it might stress the interest that people have in being able to communicate with a sufficiently extensive network of people so as to leave them with a fully adequate range of social and economic opportunities (the "social mobility" version). Or, finally, it might emphasize the interests that people have in being able to communicate with fellow citizens in the context of the informal deliberation and discussion that is part of the democratic process (the "democratic participation" version).[4]

In seeking to defend the priority principle, the social mobility version of the argument is, in my view, the most promising. This version of the

---

[4] For the distinction between these three versions of the communication argument, and for further discussion of each, see Patten 2003b.

argument appeals to the interest that people have in being able to access what Kymlicka (1989a, 1995) terms an adequate "context of choice." People have an interest – grounded in considerations of well-being and autonomy – in having at their disposal an adequate range of opportunities and options. Competence in the language(s) in which opportunities and options are offered is a precondition of having this context of choice. Without competence in the language spoken by those around her, a person will encounter difficulties in finding a job, getting promoted, doing business, making friends, practicing a religion and so on. For any given individual, this linguistic precondition can be satisfied in two different ways. There can be a sufficiently healthy context of choice operating in her own native language. Or she can achieve sufficient competence in a second language in which there is an adequate context of choice available.

Adapting some of Will Kymlicka's terminology, I will say that a language supports a "societal culture" when an adequate context of choice is available in that language.[5] To say that there is a Francophone societal culture in Quebec, for instance, is to say that a French speaker in Quebec has access to an adequate range of options and opportunities operating in the French language. To say that there is no Italian speaking societal culture in the United States, by contrast, would be to deny that an Italian speaker in that context has an adequate range of Italian-language options and opportunities. To enjoy social mobility, an Italian speaker in the United States must learn English and access the English-language societal culture that dominates the country. As these examples suggest, an individual's interest in social mobility can be satisfied in two different ways. There can be a societal culture operating in a language that the individual speaks. Or the individual can integrate into a societal culture by learning the language in which it operates.

To locate the connection between social mobility and language maintenance, one further distinction is needed: the distinction between what I shall term "secure" and "vulnerable" societal cultures. A secure societal culture is one that remains intact as a societal culture even in the face of a range of different demo-linguistic shocks and changes. In a secure societal culture, there could be fairly significant demographic changes, or a fairly significant number of people who shift to another language, and the language community would still be able to offer its members an adequate context of choice. A vulnerable societal culture is one that is insecure. Even fairly minor changes in demographics, or a modest accumulation

---

[5] Kymlicka (1995: 76) defines a societal culture as a "culture which provides its members with meaningful ways of life across the full range of human activities."

of individual decisions to use another language, can leave such a culture in a position where it is unable to provide an adequate context of choice to its members.

Vulnerable societal cultures raise a specific concern from the point of view of the interest in social mobility. The concern is that, just as Laponce predicts, competition between several languages will end up undermining a vulnerable societal culture. Attracted by the options and opportunities that it provides, some members of the vulnerable culture may increasingly choose to live aspects of their lives in the more secure language. The unilingual members of the vulnerable culture will, as a result, become stranded: their own language community will no longer be able to afford them an adequate context of choice, and they would not have the linguistic capacities to access options and opportunities in the other language.

The argument for adopting a language policy that prioritizes the maintenance of the local majority language appeals to the possibility that the local majority-language societal culture may be vulnerable. Suppose that the following conditions are satisfied:

(a) If RILMs are recognized, it is likely that there would be demolinguistic changes that leave the local majority language unable to support a societal culture.
(b) These changes would not occur if RILMs are refused.
(c) Some local majority-language speakers are unilingual, and it is unlikely that they can be made proficient in the internal-minority language.

When these conditions are met, it is at least plausible to think that a concern for the interest in social mobility of local majority members indicates that language maintenance should be prioritized. Unless RILMs are refused, the internal minority language would tempt enough people away from the local majority language so as to undermine the social mobility of unilingual majority language speakers.

It might be objected that condition (c) ignores the ease with which people (or, at any rate, their children) can learn new languages. If the local majority-language community is vulnerable, then the best course of action may not be to prop it up by adopting special measures but to embark on an intensive program of language training aimed at ensuring that *all* members of the local majority-language community are able to enjoy social mobility in the state-wide majority (or internal minority) language. The main response to this objection should be to concede that the empirical conditions needed for this version of the social mobility argument to go through are indeed very demanding. Given that condition (a) reflects the power and attraction of the internal minority language for members of the majority, it is not obvious that it will be satisfied in conjunction with condition (c).[6]

This concession should be qualified in two ways, however. It is possible that different sections of the majority community may have very different propensities to be fluent in the internal minority language. Knowledge of the minority language may be disproportionately concentrated in an urban middle class oriented around white-collar employment. Competence in the minority language may be considerably less common amongst working-class majority members or amongst those who live away from the metropolis, and training these majority-language speakers in the minority language may be fairly difficult if they do not have much exposure to it. Under these kinds of circumstances, the third condition may not be impossible to satisfy.

The second qualification is connected with the ease with which local majority speakers could reasonably expect to become fluent in the language of the internal minority (so that they can enjoy access to the options and opportunities that are increasingly available in that language). Even if the response to the erosion of the local majority language were to be an accelerated program of training and education in the language of the internal minority, this would take a great deal of time. In the meantime, adult unilingual members of the majority community would be disadvantaged by the declining options and opportunities available in their own language. Although ideally (i.e. if the education and training program is effective) this disadvantage would only last for a generation or so, it may be grave enough to warrant the introduction of special measures designed to protect the local majority language.

My conclusion about the communication argument for the priority principle, then, is that it may sometimes be valid. It is imaginable that language maintenance and the recognition of RILMs could conflict with one another. The presence of RILMs could make a crucial difference in tempting speakers of the local majority language away from their usual habits of speech, or it could mean that certain key domains of language use (e.g. white-collar employment) become increasingly conducted in the language of the internal minority. The loss of speakers and of high-status language domains may then strand unilingual members of the local majority community. It is plausible to think that a concern for the social mobility and equal opportunity of these stranded unilinguals should, in some contexts, outweigh the reasons that could be marshaled in favor of

---

[6] A variation on (c) would allow that local majority-language-speakers can be made proficient in the internal-minority language but worry instead that their access to options and opportunities will be blocked by discrimination on the part of members of the internal minority.

recognizing RILMs. Securing social mobility and equal opportunity for all citizens is an important liberal priority and a liberal state is justified in adopting fairly strong measures in pursuit of this objective. By contrast, the argument in favor of recognizing RILMs, as I will suggest in the next section, is more concerned with the identity interests of internal minorities, and thus seems less urgent within a liberal framework.

The tentative language of the preceding paragraph should, however, draw attention to the special empirical conditions that would have to be satisfied for the priority principle to be defensible on communicative grounds. It is not every case of a vulnerable language community that will give rise to the form of argument I have been sketching. It has to be true, not only that (1) the language community is vulnerable, but also that (2) recognizing or refusing RILMs will make a crucial difference in tipping the vulnerable community one way or another, and that (3) the decline or collapse of the vulnerable community (if that is the way in which things tip) would leave significant numbers of unilinguals stranded without an adequate range of options and opportunities.[7]

Identity

For many people who would defend the priority principle, the speculative remarks in the previous section about the ease with which speakers of a vulnerable language could be encouraged to acquire the more secure language are entirely beside the point. Even if members of a vulnerable local majority community could easily be made proficient in the more secure language of the internal minority – indeed, even if they are *already* fluent in this language – the members of the majority still have a legitimate interest in the survival and flourishing of their own language. For a defender of the priority principle, this interest is weighty enough that policies designed to maintain vulnerable language communities should be considered more urgent than the recognition of RILMs.

But what is this interest? It is clearly not an interest that derives from the importance of communication, since it is one that people are said to have even when they are perfectly fluent in some other language that provides them with an ample range of communicative possibilities. Instead, as I mentioned in the introduction, the case for language maintenance is commonly made by arguing that one's own language is intimately connected with one's identity and culture.

It is important to note, however, that it will not be just any kind of argument from identity or culture that will do the trick, since some such

---

[7] See Laitin 1998 and 1999 for a discussion of language shift as a "tipping" phenomenon.

arguments end up appealing, in a round-about way, to the interests in communication and social mobility that we are now bracketing. Consider, for instance, Kymlicka's theory of culture as a "context of choice." On this theory, culture is viewed as a framework of meanings and practices that provides choice and opportunity to its members. If we ask why individuals need to access this framework through their *own* culture – i.e. the culture in which they were born and raised – the answer Kymlicka offers stresses the difficulty and costliness of adjusting to a new culture (1995: 85, 89). And, if we ask why it is difficult and costly for people to integrate into a new cultural context of choice, a major part of the explanation appeals to communicative considerations. People cannot access the meanings and options provided by a cultural context of choice if they do not speak the language in which that culture operates. And it is difficult and costly for people – especially adults – to learn a new language.

So on at least one reading of Kymlicka's cultural argument, that argument relies in an important way on the considerations of communication and social mobility canvassed in the previous section. It would not, on this reading, be an argument that someone could appeal to in support of the view that members of a vulnerable local majority community who are already fluent in the more secure language of the internal minority still have an overriding interest in the survival and flourishing of their own language.

The question we need to consider, then, is whether there is some argument in favor of the priority principle that appeals to identity or culture *and* is not reducible to the communicative considerations that have already been explored. Presumably there are any number of such arguments that might be advanced. In what follows, I consider one possible way that an identity argument could go, based loosely on the view put forward by Charles Taylor in his well-known essay, "The Politics of Recognition" (1994).

The argument I have in mind makes three key claims:

1. A secure identity is an important condition of individual well-being (the *identity* claim).
2. The security of a person's identity is, in part, a function of the degree to which that person's own language community (i.e. the language community in which they were born and raised) is flourishing (the *language* claim).
3. A person's identity can be damaged by a failure of "due recognition" on the part of public institutions (the *recognition* claim).

Although important and complex issues might be raised about each of these three claims, I will focus my attention on the recognition claim. The recognition claim talks of "due recognition" but it is not really clear how this should be interpreted. It is only if "due recognition" is taken to have certain policy implications that an argument drawing on these three claims can be taken to support the priority principle. My argument will be that the most plausible understanding of "due recognition" can only offer support for the priority principle under certain special circumstances. It must be the case that the local majority is struggling to maintain itself under conditions of *market unfairness* and/or *historical injustice*. In the absence of these conditions, the best account of "due recognition" – and the best reading of identity considerations more generally – suggests that RILMs should be embraced and the priority principle rejected.

So what, then, should count as "due recognition" for the purposes of designing public institutions and formulating public policies? In considering this issue, Taylor distinguishes two different views. The first, which he refers to as the "politics of universalism," takes as its model the standard liberal approach to religion. For liberals, the appropriate way for public institutions to respond to the religious beliefs and identities of their citizens is two-fold. It involves (a) carving out and protecting a range of individual freedoms (conscience, association, speech, etc.) and areas of equality (non-discrimination, equality of opportunity, etc.) that leave individuals with a high degree of latitude to shape and express their own religious outlooks; and (b) otherwise refusing, through a policy of "disestablishment," to grant positive recognition or assistance to any particular religious way of life. Generalized to non-religious forms of identity, the politics of universalism sees "due recognition" as calling for standard liberal rights for individual bearers of identities, together with a policy of "culture-blindness" that refuses to grant any other positive recognition or assistance to particular identities.

As Taylor points out, there is a problem with applying this "politics of universalism" model to identity claims based on language. The idea that there could be a policy of "language-blindness" or "linguistic disestablishment" is an illusion. Although the state can avoid regulating, or interfering with, the language choices people make away from public institutions – it can respect a set of "tolerance-oriented" rights – there is no way for it to avoid taking a stand on a whole series of other language policy issues (Kymlicka 1995: 111; Carens 2000: 77–8; Patten 2001: 693). Public services have to be offered in some language(s) or other, and the same is true of public education. Where the state does present itself as striving for a kind of culture-blindness this usually means the exclusive recognition of the particular identity and language associated with the majority. In Taylor's memorable formulation, the idea of "culture-blindness" typically involves a "particular masquerading as the universal."

Taylor's alternative to the politics of universalism – the "politics of difference" – takes seriously the "fact of linguistic establishment." Under a politics of difference, "due recognition" involves a respect for fundamental individual rights (this much is shared with universalism), but, within the constraints set by this requirement, then calls for public institutions to actively protect vulnerable cultures in order to give those cultures the tools they need to survive and flourish. Taylor's sympathies clearly lie with this second model of recognition. "If we're concerned with identity," he argues, "then what is more legitimate than one's aspiration that it never be lost?" (1994: 40).

This second interpretation of "due recognition" has the advantage of connecting the recognition claim in a straightforward way with the identity and language claims. What promotes well-being is a secure identity, and what secures identity is a flourishing language community. It is no great leap from these assumptions to the idea that the "recognition" that people are "due" takes the form of policies designed to ensure that their language community does indeed flourish.

So is this the best way to understand "due recognition"? A striking feature of the argument that I have been sketching is that it makes no reference at all to the presence in the community of other languages besides the language whose flourishing is said to require the attention of public institutions. This omission points to an obvious worry about the interpretation of "due recognition" being considered for jurisdictions containing more than one language group. For if the identity, language and recognition claims hold true for the members of the majority, then presumably they also hold true for the members of a language minority; that is to say, if the three claims are accepted as true for the majority, then it should also be allowed that:

- having a secure identity is an important condition of well-being of members of the language minority;
- the security of identity of members of the minority is in part dependent on the degree to which their language community is flourishing;
- the members of this group can have their identity damaged by a failure of "due recognition" on the part of public institutions.

The worry is that, on the interpretation of "due recognition" being considered, due recognition for the majority will not be compatible with due recognition for the minority.

The set of policies that public institutions would need to adopt to ensure the flourishing of the majority language community may be quite different than – and incompatible with – the set of policies those institutions would have to follow to achieve the same outcome for the minority language community. On Taylor's "politics of difference" interpretation of the due recognition requirement, due recognition would be in conflict with itself.

To see this problem more concretely, consider the relationship between due recognition, as formulated by Taylor, and the priority principle. At first glance, it might seem that Taylor's argument could be marshaled in favor of the priority principle. If Laponce's empirical conjecture is true, then the only way to ensure that the language of the local majority flourishes is by refusing RILMs. Taylor's preferred understanding of due recognition seems to offer a reason for caring more about the flourishing of the local majority language than about the recognition of RILMs. Refusing RILMs extends a form of recognition that is "due" to members of the local majority, and in the process secures their identity and promotes their well-being.

The problem becomes apparent, however, once we check the situation of the internal minority under this scenario. If refusing RILMs is the policy necessary to secure the flourishing of the majority language, then this is the policy that would be required to give the recognition due to the majority. But refusing RILMs could easily undermine the flourishing of the minority and thus violate a requirement that they be accorded due recognition too. Although one could imagine cases in which the conditions of flourishing of the two language communities fortuitously converge on a policy of refusing RILMs, in general there is no reason to expect that this will be so. In general, a policy of promoting the identity of the majority by refusing RILMs will end up damaging the identity of the minority.

Both of the interpretations of "due recognition" mentioned by Taylor turn out, then, to be unworkable and incoherent. For the politics of universalism, this is because it is impossible for public institutions to avoid recognizing one or more languages. In the case of the politics of difference, the problem is that, applied consistently to both the majority and the minority, due recognition generates conflicting requirements.

There is a third way of understanding "due recognition" that is not sufficiently considered by Taylor and points a way out of this morass. In the spirit of Taylor's suggested labels, one might call this third proposal the "politics of fairness."

This view, as I will understand it, shares a commitment with Taylor's two formulations to extending equal basic rights to all citizens. Its distinctive feature lies in its attitude to the public recognition of linguistic and cultural differences. Whereas "the politics of universalism" calls for culture-blindness, and "the politics of difference" equates recognition with ensuring survival and flourishing, the "politics of fairness" involves designing public institutions, and formulating public policies, so as to provide *fair treatment* to different cultures and languages.[8]

The intuition is that, where public institutions cannot simply withdraw from the terrain of identity politics, and where they cannot guarantee that everyone succeeds, they can at least seek to establish a framework of rights and entitlements that is fair to everyone. Within the space left to them by this framework, individuals will develop their linguistic identities and make choices about language use. Some languages will flourish under such conditions; it is likely that others will not. But nobody will be able to say that they did not have a fair opportunity to realize the language-related identity commitments that they hold dear.

But what more concretely would "fair treatment" entail? Let me begin with an initial proposal and then go on to consider various possible objections and amendments. The key idea behind the initial proposal is that fair treatment requires *equal* treatment. Equal treatment means that each language spoken in the community enjoys the same recognition. The same public benefits, protections and privileges that are extended to one are also extended to the other(s). For instance, if a particular public service (e.g. advice about tax matters from a government office) is offered in one language spoken in the community, then that same service is also offered in other languages spoken in the community. Or, if a particular piece of public business (e.g. filing a suit in a court of law) can be conducted in one language, then it can also be conducted in the others. On this initial proposal, then, the recognition that is due each language group takes the form of a bundle of rights and entitlements that is comparable in content to the rights and entitlements enjoyed by other language groups in the same community.

It is hard to see how the priority principle could be justifiable under this proposal. The refusal of RILMs seems plainly incompatible with equality of treatment. In the absence of RILMs, the community's language policy would help to secure and promote the language of the local majority and, to this extent, would accommodate the language-based identity of those in the majority. At the same time, no assistance at all would be given to those in the internal minority with a language-based identity. A bearer of an internal minority-language-based identity could reasonably object that he does not have a fair chance to realize his identity under such a policy disposition. By contrast, under a language regime that recognized RILMs, this unfairness is absent. Public institutions would operate in both the

---

[8] I develop this third position more fully in Patten 2003a.

majority and the minority language and to this extent offer roughly equal kinds of assistance to bearers of minority-language and majority-language identities.

As I mentioned earlier, fairness in treatment of one's language does not guarantee that that language will survive or flourish. The degree to which a language flourishes is a function of the public rights and entitlements associated with the language *and* the totality of decisions about language use that people make within the framework established by these rights and entitlements. If Laponce's empirical conjecture is correct, and we accept the initial proposal, then we have to worry that the local majority language may not flourish or survive under institutions establishing fair treatment. And for some proponents of the priority principle this possibility would be enough to call into question the "fairness" of the initial proposal. The initial proposal, it might be objected, offers an empty and formal interpretation of fairness, in which it is predictable that the strong will race ahead and the weak lag behind.

I will make some concessions to this sort of objection in a moment but first I want to caution against accepting too crude a version of it. It cannot be a criterion of fairness that every language survive and flourish, and thus the mere fact that, predictably, some languages will do well and others will not cannot be sufficient to reject the initial proposal. As I argued above, it is likely that there is *no* possible set of public institutions that guarantees to every language that it will survive and flourish. Since no arrangement of public institutions can meet this standard, it is not an objection to any particular arrangement that it does not. We have to find some different kind of standard for assessing the linguistic character of public institutions, and this is precisely what the initial proposal offers.[9]

Still, I think that the initial proposal is not entirely adequate as it stands and that the "empty formalism" objection is on to something. The problem is not that equal treatment can lead to unequal outcomes but that there may, in some cases, be more immediate reasons to think that equal treatment would not be fair treatment. Let me focus on two sources of unfairness that are not addressed by the initial proposal.

Market unfairness[10]   The success of a language, as I have suggested, is not just a matter of the framework of public rights and entitlements the language enjoys but also depends on the decisions that people

---

[9] See Rawls (1993: 197) for a more general statement of the argument sketched in this paragraph.
[10] I'm grateful to Arash Abizadeh for pushing me to think more carefully about this case.

make within that framework. These decisions, however, are often made in the context of market interactions. And it is easy to be suspicious that markets do not always – or even generally – realize or promote fairness. Market interactions reflect the economic assets of the various participants, and there may be nothing fair about how those are distributed. More specifically, the distribution of economic assets may be systematically skewed towards members of one language group in a community (e.g. the internal minority) and away from the other (e.g. the local majority). Under conditions like these, equal treatment of the two language groups may be unfair treatment if it means doing nothing to correct or compensate for the kinds of unfairness that are predictably thrown up by market processes. It would be hard to argue to members of a disadvantaged local majority that a policy of equal treatment leaves them with a "fair opportunity" to realize their identity if, in fact, their lower economic position systematically thwarts the realization of their identity-related goals and projects.

Historical injustices   A distinct but often related worry about equal treatment is that it may work as a kind of rubber stamp on historical injustices. A language community may find it hard to flourish under conditions of equal treatment because it is hobbled by injustices it has suffered in the past. The members of the group may have faced significant forms of discrimination, contempt and denigration in the past, and the effects of these past injustices may impact on their present capacity to realize their identity. To flourish, a language must have some success at competing with other local languages for speakers and for prestigious domains of language use. Where members of one language group are still dealing with the effects of past injustices, it is hard to be confident that such competition would be "fair" if public institutions make no effort to correct or compensate for the historic damage but instead simply insist on a policy of equal treatment.

Obviously more work needs to be done in elaborating these two possible sources of unfairness. What we need is an account of how fairness in treatment of different identity groups interacts with economic and rectificatory justice. Such an account would allow us to revise or amend the initial proposal and arrive at a richer formulation of the "politics of fairness." Although I will not try to develop such an account here, I think we do now have enough to draw some conclusions about identity arguments and the priority principle.

I argued earlier that the initial proposal should be regarded as incompatible with this principle. Is this conclusion affected if the initial proposal is amended or revised along the lines I have just been sketching? It seems possible that the answer is "yes" or, more likely, "yes, sometimes." It is possible to imagine cases in which the local language majority is so hobbled by economic disadvantage and/or the lasting effects of historical injustice that the only conditions under which its members have a fair opportunity to realize their language-related identity are when RILMs are refused. The economic disadvantage of local majority speakers, and the persisting effects of past injustices, lower the status of their language and make it less tempting for newcomers to decide to learn this language or for others to pass it on to new generations. The refusal of RILMs works to offset these effects, raising the status of the local majority language by making it a necessary tool for a range of different public interactions.[11]

It seems equally possible to imagine cases, however, in which members of a local majority cannot claim to be especially or disproportionately burdened by economic disadvantage or historical injustice (or where they can claim a special burden but not a very grave one). In these cases, the initial proposal (equal treatment) seems like the best way to establish fairness between the different language groups cohabiting a common political community. From the point of view of identity considerations, then, we should embrace RILMs, and reject the priority principle, unless some particular argument can be made that the local majority faces market unfairness or the lasting effects of historical injustice.

Conclusion

A common theme in recent discussions of identity and culture is that political theory in these areas needs to be done in a contextual way. In theorizing the normative questions arising because of cultural diversity it will seldom, if ever, be possible to lay down timeless, universal laws. Instead, theorists need to be sensitive to the particular historical, social, economic, legal and cultural contexts in which particular normative claims are being advanced, and they must be prepared to modulate their evaluation of those claims as circumstances vary from case to case.

In general I am sympathetic with this "contextual turn" in recent political theory. Still, there is a worry that any given particular case will contain an effectively limitless amount of contextual detail that could potentially be relevant to some specific normative dispute or question. A good theory should, in my view, help to prevent us from drowning in the context by seeking to articulate what particular features of a given context we should

---

[11] See Laponce (1984: 155) for the suggestion that territorial unilingualism might be justifiable in Quebec as a kind of "compensating inequality."

be especially attentive to and what questions, so to speak, we should ask of the wealth of empirical detail we face. And it won't just be the context that tells us which features of the context to pay attention to, because this simply pushes the problem back one step. Inevitably, there will be a role for political theory in reflecting on a broader set of normative questions and principles, e.g. about the nature and commitments of a liberal democracy.

My aim in the present chapter has been to put political theory – understood in broadly this way – into the service of a particular controversy arising in a number of jurisdictions around the world. That controversy concerns whether or not internal linguistic minorities should enjoy various language rights. I have been considering a specific argument – the territorial imperative argument – for the claim that internal linguistic minorities should not enjoy such rights. My objective has not been to arrive at a conclusion that the territorial imperative argument is generally true or false. Rather, I have sought to identify a number of questions that someone trying to reach a judgement about a controversy in this area might ask of the context.

We should ask:

1. Would the recognition of rights for the internal minority end up undermining the local majority language in a way that leaves unilingual speakers of that language without an adequate range of life options and opportunities?

2. Do the members of the local majority suffer disproportionately from an economic disadvantage, or from the lasting effects of a historical injustice, in a way that would leave them without a fair opportunity to realize their language-related identity commitments if significant rights are accorded to the internal minority?

If the answer to both of these questions is "no," then there is, in my view, as much reason to think that internal minorities should enjoy significant language rights as there is to think that the majority should.

Part III

Individual autonomy

7   Autonomy, association and pluralism

Jeff Spinner-Halev

Critics of illiberal groups are right to point out that these groups can too readily undermine the rights and equality of individual group members. Some groups, particularly but not only traditional religious groups, are hierarchical and patriarchal; they often shun liberal democratic values. Some liberals suggest that this opposition to liberal norms and practices is a challenge that necessitates a response. Yet in their attempt to ensure equality, these critics too easily dismiss the autonomous choices that some people make, and are too ready to undermine pluralism for other goals. Some people actually choose to belong to illiberal groups; this is a choice that liberals ought to respect. Moreover, the tendency of some liberals to want the institutions of civil society to mirror the norms of the liberal state, dangerously undermines pluralism which we ought to accept as an inevitable outcome of liberty.

This hardly means that illiberal groups ought to be given all the autonomy they want. Some supporters of group life suggest that all groups – illiberal or not – be left alone to conduct their affairs as they wish. This view, however, would make individuals vulnerable to the decisions and power of groups, and would dangerously undermine individual autonomy and equality. My goal here is to find a middle course between these two views, one that tries to uphold individual autonomy *and* pluralism. Doing so does not mean finding the magic bullet that satisfies the concerns of all, dissolving all tensions between pluralism and autonomy. Rather, it means finding reasonable ways to balance the different concerns involved, realizing that there is no perfect balance between pluralism and autonomy, but that it is important to try to find the balance, shifting though it may be. Liberalism ought to be able to tolerate minority groups that do not adhere to some liberal norms, while also granting some protection to the minorities within the minority group.

Thanks to Sigal R. Benporath and Avigail Eisenberg for comments on an earlier version of this essay.

My views on this issue, the issue of minorities within minorities, are fueled by three concerns. There are tensions between these concerns, but these tensions are not fatal. We should worry more about views that lack any tensions in them than about those that do. My first concern is that individual autonomy is secured for as many people as possible. This means ensuring that people have a real right of exit from their group. Second, that liberalism does not reach into the confines of every group and insist that each group adheres to liberal principles. Once exit is secure, the state should usually leave groups alone (unless they break general laws, like torturing animals, or selling illegal drugs). Third, that the liberal state use its authority legitimately, and not imperially. This means that the state should be mindful of how it has used – and abused – its power in the past when it formulates policies towards groups today, particularly those groups whose experience with the state has been an unfortunate one. I would characterize my view as a pluralist one, as it emphasizes the importance of both maintaining a plurality of liberal values in the state, and a plurality of groups.[1]

I begin by defending the right to exit. I defend my position against those who would do too little to ensure that groups uphold the autonomy of individuals, and then against those who would interfere in groups too much. The groups that I have in mind in this section are usually traditional religious groups. These groups usually have little in the way of formal group rights – Western states usually do not grant one religious group the right to be exempt from certain laws.[2] Yet under other broad liberal principles and laws – the right to associate, freedom of religion, the right of parents to have a say in their children's education – these groups exercise some authority over their members. In the second section I turn to subordinate groups that do have (or perhaps ought to have) some measure of group rights, like indigenous peoples in many states. I take these groups to be a special case within liberalism, since the liberal state has been the cause of the group members' misery for a long time, which puts into question the legitimacy of the state intervening in the group. In all cases, however, I argue that for coercive authority to be legitimate it must be democratic. When authority is not coercive – when there is a real opportunity to leave the group – then that authority can be constructed in a variety of ways.

---

[1] For a full expression of liberal pluralism, see Galston 2002.
[2] There are some exceptions to this rule (Ontario, Canada, for example, grants state funding to Catholic schools but not to other religious schools), but I will pass over them here.

Defending a meaningful right to exit

Theorists who want to intrude into group life are motivated by two basic worries. First, that the autonomy of some group members, particularly children, will be undermined by the group's values and practices. Children of insular groups like the Amish or Hasidic Jews, or some conservative Christian groups, for example, are often raised within the values of the group, and are taught to carry on the group's traditions. These groups are typically hierarchical, and little attention is spent on liberal or democratic ideals. Living in such insular communities with a restricted education will lead, some charge, to the inability of many children to really choose the kind of life they want to lead as they grow up.

The second worry is that women and girls will unfairly face discrimination. Many traditional groups often discriminate against girls and women, who are taught that the man is head of the household. In a variety of ways, the charge goes, these communities unfairly restrict the choices of girls and women. Patriarchy does not necessarily mean that men are free to do what they want, since men's lives are often constrained in many ways by group norms. Yet in these traditional communities, men are in charge of both the community and the household, and are often given more leeway in their lives than women.

The minimal standard argument

The traditional liberal response to these worries, a version of which I mean to defend, is that people ought to have the freedom to organize associations and to leave them if they wish. They can be kicked out of the association as well. These views date back to John Locke's *Letter Concerning Toleration* (Locke 1983). My arguments are inspired by Locke's *Letter*, but do not mirror them. The basic ideas behind my exit argument are twofold. First, that the argument that democracy be legally instituted only has resonance with institutions that have coercive authority. In institutions without coercive authority, the state and its laws should show little concern with how these institutions are structured. Second, certain minimal standards, which I will spell out, are needed to ensure that exit is really an option.

Associations and privacy go hand in hand: one of the ways in which people's privacy is protected is by granting them large leeway in how they act and whom they associate with in private. Associations in a liberal society lack coercive authority: a religious group may claim authority over every aspect of their members' lives, but this authority is not backed up with any legal force in most liberal societies. When authority is coercive, then worries about democracy and discrimination must set in. If people must follow the rules of a community, then that set of people ought to have a say in the construction and change of that community's rules under normal circumstances. When authority is not coercive, however, then usually there is not any claim for democracy. There is no liberal or democratic reason to insist that voluntary associations are democratic or egalitarian. As long as people can leave these groups, they ought to be free to join the groups they want. Indeed, given the plurality of people's interests and values, we ought to expect that people will join a variety of groups with different sorts of structures. Some will be attracted to egalitarian groups, others to hierarchical ones, and some to those with a mixture of the two.

Yet to say an association is voluntary does not ensure that people have a real right to exit. Minimal standards are needed to make the right to exit meaningful. These standards include freedom from physical abuse, decent health care and nutrition, the ability to socialize with others, a minimal education – basic literacy in the basic subjects of reading, math, science, etc. – and a mainstream liberal society. These standards are needed so that people can evaluate the choices they make, and have the minimal skills needed to leave their group. A person who cannot read or is very ill or undernourished will have a very hard time leaving her group. A mainstream society is needed so that if people want to leave they have a place to go to, where they choose the kind of life they want to lead. Exit is only meaningful if people are able to make the choice to leave, and can enter a society that cultivates different ways of living.

The libertarian challenge

Some critics argue that this "minimal standard argument" is too robust. Chandran Kukathas maintains that neither the state nor groups have any responsibility in ensuring the well-being of any of their members, including children (Kukathas 1997). As long as one can formally leave – that is, as long as one can walk away from one's group without restraint – then enough of a right to exit is assured. Kukathas defends this right to exit as sufficient even if the members are abused, denied an education, or lack any job skills. Kukathas recognizes that groups might do terrible things to their members, rendering the right of exit hard to exercise, but he argues that states, even liberal democratic states, often do terrible things to their members as well. Why, Kukathas asks, should we trust the state more than the group? Kukathas is right to point out that states are not always benevolent actors, but if a state insists that all the citizens under its purview receive the minimal standards I have discussed, then worries about the state acting malevolently should be eased.

Kukathas worries about the tyranny of the state, but you don't have to eliminate state power to ease this worry; you can, instead, limit its power. It is not the state's responsibility to raise children by itself, or to take children away from non-abusive families and hand them to others. When states do so, they overreach their authority. We can reduce the potential harm the state can do by ensuring that it has a limited role in ensuring the well-being of children. The state can, for example, insist that parents ensure their children are educated, but the state need not insist that the state do the educating. A state education can be offered as one option among several. Parents, groups and the state all share the responsibility in raising children, which reduces the ability of any one agent to use its power over children tyrannically.

The liberal challenge

While libertarians and their fellow travelers object that my minimal standard argument is not very minimal at all, many liberals today think that this argument gives the state too small a role in ensuring individual autonomy. Before I discuss the specific charges aimed at my argument here, I want to note that the path these liberal critics are led down is an alarmingly interventionist one. The right to association and the right to privacy are two fundamental liberal values. Liberals that argue for ending all forms of discrimination or supporting a robust version of autonomy are placing one liberal value very much above others. It is also a liberalism that is in danger of becoming imperialistic, by trying to root out all forms of life that are non-liberal. Liberalism's traditional strength, however, is its ability to balance different and important values, between autonomy and pluralism, equality and tolerance. There is no reason to give up one value for another, because each value restrains the others. A liberalism without balance is too much in danger of overreaching itself.

The suggestion that the minimal standard argument undermines individual autonomy rests on the idea that children need to have wide exposure to the outside world in order to be autonomous. Without seeing other ways of living up close, this argument suggests, children who are raised in closed environments will not really understand and be able to evaluate their own and other ways of living. Without this understanding, the ability of children to really choose the kind of life they want to lead – their ability to be autonomous – is dangerously undermined. Since autonomy is a fundamental liberal value, groups that do not expose their children to a wide variety of lifestyles ought to be made to do so (Gutmann 1995; Raz 1994: 182–90).

The main flaw in this argument is that it fails to recognize that in the consumer, materialist societies of the West, the lure of exit is always present. It is partly because our societies are so materialist, including our public schools in many ways, that some people retreat to religion. Some people complain about the hold that certain groups have over their children, but the hold that popular culture has over many people is not exactly uplifting. It is the actual condition of mainstream society that is often missing in the arguments given by critics of the exit argument. In their arguments they compare actual traditional religious groups with an ideal version of liberal society. These critics note that certain religious groups do not raise their children to be autonomous, to think for themselves and so on. The state then needs to ensure either a better education for them, or that they have more exposure to the mainstream society, or both. The unstated assumption here is that children become autonomous in mainstream, Western societies. This may be true in an ideal liberal society, but the ideal is hardly matched in practice (Carens 2000).

It is certainly true that *some* people become autonomous in Western societies. It is also true that other people find themselves subject to many influences that they find hard to resist. In the USA today *public* schools routinely make marketing deals with Pepsi or Coca Cola; where other private companies are allowed to buy advertising within the schools; where private television networks are shown for free in schools in return for the ability to show advertising to the children; where peer pressure is often intense and sometimes harmful. Are these the sorts of schools that produce autonomous adults? Then, of course, there are the private media that children in mainstream culture often find themselves immersed in. I won't subject the readers to the details of that, but suffice to say that autonomy is not what much of popular culture is after. As William Galston (2002) remarks, "Children immersed in a culture defined by advertising, entertainment media, and peer pressure are often dominated by influences they neither understand nor resist. In the face of such challenges, to have any realistic possibility of exerting some countervailing formative power, parents may be compelled to take a strong countercultural stance" (105–6). In a society where public schools allow advertising for commercial products, where conformity is often prized by students, who often indulge in illegal drugs and alcohol, and where the education is often of uneven quality, it should not be surprising that some choose to opt out of these schools or try to avoid many aspects of mainstream society.

Not all schools are terrible, and not all parts of mainstream society are best avoided. My argument is not that liberal societies are really modern-day Babylons, but neither are they utopias, and liberals should understand that some people have good reason to opt out of public schools and mainstream institutions. Forcing children into the mainstream society hardly ensures that they will become autonomous. However, having the *option* of living in the mainstream is important for autonomy. While some object that religious groups may make exit difficult by sheltering their children, this is hard to do in our society. Some religious groups do keep a tight grip on their children, but the range of popular culture is farreaching, and extends to almost all groups in our society. It is hard for traditional religious children not to see that other kinds of life exist in our society. The streets are full of different kinds of people; advertising is ubiquitous; computers allow people to virtually travel around the globe. The kind of insularity needed to live a life where others are not encountered is extraordinarily rare in Western societies.

Between the minimal standards I have described here, and the lure and ubiquity of popular culture, not much more is needed to ensure that people have the right of exit.

A second argument against the minimal standard argument is that the right to exit simply underestimates the psychological difficulties of leaving one's group (Reitman this volume; Weinstock this volume).[3] This is not true for all groups – it may not be so hard to leave one's chess club – but it often is hard to leave what Weinstock calls "identity-conferring" groups, like a religious group that one was born into. A Catholic woman may dislike the fact that the Catholic Church hierarchy is all male, but she still may find it hard to leave. Having grown up within the Church, her identity may be closely intertwined with it, meaning that leaving the Church is akin to changing's one identity. There may be parts of the Church that she loves. To force her to choose between her identity and her church is simply cruel (Shachar 2001).

Yet the degree to which people identify with their religion varies quite a bit: for some people it is quite important, and for others it is less important. Religious groups are "identify-conferring" groups for only some people. In liberal societies, some people more closely identify with sports teams than with their religion, but this hardly justifies a greater worry about what to do with teams that do not act as their fans wish. It is also unclear why the psychological argument should apply mostly or only to groups. Parents often exert psychological pressure on their

---

[3] Ayelet Shachar also points to the psychological difficulty of leaving one's group, but her work focuses mostly on groups that have state support for institutions, as in India and Israel where religious family law has the backing of the state. Reitman and Weinstock's concerns are broader, and extend even to groups whose rules receive no state backing, and need not be followed by anyone (Shachar 2001).

children. Indeed, the woman who is torn between her egalitarianism and the Catholic Church may be experiencing a more fundamental conflict between disappointing her parents, who are devoted Catholics, and fulfilling her ideals. When people experience psychological conflict about leaving one's group, it is often unclear whether the psychological pressure point is the group or one's parents. Since it is often the parents, should the state then worry about parents who put undue pressure on their children? That certainly would be overreaching the state's purview.

Moreover, people have been changing religions for quite some time now, and continue to do so. Some people do disappoint their parents. Some people throw up the clutches of their identity-conferring group, sometimes in exchange for another one. People in the West have been leaving their religions in droves since the Reformation. Is it really harder to leave one's religious group now than in, say, 1650 or 1750?

Finally, the psychological argument is flawed because it is impossible to reach the goal of ensuring that each group responds to the wishes of all its members. If the state then intervenes to make the religion accommodate the view of the dissenters, it will simply create a new set of dissenters, those who dislike the new changes. No religion can be responsive to the needs of all its members. Change, even one that we liberals think is progressive and right, will always leave some people out in the cold. Some Catholics want the Church to open the priesthood up to women; others do not; and still others think that the role of women in the Church ought to be reduced. The Church cannot respond to the wishes of all groups, and members of each group may closely identify with the Church as a whole. The argument that religions ought to respond to the wishes of their members otherwise their identity will be harmed, cannot work because no religion can coherently secure the identity of its dissenters and fully-fledged supporters alike.

The third argument against the minimal standard argument is that illiberal groups that undermine equality, even in private, are a problem for liberalism that must be dealt with somehow. Religions that discriminate against women may appear to be private, but they violate a fundamental liberal value that will harm the women facing the discrimination, and perhaps make it harder to establish a public culture of equality. Such a violation of liberal norms cannot be ignored. Abolition of these groups may be impossible, but other ways ought to be found to make it harder for them to discriminate (Okin 2002; Reitman this volume; Weinstock this volume).

This argument, however, undermines both autonomy and pluralism. Tolerating different groups protects liberty and choice. If all groups adhere to robust liberal standards on individuality, equality and discrimination, the pluralism within the liberal state would be reduced. This would diminish the choices that people can exercise, undermining their autonomy. Pluralism and autonomy are not very meaningful if the only pluralism that is available is completely compatible with the ruling public philosophy. Meaningful choices means having the choice to belong to a hierarchical religion. If all private groups are remade in the image of the liberal state, then everyone's choices are reduced. If we are to take toleration and diversity seriously, then we have to be willing to put up with private groups with illiberal values.

The need to protect toleration and diversity is why we should reject the argument that religions that practice gender discrimination should be denied their tax-exempt status because of their violation of a key liberal value (Okin 2002; see Altman 2003 for a nuanced argument). The idea behind tax-exempt status for non-profit groups is to encourage the existence of a vibrant civil society. This is surely a laudable goal. It will be the case that liberals will not agree with the goals or the institutional structure of some of these non-profit groups. Yet many of these non-profit organizations can still contribute to civil society: they can encourage people to interact, offer people a sense of community, and offer them opportunities to engage in social and political activities. These are all important functions and they are helped by many non-profit groups, even many of those that do not have a liberal agenda or structure. It is probably the case that many non-profit organizations have a mixed record from a liberal point of view. Many Baptist churches, for example, are patriarchal, yet they give many women important opportunities to learn a variety of skills, since women participate in church activities in larger numbers than men (Verba, Schlozman and Brady 1995: ch. 11). If we only look at their institutional structure we may miss the liberal and democratic opportunities that many non-profit groups offer to their members. Furthermore, if we begin to walk down the path of selectively determining which non-profit groups should be tax-exempt and which should not be, then we will politicize the non-profit sector to the detriment of democracy. The political party in power will try to shape civil society in its image, which is surely not a benefit for democracy. The strength of a vigorous civil society is its ability to support democracy in a general way, by encouraging such background virtues of a democracy like participation, moderation, compromise and the building up of communities. To overtly politicize these virtues is to undermine them.[4]

---

[4] If in the rather unlikely event that Congress passes and the president signs a bill revoking the tax-exempt status from the Catholic Church and other religious institutions that do not practice gender equity, what is to prevent a bill passing that denies tax-exempt status to religious institutions that recognize gay and lesbian marriages? The latter is of course more likely to pass than the former with the US Congress that exists while I write these words.

A strong civil society also does not mirror all the values of the state. One of the ways in which tyranny is checked in a liberal society is by having different sources of power and different values. A relentlessly liberal society, one that was liberal in all of its institutions, which mirrored the state's values, could too easily become tyrannical: it would too readily stamp out any non-liberal dissent as dangerous. Non-liberal groups can help point out when liberals make mistakes or overreach themselves. They provide a source of refuge for those who do not particularly like liberalism. Non-liberal groups are both a reflection of liberty and one way in which it is protected.

It is worth noting that the fastest growing churches in the USA in the 1990s were the conservative ones, while the more liberal churches lost members. The Church of Latter Day Saints (as the Mormons prefer to be called), is the fastest growing church in the USA (Goodstein 2002). It is also the case, surprising as it may seem to some liberals, that some women may really choose to belong to hierarchical religions. Jan Feldman (2003) may be too uncritical of Hasidic Jews in her book supporting their way of life, and their choice to lead it, but after immersing herself in their community, she clearly thinks that Hasidic women really do choose their way of life. It is hard to deny that at least some women are making that choice. Moreover, Feldman argues that Hasidic women make this choice for good reasons, not because they are unduly influenced by sinister patriarchal forces. Feldman's argument cannot easily be completely dismissed. Adults are *choosing* on a regular basis to become members of conservative religions. Instead of trying to figure out ways to intervene in these churches to make them more liberal, explain away their success, liberals ought to work to make liberal society more attractive so perhaps liberal churches will gain members. But liberals also need to realize that some people want to belong to conservative churches for any number of reasons, regardless of how well-functioning the larger liberal society is. It is simply mistaken to think that a world without poverty or oppression, and where everyone was treated with respect, would be a world where everyone embraced all liberal values.

The argument that illiberal social institutions dangerously undermine public liberal values also overstates the hold most religions have over people. The Catholic Church may be a patriarchal and hierarchical institution, but its teachings are routinely ignored by many of its members. Italy, after all, has the second lowest birth rate in the world, right after Spain (PBS.org 2003). Many Italian and Spanish Catholics are presumably religious practitioners of birth control, contrary to the teachings of the Church. You do not even have to exit if you disagree with the Church. Church members routinely and readily find themselves disagreeing with its teachings and yet remain members of it. Since the Church lacks any coercive authority, there is little it can do about this situation. Occasionally the Church may kick some members out, but its reliance on its members for funding means that it resorts to expulsion only rarely. The power of liberal public culture is quite strong, as it lures people in despite and because of themselves. Nonetheless, if we are to respect the ideal of autonomy, we need to respect the choice that some do make to belong to patriarchal institutions.

Most of the liberal arguments against the minimal standard argument come too close to being illiberal by using one liberal value to justify the intervention into group norms and practices that do not physically harm others; that prevent many parents from teaching their children as they wish, alongside minimal standards; and by refusing to respect the choice that people make to live non-liberal lives. We must recognize that the diversity of people means that different choices will be made that we have to respect. Yet the lure of liberal societies – for better and for worse – will be hard for many people to resist.

Exceptions to the rule: justice and legitimacy

Generally patriarchal groups ought to be left alone as long as they adhere to the minimal standards I have described here, and as long as they do not have coercive authority. But general rules sometimes admit of exceptions, and here the main exception is for those groups that have a deep-seated history of being oppressed by the state (or by others in society, with the state doing little about it), and have been or are in a position to exercise some group authority. My claim here is that the legitimacy and justice of the liberal state imposing liberal values on long-oppressed groups is questionable, even if the values that the state wants to impose are themselves just. There is here sometimes a conflict between two sorts of justice: the justice of authority and the justice of rights.

Liberal justice focuses on procedures and rights: an individual's rights should be respected, he or she should not face undue discrimination, should be allowed to live a dignified life, and have decent and reasonable opportunities to pursue his or her life. Liberal justice demands that people be treated equally under the law. Since the role of the state is to protect the rights and equality of its members, few liberals ask whether the state has the authority to intervene in different communities to do so. Similarly, democracies gain legitimacy by granting their members the right to vote upon and change their government at regular intervals. But if a group of people in a democracy are not given the right to vote – and are denied other rights as well – then the legitimacy of the democracy's authority over that group is clearly questionable. The clearest (but not only) example of this is the indigenous peoples in most Western states. For years these democracies have used their armies, legislatures and courts to displace indigenous peoples, deny them equal rights within their jurisdiction, and generally make life miserable for them. This suggests that the legitimacy of Western states to exercise authority over indigenous peoples is dubious, since they have been denied their democratic rights. Critics of multiculturalism like Brian Barry may claim that the model of universal citizenship – that all adults in the political community receive the same rights and protections – is one of the great triumphs of liberalism (2001a: ch. 2), but the theory of liberalism has often not been matched in practice. To tell indigenous peoples that if only the theory of liberalism had been upheld their ancestors would have been better treated and their lives now much better – a controversial enough argument – is hardly enough to convince them that in fact they all ought gleefully to become liberals now. The damage has been done, the intent to treat indigenous peoples fairly now is dubious, and the legitimacy of most Western states to treat indigenous peoples like other citizens has been greatly undermined (Ivison 2002).

Legitimacy matters not only because it is an important principle in and of itself, but also because illegitimate governmental decisions can have bad consequences. When a government exercises its authority illegitimately, it often loses the trust of the people it exercises authority over. Unsurprisingly, Black Americans often mistrust the criminal justice system in the USA, since they have often been unfair victims of it. The same is true of many oppressed minorities the world over. The consequences of mistrust are often severe: fear, riots, a weakened criminal justice system, an increase in crime, and sometimes a refusal to co-operate with the authorities. A focus on liberal justice that ignores the question of authority will not be able to achieve justice.

My argument here on the importance of legitimate authority does not mean that any group that wants to reject the government's legitimacy should be able to do so. Lucas Swaine (this volume) argues that some religious conservatives do reject the authority of the state. Some of these people – Swaine's "ambitious theocrats" – actively engage in political life, aiming to "topple the liberal establishment," in his words. While these theocrats may deny the legitimacy of the state, a simple denial is not enough: the denial of legitimacy has to be justified. If any group can simply claim that they do not like the government, so its authority is illegitimate, or that the government is not properly constructed to their liking, chaos might very well ensue. The argument that some groups are right to limit the state's authority must be restricted to those groups that have a good claim for this limitation. Since one of the aims of ambitious theocrats – to change government policies – affects all citizens, they appear to be engaged citizens, who have the same rights and responsibilities as others. It is hard to see what makes them good candidates to successfully deny the state's authority over them. Nonetheless, Swaine is right to warn about the consequences of the liberal state overreaching itself – when the liberal state becomes an imperial state, insisting that as much of private and public space as possible adheres to liberal norms, we should expect to have an adverse and possibly even violent reaction. To prevent this, the liberal state ought to ensure that its reach into the private sphere is limited. This is what liberal toleration and liberal privacy demand.

The legitimacy of authority is important, but difficult questions arise when groups deny their members rights or discriminate against some of them, and claim the state lacks the legitimacy to intervene. Some indigenous tribes, for example, discriminate against Christians, while others discriminate against women. Few indigenous peoples adhere to a classic conception of individual rights like liberal states do. What we have here is the need to balance the claims of two kinds of justice, the justice of authority and liberal justice, in these sorts of cases. As with many times when a balance is needed, there is not always only one way to establish this equilibrium. Nonetheless, a couple of guidelines can be offered.

First, when group rights are possible or already exist, the state's pressure on the group to alter its illiberal practices should rely in part on how much of a right to exit exists. When there is a right to exit, there is less concern about the group's illiberal practices, since people who dislike the group's practices can leave. This is the case with most indigenous peoples, whose members are usually citizens of the larger state. I do not want to diminish the difficulty in leaving, which can clearly be psychologically hard to do. (Though in fact the issue with many tribes in the USA and Canada is more often entrance than exit: more people want to enter the tribes than the tribes are willing to admit.) As long as authority is not coercive, however, the state's need to intervene is diminished; when the question of whether the state has the legitimacy to intervene is added in, then it is hard to see what justifies state intervention in indigenous peoples.

Second, there are cases when exit is not an option, such as the personal (or family) law systems in Israel and India. In these countries one almost always must get married according to the rules of one of the officially recognized religions; one must get married as a Christian, Muslim or Hindu (India) or Jew (Israel). The rules are often made by men who want to sustain a system of patriarchy (a system which gives them priority as men from which they benefit). For the state to simply change the rules would usually provoke an outcry from the minority. Israeli and Indian Muslims are subordinate populations who feel oppressed. There is little doubt that the majority in each community cling to their rules and would resent the state's intervention to change them (Spinner-Halev 2001). The interesting issue raised by this is why most women put religious/national identity and group solidarity ahead of their interests as women. I cannot fully answer this question here, except to note that national identity is especially strong among groups that feel under threat. When a group feels threatened, people's collective self-esteem becomes tightly woven to their group. When under threat, the group becomes more cohesive, puts up with little internal dissent, while a centralized leadership becomes ever more powerful. People's allegiance to a threatened group that is important to their identity becomes very strong (Spinner-Halev and Theiss-Morse 2003).

This leads to a difficult dilemma: a threatened group is less likely than ever to change when the change is demanded by the state that is perceived to be the oppressor.[5] The solution in these sorts of cases may lie within the community: instead of leaving change up to the state or to the community's leaders, it may be best to agree to allow the community to continue to construct or maintain its own rules, but insist that it do so democratically. Coercive authority is only legitimate when it is democratic; what is true for the state is also true for subordinate communities. Some may object that this proposal invites the state to intervene into the subordinate community's affairs, but the state must decide who in the community should be allowed to make up the community's rules. Since a minimal amount of state intervention is inevitable, the fairest route is to ask the entire community to make up its rules, rather than a band of self-selected leaders.

Conclusion

I offered two ways to treat minorities who do not discriminate against some of their members. First, in groups that lack coercive authority, the state should ensure that there is a real right to exit by insisting that all members be treated with the minimal standards I have described here. Second, in subordinate groups that have a good claim to partly reject the authority of the state, I have suggested that some balance between granting these groups some authority to govern themselves and ensuring justice within the group must be sought. The less there is a right to exit from these groups, the more the state should ensure that the group's rights are

---

[5] Shachar calls this phenomenon "reactive culturalism" (Shachar 2001).

democratically established. These two methods of treating subordinate communities do not, of course, exhaust all the possible ways to conceive of the relationship between the state and the oppressed communities.

My proposals here do not leave us a world without anguish or difficult problems. Liberalism treasures different values – autonomy, equality and tolerance – which do not always lead in the same direction (Berlin 1969). Even those liberals who maintain that one value trumps all others will sometimes find that the one triumphant value tugs in different directions. Autonomy may mean leading one's own life according to one's own lights, which can easily be interpreted as allowing parents to raise their children as they see fit (within the bounds of physical harm). But autonomy may also mean trying to ensure that children are able to free themselves from the grip of their parents. Moreover, autonomy, toleration and equality are not values that either exist or not; all admit of degrees. Giving or protecting the autonomy of indigenous peoples may harm equality to some degree. Giving religious parents wide latitude in raising their children may mean that their children have a less robust version of autonomy than others have. This does not mean that equality or autonomy do not exist for some indigenous people or for some religious children, but that certain robust versions of these values may be out of reach for some people, in order to give space to other liberal values.

A single-minded liberal theory is in danger of losing sight of crucial liberal values. A heavy emphasis on toleration threatens equality and individual autonomy by allowing all kinds of groups to exist, regardless of their practices. A strict emphasis on equality threatens individual autonomy and toleration by allowing the state to tell parents and religious bodies how to raise their children, treat their members, and so on. Liberal pluralists argue that different liberal values must be balanced, that we should not emphasize one value to the point of losing sight of other liberal values. There is no single way to balance different liberal values; my point is that they somehow must be balanced so they can all coexist, however uneasily. Any pluralist view like my own openly acknowledges that the liberal state needs to accommodate different, and sometimes conflicting, values, and so tensions between these values are inevitable. I worry less about a theory that admits to internal tensions than I do about a theory that is much too singular in its aims. A relentlessly consistent political theory can too easily become relentlessly tyrannical.

8   Sexual orientation, exit and refuge

Jacob T. Levy

Some kinds of minorities-within-minorities problems can be characterized as: this minority community relegates some of its members to second-
class status and membership. Can this be morally legitimate? If it is not,
who is morally permitted to act to change it, and using what means?
Questions concerning the status of women in conservative cultural and
religious communities are typically of this form.

But it is important to remember that *not all* minorities-within-
minorities situations have this form. Conservative religious and cultural
groups do think that women have *some* place in their societies; this is often
not so for, for example, gays and lesbians. The problem of second-class
membership is different in kind from the problem of those who are, in
principle, denied any kind of membership at all. I propose to examine this
latter kind of problem, focusing on the case of gay and lesbian members
of religious and cultural communities that are hostile to homosexuality.
Shifting our focus in this way reemphasizes the importance of exit rights,
an importance that has been somewhat obscured by the recent turn to
"transformative accommodation"[1] in thought about minorities within
minorities. And it refocuses attention on what the society surrounding
minority cultures must be like, for exit to do the moral work that we
demand of it.

I

Gay and lesbian members of religious and encompassing cultural communities that are hostile to homosexuality have morally serious interests
that are in inescapable tension with each other, to wit:

I thank Emily Nacol for valuable research assistance.
[1] The phrase is, of course, Ayelet Shachar's (2001). But, as will become clear, I use the
term to refer to more arguments than only hers. Some of the approaches I characterize
here as "transformative accommodation" Shachar would understand as falling into one
of her other analytic categories.

(1) the interest in living a life in which romantic and sexual intimacy play their part, free from guilt, shame and the psychologically tortuous project of trying to deliberately control and alter one's sexual orientation;

(2) the interest in remaining a good-faith member of one's cultural or religious community, in living a life consonant with its commitments and norms, and in seeing the continuation of that community.

The latter interest may be characterized more precisely in the case of religious communities that are committed as a matter of religious principle to some body of behavior-governing religious law, issued or authoritatively interpreted by some religiously significant agent:

(2a) the interest in living a life consonant with the rules and values one believes, as a matter of religious conviction, to have been issued or authoritatively interpreted by the appropriate religious authorities or divine power(s).

Of course, not all gay Catholics, gay Muslims, gay Orthodox Jews and so on will experience this as a dilemma. Some are only weakly committed or are not committed at all to their respective religion's claims to moral truth or knowledge of the divine. Some remain attached to the religion only because of a desire to remain associated with their families or their ethno-cultural communities. Some are willing and able to give up their religious attachment altogether. And, conversely, some committed believers will experience their homosexuality as a temptation to sin, one that ought to be overcome even at the cost of, for example, celibacy.

But for many, the dilemma will be all too real.[2] In describing this as a dilemma I mean to say more than that such people want two different things. Each of these "two different things" is a matter of very great importance. Those interested in the concept of identity might say that each is partially constitutive of a person's identity. Others might put it differently: the capacity for romantic and sexual intimacy and the capacity for religious experience are both fundamental capabilities; the experience of each is a primary good; each is part of the foundation for self-respect, or simply for a complete and flourishing human life. I am not so much interested in the differences among these ways of characterizing

---

[2] Probably the best-known writing documenting this dilemma from the inside in recent years has been by the gay Catholic intellectual Andrew Sullivan. Sullivan (1995), in his work in liberal political theory, does not spend much time on the dilemma as it is primarily about the proper role of the state. But the argument in that book about Catholic doctrine is, so to speak, an insider's argument. Sullivan (1998) contains his most sustained account of the dilemma. These two books have contributed a great deal to my thought about these questions – though Sullivan continues to remain within Catholicism, not to exit.

the dilemma as I am in understanding that there is a dilemma at all. This must, I think, be granted by any theory of human well-being that sees both romantic/sexual intimacy and religious experience as central components of (many people's) good lives, and that does not consider the two strictly commensurable with each other.

The dilemma is the same one that Ayelet Shachar has memorably but tendentiously characterized as "your culture or your rights." But while Shachar sees this as a dilemma unfairly foisted upon dissenting or vulnerable members of minority cultures by emphasizing exit rights, in this context I think it is useful to see the dilemma simply as characteristic of life in a world of religions with rules of conduct and religiously ordained interpreters of such rules.[3] "[T]he right of exit argument," Shachar maintains, "suggests that an injured insider should be the one to abandon the very center of her life, family, and community. This 'solution' never considers that obstacles such as economic hardship, lack of education, skills deficiency, or emotional distress may make exit all but impossible for some" (2001: 41). To avoid this suggestion, to escape placing the burden of exit on those who are already burdened, Shachar constructs an elaborate model of "shared governance" that accommodates minority cultures while transforming the content of their rules. In the examples of greatest interest to her, the institutional solutions are to prevent the need for burdened women to exit by gradually transforming groups' gender-inegalitarian internal rules and norms.

I do not mean to deny that transformation of inegalitarian cultures can take place, or that it is sometimes a desirable goal. But we should not treat the hope of transformative accommodation as an excuse for wishful thinking, for imagining that eventually all good things will go together. Religious and cultural groups will persist, and will persist in embracing divergent views of morality, family, gender and so on. We should not expect all religions and cultures some day to come around to internal egalitarianism, libertarianism and democracy. There will continue to be groups that differentiate internally between, say, men and women, typically in ways disadvantageous to the latter. There will continue to be groups that consider as sinful conduct that the liberal state holds to be within the rightful range of individual freedom and choice. There will continue to be groups governed by internal hierarchy. Indeed, insofar as some religions and cultures liberalize and democratize, others will respond with reaction and ostensibly purifying reformation, and new

---

[3] The "or your rights" part of Shachar's phrase, of course, depends on an already-assumed answer about which internal rules of a culture or religion (a *nomos* group, in her useful wording) violate the rights of their members.

conservative or hierarchical groups will arise. Transformation is not only one-way.[4]

And people will still feel bound in conscience to leave some groups, because the groups are illiberal. This may violate our sense of fairness, if the religion's internal rule is one that we reject; the already-burdened believer – e.g. the gay or lesbian condemned by his or her faith and co-religionists – may feel obliged to pay the price of exit, or may even be forced out. But the sense of fairness that is violated there is not liberal political justice. It is something more akin to Isaiah Berlin's recognition that there can be no social world without loss. If people are to be free to believe in norms of conduct that are stricter than the basic Humean rules of justice, then they will sometimes find that those norms are in irreconcilable conflict with something else in their lives or their basic make-up. If they are to be free to belong to institutions and groups that subscribe to such norms, then they will sometimes find that this conflict leads to voluntary exit or involuntary expulsion. And those of us who do not subscribe to the norms in question will, over and over again, see this as a kind of double-burdening.

What this means is that exit turns out to be central to moral thought about conservative religious and cultural groups after all, and despite all of the abuse that has been heaped upon it. It also means that exit is *possible* after all, despite theorizing that seems to suggest that it could never be without massive state intervention to make exit rights effective.

Brian Barry (2001a: 150–1) has suggested that a discussion of costs of exit must distinguish among intrinsic, associative and external costs. Barry illustrates the trichotomy with reference to excommunication from the Roman Catholic Church. Intrinsic to departure from the Church (voluntary or otherwise) is the loss of the good of membership in the Church, with all that that entails. To a believer, joining in communion with the true Church entails a good of a terribly important kind. "[T]he cost could be described as infinite [but] it is not one that can be detached from the phenomenon of excommunication itself; it cannot be altered by the actions of states or anybody else." Leaving the church (will-ye or nill-ye) may also prompt those who are still members to "break off social relations with you"; this is not intrinsic to excommunication but is rather a deliberate choice to dissociate on a personal level. These associative costs may also be very high – the loss of family, friends and loved ones is a personally serious matter – but "people in liberal societies cannot be

---

[4] Shachar (2001: 35–7) discusses this under the rubric of "reactive culturalism," though I do not think that she takes full account of the permanent and recurring character of such reaction. See also my discussion in Levy (2000: 40–1, 53–4).

prohibited from being narrow-minded and sectarian in this way." External costs are those "not legitimately imposed," "gratuitous" losses that the church or church members have "no right to impose." The example Barry offers is being fired by a Catholic employer, or even by an employer owned by the Church if one's job does not (like being a priest) intrinsically depend upon church membership.

This classification is question-begging; associative and external costs are distinguished only by moralized fiat. If we knew *ex ante* which costs were "not legitimately imposed," then we would hardly need a classification on which to build a theory. In other words, Barry's definitions make it impossible to offer an argument in favor of the freedom to impose "external costs" – they are *ex hypothesi* illegitimate – but people have offered arguments based in associational freedom for the right of religious employers to discriminate in hiring and firing. Still, the intuition Barry is building on is a plausible one. It is not coherent to treat the existence of inherent costs as a problem for the state to remedy, as an injustice to be repaired. If people are to be free to have serious commitments in their lives, and if they are to be free to join together in pursuit or honor of those commitments, then we will always have inherent costs with us. And this is particularly true for religious commitments. I suppose that one could imagine a world with serious commitments but without associative costs, but I find it difficult. People's shared commitments bring them together personally; their shared sense of justice or of the divine or of the familiar and comfortable provide foundations for friendship and more. It is implausible to think that people will not be driven apart when those commitments change.

I will leave aside the question of external costs, some of which I think are legitimate and some of which clearly are not (at the limit, submitting to bodily violence as the price of departure). Some interesting political philosophy has been written about external costs, focusing on a few pretty exotic cases such as the Hutterites and pretty complex ones such as the Pueblo. But when considering exit from most religious or cultural groups in most liberal democracies, it is typically intrinsic and associative costs that make exit such a grave choice. It is intrinsic costs that Shachar complains about with the formulation "your culture or your rights"; it is intrinsic costs that I described above as weighing on the good-faith gay or lesbian believer in a religion that proscribes homosexuality. It is associational costs – the loss of family and friends and familiarity – that can make it so dreadful to leave a religion even when one ceases to believe. It is associational costs that weigh so heavily on the case made much of by Okin (2002: 222, quoting in part Olsen 1997: 136, 138; see also Spinner-Halev 2001: 89–90):

The words of a seventeen-and-a-half-year-old Indian student from Fiji capture the dilemma such young women face. Suddenly faced with a coerced [*sic*] marriage that would not allow her to graduate from high school, she said, "I don't know what to do now. My dreams and plans are all messed up . . . I am tormented." But when a teacher suggested that she need not, perhaps, go through with the marriage, she responded indignantly, "In our religion, we have to think of our parents first. It would kill them if I ran away or disobeyed them . . . For me, I couldn't marry someone who wasn't a Muslim. I will do it the Muslim way. And I would never go against my parents!" A young woman like this has a formal right of exit.

But exercising it is not "thinkable to her," since by doing so "she would lose much of what she most values in life." The young woman does not in fact face a risk of excommunication; she would not have to renounce Islam in order to reject this particular marriage. But she faces crippling associational costs: rejecting this marriage would (she believes) require rejecting her parents.

Okin does not prescribe a policy solution to the case, and it is unclear to me what one could possibly look like. No liberal state may, and I doubt that any state successfully can, intervene to force parents to regard their children's religious or marital choices as matters of indifference, or to force children to be free of their parents' wishes. Neither may it or can it intervene to force parents to regard their children's sexual orientation with indifference. Okin implies that exit is unthinkable, impossible, unavailable. But exit in such circumstances is precisely what countless gays and lesbians do and have done for many years. It is wrenching; the intrinsic and associational costs are both very high. And it is no doubt a good thing that, in liberal democracies, many fewer gays and lesbians are rejected by their families and their communities than were in years past. But as long as there are religions that proscribe homosexuality, exit will continue to be what many similarly situated gays and lesbians do. Abolishing or even deliberately radically transforming the religions is not an option for a liberal state. We outsiders are limited to providing a safe, free and just place for them to exit *to*.

II

The problem of what it means to provide such a place will be returned to in the next section. A partially separate question from the perspective of liberal theory – though not entirely separate in political practice – involves the social foundations of the legal and political institutions of liberalism. When do those religious and cultural groups undermine the ability of the liberal state to offer a site of refuge? Religious groups have an impeccable right, according to the liberal theory of freedom of religion, to consider homosexuality to be sinful, and to condemn, shame or excommunicate gays and lesbians. They do *not* have the right to use the state to enforce that religious view – to enact or enforce sodomy laws, to deny gays and lesbians equality before the law in arenas such as marriage and military service and adoption, or to censor publications or broadcasts because they depict homosexuality in a favorable light (or depict it at all). Still less do they have the right to use or threaten private violence against gays and lesbians, publishers and broadcasters, and so on. These distinctions are drawn from liberal theory, however, and may not be reflected in the internal moral views of the various cultural and religious groups. Some religious world-views may deny the distinction between (for example) sin and crime. Others may have internally principled reasons for drawing such a distinction, but for drawing it in a way that differs dramatically from liberalism. As is well known, Catholic natural law theory holds that the reasons for condemning abortion, contraception and homosexuality are not internal to Catholicism or the Christian revelation, but are matters of objective reason binding upon all.

This difficulty is a familiar one from debates about political liberalism (Larmore 1990; Rawls 1993; Macedo 1995a, 2000; Tomasi 2001). It intersects with multiculturalism in a couple of ways, at least one of which has not been much discussed in the political liberalism literature. Rawls famously developed his theory assuming the model of a closed society, entered only by birth and departed from only by death. But arguments about multiculturalism cannot assume away immigration. And, from the perspective of Western liberal democracies, immigration may well strengthen the threat to the liberal separation of public and private. It may increase the share of the population who are "unreasonable" according to Rawls's criteria, the number of threatening "D people" in John Tomasi's typology.[5] It may not only increase the absolute numbers of adherents of religions that reject that separation. It may increase their conservatism, the strength of that rejection, by constantly reinfusing the population with believers who have not experienced the host country's liberalizing influences.

---

[5] Rawlsian unreasonableness is the inability to affirm the liberal democratic consensus in good faith, for non-strategic reasons, from within one's own comprehensive understanding of the good. "D people" "affirm various comprehensive doctrines that conflict with even the general values on which political liberalism is founded. This category may include racists or sexists of such a virulent kind that they reject the idea that people should be treated as free and equal even for political purposes . . . More typical of this category, however, are religious believers who express their piety by seeking to impose their views on other citizens" (Tomasi 2001: 17–18).

I want to stress that this only *might* be true. It is possible, of course, that immigrants will tend to liberalize the relevant cultural and religious groups, because they are drawn from those fleeing oppression elsewhere. It is also possible that immigrants will have little effect, because the members of the groups already present have not done much liberalizing, or have even reacted against the host society's perceived moral laxity by becoming more rigid. All the complexity mentioned in the previous section – all of our reasons for doubting that cultural and religious groups have any simple tendency to become internally egalitarian, libertarian and democratic simply because they are surrounded by a liberal polity – means that religiously illiberal immigrants might not move the political center of gravity in an illiberal direction. But they might, and complexity does not spare us the obligation, as citizens, to figure out whether and when this would take place in our society. Policies regarding immigration, citizenship and state support for immigrant cultures may all be affected by the answers.

This, I take it, was at the center of the critique of Muslim immigration to the Netherlands offered by the gay politician Pim Fortuyn before his assassination. Fortuyn campaigned on a platform of protecting Dutch social liberalism, its feminist and gay-friendly public policies. He argued that – especially in a state with such a small overall population – growing Muslim immigration could threaten that liberal political consensus. Though the American media sometimes lumped him in with figures of the European racist right such as France's Jean-Marie Le Pen, his arguments for restraining Muslim immigration rested on a very different foundation from theirs.

This is not, or is not only, a problem of "minorities within minorities." That is, this is not only a question regarding how traditional religious and cultural groups treat gay and lesbian *members of the groups*; it is also a question of whether those groups will affect the political and legal treatment of gays and lesbians who were never members (as well as those who are no longer, and those who still are). But it does seem plausible that religious believers who wish to use the power of the state to enforce their religion's prescriptions will be particularly eager to exercise power over those they view as "internal" sinners or apostates.

In the political liberalism literature, mostly centered on the United States, the examples usually given of religious minorities that might threaten the liberal consensus are various types of conservative Protestants and pre-Vatican II Catholics. But in Western Europe, where – Ireland excepted – neither Catholicism nor conservative Protestantism has much remaining strength as a political force, it is Islam that stands as the most plausible threat to the liberal political settlement.[6] I do not say that it is a very plausible threat; I am not in a position to judge that, and the answer may (as Fortuyn suggested) depend on the size of the country's population.

And Islam is, of course, internally diverse. Sheikh Omar Bakri Mohammed is a clear example of someone who would threaten the liberal political order in Britain if he had the power to do so; he explicitly holds that Britain ought to become an Islamic theocratic state on the model of the former Taliban regime in Afghanistan. Bakri and his affiliated self-styled "Shariah Court of the United Kingdom" have gained a great deal of publicity by issuing *fatwas* of death against both the gay Muslims in Britain who formed a chapter of the international group Al-Fatiha ("The Opening") and the gay playwright Terrence McNally for portraying Jesus as gay in the play *Corpus Christi*.[7] It is very clear that Bakri and his organizations represent only a very small fraction of the Muslims resident in Britain, even of the immigrant Muslims there; and some Muslim organizations have complained that the publicity is disproportionate and stigmatizing.

But it cannot be unfair to take any notice at all of Bakri and those like him. If wholly open borders are not a requirement of liberal justice (a question I bracket here), or if some good-faith affirmation of liberal democratic values is required before immigrants can become citizens, then the liberal state has some authority to prevent would-be theocrats from becoming citizens. It obviously has the authority to prevent them from committing violent acts; but the question is whether it also has the authority to prevent them from immigrating and/or becoming citizens and using their new political power to threaten the liberal order. I do not really mean to answer that question here, but to raise it as a serious one for the debates about political liberalism and the kind of citizens necessary to uphold the liberal democratic order. That debate is mostly conducted around how the state educates future citizens, not around how it makes its decisions about whom to admit to citizenship from outside; but the relevant debates in real politics are increasingly about the latter. As I said, this is not strictly speaking a part of the same "minorities-within-minorities" question as the remainder of this essay. But the two are likely

---

[6] In Israel, by contrast, the threat comes from the Haredim and the ultra-Orthodox Jewish political parties, which have leveraged their frequent position as political kingmakers into a veto over, for example, changes in the marriage law that governs even secular Israeli Jews.

[7] These *fatwas* have avoided being criminally punishable incitements to murder because they declared that only an Islamic state, not a private individual, was authorized to carry them out.

to intersect in practice; Bakri threatens gay Muslims as well as outsiders such as McNally.

In addition to having an effect on deliberations about immigration and citizenship policy as such, considerations such as these matter for one's view about the proper way to structure policies of multicultural accommodation. That is, *in addition* to worrying about designing policies that tend to artificially enhance the power a particular group of conservative elites has over group members, we need to worry about designing policies that inflate and entrench the political weight and resources such leaders have in their negotiations with the polity or the electorate as a whole. And we need to worry about this both as a matter of preserving the political liberal order in general and as a matter of protecting the polity's ability to offer refuge from the group to those who seek it.

III

Since Chandran Kukathas (1992a, 1992b, 1997) first made the idea of exit central to the cultural rights debate more than a decade ago, he has attracted much criticism for suggesting that the existence of a surrounding open market society would suffice to ensure the viability of exit rights. This has been taken as the language of complacency, as meaning that a standard involving freedom of exit was tantamount to inaction. Critics of Kukathas have mostly argued that real, effective freedom of exit required the state to constrain the internal activities of minority cultures, and that the *de facto* barriers that exist to exit mean that membership in minority cultures cannot be understood as voluntary in a morally meaningful way.

But perhaps the idea of the open society should not be assumed to be synonymous with our presently existing, unreformed liberal democracies. Once we understand that exit is a permanent part of the structure of relations between cultural communities and surrounding societies, that cultural and religious diversity entails that there will always be some who face a burdensome and wrenching need to leave their existing cultural or religious community, then we can begin to see freedom of exit as a standard that allows critical evaluation of the society being exited *to*. What kind of a society, governed by what kind of a state, will allow exit in a suitably safe way?[8]

---

[8] I think that much of what follows is compatible with Kukathas's most recent judgements, expressed in Kukathas (2003), but there are substantially different emphases. Others who have written in support of taking exit morally seriously and have paid attention to what this demands of the society being exited to include Spinner-Halev (1995, 2000) and Galston (2002).

It should of course be noted that this way of evaluating a liberal society is controversial. Michael Walzer (1983) famously criticized images of liberal politics that make the liberal polity into a safe, clean, characterless hotel room instead of allowing it to be a home. Evaluating the liberal polity as place of refuge is certain to cut against evaluating it as a solidaristic thick community, and this is true whether refuge is to be offered to inter-state migrants (the case Walzer had in mind) or to migrants from internal cultural and religious communities. But the more we remember the legitimate range and scope of internal rules governing such communities, the more we see that solidaristic thick communities are not absent from the liberal state. Reaffirming the rights of such communities is eminently compatible with evaluating the liberal society as a place of refuge (see, partially in response to Walzer, Shklar 1998a, 1998b, 1998c).

First of all, providing a safe place of refuge means providing safety. This is the sort of truism that is easy to overlook in theoretical discussions. But violence and threats of violence against dissidents and those who exit are far from unheard of; Bakri's *fatwas* are still in effect. Similarly, reports of death threats against Muslim or formerly Muslim women who publicly criticize Islam have become distressingly common even in Western societies.

A closely related point is that no religious or cultural body can be allowed to have a veto over the speech and association of dissidents and exiters – whether that veto is enforced by private violence or public law. Not only laws against apostasy and heresy but also statutes forbidding group libel or hate speech require the state to immunize orthodox groups against criticism, and therefore to silence their critics (who are, very often, members or former members). To the traditional liberal freedom of the schismatic we must add the freedom to form associations of gay Muslims, of Orthodox Jewish feminists, of Catholic supporters of abortion rights, and so on. The relevant religious bodies are of course free to excommunicate the members of these groups. But the associational rights of the dissidents must be as protected as the associational rights of the orthodox; and the orthodox cannot prevent the dissidents from referring to themselves as Muslims/ Jews/ Catholics and from criticizing orthodoxy. This, too, is a reason for worrying about the excess political power that some kinds of cultural rights deliver to status quo cultural and religious authorities.

These requirements are familiar ones, though they are neither trivial nor everywhere observed. One consideration not typically thought of as the sort of thing that is very relevant to a theory of justice is that the liberal society of refuge must be, to some significant degree, an urban one. Since the medieval birth of modern European cities and the civil society (in the original meaning) they embodied, cities have been a kind of refuge from the inequalities and unfreedoms of the surrounding world. The civil society ideology of the cities, which predated and helped to shape liberalism, did not recognize feudal hierarchies; it promised freedom from hereditary burdens to those who escaped to a city and lived there for a year and a day. And, as Walzer (1997) notes, the urban center of an empire (while typically not a civil society-city in the juristic sense) can serve a similar role, providing, for example, a place of refuge to those who inter-marry in violation of the code of separation and stability by which the empire governs its various populations. To this day, of course, celebrations of the city are likely to emphasize the possibility for self-recreation, for liberation from the past. Greater population densities, greater cultural plurality, and the self-reinforcing selection effects created by centuries of seeing cities as sites of refuge from provincial conservatism have combined to make cities attractive to those who find themselves unwelcome outliers elsewhere.

It is no accident that liberal (in multiple meanings of the word) cities have figured so prominently in the last few decades' progress for gays and lesbians. Cities provided, first, a place of refuge and safety from deeply hostile families and religions; second, sufficient populations to overcome the fact that homosexuality seems to be more or less randomly distributed through society with each generation, leaving gays and lesbians in thinly populated areas with little ability to find each other; third, sites for the development of increasingly self-conscious gay cultures and societies; and then, finally, a critical population mass and an institutional network that allowed for the increasingly confident insistence on justice from the state.

I do *not* mean to endorse the thought that cities embody liberalism and the provinces embody illiberalism, or to join in the urbanist critique of suburbia, each in their own way the expression of a vain hope that society will become more or less *completely* urban. I mean rather to say that liberal cities are a necessary complement to the fact that religious and cultural diversity on the societal level frequently means homogeneity on the local level. Given religious freedom and freedom of movement, local religious majorities tend to build up and to become self-perpetuating, even without committing any injustices. The diversity that liberal freedom allows will always mean that there are some societies and communities that are internally illiberal and inegalitarian in a variety of ways; if it were otherwise, we should have some reason to doubt that the polity really respected religious freedom. The liberal polity should not aim to remake all of these communities as civil societies or cities. But it must make sure that, for those in each generation who find themselves needing to leave such communities, there is another place to go.

Exit and refuge as tools for evaluating the liberal state suggest more ordinary legal and policy reforms as well. If the liberal polity is to offer freedom and refuge, it must genuinely differentiate itself from the communities being exited from. If the state's laws mirror the internal rules of the religious and cultural communities, then it can hardly claim to offer a viable alternative to them.

In the case of gays and lesbians this means first, and one would think most obviously, the state must not criminalize or prohibit consensual same-sex relations between adults, including sexual relations. If such laws are widely enforced, then the wider society will look at least as hostile as the original community. If they are not widely enforced, then they remain a tool for arbitrariness in the police and judicial systems, a standing threat against and reproach to gays and lesbians. Not regulating the sex lives of consenting adults is, of course, part of what it means for a state to be a liberal one that protects freedom. We do not need the idea of refuge or exit in order to justify the abolition of sodomy laws. But in this context it is worth reiterating that such abolition is a required part of the idea that the society into which exit is possible should be a liberal one.[9]

Second, and apparently much more controversially, the state must offer full equality before the law. In particular, the acceptance by the state of religions' full self-governance on matters of marriage and family has as a sort of flip-side that the public law of marriage and family ought not to be religiously governed. That is, same-sex marriage should stand on an equal *legal* footing with heterosexual marriage, in all matters including adoption. Doing so does not commit the liberal state to any view about how Catholicism, Judaism or Islam ought to govern marriage, any more than the existence of a no-fault divorce regime constitutes an attack on Catholic doctrine concerning divorce. The point is that the liberal state ought to make exit *really possible*, and not compel those who leave one of these religions to still be tacitly governed by it. Refocusing attention on exit forces us to refocus attention on the boundary between inside and outside, and to keep the public law of society here, outside, free from excessive influence by matters of religious doctrine.

It is not difficult to think of further examples of injustices committed against gays and lesbians by ostensibly liberal states that make the liberal polity's promise of refuge a partially hollow one. Printed and other media have been censored for their "homosexual content." Various state

[9] There is of course a very large literature on this question alone. Some of the most important contributions include: Hart 1963; Devlin 1965; Dworkin 1977; Finnis 1980; Feinberg 1985; Posner 1992; George 1994, 1996; Macedo 1995b; Sullivan 1995; George and Wolfe 2000. Obviously, for purposes of this piece I assume that the liberals are right and the new natural law theorists are wrong about the permissibility of sodomy laws.

employers, from the armed services to public schools, have been required to discriminate on the basis of sexual orientation. Each of these is unjust in its own right as well as being a violation of the obligation to provide genuine refuge. But there is something centrally important about marriage and family law. This is not only or even primarily because the injustice of discriminatory marriage law falls on many more people than does discriminatory military personnel policy. It is because marriage and family law represents the most direct, and most intentional, mirroring by the state of the internal rules of religious groups. In the modern world, churches *qua* churches have no militaries (other than the Vatican City's few rented Swiss guards) and they typically have no internal doctrine governing how armed forces should be structured. But religious rules governing marriage, family and sexual relations are ubiquitous; and they are treated as having authority in debates about the legal content of civil marriage. Even some liberal polities that have gone far towards the creation of same-sex marriage have retreated from the *word* "marriage," creating a new category called "civil unions." The religious meaning of marriage is treated as constraining its permissible legal meaning. But civil marriage has long since been desacralized in most Western states.[10] Marriages need not be performed by members of the clergy; indeed in some liberal democracies a marriage *must* be performed by a civil official in order to have legal force, and clerics do not have the status of "justice of the peace." Inter-religious marriage is freely allowed. Divorce is legally available regardless of the religious commitments of those in the marriage, even if those forbid divorce. Yet when the possibility of same-sex civil marriage is raised, it is treated as an assault on the religious traditions that deny the possibility of such a thing.

It need not be the case that legalizing gay marriage must be taken by members of the religious and cultural groups in question as constituting any kind of public attack on them. It could be the case that such groups are also well served by the availability of a secure site of refuge in the wider society, and by maintaining a clear separation between law and doctrine. One could at least easily imagine a religious group that (a) was firmly committed to its opposition to homosexuality and (b) would rather have ex-members than hypocritical members. The availability of genuine exit to a liberal society that is not governed by religious rules may offer a sort of safety valve for particularly strict religions; those who remain within the group will be those most able and willing to live according to its strictures. As I have said, the views of such groups towards exiting gay and lesbian members may vary; they may view them as sinners but prefer

---

[10] Israel, of course, is a prominent exception.

that they sin outside the tent than inside it. Conversely they may hold that it is better to be a sinner in communion with the true faith than a sinner not in such communion, in which case exit is not to be welcomed. But that is not the view taken by *all* the relevant religions.

More generally, religious views about homosexuality among non-members may vary. Some believers may view homosexuality as immoral for reasons internal to the faith, and have limited expectations for the godliness of outsiders in any event. Religions that view their religious morality as all of a piece may well take this view. This is, arguably, the perspective to expect from the Amish and from Orthodox Judaism. Some sects of conservative Protestantism might also take this approach, viewing the civil state as suspect and worldly, and therefore not viewing the state's actions as impugning or contaminating internal religious understandings. Conversely, Catholic natural law theory holds that homosexuality is prohibited, not by that aspect of divine law accessible only through revelation, but by natural law accessible to reason and binding on all. The reasons that Catholicism adduces to condemn homosexuality (like those it adduces to condemn abortion) are in principle reasons that apply to Catholics and non-Catholics alike. Islam, it seems to me, has a foot in each of these camps; but it considers exit doctrinally unacceptable in any case.

What the liberal state ought to do is not, in the final accounting, dependent on what conservative religious groups would like it to do. If such groups do construe the legalization of gay marriage or of same-sex sex as an assault on their integrity, then there may be nothing more to be said than "so be it." But the liberal state and its advocates can and should insist upon the difference between civil laws justified by public reason and the internal norms governing religious and cultural groups. They can and should reiterate that offering a genuine site of refuge, a place to exit to, is the flip-side of the considerable freedom such groups have to govern themselves and their members.

IV

The dilemma of gays and lesbians in minority religious groups or traditionalist cultures has not been much considered in the literature on multiculturalism and group rights. Sometimes gays and lesbians are listed as an oppressed group *alongside* members of minority cultures, as if these were non-overlapping categories, all subject to persecution at the same sets of hands. Even if the overlap is noticed, it may be only to say that, for example, African-American lesbians are doubly or triply oppressed by a heterosexist, sexist and racist society. There has been some work in recent years documenting the tensions about homosexuality, and the sometimes very anti-gay political movements, in relatively uninstitutionalized US ethnic groups such as African-Americans (e.g. Cohen 1999) and Hispanics. But criticism of the internal rules of more-institutionalized or normatively thicker cultures and religions has proceeded mostly in terms of women and unconsenting children. Nussbaum (1999), for instance, contains extensive treatments of both religion, culture and cultural relativism, on the one hand, and of the rights of gays and lesbians on the other, but these topics are not brought together. When she looks at cultural and religious traditions and their potential for illiberalism, she is discussing gender equality and the freedom of women. When she considers discrimination based on sexual orientation, she is discussing the public law of the United States. Female genital mutilation, forced marriage, polygamy, *Sati* and gender-discriminatory religious legal codes are all analyzed as part of a discussion of cultural relativism and moral universalism that ranges from sub-Saharan Africa to India to China to Eskimo tribes. Discrimination against gays and lesbians is absent from those discussions, and the chapters on gay and lesbian rights hardly glance outside the boundaries of the United States.[11] I single out this book only because it at least treats gay rights and multiculturalism within the same set of covers. Typically in treatments of the latter subject, the former is absent altogether. *Mea culpa*; this is as true of my own discussion of internal rules, customary law and internal cruelty (Levy 2000: 51–62, 142–50, 161–96) as it is of anyone else's.

This may be because the mistreatment of women has a kind of exotic variety from case to case and culture to culture – foot-binding, veiling, virginity testing and all the rest – while the enforcement of taboos on homosexuality are depressingly similar from case to case. But I think the greater reason for the silence lies elsewhere. (In my own case, I hope that it does.) I suspect it has simply been assumed that gays and lesbians in religions – and encompassing cultures, such as Romany culture (Lee 2001) – that forbid homosexuality will *of course* sometimes have to exit.[12] Preventing Indian tribes from discriminating against religious minorities or preventing religious minorities from discriminating against women seems possible; preventing cultural and religious groups

---

[11] This is all the more remarkable, and unfortunate, because Nussbaum has taken very public positions in defense of gay and lesbian rights in India, and has written elsewhere about such matters.

[12] As a sociological observation about academia, it might seem odd to think that this assumption has been widely made, given that no such assumption was automatic in the case of a purely voluntary association, the Boy Scouts of America. Nonetheless, I think that the assumption has been, tacitly, very widespread.

from condemning homosexuality seems implausible. But if this is so, then we have been taking for granted both that conservative religions and encompassing cultures have the right to have deeply illiberal and inegalitarian internal rules, and that exit even from such encompassing groups is not only possible but routine. These assumptions have not then been carried over into other discussions of minorities, or women, within minorities.

9   On exit

Oonagh Reitman

The idea that a member of a cultural minority ought to be able to exit from his or her community plays many roles in thinking about multicultural-ism. I can see three roles for exit: first, in its most passive role – which I shall refer to as exit's "basic role" – exit simply figures as an option open to a member of a minority community as a citizen of the wider society. Here, exit exists as a derivative feature of a certain type of social ordering of culturally diverse – that of contemporary liberal democratic states.

However, when exit appears in multiculturalism theory, the roles it is asked to perform tend to be more active. One role – which I shall denote exit's "protective role" – calls upon exit to protect vulnerable group members against the oppression which they may suffer at the hands of their groups. The argument here is that exit can be relied upon to enable the group member to escape oppression by leaving the group.

The other role – which I shall label the "transformative role" – is related to the protective role in that both are concerned with remedy-ing oppressive minority practices. Here, the claim is that exit can help cure a group of the oppressive elements of its distinct practices by exert-ing pressure to bring about their reform. Change will become desirable, perhaps inevitable, according to the argument for exit's transformative role, in order to prevent mass exodus through exit and thereby cultural annihilation.

In this chapter, I defend exit's basic role but reject its protective and transformative roles. The chapter is in three parts. The first supports the

I am grateful to Jeff Spinner-Halev and Avigail Eisenberg for the chance to participate in the Minorities within Minorities Conference and for very helpful comments on the paper presented there, and thanks to the other participants. I received helpful comments from Anne Phillips and Moira Dustin on an earlier draft. Many thanks to Sophia Reitman-Voignac, Cecile Fabre, Bernard Jackson, Tariq Modood and Joseph Raz who read and commented on material on which this chapter is based. A conversation with Jeremy Rosen helped me to think more clearly about exit and the Jewish law system and a conversation with Susan Weiss gave me insights into divorce practice in Israel. Thanks are due to the British Academy and Nuffield Foundation for financial support.

basic role of exit. The second, principal part argues that exit cannot be relied upon to justify a given regime of multicultural accommodation or toleration through its alleged protective and transformative properties. The conclusion of this section is that whenever we are tempted to give exit either of these two additional roles, we ought to take this as a sign that further avenues ought to be explored so as better to discharge the state's duties in respect of oppression suffered by minorities within minorities.

In the final part of the chapter, I argue that reliance on exit can be attributed to a misplaced non-interventionist reticence to become involved in the internal regulation which goes on within cultural minority communities. When theorists rely on exit, I sense they do so because they misguidedly think that there are no more promising avenues to be explored and that exit is the best mechanism on offer. Here, I shall suggest, albeit only superficially in the space available, that it ought to be possible for the state to provide remedies to internal oppression which are more effective than exit, in both its protective and transformative properties, but which do not, at the same time, necessarily give reason for anti-interventionism.

Exit's basic role

The basic role of exit is a component of a larger theory of justice. It is a by-product of a particular type of multicultural nation state – not the millet nor the empire (e.g. Kymlicka 1992: 35–40 and Walzer 1997: 14–19 respectively), in which each cultural grouping engages in self-regulation; nor the association of communities model (e.g. Kukathas 1997), in which the state's primary regulatory function extends only to the superstructure in which the various communities coexist. It is, rather, the contemporary, cosmopolitan liberal democratic state which engages in extensive regulation. Here, a right of exit is essentially the opportunity for a member of a particular cultural community to be or become a member of society in an unmediated manner, without going through the group and without becoming subject to its regulatory power. The basic right of exit exists when there is a direct regulatory link between the individual and the state.

Take the regulation of divorce under Jewish law. Members of Jewish communities around the world are required by Jewish law to respect particular rules in order to terminate their marriages. Now compare the situation of Jews settled in France with those settled in Israel. The French Jew has the benefit of the locally applicable French divorce regime. Her conscience may require her to submit to the Jewish divorce regime – most interpretations of Jewish law would not recognize her French divorce. But she would not be compelled to do so: she has a right of exit by virtue of her relationship to the French state since there is another system of regulation available to her under French law.

Compare this with divorce under Israeli law, essentially a relic of the colonial/Ottoman millet-model for ordering culturally plural societies, in which each cultural group is accorded regulative autonomy over its own members. Here, there is no formal right of exit – there is no state alternative given that group divorce is state divorce. Informal mechanisms of exit have been attempted: some take advantage of overseas civil marriage regimes whose acts are given recognition under Israeli (private international) law. Others may opt to forgo marriage in favour of a regime of cohabitation, itself increasingly bolstered by state protections to bring that regime closer to that of marriage. Statistics suggest that Israeli couples are increasingly taking this option (Hirschberg 1998: 9).

A couple may not succeed in escaping the regulatory reach of religious law on divorce in this way. Under Jewish law a marriage can be deemed to have taken place quite easily – even in the absence of an Orthodox marriage ceremony – and therefore these quasi-exit strategies may be of limited use, at least at the official level, although they would no doubt offer greater leeway for maneuvering around problems shorn up by Jewish law should the relevant arbiter of that law be amenable and sympathetic.

The difference between France and Israel here is that the former offers a formal basic right of exit in respect of divorce regulation whereas the latter does not. In fact, in the French case, the right is more a right not to opt in than a right to opt out. That is, submission to Jewish law is, from the perspective of the state, something which a Jew may or may not decide to do as a matter of conscience. Although most interpreters of Jewish law will not regard submission to French law as sufficient, a French Jew can choose to submit to the French divorce regime alone, without (also) submitting to the Jewish divorce regime. In Israel, where this choice is not available, the campaign for a right of exit is made in the context of larger debates about the character of the nation state and, in particular, how to pursue its parallel goals of being a Jewish homeland and a modern democracy. The right of exit emerges as the present model gives way fully to that of the modern democratic state.[1]

---

[1] The reason there is no exit in Israel is bound up with Jewish nationalism and, as we shall see later, with the place of Jewish marriage laws in the constitution of the Jewish people. Submission to these laws acts as a symbol of, and is perceived as a precondition for, the state's Jewish character (see generally e.g. Raday 1996; and Halperin-Kaddari 2000). The success of Shinui in the 2003 elections, standing largely on the issue of secularism, can be taken as a sign that the argument at this more general level has gained significant ground. Where I use the example of Jewish divorce law in the ensuing discussion, I am referring to that law as it is applied in the Diaspora and not in Israel except where expressly stated.

Exit's protective and transformative roles

The argument for the basic role of exit does not depend on a showing of oppression – the argument about religious compulsion is sufficient. However, the existence of oppression makes the argument all the more compelling. In the Israeli case, for instance, the fact that there is no formal right of exit exacerbates the oppression which arises in the operation of Jewish divorce. The patriarchal essence of these rules can be abusively deployed by unscrupulous husbands, with few or inadequate mechanisms of protection. The scope for harm stems particularly from the rule that divorce is dependent upon the husband's consent – there is no judicial divorce under Jewish law, albeit that the procedure for divorce has a judicial feel in that, owing to its complexity, the expert supervision and counsel of a court of law (*beth din*) is required. At the core of that procedure, however, lies the husband's consent – only he can give his wife the *get* (the bill of divorce) without which she stands to suffer greatly: quite apart from the impossibility of achieving closure and the clean break needed in order to move on, she cannot remarry within the Orthodox faith. Until she receives her *get*, sex with another man constitutes adultery. (The refusing husband, on the other hand, need worry only about the marital status of his subsequent sexual partner since Jewish law's definition of adultery refers solely to female marital status.) Any issue of an adulterous union is stigmatized as a *mamzer* – a status which bars that person, and that person's issue and generations thereafter, from full membership in the community.[2]

To avoid these consequences, women are blackmailed into striking patriarchal bargains: in exchange for the husband's consent, they strike unfair deals in respect of matters ancillary to the divorce – as regards the distribution of income and capital and even arrangements in respect of children.[3]

Exit is called upon in debates about multiculturalism in order to attend to oppression of this kind and to the plight of minorities within minorities more generally (e.g. Barry 2001a: 148–54; Benhabib 2002: 19–20, 131–2 and 149; Galston 1995; Kukathas 1992a and 1997; Shachar 2001: 122–6; Spinner-Halev 2000: ch. 3; and Raz 1994: 184, 187). Women should be protected against oppression by ensuring access to an alternative forum

---

[2] This is the Orthodox account of Jewish law. As we shall see, although other branches of Judaism have developed different rules, they tend to conform to the Orthodox standard as much as possible because of problems of community cohesion.

[3] Although women also have to consent to a Jewish divorce, there are two key differences: first, Jewish law solutions have been found to get around the wife's refusal to consent; second, given the definition of adultery, a man does not necessarily suffer the same sorts of consequences if he proceeds without a *get*.

for the regulation of divorce – one which offers women terms which are more just.

Here, the argument for exit appeals to the protective and transformative roles and applies just as well to Israel – where the basic role is also canvassed – as to France, where the basic right is already available. Yet it is at this point that the argument weakens. Both the protective and the transformative roles are hindered by the limited realizability of rights of exit. A comparison between France and Israel here is instructive, especially one which compares the secular sector of society, for whom communal membership may be of less value, on the one hand; and the more religious and communally affiliated, on the other. The position of the former differs radically as between France and Israel given the possibility of exit. But for the religious and committed members of the community, the position is broadly the same in both countries, notwithstanding that only one offers the possibility of exit.

The reason is that the formal right of exit suffers from difficulties of realizability which are especially marked as regards the more religious and communally affiliated members of society. Here, it is difficult to see what might be done to erase these difficulties and secure conditions which would make exit a realizable option. The argument of the next section is that if exit is not possible for some people then it cannot be relied upon to further the protective and transformative roles claimed of it as regards these people.

The cost of exit

Broadly speaking, there are two orders of obstacle to exit: a material one and what one might term a socio-psychological one. The material obstacles to exit are remediable to some degree by way of state policy. Although many exit defenders attend to this question, not all do – Chandran Kukathas, for instance, probably exit's most influential defender, is minimalist on this point: although he acknowledges that the right of exit is much more potent when the "formal right comes with substantive opportunities" (1992a: 128), and although he speaks in terms of an individual having "*substantial* freedom to leave" (1992a: 133), he seems unwilling to impose any minimum guarantees. On education, for instance, he is explicit that it is not the business of the state to interfere in the education of the young, even when it is of such a nature as to deprive them of the education needed in order to appreciate and manage their options, including that of exit (1992a: 126).

In his early writing, Kukathas suggests the state would be entitled to enforce certain minimum guarantees, which he lists as freedom from slavery; physical coercion; and cruel, inhuman and degrading treatment (1992a: 128). In later writing however, he seems to advocate the toleration of practices which he had earlier suggested might be covered by these minimum guarantees, notably female genital mutilation (compare 1992a: 138 n.88 with 2002: 195 and 197).

Some of exit's defenders are, however, more concerned to see that the conditions necessary for the exercise of rights of exit are met. Some address these worries by way of more comprehensively drawn generally applicable laws. No doubt Kukathas is assuming that generally applicable laws would be likely to provide the minimum guarantees enumerated in his earlier work, the nub of the issue lying in the question of how widely to draft generally applicable laws – Kukathas would want only those laws necessary for the ordered functioning of a scaled-down libertarian state; others would want more comprehensive state policies which would serve better to guarantee the material conditions necessary for exit. These include minimum standards of education so as to enable the exiting member to have an appreciation of his or her lifestyle choices and to acquire the basic skills necessary to survive in a different cultural environment; as well as the minimum economic wherewithal to enable the member to survive without the financial support of family and community (e.g. Spinner-Halev 2000; Galston 1995; Barry 2001a).

A number of theorists provide for specific measures to address the difficulties of exit, not content to rely on generally applicable laws. Jeff Spinner-Halev, for instance, suggests an exit fund to enable people to be compensated for the economic disadvantage of exit (2000: 77–9). Ayelet Shachar focuses on economic conditions for exit as well and, helpfully in this context, uses the Jewish divorce example to illustrate what she claims to be an enhanced version of exit which addresses obstacles to its realizability. She wants the economic aspects of divorce to be automatically regulated by the state's more egalitarian or equitable system of wealth distribution so as to ensure that economic factors do not bar the freedom of women (see 2001: 124–5 and 134–5).

Shachar's exit may well look enhanced or advantageous in a country such as Israel, where the option is not available. It is not clear why it would help in a country such as France, where there is both a formal right of exit and (something approaching) equitable distribution as regards financial matters.[4] Many women who do not exercise their rights of exit from

---

[4] As we shall continue to see, Shachar's work makes best sense in relation to the Israeli multicultural context (see 2001: xi) but may not transpose well to many other contexts given that Jews form the Israeli polity's dominant majority. Cf. Spinner-Halev 2001: 93 (criticizing Shachar for failing to distinguish between oppressed and non-oppressed groups, Jewish Israel being a bad example because the protected group is not oppressed).

Jewish divorce regulation – facing entrapment and blackmail instead – are not prevented by material obstacles. Many are highly educated and many are rich – indeed, material wealth is at the very root of the blackmail here. Jewish divorce offers husbands the occasion to bargain for something which women have, whether by private wealth or state law entitlement (although, there are also clearly cases where men act simply out of spite, with no material motive). As Sharon Shenhav, an influential advocate and campaigner on Jewish divorce, has said, "a norm . . . all [in the community] accept [is] . . . that when there is a Jewish divorce . . . the wife, has to pay something for that divorce, and it can be an amount that is commensurate with her financial position" (1998: 4; cf. Mizrahi 1992, confirming the practice to be widespread in Canada where women have both exit rights and financial guarantees under state law). The provision of substantive financial guarantees would act, if anything, as a bargaining chip, swallowed up by the patriarchal undercurrent created by the operation of Jewish law in the informal sphere, rendering ineffective the guarantees formally provided in the public sphere in which state law officially operates.

The obstacles faced in these circumstances are more socio-psychological than material – they are born of belief and psychological make-up; of fear of ostracism by family, friends, associates and community. One may fear the loss of moral support and the sense of belonging and rootedness derived from community. Or one may simply fear change and the unknown. The idea of rupture with one's family and the people with whom one is closest is pretty hard to conceive in any situation. On top of these difficulties, one can add obstacles which stem from the fact that cultural membership can be pervasively defining of one's sense of self.

Take the case of Jewish divorce – here, exit would mean not abiding by what is perceived to be God's command. For some, this might be tantamount to suggesting that they cut off a limb or undergo a procedure which would render them unrecognizably different. It is simply not an option which they are capable of taking given who they are and the life they have, the commitments they have formed and the projects they have acquired and nurtured (e.g. Green 1994: 111; Razack 1994: 910–12).

Even for those whose affiliation is more ethnic than religious, exit may be equally unrealizable given that abiding by Jewish law on divorce is considered a significant, even constitutive, part of what being Jewish means. The influential Orthodox Jewish feminist Blu Greenberg lists divorce as one of a small number of acts which are, "quite simply, the way a Jew lives. This is how Jews have done these things for several millennia; this is the manner in which one marks oneself as a Jew today" (1981: 140).

Jewish divorce rules should not be written off as those adhered to by a small minority "frozen in the shtetl" (Barry 2002: 224). To the contrary, even some of the most modern and secular of community members may be committed to their observance. The reason is that divorce rules are boundary-marking – the penalty of non-observance under Jewish law is a form of communal exclusion (the *mamzer* status) which endures in one's progeny.

While the material obstacles to exit can be satisfied by the kind of background state commitments to education and welfare ordinarily defended within comprehensive liberal theory, the socio-psychological costs of exit are not so readily addressable by state action. Here, there is little the state can do (e.g. Spinner-Halev 2000: 72; Barry 2001a: 150–1). Even once the material difficulties of exit are addressed, the socio-psychological costs endure and they are likely to do so for as long as the underlying patriarchy endures. In these circumstances, the protective properties of exit are seriously circumscribed.

The mechanism of exit is also usually claimed to have transformative properties, over and above, and intertwined with, its protective properties. These are called upon to attend to oppression such as that occasioned in the Jewish divorce example, but the next section gives reason for doubt.

The counter-productive ricochet of exit's transformative potential

To focus on exit's costs and difficulties is to overlook the transformative effect of the mere threat of exit, a force which works without actual exit having to take place; that is, without having to pay the kinds of costs and difficulties just discussed. As Albert Hirschman argued in another context, the simple power to threaten exit allows one greater voice in influencing the course of events so as to take away the need for exit (1970), a thesis which has inspired similar arguments in the minority context, with regard to minorities within minorities (e.g. Kukathas 1992a: 128 and 133; Shachar 2001: 117 and 122; Spinner-Halev 2001: 89–90; Raz 1994: 180; Barry 2002: 224). The mere possibility of exit can exert a transformative force on the oppressive culture, leading to its progressive cultural reform. Here, protection against oppression suffered by minorities within minorities can be afforded without or with significantly reduced socio-psychological costs.

Those who see in exit a transformative potential tend to rely on minority groups displaying group self-preservation instincts which would cause evasive action to be taken to prevent women from exiting (e.g. Shachar 2001: 140). The thinking seems to be that the leaders of a minority culture would reform the patriarchal aspects of that culture in order to avoid mass exit.

While this is a reasonable definition of survival, it is not the only one and may not be the one most likely to arise in the multicultural context, especially not that involving a minority whose existence is beleaguered under conditions of cultural diversity (as most are, to varying degrees). In such circumstances, cultural change can be resisted in reaction to contact with the surrounding multicultural environment, a contact which exit and even the threat of exit merely exacerbate.

Cultural identity is constructed relationally. It consists in marking off that which is other, that which a given group of people with a common identity asserts itself not to be. Gender is highly significant to this process. Whereas sex difference is universal, gender difference, as a cultural construct, tends to vary from culture to culture, and these differences in gender ascriptions serve to distinguish cultures from each other.

One manifestation of this differentiation process is when cultures stake their difference with reference to the values of feminism. Leaders of traditionally patriarchal cultures sometimes define their cultures in opposition to feminism – almost as if feminism defines what the culture is not. It is perceived as a force which arises and ought to exist outside of the community, as antithetical to its core values and beliefs.

It is not clear that the definition of survival which undergirds the thesis on exit's transformative properties would tally with the definition of survival given by a minority's leadership. If, for them, feminism has become defining of what the group is not, then survival means resisting rather than acceding to claims for feminist reform. Here, change in regard to issues concerning women might well be viewed as the first step down a slippery slope at the end of which lies cultural annihilation and full-scale assimilation.

The case of Jewish law, and Jewish divorce in particular, does not support the claim as to the transformative potential of exit. In this section I argue that, although exit has acted as a spur to the emergence of break-away movements within Judaism, offering women alternatives to Orthodox regulation, as regards the prospects of achieving reform of the underlying patriarchy within Jewish divorce regulation, the picture is unsatisfactory because of two factors. First, Orthodoxy's self-definition can be viewed in relational terms as an opposition to the very movements which have suggested reform as a way of avoiding total exit from Judaism. The reforms of the more progressive streams tend to be cast as a corruption of Jewish law and ruled out, resulting in a retrenchment within Orthodoxy. The second factor is that the different denominations within Judaism have limited regulatory autonomy in the domain of status regulation because of its work in the constitution of the larger group to which all the denominations belong – the Jewish people. Here, there is a degree of harmonization between the different denominations. Were the harmonization generally in the direction of greater reform, the thesis as to exit's transformative potential would be satisfied. In the Jewish divorce example, the opposite is true: harmonization is to the position of the most unyielding, namely that of Orthodoxy. This example shows how the transformative force of exit can perversely end up making it harder to achieve change in the multicultural context and so prove counter-productive in the long run.

Exit and factionalism within Judaism   A slightly modified version of the argument as to exit's transformative potential highlights the possibility that dissident members could join or form a more egalitarian version of their culture (e.g. Kukathas 1992a 117; cf. Barry 2002, 224, noting that this is what most have done). Here, although exit is indeed exercised, its costs are minimized by the fact that exit takes the form of entry into a community with similar characteristics to that left behind – indeed it could in theory be the same, in all characteristics, other than those which caused the need for exit.

One imagines, for instance, that an Orthodox Jew could choose to join an alternative movement within Judaism – Conservative, Reform, Reconstructionist and so on. The desire to avoid exit was a significant driving force behind the emergence of branches Ashkenazi Jewry which have come to rival Orthodoxy. For instance, in a letter explaining the reasons for their "Great Secession," the label given to the nascent Reform movement in Britain in the mid-nineteenth century, the reformists explained that their movement was intended

to arrest, and prevent secession from Judaism – an overwhelming evil . . . Most fervently do we cherish the hope that the effect of these improvements will be to inspire a deeper interest, and a stronger feeling towards our holy religion, and that their influence on the minds of the youth of either sex, will be calculated to restrain them from traversing in their faith, or contemplating for a moment the fearful step of forsaking their religion, so that henceforth no "Israelite born", may cease to exclaim, "Hear, O! Israel, the Lord our God, the Lord is one!" (quoted in Englander 1994, 197; emphasis omitted)

While this shows that exit has transformative potential, it yields a counter-productive secondary effect stemming from the fact that the different denominations within Judaism define themselves largely in opposition to one another and their differing positions on various matters including, in near unrivaled primacy, the question of gender.

If non-Orthodox movements become defined as reacting to exit by reforming gender oppressive laws then Orthodoxy risks becoming defined as not doing so. On this view, survival of Orthodoxy might be considered best assured by resisting the appeasement shown by progressive movements in the face of modernist demands such as feminism. The key to survival may not be to avoid exit but the reformist ideology the threat of exit encourages. Indeed, tenacity and fidelity to existing interpretations of the law may themselves become the mark of the culture's resilience, the feminist calls of women standing here as a symbol of the encroachment of the surrounding culture. Orthodox leaders want to ensure ideological purity and the pursuit of what is perceived to be God's command. They may have little interest in bolstering numbers as such, preferring to soldier on with those whose commitment is beyond question. Better, the leaders might think, to let those of dubious commitment exit, while perhaps putting pressure, instead, on remaining members to make up the numbers with yet higher birth-rates. To do otherwise, so the argument goes, would be survival in some kind of diluted and mangled form and, although numbers might be propped up for a generation, perhaps two, this would not be survival but eventual assimilation.

The existence of break-away factions can serve to delegitimize the campaigns of those seeking to change the patriarchal aspects of Orthodox understandings of Jewish law. Since ideas about gender significantly differentiate the various Judaic branches from one another, one might argue that a member who objects to the patriarchy of Orthodox understandings of Jewish divorce law is free to find a more suitable community in one of the more progressive streams which explicitly define themselves, and are differentiated from Orthodoxy, in reference to patriarchy. If the original community is, in some significant way, constituted by adherence to a hierarchical, indeed patriarchal, normative system (as is the case, say, of Orthodox Judaism), then questioning that hierarchical and patriarchal ordering, as many Orthodox feminists do, could be taken as a loss of cultural membership which exit merely confirms. Indeed, as we have seen, some of exit's defenders rely on something approaching this argument in downplaying the costs of exit.

Those who challenge minority patriarchy may be branded traitors to the culture – they are said to be "puppets of western feminists"; and "offshoots of western imperialism" (Yuval-Davis 1997: 121). Their demands are perceived as the product of "'outside' influences" (Moghissi 1999: 216) "and therefore not legitimate" (Yuval-Davis 1992: 284; cf. Aull Davies 1996: 166).

The symbolism of exit, as egress, may undermine efforts to reform the underlying patriarchy within a culture by linking reform and remedies to internal oppression with what goes on outside, in the surrounding society. To win adherents to their arguments, those campaigning for feminist reform face the additional hurdle of having to demonstrate that their arguments are not those of the break-away movements; that they are, rather, legitimate arguments made in the language of authentic Orthodoxy.

The relational nature of Orthodoxy's self-definition is manifest on the question of divorce: in her description of what the different branches of Judaism have done in response to the oppressions of Jewish divorce, after detailing the various measures taken by the other streams, Blu Greenberg summarily states that "[b]eyond rejecting the strides taken by Conservative Judaism [which is the closest of the more progressive branches to Orthodox Judaism] there has been little movement" within the Orthodox world (1981: 138).

Retrogressive harmonization: the resilience of orthodoxy   While the experience of bifurcation within Ashkenazi Judaism can be taken as a sign of the transformative potential of exit, it is hard to describe the overall result as progressive. Where transformation has been most effective is in matters such as the participation of women in religious ceremonies and the elevation of women to positions of leadership within the religious structure – matters on which each denomination has greater regulatory autonomy and in relation to which women can truly be said to be offered an alternative to Orthodoxy.[5] The position is different as regards the regulation of divorce because of its work in delineating the physical boundary of the larger group of which the different denominations are part.

Orthodoxy has been the most intransigent of the denominations in the face of demands for law reform on divorce. Yet it is to the Orthodox position that all ultimately conform so as to ensure cohesion of the group as a whole. While the more progressive Judaic movements have departed, to varying degrees, from the gender inequality of Orthodox understandings of Jewish divorce, in practice they tend to conform to Orthodox standards in the interests of fostering community cohesion. This is done in view of the divisiveness of the communal exclusions which ensue as a result of non-compliance with Jewish law on divorce. As we have seen, the progeny of women who flout these rules will be branded with the status of *mamzer*, which effectively creates a two-tiered community with marriage between the tiers impossible according to Orthodox understandings. As a result,

---

[5] Not that this would necessarily make exit easier since gender issues, though significant, are not the sum total of that which distinguishes the different branches from each other. A woman accustomed to the Orthodox way of life may feel unable to belong in a non-Orthodox setting (and *vice-versa*).

the more progressive movements are reticent entirely to dispense with the patriarchal rules for fear of communal fragmentation. Many promulgate a more egalitarian interpretation of the rules while privately recommending compliance with Orthodoxy. In Britain, for instance, the Liberal and Progressive movement, which diverges most from Orthodoxy, deems a civil divorce sufficient to terminate the couple's marriage – there is no official need for the *get* (Goodkin and Citron 1994: 81). The American Reform movement adopts a similar attitude. Yet even though the *get* has been officially dispensed with, rabbis in these movements continue, on the whole, to recommend that their divorcing congregants proceed with the *get* under the auspices of an Orthodox rabbinical court (Jacob 2001: 187–97, especially 193). The British Reform movement goes one stage further by making this official policy (Montagu 2001).

True, these movements do offer women an exit option when faced with an absolutely intransigent husband. The Reform movement, for instance, will issue a document permitting remarriage in such cases (Jacob 2001: 187–97). The non-Orthodox streams bend to Orthodox standards but not to the point of endorsing the husband's entrapment of his wife.

That said, the patriarchy of Orthodox interpretations of Jewish law continues to have an effect in the regulation of divorce even amongst members of the non-Orthodox movements. Many members of the more progressive movements continue to be reluctant to take up the opportunity of exit even though doing so would be in compliance with non-Orthodox understanding. Many take advantage of provisions within state law which have been put in place to help fight against entrapment and blackmail arising under Orthodox interpretations of Jewish law (Syrtash 1992: 117–18). They do so in the hope of avoiding the negative consequences of exit. Unjust bargains are reached when the climate in which people bargain is unduly weighted in favor of one side. The fact that state law mechanisms are being used here, and the fact that non-Orthodox rabbis privately continue to advise compliance with Orthodox standards, suggest that unjust background conditions are likely to be present in the divorce bargaining which takes place even amidst non-Orthodox Jewry. The patriarchal shadow cast by Orthodox understandings of Jewish divorce requirements extends as far as the non-Orthodox realm – perhaps, in these reaches, the shadow is less dense because of the existence of exit but it is cast nevertheless.

Designing exit

I want here to consider Ayelet Shachar's proposal for a formalized, institutionalized type of partial exit. It is exemplary of the types of claims which are made of exit yet attempts to sidestep some of the objections highlighted in the foregoing discussion. Like many of exit's defenders (e.g. Kukathas 1997: 87), Shachar is cognizant of exit's weak realizability. Indeed, she criticizes others for their reliance on exit on this very ground (2000a: 79–80; cf. 1998b: 111 n. 77). Yet exit continues to play a significant role in her proposals and as such her design of exit offers a good testing-ground for seeing whether exit can survive scrutiny.

Shachar envisages that the minority group and the state would deliberate over and agree a form of regulative power-sharing arrangement whereby the group would get a tranche of regulation, one condition of which is the provision of a pre-agreed form of partial exit in favor of state regulation so as to protect the group member against entrapment and oppression should the need arise (2001: 122–6).

Exit may well continue to be pretty ineffective notwithstanding the institutional fortification and the other measures which Shachar proposes to reduce the costs of exit. In the Jewish divorce example, this is especially true when one considers the case of observant members.

Jewish law requires disputes to be resolved by a religious court. If an observant woman wants to submit to civil law, she must obtain permission from a competent rabbi and that permission can only be granted if specified circumstances exist (e.g. Epstein 1989: 19, 23–4). While Jewish law encourages respect for the law of the land (under the principle of *dina demalchusa dina*), that law cannot contradict Jewish law.

From the perspective of Jewish law, the act of submission to a state court tends to be recast as confirmation of the religious court's determinations. The state court is here the religious court's rubber-stamp: the latter's determinations are presented in state court as an out-of-court settlement between the parties which is barely vetted by an already overstretched state court system. Submission to civil law serves to give the determinations of the minority legal system greater force of law by having these incorporated into the acts of the state legal system, and thereby benefit from greater coercive powers of enforcement in ensuring that minority legal acts are given effect in the multicultural environment in which minority law is relegated to the private sphere.

If a woman goes to the civil court in order to obtain treatment she deems more favorable than that which she can expect at the hands of the religious court – say, on ancillary matters – she may well suffer negative consequences, in terms of social ostracism and communal reprimand, for deigning to flout the authority of the religious legal system (cf. Raday 1996: 233). Going "to the civil courts because [one] can get a 'better deal' there is tantamount to stealing" since one is not deemed entitled to that which is surplus under Jewish law (Epstein 1989: 23). Nadine Brodsky, of the advocacy group Jewish Women for Justice, has said that "[t]o go to secular court is considered the greatest offense a Jewish person can commit" (quoted in Graham 2000: 46). A rabbi writing on divorce has described the act of going to a secular court as being as bad as blasphemy and "taking up arms against the torah" (Malinowitz 1994).

Shachar envisages that exit would be pre-agreed in advance by the group, suggesting that it would set in place a kind of exit which might be considered most acceptable from its perspective – one which would not give rise to these impediments. But in the Jewish divorce case, it is hard to see what sort of exit might be designed to fit the bill. The fact that the group may pre-agree a right of exit as part of the multicultural deliberation Shachar proposes does not, of itself, help here for that agreement may simply be the product of the politics of multiculturalism – a necessary expedient to which the group would accede as a formal matter in order to obtain its slice of the regulative pie. Informally, however, exit may well continue to be made sufficiently unattractive that women feel they cannot opt for it. Whether partial exit would be possible depends on many factors, including, most centrally, the attitude of others in the group and the significance of the domain of regulation from which exit is made. If the practice is of constitutive importance to the group, and if abidance by it is an important signifier of membership, it may well be that exit would be little tolerated, with the exiting member being shunned and ostracized, even if a formally agreed exit option has been put in place.

For women who presently cannot or do not exit, Shachar's version of exit is unlikely to change matters. But what of women who presently can and do exit? In the Diaspora, exit simply means not exercising one's voluntary right to submit to the additional minority regulatory system operating in the private sphere. Indeed, some women currently exit without even knowing that they are doing so, unaware of the need for a *get* because of assimilation and secularism. One feature of Shachar's transformative accommodation is that groups would acquire compulsory and automatic jurisdiction over status determination. For these women, exit becomes a much more formal procedure since they would have compulsorily to submit to the minority's regulation and then formally to exit from it after a given period of time. (She does not suggest how long the "specified separation period" would have to be but presumably it would have to be long enough to enable the condition for its exercise to have arisen, namely the group's failure to "offer a meaningful remedy" (2001: 135)). An advantage to group leaders concerned about community cohesion perhaps; but hardly a victory for women subject or potentially subject to the patriarchy of Jewish divorce regulation.

To the extent that exit proves to be necessary and exercisable, Shachar's exit has the advantage of offering a "comprehensive policy approach" rather than "a case-by-case approach" (cf. 2000a: 79), enabling the exiting member to take advantage of a predetermined exit procedure (rather than having to navigate through the various obstacles from scratch), presumably with some kind of institutional back-up which would smooth the process and take away some of the pressure. But this advantage is gained at too great a price, since it entails compulsory submission to a patriarchal divorce system, and could be achieved by means which are less costly – for instance, a non-governmental organization could be set up within civil society with the aim of helping women through the process of exit by pooling resources and sharing experiences. One can think here of the work of Hilel, an Israeli volunteer organization set up by ex-members "to help ease the transition from the strictly Orthodox . . . world to a more secular lifestyle" (Cowan 2000).

Non-interventionism and exit

In the remaining space, I shall briefly argue that reliance on exit is born of an understandable but misplaced reticence to become involved in struggles to eliminate patriarchy arising in the minority context. Exit appears to be an attractive option for managing the problem of minorities within minorities because it is perceived to involve minimal interference with minority life.

First, one should note that measures to make exit more realizable are likely to detract from its non-interventionist nature. Hilel, for instance, has unsurprisingly "provoked the ire of many in strictly Orthodox circles" (Cowan 2000), precisely because it is perceived to be intervening to encourage people to exit. In such circumstances, the non-interference properties of exit appear lost.

The answer is not to retreat to a less interventionist form of exit, such as that proposed by Kukathas. The foregoing critique has given reason to doubt the protective and transformative properties of exit. Something else must be sought to attend to internal oppression. In looking for such an alternative, we ought not to lose sight of the risks of intervention, for these are quite considerable.

There is the risk that the struggle against patriarchy could become conscripted to racist or xenophobic forces in which the minority culture would be denigrated and attacked in the guise of concern for women's rights (e.g. Kukathas 1997: 88–9). This phenomenon is no stranger to the political landscape nor to popular imagination, where perceived maltreatment of women is ever present as the negative stereotype of minority cultures. The phenomenon of Islamophobia is the prime example of this for our time, in which "claims about otherness and inferiority" rely on a central claim that "Muslim cultures mistreat women, but that other religions and cultures have outgrown patriarchy and sexism" (Runnymede Trust 1997; cf. e.g. Saharso 2000: 227, n. 2; Phillips 2001: 8; Raz 1994: 179).

Even at a more benign level, there is a danger that the state could simply get it wrong. It might not have enough information to help effectively – say because information is hard to come by and because it requires specialist local knowledge to which access is privileged. In the hope of making up for this disability, the state might end up listening only to the group's elites, those represented as the most learned, but who might present a solution on terms that would maintain or augment their power (Kukathas 2001: 94). Alternatively, the state might choose to listen to those within the group with whom it is most in sympathy – to the victims of oppression and those who might otherwise be silenced. Without achieving sufficient consensus within the group (Kymlicka 1989a: 197), the state might implement what dissidents believe to be a good solution to the oppression in question. This, however, could end up backfiring, since the recognized group's authorities would be likely to feel slighted, their authority having been by-passed. In these circumstances, a solution which might otherwise have passed muster is rejected out of reactionary resistance.

A good example can be found in legislation passed in New York in 1992 to attend to problems of oppression in the operation of Jewish divorce law (NY Dom. Rel. Law 236(B)(5)(h), (6)(d) (McKinney Supp. 2004)). There is strong disagreement over whether the measure is acceptable from a Jewish law perspective. Even some of those who say that the law is acceptable nevertheless argue that it ought not to have been passed because it was enacted with insufficient consensus amongst the recognized authorities on Jewish law (e.g. Broyde 1997).

The state's involvement might end up worsening the lot of women, its "solution" giving vent perhaps to a more reactionary interpretation of the cultural norm, codifying one interpretation when a number of others were hitherto available. Similarities between Jewish and Muslim divorce laws have sometimes caused multicultural states to want to attend to both communities by the same measure, perhaps to avoid singling out a particular minority for special treatment (e.g. *Hansard* HC Deb vol. 61 cols. 928–9 (13 June 1984)). But this runs the risk of assisting reactionary forces striving for a "return" to more patriarchal interpretations of Muslim law (Carroll 1997). Unlike their Jewish counterparts, Muslim courts, such as the Islamic Shari'a Council in London, can grant judicial divorces to women whose husbands refuse to co-operate in the divorce (e.g. Shah-Kazemi 2001).

Or the state's involvement could perversely serve to make recourse to civil law more difficult for women. This may be the effect of the New York Jewish divorce legislation mentioned above. A number of rabbinical authorities have voiced concern regarding *all* use of state divorce law following the introduction of the measure in question (and not simply reliance on that measure specifically), on the ground that its mere presence on the statute books taints aspects of state divorce law which had not hitherto posed difficulty from a Jewish law perspective. Wives may now be required to renounce their rights under state law (as happened, for example, in *Becher v. Becher* 245 AD 2d 408; 667 NYS 2d 50 (NY App Div 1997); cf. Zornberg 1995: 762).

Although the risks of intervention are not to be taken lightly, they do not militate against the state becoming involved in remedying problems faced by minorities within minorities. That seems too defeatist, especially where the state otherwise pursues comprehensive policy objectives tending towards the elimination of oppression. Why should its duties in this regard be stopped by walls of cultural membership (e.g. Okin 2002)?

The risks of intervention ought to be considered matters by which to guide the design of policy. The manner in which the state acts should be set by the very considerations which motivate objections to intervention. That is, the contours of policy are to be framed by reference to the same reasons which fuel the reticence which, I have suggested, explains reliance on exit. In the manner of becoming involved, the objection to intervention ought, with careful policy design, to dissipate. That the policy-making process here is likely to be difficult is undeniable but it ought to be possible.

All important is the process of deliberation over the forms of intervention which would be most likely to help attend to the oppressions suffered by minorities within minorities. In the foregoing I have tried to give reason to downplay exit in these deliberations. But I have not criticized the framework proposed by some of exit's defenders, notably Shachar, within which a designed exit is to be deliberated and agreed upon. Exit is the problem here; not deliberation.[6]

One ought not to overlook the quite considerable experience of exit in relation to Orthodox Jewish divorce regulation in the Diaspora, where many divorced Jews do not have a *get* (Schmool and Miller 1994: viii).

---

[6] While deliberation is crucial to the success of multicultural policy (see generally, Parekh 2000; Kymlicka 1995: 167–68; An-Na'im 1999; Benhabib 1999, 2002; Deveaux 2000a, 2000b), doubts can be raised regarding the particular form of deliberation which is retained by Shachar. In this paper, I have argued that the place to exit in her blueprint for deliberation is likely to be problematic and I draw similar conclusions elsewhere regarding certain of its other aspects (see Reitman (forthcoming)).

While this has certainly caused consternation,[7] there is little sign, as yet, of much reform of the patriarchal rules themselves. Exit here does not seem to have exerted much of a progressive transformative force.

Yet the state has become involved in ingenious ways in alleviating the problems occasioned by Jewish divorce rules, at the behest both of the community establishment and the victims of the system of Jewish divorce regulation. The picture is not entirely rosy since state law mechanisms have not managed to eliminate the effects of patriarchy in the operation of Jewish divorce law but there is nevertheless something of value in the state's engagement.

At its best, state action exerts a co-operative force rather than the sort of competitive force which exit defenders, Shachar most active among them, rather counter-productively want to engender through exit. The foregoing description of intransigence in the face of problems shorn up by Jewish divorce law is an example of reactionary resistance produced by multicultural anxiety. Shachar calls this "reactive culturalism" which she says occurs when the minority "adopts an inflexible interpretation of its traditions *precisely because of the perceived threat from the modern state*" (2000b: 423; emphasis added). The problem with exit as a transformative force is that its transformative potential is derived from the very competition she wants to harness between group and state. That is, by counting upon exit as the catalyst for change, one runs the risk of aggravating precisely those forces which stand in the way of change.

In the Jewish divorce example, the process of deliberation would be unlikely to lead to a form of compromise in which exit has an active role to play. The best type of state action which can be singled out from the experience of accommodation in respect of Jewish divorce can be understood as that which helps a weakened minority regulatory system make up for its powerlessness by harnessing the coercive power of state law-enforcement mechanisms so as better to police abusive men. State action meshes with the cultural system out of which the patriarchy arises in order to take up whatever adjunctive role may be appropriate in the circumstances.

There is little room here to do more than merely make this announcement of a form of multiculturalism in which no reliance is placed on exit (cf. Reitman (forthcoming)). Although exit must be available, it appears in this theory only in its most basic role, as a generally applicable form of regulation by the state, available to all members of society, whatever their cultural membership.

---

[7] Organizations have been set up in order to try to prevent exit, particularly when it happens out of ignorance of the requirements of Jewish law (e.g. Kayama <http://www.kayama.org/aboutus.htm> (accessed 16 December 2003)).

My purpose in this chapter has been to argue against thinking that exit has any additional, operational or justificatory roles to play in theories of multiculturalism. There are alternative, more promising avenues to be pursued in seeking solutions for the problem of minorities within minorities. In looking for them, if we should be tempted to say that this or that arrangement concerning minority cultures is acceptable because there is a right of exit for minorities within minorities – which would protect them against internal oppression or would enable that oppression to be reformed – then we ought to take this as a sign that we have given up too soon; and that further work needs to be done in order to come up with more just arrangements.

10 Minors within minorities: a problem for liberal multiculturalists

Rob Reich

Liberal multiculturalists seek to base the extension of group rights and accommodations to ethnocultural minorities on the claim that it is the interests of individuals and not groups themselves that warrant such rights and accommodations. Individual freedom and flourishing, liberal multiculturalists argue, is only possible within a cultural context. Traditional liberal policies of individual rights ought therefore to be supplemented with multicultural policies of group rights and accommodations that will promote individual freedom and flourishing. There is now a wide body of literature on the appropriate kind of group rights and accommodations for different circumstances and for different kinds of minority groups.

But the extension of group rights and accommodations to ethnocultural minorities within a liberal state leads to a clear tension. When the state seeks through collective rights to improve the status of minority groups and their members with respect to the larger society, it can also undermine the status of the weaker members within the group. Susan Moller Okin criticizes multiculturalism for this reason, arguing that group rights often reinforce the subordination of women within groups (Okin 1998; 1999a). And Ayelet Shachar, more sympathetic to the multicultural project, nevertheless finds that multicultural accommodations can reinforce power dynamics that render the most disadvantaged group members, especially women, even more vulnerable. She labels this the "paradox of multicultural vulnerability" (Shachar 2000a; 2001). Each is concerned to ensure that attempts to secure justice for minority groups do not undermine the already vulnerable position of women within such groups.

I agree with their diagnoses and have broad sympathy for their recommended remedies. I believe, however, that scholars have overlooked the class of persons for whom the paradox is most threatening: children. It is minors within minorities who are the most disadvantaged and therefore the most vulnerable to the underbelly or unintended consequences of a multicultural politics.

This is so for a variety of reasons. But chief among them is the fact that the kinds of rights and accommodations sought by ethnocultural minorities often have considerably greater impact on children than on adults. I shall focus here on one of the most familiar of these rights and accommodations: exerting control over educational arrangements. Such control comes in two general forms, either via the right to separate schools or culturally centric curricula, sometimes at public expense, or via the right to exemptions from educational requirements, such as compulsory attendance laws.

It is easy to understand why in culturally diverse states control over education is so important. First, and most obvious, schools are a central vehicle of cultural transmission, perhaps the most important vehicle next to the family. Beyond socialization within the home, schools play a crucial role in initiating children into the norms, beliefs and rites of the larger group, forming and deepening their cultural identities in the process. It is for this reason, historically as well as presently, that many parents choose a school for their children not (only) on the basis of academic quality but (also) on what the child in the seat next to their son or daughter looks like or believes in. Second, when children of ethnocultural, religiocultural, or national minority groups attend common schools, they have often been discriminated against or marginalized within the curriculum, both as an explicit aim of state policy. Schools in many parts of the world, and especially in the United States, have historically attempted to strip away cultural attachments and beliefs in an effort to assimilate children of the adult members of minority groups to the majority culture. More subtly, schools have often failed in their curricula to recognize the existence and history of many minority groups, leading minorities to feelings of invisibility, inferiority and second-class citizenship. And third, control over schooling also means that those in charge can decide who gets an education at all. Schools often restrict attendance to certain children, reinforcing particular norms about those who are considered educable or worthy of education. Consider the history in the United States of preventing African-Americans from attending schools, or forcing them to attend impoverished schools, or the current practice in many parts of the world of educating only boys.

In this chapter I examine the educational presuppositions and implications of the work of several multicultural theorists who identify themselves as working within the liberal tradition: Avishai Margalit and Moshe Halbertal, and Joseph Raz. I contend that their defense of multicultural accommodations in education neglects the potential perils of accommodation. I do not wish to press the typical fear, however, that extending cultural rights threatens the value of common citizenship and leads to balkanization. My sense is that, at least in the US context, such fears are greatly exaggerated. My concern is that accommodation policies meant to promote or preserve cultural groups potentially place the integrity of the group above the freedom and equality of the individuals within, especially children. In particular, multicultural accommodation policies in education that grant rights to separate schools or wholesale exemptions from state regulations amount in some circumstances to sanctioning the oppression of children.

Margalit and Halbertal, and Raz claim that their respective theories remain distinctively liberal because they aim to guarantee a so-called "right of exit" from any group. While the freedom to dissociate from a group, seeking happiness elsewhere, is indeed central to the liberal tradition, I argue that group rights, especially when extended to groups who wish to deny their children a liberal education, may serve to disable or severely impoverish the capacity of children to exit; they may serve instead to incarcerate children within a cultural group. While the aim of the chapter is almost entirely critical, my comments point towards some very obvious constructive proposals concerning education for autonomy which I have defended at greater length elsewhere (Reich 2002). Regulation of schools that are attended by the youngest citizens of the state is not something to be given up lightly, and, I conclude, certainly not something the liberal state should cede to ethnocultural minorities as a matter of multicultural principle.

A right to culture?

Consider first the strongly worded work of Margalit and Halbertal, who articulate the most basic claim of almost all multicultural theories: individual freedom and flourishing depend crucially on one's cultural attachments. This rather unobjectionable claim leads to what, at bottom, is a strikingly elementary argument: if culture matters to individual freedom and flourishing, then liberals, who seek to safeguard freedom and facilitate individual flourishing, should also concern themselves with culture. Margalit and Halbertal thus begin their argument with the simple but dramatic assertion, "Human beings have a right to culture – not just any culture but their own" (Margalit and Halbertal 1994: 491).

Note here, however, that the key assertion is not that cultural attachments are important *per se*, but rather that attachments to *one's own* culture are important. Now it is probably trivially true that people need cultural attachments in order to lead satisfying lives, but it is another question entirely whether or not people need to be attached always to their own cultural groups in order to lead satisfying lives. And prior to this question, we must ask a host of others about the meaning of "one's own culture": How will one's own culture be identified? Who shall be the identifying agent(s)? Is there a possibility of multiple cultural attachments? Can people change cultural allegiances?

These familiar questions raise some initial problems for Margalit and Halbertal, but it is important first to ask what follows from their notion of a right to culture. For Margalit and Halbertal, "the right to culture may involve giving groups a status that contradicts the status of the individual in a liberal state" and that "[p]rotecting cultures out of the human right to culture may take the form of an obligation to support cultures that flout the rights of the individual in a liberal society" (Margalit and Halbertal 1994: 491). Moreover, they say that the liberal state must "abandon its neutral position and actively assist needy cultures" not because this is in the interest of the majority but because it is necessary "to make it possible for members of minority groups to retain their identity" (Margalit and Halbertal 1994: 492). Thus the motivating force behind the right to culture is an interest in protecting the existence of minority cultural groups.

For Margalit and Halbertal, then, identification with one's own culture is of such importance that it generates a right that overrides other traditional liberal beliefs in freedom of choice, association and movement. Minority cultural groups may be allowed to impose certain restrictions on their members as well as certain regulations on outsiders. Margalit and Halbertal say, for example, that the right to culture will permit groups to recognize only arranged marriages, or to forbid outsiders from entering or living in a particular geographical area. Moreover, using as an example the Ultra-Orthodox Jews in Israel, they assert that defending a right to culture issues in a defense of the subordinate status of women within the group (Margalit and Halbertal 1994: 491–2).

The most significant implications of a right to culture, I believe, concern schooling. The right to culture justifies for Margalit and Halbertal the right to publicly subsidized separate schooling. They argue that the right to culture and the privileges that follow from it are not meant merely to protect cultures in danger of disappearing, but also to aid a minority group that finds it difficult to "maintain specific aspects of its culture without these privileges" (Margalit and Halbertal 1994: 506). Thus for those groups whose ability to transmit their cultural values and beliefs to children may be compromised or undermined by attendance in public schools, the state ought to provide public assistance for separate educational institutions. Margalit and Halbertal say that, within the Israeli context, both Ultra-Orthodox Jews and Arab Israelis should be permitted to establish and maintain separate schools at public expense (Margalit and Halbertal 1994: 493, 507). Should the state continue to regulate or oversee the structure and content of the separate educational institutions desired by each particular cultural group? Referring to Ultra-Orthodox society, Margalit and Halbertal note that "the school curriculum is controlled exclusively by the community, and there is a clear discrimination between the education of girls and of boys" (Margalit and Halbertal 1994: 493). Boys engage in lifelong study of the Torah, learning almost no secular subjects; girls receive a different curriculum and complete their studies before the age of twenty. Summing up their position, Margalit and Halbertal contrast the *conditional* right to control access to a community's neighborhood, based on a balance of the community's interest and the burdens that restricted access place on outsiders, with the apparently *absolute* right to maintain separate educational institutions. A right to culture, for Margalit and Halbertal, means that cultural groups, without state oversight but with state financial support, ought to be permitted to direct and control the education of their youngest members.

Given this list of implications regarding marriage, geographical access and education, it is not difficult to discern how establishing a right to culture leads to potential conflicts with basic liberal beliefs. If the liberal state takes the freedom and equality of individuals seriously, it cannot permit a cultural rights program of the sort suggested by Margalit and Halbertal. The reason is that in the interest of preserving the culture, the rights extended to groups may sanction illiberal treatment of group members, not to mention the potential neglect of the development and sustenance of civic and political virtues in children.

Permitting, as Margalit and Halbertal do, "judicial autonomy in marital and family matters" (Margalit and Halbertal 1994: 507) might qualify as a *prima facie* case against the supposed liberalism of their theory.[1] But consider their stance on separate education and their own example of the Ultra-Orthodox. How on liberal grounds can one defend an educational system where girls are denied simple equal educational opportunity, by which I mean equal access to schools and curricula? Equally worrisome from a liberal perspective is the fact that boys are denied the opportunity to study anything secular.[2] Given, as Margalit and Halbertal admit, that "Ultra-Orthodox culture is essentially illiberal" and that "there is no aspect of its members' lives in which it does not actively interfere, sometimes to the extent of compulsion" (Margalit and Halbertal 1994: 492–3), schooling that perpetuates a second-class status for women and that shields boys from engagement with secular culture is inconsistent

---

[1] Ayelet Shachar's criticism of multicultural accommodations is aimed directly at issues of family law. See Shachar 2001: ch. 3.
[2] For a similar complaint, see Okin 1998.

with a liberal's interest in freedom, equality, and participatory citizenship. Group rights of the sort described by Margalit and Halbertal allow for illiberal treatment of individuals within groups.

Margalit and Halbertal might reply in two ways. First, they might say that cultural rights are valuable only insofar as they are in the interests of individuals. What they do say is that "the individual's right to culture stems from the fact that every person has an overriding interest in his personality identity – that is, in preserving his way of life and the traits that are central identity components for him and the other members of his cultural group" (Margalit and Halbertal 1994: 505). But the notion of personality identity as the grounds for a right to culture seems to me controversial at best and incoherent at worst. Do all individual adherents of a culture have similar personality identities? Must personality identities derive from the cultural unit into which he or she is born? Do they alter over time? Can a person construct a personality identity out of multiple cultural materials? I shall comment at greater length on the importance of this cosmopolitan alternative later in this chapter.

Second, reminding readers that "the right to culture is based on its contribution to the basic interests of individuals," Margalit and Halbertal argue that each individual must always retain the right to exit a culture if he or she wishes to do so.[3] The right to culture does not, they write, "justify coercing those who wish to leave the culture to remain within it on the pretext that if people begin to leave, the culture will be destroyed" (Margalit and Halbertal 1994: 508). Consistent with the value of personal autonomy, they aim to honor the capacity of individuals to examine their lives and preserve freedom of association by denying cultural groups the right to forbid exit.

But are the group rights they endorse themselves consistent with a meaningful right of exit? Given the restrictions Margalit and Halbertal are willing to tolerate even among self-described illiberal groups, this hardly seems the case. It is one thing simply to announce that cultural groups may not forbid their members from exiting; it is an entirely different matter to create the capacity for individuals to exercise this right. The distinction here is a familiar one, namely between formal liberties and the actual worth of liberties. Margalit and Halbertal are too willing to sacrifice basic conditions for exercising a right of exit in the name of ensuring the continued existence of the group, all in order to preserve an individual's personality identity.

---

[3] Presumably this would imply the conscious rejection of one's personality identity and subsequent adoption of a new one, although Margalit and Halbertal never make this clear.

Consider the (absolute) right of cultural groups to separate educational institutions that Margalit and Halbertal defend. The Ultra-Orthodox education they describe – in its effort to shield students from secular society, in its reinforcement of gender inequality – seems unlikely to play a role in creating the conditions where students might be capable of revising or rejecting their religious attachments. (It seems equally unlikely to teach children the civic skills and behavior they need to be informed and active citizens.) Indeed, the Ultra-Orthodox education is designed exactly to prevent that. But we can imagine far worse scenarios. If the norms of a cultural group continually reinforce a message that girls and women were sources of evil, sexual temptresses, or merely unequal in all respects to men, would Margalit and Halbertal defend schools that taught these lessons? If the norms of a cultural group aim systematically to disable the ability of boys to think critically except with relation to the Talmud, or to accept unerringly the dictates of elders, would Margalit and Halbertal defend an educational system designed to further this end? If the answer is no, Margalit and Halbertal offer no criteria by which to distinguish acceptable from unacceptable aims and forms of separate education. On their own admission, the relative liberality or illiberality of group practices would *not* count as such a criterion. In fact, far from distinguishing between liberal versus illiberal educational practices, they suggest that the state must not only tolerate separate schools, but actively support them financially. Yet when cultural groups are illiberal in their educational practices, it is hard to believe that the right of exit Margalit and Halbertal guarantee individuals will have any real substance. Rights of exit are meaningless without the capacity to exercise them.

Margalit and Halbertal are not alone in their reliance on the right of exit strategy. Multicultural theorists often seem to condition the justice of proposed group rights or accommodations on the right of individuals to exit. Yet, as Cass Sunstein has argued, a person's preferences often adapt to the environment in which they form, all the more so when the environment puts up barriers to exposure to diversity. As a result, people's preferences, Sunstein writes, "need not be respected when they are adaptive to unjust background conditions; in such circumstances it is not even clear whether the relevant preferences are authentically 'theirs'" (Sunstein 1999: 88). We may wonder, therefore, about the expressed preferences of adults *not to exit* who have received exceptionally illiberal educations; we may wonder, essentially, whether they have been indoctrinated. It is hard to see how a liberal state could justify multicultural accommodations in education that permitted indoctrination. But unless an education is provided that does not indoctrinate, that does not systematically adapt one's preferences and, over time, one's very character to uphold cultural norms, the right of exit strategy inevitably fails. If the right of exit strategy is even to be coherent, individuals must acquire the capacity to question the value of continued allegiance to cultural norms and practices, and ultimately to the group itself (and, of course, to the larger state as well). This is necessary simply to begin the process of deciding for oneself whether exiting the group is, all things considered, a desirable pursuit.

In fact, we might express another concern about the right of exit strategy precisely because, even if one is capable of it, exiting one's group is in the real world a momentous and highly consequential decision. Since children are still dependent on their families for care, it is highly unlikely that many children would ever avail themselves of the exit option, even were they able to consider it. As for adults, those who would consider exiting are likely to be those who are already subject to illiberal and unjust treatment – internal dissenters or women, for example. To the extent that group rights or accommodations come conditioned on the ability of persons to exit, the burden of such accommodations is often borne by minority group members who are already most vulnerable. As Ayelet Shachar notes, if a state extends collective rights to a minority group and tensions then arise between an individual and the group, it is the individual who must resolve the tension by deciding whether or not to stay.

> By turning a blind eye to differential power distributions within the group hierarchy and ignoring women's heightened symbolic role in relation to other group members, the right of exit rationale forces an individual member into a choice of penalties: either accept all group practices, including those that violate your fundamental citizenship rights, or (somehow) leave. (Shachar 2000a: 80)

Thus, even if education were to provide children with a substantive as well as formal ability to exit, we might worry about the overall justice of the right of exit strategy.

I conclude that even if Margalit and Halbertal can answer successfully the difficult questions about what it means to have a right to *one's own* culture with which I began this section, and assuming that the confusing matter of a personality identity can be made clear, their theory fails on liberal grounds. If the right of exit is what makes their theory a *liberal* multicultural one, the group rights they defend, especially the allowance for separate and publicly subsidized educational systems, potentially undermine the very possibility of exit from the start. At a very minimum, we can say without any controversy that, given separate schools, the capacity to exit a group will be distributed differentially amongst citizens.[4] The

---

[4] Certainly the capacity for exit will be distributed differentially even in societies in which all persons receive the same education, or even in the most liberal of societies. My point

liberal multicultural theory of Margalit and Halbertal is deeply trouble-some, then, for while it claims to have the flourishing of individuals in mind, it serves to preserve the integrity of cultural groups at the potential cost of the freedom and equality of individuals within groups. We could put the problem more generally by asking whether a multicultural theory that protects the right of cultural groups to treat their members illiberally deserves to be called a liberal theory at all. Margalit and Halbertal have provided no reason to answer in the affirmative.

The myopia of Raz's liberal multiculturalism

Joseph Raz has argued that liberalism in a sense entails multiculturalism. Raz presents a staunchly liberal version of multiculturalism, defending individual autonomy in emphatic terms and supporting choice-making within and among cultures. Yet despite Raz's liberal multiculturalism, his theory suffers from two significant problems. First, Raz falsely pre-supposes that individuals possess an allegiance or affiliation to a single culture. Just as societies may be multicultural, so too may individuals. Second, Raz's theory is too often blind to the existence of children. This lacuna leads him to give arguments about autonomy that ultimately are contradictory; Raz strongly supports autonomy for all individuals yet appears prepared to exempt autonomy-retarding cultural groups from any state effort to develop autonomy in their children. Taken together, these problems call into question the practical usefulness and ultimate coherence of Raz's liberal multiculturalism.

Raz builds his case for liberal multiculturalism from an interest, at heart classically liberal, in the freedom and well-being of individuals. In Raz's view, liberalism exalts autonomous choice, which in turn gives individu-als freedom of self-definition and makes possible individual flourishing. "Liberalism upholds the value for people of being in charge of their life, charting its course by their successive choices" (1994: 175).[5] Further, the freedom to make choices, however, is not a capacity that springs forth from within individuals. Radical self-creation is a utopian (or per-haps dystopian) fantasy; we do not create ourselves, or choose among life's options, untethered to the social world. On the contrary, choices only make sense within a social context. Autonomous choice presupposes shared meanings and common practices among individuals.

---

here is not that unequal capacity to exit is unjust, but rather that a theory of group rights that institutionalizes the discrepancy should be called into question.

[5] Joseph Raz, "Multiculturalism: A Liberal Perspective," in *Ethics in the Public Domain* (Oxford: Clarendon Press, 1994: 175). All subsequent references to this article are located in parentheses in the main body of the text.

For Raz, however, the social context he has in mind is quite specific: it must be a *cultural group*. "Only through being socialized in a culture can one tap the options which give life a meaning. By and large one's cultural membership determines the horizon of one's opportunities, of what one may become, or (if one is older) what one might have been" (1994: 77). Furthermore, Raz argues, an individual's connection with a cultural group constitutes one's sense of identity.[6] With the honor and dignity of one's identity at stake, it follows that slighting or, worse, persecuting a cultural group insults or discriminates against members of that group.

If liberal governments are interested in the flourishing of their citizens, then, they must necessarily take an interest in the well-being of the variety of cultural groups living within their borders. This, according to Raz, is not because cultural groups have some independent and overriding moral importance, but rather because integration within a cultural group is a "precondition for, and a factor which gives shape and content to, individual freedom" (1994: 178). Because liberals concern themselves with the freedom and prosperity of individuals they must also concern themselves with the vitality of cultural groups. An awareness and support of multicultural policies thus arises directly from liberalism's basic emphasis on individual freedom and well-being.

Two additional features of Raz's liberal multiculturalism are worth noting here. First, Raz comments that autonomy – the ability to choose freely – is meaningless without a diversity of valuable options from which to choose. A liberal's interest in fostering autonomy means that an individual's connection to a cultural group must be respected and secure, that the individual must enjoy some real measure of choice *within* that cultural group, and more significantly, as Raz sometimes seems to say, *among* cultural groups. Autonomy, Raz writes, "is valuable only if one steers a course for one's life through significant choices among diverse and valuable options." He stresses that, "The picture this pluralistic and autonomy-based liberalism suggests is one in which the community and its institutions foster and encourage a wide range of diverse forms of life among which individuals are left freely to choose" (Raz 1994: 119, 123). Freedom and flourishing, for Raz, mean having the autonomy to make choices both within and among cultural groups. For this reason, Raz also champions a "right to exit," by which he means "the right of each individual to abandon his cultural group" (181). Valuing autonomy *within*

---

[6] I have chosen the strong formulation of Raz's argument here. What Raz actually writes is rather revealing. Perhaps anticipating the problems associated with cultures constituting identity, Raz writes "In this way one's culture constitutes (contributes to) one's identity" (Raz 1994: 178).

groups places limits on what the state can do to groups and individuals.[7]
Valuing autonomy *among* groups places limits on what cultural groups
can do to their members.

Second, Raz makes plain that liberal multiculturalism does not imply
the museum-like preservation of cultural groups. Change is inevitable,
cultures are dynamic. "[Liberal multiculturalism] is not a policy of con-
serving, fossilizing some cultures in their pristine state" (Raz 1994: 181).
Cultural groups are valuable only insofar as they contribute to the well-
being of their adherents. When cultural groups are repressive or stagnant, liberal multiculturalism counsels intervention, for "fossilized cultures cannot serve their members well in contemporary societies" (182).
Some cultures, like slave cultures, racially discriminatory cultures and
homophobic cultures, can be supported only by "neutraliz[ing] their
oppressive aspects" (184) and guaranteeing a right of exit from them.
In all cases, however, Raz urges "restraint and consideration in thinking
of the means" (185) of intervention.

Raz's presumption of individual monoculturalism

Raz's liberal multiculturalism is a policy of fostering and encouraging
the cultural and material prosperity of cultural groups within a society
while also protecting the right of individuals to exit a cultural group. It
means, for example, that the state should generously support independent
cultural organizations and that public institutions and private companies
should respect the traditions (clothing, holidays, etc.) of cultural groups.
It also has important implications for education: while all should learn
and respect "the history and traditions of all the cultures in the country,"
children should be educated "if their parents so desire, in the culture of
their groups" (Raz 1994: 189).

Raz's language throughout his essay, particularly in the latter remark
about education, betrays one of his fundamental assumptions: individuals
belong to only one cultural group. Everywhere Raz emphasizes that individual freedom and well-being are possible only with "unimpeded membership in *a* respected and flourishing cultural group" (Raz 1994: 189;
also 174, 177–8); he notes that children should be educated in "*the* culture of their groups"; he thinks rights of exit are important as a safeguard
"for members who cannot develop and find adequate avenues for self-
expression within their *native* culture" (187; my emphases). Nowhere

[7] Raz says that, "Governments, and other people generally, can help people flourish, but
only by creating the conditions for autonomous life, primarily by guaranteeing that an
adequate range of diverse and valuable options shall be available to all. Beyond that they
must leave individuals free to make of their lives what they will" (Raz 1994: 120).

does Raz countenance the possibility of multiple cultural allegiances and loyalties.[8] According to Raz, societies are multicultural, but individuals are monocultural.

Why does Raz assume this? Here we must turn to Raz's definition of "cultural group." He fails to offer a precise definition of cultural group in the liberal multiculturalism essay. He offers, however, a careful and detailed definition of a very close relative, perhaps twin – "encompassing groups" – in a separate essay co-authored with Avishai Margalit.[9] Encompassing groups are "groups with pervasive cultures" and groups where membership "is important to one's self-identity" (Raz and Margalit 1994: 133). This already sounds like a "cultural group." But more significant for the comparison is Raz's statement that "the key to the explanation is in the importance of these groups to the well-being of their members" (Raz and Margalit 1994: 133). The argument of this essay, moreover, parallels the argument of the multiculturalism essay. Raz discusses, for example, the importance of membership in an encompassing group for the ability to make choices; since identity is tied up in such groups, it is harmful when groups are not respected. In almost every respect, then, when Raz talks about cultural groups, it sounds very much like the encompassing groups he discusses elsewhere.[10]

Let us be more specific. Raz says that encompassing groups are usually nations or peoples, but could also be racial, religious or social classes (Raz and Margalit 1994: 132). Given this definition, one might expect that membership in multiple encompassing or cultural groups would be a normal phenomenon. Many people are simultaneously members of a racial group with a pervasive culture, a religious group with a pervasive culture, and a nation. Each of these memberships, individually and collectively, may be important for the person's identity and well-being. Yet Raz still does not recognize the possibility. He notes that though "people growing up among members of the group will acquire the group culture," they need not be "indelibly marked." He explains, "People may migrate

---

[8] To be fair, Raz does argue that liberal multiculturalism "requires the existence of a common culture in which the different co-existing cultures are embedded" (Raz 1994: 187). This, however, is not the kind of multiple membership I have in mind. By multiple cultural allegiances and loyalties, I mean to indicate attachments to the distinct cultural groups that are embedded within this larger, but vaguely defined, "common culture." Raz never raises the possibility of these multiple memberships.

[9] Raz offers this careful definition in an article co-authored with Avishai Margalit. See Raz and Margalit 1994.

[10] This leads to a puzzle. In general, Raz equates encompassing groups with nations or people, and he argues for their right to self-rule. Cultural groups, however, do not enjoy the same measure of self-rule, though they resemble in almost every possible way encompassing groups.

to other environments, shed their previous culture, and acquire *a new one*" (Raz and Margalit 1994: 129; my emphases). Cultural emigration is possible; cultural *mélange* is not. The obvious assumption about mono-cultural individuals remains. Raz's explicit definition of encompassing groups provides no help in understanding why he never considers the possibility of multicultural persons. To the contrary, it only reinforces the impression that he views individuals as possessing, at any given time, membership in one and only one culture.

What evidence or argument exists to support my contention that indi-viduals can be multicultural? Two reasons come immediately to mind: the facts of demography and biology; and philosophical arguments for "cosmopolitanism."[11] By the "facts of demography and biology," I sim-ply mean to call attention to the increasing prevalence of mixed race and mixed-cultured persons.[12] Take for example, Tiger Woods. Woods is by birth part Thai, part Caucasian, part Native American and part black. If racial groups can constitute cultural groups, as Raz admits, then at least two of these – Native American and black – qualify under current American social understandings as clear cultural groups. Furthermore, Woods was raised as a religious Buddhist, which again qualifies as a cul-tural group under Raz's standards. Woods would appear to have alle-giances to at least three cultural groups, by birth and early socialization (not by later emigration or mixing). Is it possible, or necessary, to identify one of these as primary? If schools are charged with educating children in the culture of their group, which culture will the school choose when edu-cating a Tiger Woods? Can Tiger Woods be said to have a single "native culture"?

Jeremy Waldron gives some philosophical underpinning to the idea of multicultural, or, in his phrase, cosmopolitan individuals (Waldron 1992; 1996; 2003). While Woods is rapidly becoming a multiracial icon, Waldron identifies Salman Rushdie as the paradigmatic cosmopolitan, a person who embodies and takes pleasure in appropriating and mixing himself into multiple cultural traditions. Quoting Rushdie:

[11] A third possible reason could also be cited: the voluminous psychological literature on bi- and multiculturalism. See the excellent survey by Teresa LaFramboise, in LaFramboise et al. 1993. LaFramboise et al. conclude that the most powerful theory is that of "alternation," where it is assumed that "an individual can have a sense of belonging in two cultures without compromising his or her sense of cultural identity" (246).

[12] Census data indicate that the number of multiracial children has quadrupled since 1970 (to 2 million). More significantly, a Department of Education study found that 41% of all public schools report that the racial categories used by the government are not accurately descriptive of their school populations (see "Racial and Ethnic Classifications used by Public Schools," National Center for Education Statistics (NCES 96-092), March 1996.

I was born an Indian, and not only an Indian, but a Bombayite – Bombay, most cosmopolitan, most hybrid, most hotchpotch of Indian cities. My writing and thought have therefore been as deeply influenced by Hindu myths and attitudes as Muslim ones . . . Nor is the West absent from Bombay. I was already a mongrel self, history's bastard, before London aggravated the condition. (Waldron 1996: 105; quoting Rushdie's *Imaginary Homelands*: 404)

If not the racial mixture of Tiger Woods, then the national and religious hybridization of Salman Rushdie certainly gives cause to see these individuals as multicultural.

Waldron goes on, however, to give a host of other reasons for seeing Rushdie's hotchpotch self as the norm rather than as a freakish occurrence. Waldron notes the economic, moral and political interdependence of human beings, arguing that our interdependence causes us to mix and mingle such that the borderlines of cultures are never clearly drawn and that the idea of cultural or political sovereignty so familiar today is a myth belied by the history of cosmopolitan structures and interaction (Waldron 1996; 2003).

The phenomenon of multicultural, hybrid individuals thus challenges Raz's liberal multiculturalism in three ways. First, and most directly, it undermines his assumption that individuals are monocultural. Second, the admixture of cultures, both within individuals and within societies, makes it increasingly difficult to identify cultures as having clear boundaries; they are no longer Herderian wholes. It may be the case that cultures are most like weather patterns, blurred at the edges, one area seeping into the next. And third, if the previous two are correct, Raz must revise his belief that secure location within only one cultural group "is a precondition" for individual freedom (Raz 1994: 178). On the contrary, individuals may construct their identity and exercise their autonomy within a multiplicity of cultural frameworks. As such, cultural groups must still be respected and supported, for they provide the material from which individuals gain sustenance and meaning. But Raz must now admit that programs of cultural support should not be aimed at protecting the integrity and flourishing of cultural groups, but rather provide for the possibility of blurring and admixture.

Autonomy for illiberal cultures?

The previous objections call into question the practical utility of Raz's liberal multiculturalism. The existence of multicultural individuals poses, as it were, an empirical challenge to Raz; it does not necessarily call into question the internal coherence of his argument. Multicultural individuals, in other words, may still fit into Raz's theory, for the importance of culture for individual freedom and well-being has not been called into question.

It seems to me, however, that problems with Raz's views on autonomy threaten to undermine the very logic of his argument. Raz argues for autonomy as a key value, one which enables individuals to chart their own course through life by making successive choices about who they are and what they will become. Yet Raz is also prepared to exempt certain cultural groups, even those which are autonomy-retarding, from state intervention. Raz is able to do this, I suggest, because he fails to consider the position of the child and instead focuses his attention on the fully developed autonomy of adults. Ignoring the potentially precarious position of children, his liberal multiculturalism forwards policies that may leave children within illiberal and non-autonomous groups a life without choice.

This is a strange and counter-intuitive objection with respect to Raz, for within the range of contemporary liberal theorists, Raz is perhaps the pre-eminent defender of autonomy. Indeed, throughout much of his writing Raz notes again and again the central importance of autonomy. To wit: "We regard the fact that a life was autonomous as adding value to it. We think of our own lives and the lives of others as better for having been developed autonomously" (Raz 1994: 120). Raz would certainly seem to elevate the capacity to choose over the maintenance of diversity. Raz notes, "Autonomy is, to be sure, inconsistent with various alternative forms of valuable lives" (395). Hence, a liberal society that prizes autonomy may be less diverse than a liberal society that prizes diversity. Raz doesn't hesitate here: "For those who live in an autonomy-supporting environment, there is no choice but to be autonomous: there is no other way to prosper in such a society" (391).

To what extent is Raz prepared to promote autonomy amongst the various cultural groups in an autonomy-based liberal society? At times, Raz appears prepared to go to great lengths to ensure that all citizens are autonomous: "One particular problem concerns the treatment of communities whose culture does not support autonomy. These may be immigrant communities, or indigenous peoples, or they may be religious sects . . . Since they insist on bringing up their children in their own ways they are, in the eyes of liberals like myself, harming them" (Raz 1986: 423). Raz contemplates the coercive closure of separate schools for illiberal cultural groups. But he finally decides that the viability of a culture is what should decide the level of intervention. The less viable and more stagnant a culture may be, the greater justification for intervention. As Raz says, the claims of multiculturalism "should not be pursued regarding cultural groups which have lost their ability to perpetuate themselves"

(Raz 1994: 173). One indication of a stagnant cultural group, Raz notes, is when "the allure of surrounding cultures means that the vast majority of their young people wish to assimilate" (173). Thus, one strain of Raz's thought appears unshakably committed to the development of autonomy, even at the price of assimilating youth into other cultural groups.

Within this strain, children seem to figure prominently in Raz's considerations – he worries about the education of youth in an autonomy-retarding environment; he looks to children's choices in perpetuating their communities as an index of the cultural group's vibrancy. How odd it is, then, when another strain of Raz's thought is blind to the existence of children and exempts clearly illiberal groups from state intervention.

There is the previously cited passage where Raz says that if the parents desire it, children should be schooled in the culture of their group (Raz 1994: 189). This stands in simple contradiction to his statement that groups unsupportive of autonomy actually harm their children by raising them in their own ways. But the problem is larger than this simple contradiction.

The heart of the problem lies in Raz's consideration of the limits of tolerance, or namely, the limits of how tolerant the autonomy-based liberal state that Raz supports can be of illiberal, autonomy-disregarding cultural groups. Raz states outright, "The limits of toleration are in denying communities the right to repress their own members, in discouraging intolerant attitudes to outsiders, in insisting on making exit from the community a viable option" (Raz 1994: 190). Yet Raz understands "repress their own members" to refer to adults in whom the capacity to choose is already developed. Repression would not include, to his mind, teaching children in ways that were not supportive of autonomy; therefore schooling within one's own group is not only tolerated, but encouraged.

Elsewhere Raz justifies restraint in intervention on the grounds that it violates the very autonomy of the adults within the illiberal cultural groups. "Governments should not use repressive measures . . . to discourage victimless immoralities. For such measures interfere with people's general standing as autonomous human beings" (Raz 1994: 124). It is clear from the context that the "autonomous human beings" of whom Raz speaks are all adults. A victimless immorality includes, apparently, raising children in a non-autonomous environment. How do we know this? In a footnote, Raz states that his argument "does not apply to enclaves of traditional premodern communities within our societies" (124 n. 30). The Amish or the Roma, in other words, are exempt from the framework of liberal multiculturalism. In the name of respecting the autonomy of adults, then, Raz demotes the autonomy of children.

By making children subservient to their parents' interests, by encouraging an education enclosed within a cultural group, Raz, the paradigmatic autonomy liberal thereby condemns children born into autonomy-disregarding groups to a life without autonomy. Only in cases when the cultural group is deemed to be stagnating (and who, by the way, is to make this decision?) does Raz grant the state leverage to intervene. This is extremely difficult to reconcile with Raz's other arguments for the superior value of the autonomous life. If Raz truly believes that parents "harm" their children when they discourage the development of autonomy in them, if he truly believes that the autonomous life is indeed "better," why then is he willing to tolerate illiberal cultural groups, vibrant though they might be? Raz ought to support state intervention into illiberal and autonomy-retarding cultural groups. He ought not to say that all children should be educated, if their parents so desire, in the culture of their groups. He ought to guarantee that children, regardless of their group membership, are exposed to a variety of ways of life in order to promote an awareness of other life options. Raz's own words make the case: "Since we live in a society whose social forms are to a considerable extent based on individual choice, and since our options are limited by what is available in our society, we can prosper in it only if we can be successfully autonomous" (Raz 1986: 394). By tolerating autonomy-disregarding groups, Raz not only makes it possible that their children will lead non-autonomous lives, he also makes it *impossible*, by his own argument, for them to lead flourishing lives.

Conclusion

Liberal multiculturalists promote group rights and multicultural accommodations in schooling as central to achieving justice for cultural minorities. I have endeavored to show why there is good reason to be concerned about the blanket extension of rights to separate schooling or exemptions from schooling. Education is essential to cultural transmission, but it is for this very reason that group rights or wholesale exemptions cannot be justified as a matter of principle. Because in the modern world school attendance is often mandatory, schools may represent the only significant institutional vehicle that larger societies have at their disposal to promote the freedom of its citizens and to transmit civic or political virtues. It is clear, for example, that direct state intervention into the socialization that parents give their children in the home or that cultural groups give their members in their associational lives will often be found to be too intrusive. The liberal state acts illiberally when it intrudes too directly or too deeply into family life. In other words, it is philosophically undesirable, and in addition, impossible in practice, for the liberal state to prevent parents from socializing their children in deeply illiberal ways, or to block cultural groups from promulgating norms of gender inequity, for example. But it is not impossible for the state to require an education of a certain sort for children. What this means, in my view, is that the liberal state should be reluctant to grant rights to separate schooling or to permit broad exemptions from educational requirements such as mandatory attendance. The liberal state should maintain, at the very least, regulatory authority over schooling and attempt to provide an education that aims, among other things, to foster the development of autonomy in children, as well some civic virtues, such as tolerance and civility. (The promotion of autonomy by the state is itself a controversial issue, and while I do not have the space here to defend the claim, autonomy should neither be construed so robustly as to mean individual self-creation or constant Socratic skepticism, nor so anemically as to suggest that any expression of agency or preference would count as autonomous.)[13] In the end, multicultural accommodations in education in the form of multicultural curricula, bilingual education, and many other things that typically fall under the rubric of "multicultural education" are justifiable; accommodations that mean the state may no longer regulate schooling are not.

[13] I defend a conception of "minimalist autonomy," and describe the educational implications that follow from it, in Reich 2002.

11   Beyond exit rights: reframing the debate

Daniel M. Weinstock

One of the hallmarks of liberal democratic societies is their thriving associational life. People belong to all kinds of different groups. The fairly robust guarantees of freedom of association that exist in most modern democracies have given rise to a cornucopia of forms of groups, whose members associate under often very different terms with a view to all kinds of ends.

Many such groups organize their internal affairs illiberally. That is, they enforce norms that run foul of the commitments to freedom and equality characteristic of liberal democracies. They are often structured in highly authoritarian ways. They tend not to respect the principle of gender equality which liberal democracies strive to live by. And in certain cases, they impose what would from a liberal standpoint seem like unacceptable physical abuse upon some of its members, including children.

How should the liberal state respond to such breaches of liberal principles? One prominent view, which presently dominates the philosophical literature on the subject, is that the state should abstain from intervening in the internal affairs of groups, so long as their members are provided with robust *exit rights*. When nothing objectively stands in the way of an individual terminating her membership in a group, and she chooses nonetheless to remain despite what might appear to others as harsh treatment, then the inference that ought to be drawn by the state is that she considers that continued membership in the group is worth more to her,

This paper was presented during a session of the 2002 Congress of the American Political Science Association, and at a conference on Minorities within Minorities held at the University of Nebraska, Lincoln, in November 2002. I wish to thank the participants and audience at both events for lively discussion. I would in particular like to thank Jeff Spinner-Halev, Avigail Eisenberg and Geoff Brahm Levey for extensive written comments on an earlier draft. I revised the paper during my tenure as a Visiting Fellow in the Social and Political Theory Programme of the Research School of Social Sciences of the Australian National University between January and April 2003. I presented it to audiences at the ANU and at Monash University, Melbourne. Thanks are due to all those who offered comments and questions during the various presentations of the ideas in this paper.

all things considered, than the cessation of harsh treatment. On this view, the liberal state has discharged its obligations towards members of illiberal groups when it prevents those in authority within the group from retaining members forcibly, or by trying to impose sanctions upon those who do leave. Defenders of the exit rights strategy hold that there is nothing the state can do to offset the psychological and existential costs that abandoning group membership might involve (Barry 2001a: 150–2).

In this chapter, I want to challenge the exit rights approach. I will begin by identifying three different ways in which it has been argued for. Theorists who start off with quite radically different views about the *value* of associational life have all ended up espousing the importance of exit rights as the right kind of guarantee against the kind of mistreatment that the liberal state *ought* to prohibit. This suggests that despite their differences, these rival approaches all share a common assumption.

In the second part of the chapter, I will identify this assumption, and criticize it on the basis of a number of distinctions among kinds of groups and modes of association that have been routinely overlooked. I will in the final part of the chapter present a different, and in my view more fruitful, approach to the relationship between the liberal democratic state and (apparently) illiberal groups.

I

In this section, I want briefly to describe three approaches that have been taken in recent writing to the question of the *value* of the diversity of groups that characterize liberal democracies, and to show how, from very different starting points, they are all led to endorse the exit rights strategy.

Autonomy liberalism

Many prominent liberals believe that the primary justification of liberal institutions is that they make possible the leading of an autonomous life. By an autonomous life I mean a life of one's own choosing. On this view, I am autonomous to the extent that I reflectively endorse my way of life, as well as the values that underpin that way of life, and I am able to embark upon a new course if I come for whatever reason to reject my previous values and activities. This conception of autonomy has been cashed out by the metaphor of "living one's life from the inside" (Kymlicka 1989b: 883–905).

Will Kymlicka's work has given wide currency to the idea that group membership is an important ingredient of the autonomous life. Autonomy involves choosing, after all, and the capacity for choice cannot be exercised in a vacuum. One needs a repertoire of valuable options on the basis of which to choose, and one needs a (defeasible) evaluative schema on the basis of which to rank these options. Certain kinds of groups – Kymlicka calls them "societal cultures" – provide such options and evaluative schemas to their members, and so on this view, they are ingredients of an autonomous life (Kymlicka 1995).[1]

For the autonomy liberal, though group life can contribute to individual autonomy, it has value only to the extent that it does so. That is, she recognizes no value to groups independent of their contribution to the development of the individual's capacity for choice. And when groups through their practices and norms *inhibit* the development of a person's autonomy, then there is, all things being equal, reason for the liberal state to intervene in the group's internal affairs so as to prohibit the offending practice or norm.

Now there may well be countervailing reasons not to intervene. The liberal democratic majority may very well belong to groups that have historically oppressed the groups whose internal norms and practices are now under scrutiny. Such a historical pattern might very well provide reasons for forbearance. What is more, there may be pragmatic reasons arguing against intervention. Autonomy-promoting norms are perhaps less likely to end up being autonomously endorsed through imposition than through a policy of persuasion and incentive-tweaking.

So the *prima facie* reasons for intervening in a group's internal affairs might end up, when placed alongside all other relevant considerations, giving rise to a more moderate insistence on exit rights. Though it might not be prudent to attempt to coerce change in a group, liberal principles might nonetheless require that attempts at coercing membership be prevented. And thus, explicitly in the case of Gill (2001) and implicitly in the case of Kymlicka, we end up with an autonomy-based defense of exit rights. Autonomy liberals hold that the guarantee of exit rights serves as a relatively reliable *indication* of the fact that group life is compatible with the value of autonomy, the assumption being that given the presence of exit rights, a person's continued adherence to membership in a group can be taken as an (imperfect) sign that she adheres autonomously.

Pluralism

Value pluralism has been one of the dominant themes in recent political philosophy. To a significant degree, it motivates the "political liberal" project of the later Rawls (1993), and it also drives the thought of authors such as John Gray (2000), who want to reject the liberal framework altogether. Pluralists believe that human beings appropriately pursue a

---

[1] Another recent expression of autonomy liberalism is to be found in Gill 2001.

great many different and incommensurable values and sets of values. Pluralists believe that there exists no meta-value or single metric of worth in the space of values. There are any number of ways of ordering the values that do exist. Liberalism gives expression to some of these orderings, and a liberal dispensation thus suits those people who have chosen to give autonomy pride of place in their system of values. But there are equally admirable ways of ordering values that end up being antithetical to liberalism. Some people will accord much greater importance to tradition and community for example, and they will find themselves served badly by an individualist ideology. When liberals intervene in the affairs of, say, a group that has organized itself according to a scheme of values that does not rank individual choice or autonomy highly, they do so without warrant. They are merely imposing one legitimate but not rationally commanded way of ranking values on another.

Now, pluralism is not relativism. Its claim is that there exists a plurality of values and of ways of ranking them, not that "anything goes" in the realm of value. Still, pluralism inherits at least one of the problems inherent in any attempts at generating a policy of tolerance from relativism. First, the claim that there exists no meta-value on the basis of which values can be compared sits uncomfortably with the claim that different value schemes are of *equal* value. And second, why, exactly, *should* the fact of pluralism lead directly to a policy of tolerance? Is tolerance a necessary component of any affirmable conception of the good? If not, then why affirm it? And if so, does this not do away with pluralism?

Let us leave this well-rehearsed family of problems aside and assume that we will be able to make good some argument taking the fact of pluralism as a premise and generating an obligation on the part of the state to defer to a community's norms. How thoroughgoing should such an obligation be? Should it, for example, be limited by the Millian harm principle? Thoroughgoing pluralists such as John Gray claim that it should not be so limited, as all conceptions of good will be irredeemably colored by particular conceptions of the good. "We cannot apply Mill's principle of liberty without comparing harms; but we will make different comparative judgments of harm according to our different views of human interests" (Gray 2000: 98). Bill Galston (2002), on the other hand, argues that an insistence upon exit rights can ensure that the harm principle is being satisfied without undue imposition of outsiders' values and conceptions of what harm involves. Indeed, if people do not abandon their group memberships when exit is possible, this must mean that, *by their own lights*, they are not being harmed in a manner that would warrant ending membership. On Galston's view, people, as it were, "vote with their feet." The best indication that we have of a way of life's worth is that people continue to choose to live it, or at least not to abandon it. In such cases, a group need not coerce its members; they will willingly abide by the group's strictures. "To say that a way of life is collectively worthwhile is to say (in part) that it is worthwhile *for those who are actually leading it.* It is hard to see how that claim can be sustained unless the people in question identify (for whatever reason) with the way of life in question. But if they do so, then the regime need not use coercion to maintain it" (Galston 2002: 55). In effect, Galston can be taken to be making the following argument against positions like Gray's: "Value pluralism must be distinguished from relativism. So we must have a guarantee that those groups that we exempt from laws and norms holding more broadly in liberal democratic societies actually instantiate *values.* But how can we do that, given that any one of us will be judging from his or her own evaluative perspective? The answer is that we must assume that the decision made by individuals *not* to leave a group, when that option exists, should be taken to indicate that the way of life in question is actually *valuable.*"

Associationist liberals

Associationists believe that freedom of association and conscience are the paramount liberal virtues, and that when individuals choose to associate with one another around ends and norms that might seem objectionable to others, there is no higher value to which a liberal regime can repair in order to justify intervening in a group's internal affairs. For the associationist, deference to group norms that might seem illiberal is actually quintessentially liberal. It is when groups' practices are most objectionable to the liberal democratic conscience that the liberal's commitment to freedom of association is most rigorously put to the test.

It is worth spending a moment comparing the associationist's view to the autonomist's. Both, on the face of it, attribute great importance to choice. It is on the associationist's view because people have *chosen* to associate (or at least chosen not to *dis*associate) around a set of values, practices and norms that might seem repugnant to members of a liberal majority on independent grounds that we must abstain from intervening. It is, as it were, the choice itself that we honor through deference, rather than the values, practices and norms themselves. For the autonomist, on the other hand, one of the ways in which a group might be objectionable, is precisely because its values, practices and norms fail to promote the individual's capacity for autonomous choice. They will find *prima facie* grounds for intervening in the internal affairs of an autonomy-denying group even when the group members seem willingly to go along with its norms.

The associationist's belief in the importance of freedom of association gives rise quite naturally to a defense of exit rights. For the freedom to associate is empty if it does not involve freedom to *dis*associate. People must be able through their lives to reflect upon their memberships, and to alter them when they no longer reflect their conception of what gives life value. On this view, a group to which I had previously willingly given my allegiance cannot take any steps to coerce me into continued membership. Now, associationists do not set as stringent conditions as do autonomists on what is to *count* as a choice. For the autonomist, choice must be reflective, taken in the light of a full appreciation of the relevant values, etc. The associationist honors all manner of choice, even ones that would not pass the autonomist's test. For example, the member of a religious group who may never have really considered living outside the traditions that she has inherited, and who may indeed have been raised so as to make it unlikely that she would ever quit the group, but who is not really prevented from doing so, is taken by the associationist to have voluntarily consented to whatever internal norms are imposed upon her. Jeff Spinner-Halev, who I take for present purposes to be a representative of the associationist stance, writes that "describing the religious person's convictions as a matter of choice is appropriate from the perspective of liberal institutions . . . Whether people feel their beliefs and way of life are chosen or dictated by their conscience . . . is immaterial from a liberal perspective. It only matters that people are able to live a different life if they so wish" (Spinner-Halev 2000: 27). Associationists merely require that individual members possess the opportunity to choose and to act on the result of their choosing, regardless of the nature of the mental processes that choosing involves in particular cases.

Thus, philosophers have been led to the affirmation of exit rights as a sufficient condition for the acceptability of norms and practices that offend liberal democratic sensibilities from a variety of normative standpoints. Let me take a moment to compare the arguments that have got them there. For autonomists and pluralists, the relationship of exit rights to the values which they believe should underpin associational life is *epistemic*. They believe that there is no way for the liberal state to impose these values *directly*. All kinds of practical obstacles stand in the way of the liberal state prohibiting norms and practices that fall foul of liberal values, and so individuals' decisions not to quit memberships in groups must stand as a kind of an indicator of these groups being compatible with individual autonomy. And for the pluralist, no one individual can determine whether a group whose values are quite foreign to him, actually instantiates real values. So for both the autonomist and the pluralist, exit rights increase the probability that continued membership can be taken as indicative of the requisite values being present in a group's inner workings.

For the associationist, the relationship of exit rights to his preferred value is *constitutive*. That is, given exit rights, the value of freedom of association does not require anything other than that membership in a group be voluntary in the weak sense privileged by associationists.

What I want to suggest is that the moderate versions of autonomism and pluralism that I identified above with Gill and Galston, respectively, are extensionally indistinguishable from associationism. Their theories can be taken to be claiming that, since what they embody cannot be applied directly, we should proceed as though associationism were true. Now, extreme versions of both positions are logically available. A pluralist could espouse John Gray's view that, as it were, the norms and practices of groups are self-validating. Or one could adopt a Jacobin version of autonomism according to which the state ought to prohibit any group norm that falls foul of liberalism's particular understandings of freedom and equality. These would be radical, and radically implausible, positions to adopt, for reasons that I cannot discuss here. The conclusion I want to take out of this discussion is simply that associationism is, as it were, the compromise position towards which moderate versions of apparently quite distinct theories to do with the value and import of associational life converge. In what follows I want to show that such a view is based on a deeply mistaken view of group life.

II

People in modern liberal democracies belong to a vast number of different kinds of groups. From clubs devoted to the pursuit of hobbies that might bring together no more than a small handful of people, to major world religions, these groups impose quite different conditions upon membership, they are devoted to a wide array of purposes, and are organized internally in all kinds of different ways. What I would like to suggest in this section is that the exit rights strategy is most appropriate to certain *kinds* of groups. Unfortunately for the exponent of this strategy, the kinds of group that poses most problems from a liberal standpoint are not the ones to which exit rights are most appropriate. Let me make a number of distinctions that will, I hope, make this suggestion plausible.

Let me first, however, simply flag what I take to be two fairly intuitive conditions on "groupness." First, the sharing by a set of individuals of a property does not in and of itself suffice, nor is it necessary, to constitute a group. There must be some degree of self-consciousness on the part of members of the group that they belong to a group. Thus, the fans of the Montreal Canadiens do not constitute a group on this view. But the "Montreal Canadiens fanclub" does. Second, some structure recognized by members must be in place in order for some authorized persons to act or speak on behalf of members. Thus, for example, though many (most?) women in the world conceive of themselves as sharing certain interests, on this understanding of the term they do not by this fact constitute a group. But there exist any number of women's organizations around the world that do constitute groups in the required sense.

With these preliminaries out of the way, the first distinction I would like to bring to light has to do with the way in which membership is acquired. Some memberships are acquired through an identifiable choice on the agent's part. She fills out a form and pays her dues. She turns up to regular meetings. Others are acquired by birth. Thus, I was born a Jew, a Quebecker and a Canadian. There are of course interesting and complex intermediate cases. One's membership in a linguistic community interestingly combines elements of both extreme cases. But the vast majority of groups to which one belongs are adhered to either by birth or by choice. (This is not to say that one's membership in those groups to which one belongs by birth is involuntary. Indeed, one can choose to reaffirm one's belonging, or to renounce it.) Let me mark this distinction in what follows by referring to *birth-groups* and *choice-groups*.

Second, some groups are issue-specific, while others are general. As an example of the former, I belong to the local philatelic association *in order to* pursue my interest in stamp-collecting with like-minded others. Were I to become bored with the hobby, I would simply stop paying my dues, stop attending meetings or unsubscribe to the group's list-serve. In the case of issue-specific groups, there is something that membership is *for*. General groups, on the other hand, do not have specific purposes. One does not belong to a national or to a religious group for the same kind of easily circumscribed reason as one belongs to a hobby group or to a political party. Such belongings, while they may be occasions for the forming of further groups which will be defined around specific tasks or issues, typically give expression to one's identity or underlying convictions. Taking part in the rituals and practices of such groups, and in some cases imposing their discipline upon oneself, has an expressive rather than a teleological function. They both generate and reflect our identities: they reflect them in the sense that we take them to express something about ourselves that is in a sense independent of our belonging to the group; but they also generate them in that they give greater concreteness and precision to the property the possession of which warrants our membership in the group to begin with. I will refer in what follows to issue-specific groups and general groups.

This leads directly to the third distinction between types of groups that I want to emphasize. Some groups are identity-conferring, whereas others I will refer to as identity-neutral. Were I stripped of my membership in an identity-conferring group, I would in some sense be deprived of the reference points and self-understandings around which I organize my everyday existence. I would literally become disoriented. Some memberships, that is, provide us with frameworks within which we lead our lives, rather than pointing towards goals that we set for ourselves in the leading of our lives. Other groups, on the contrary, impinge on our identities altogether less. Were my philatelic association dissolved due to lack of new members, I might view this as a great loss. I would count as a great harm any attempt to deprive me of membership in an identity-neutral association that has come to mean a lot to me. Now to speak of harm in the case of the loss of membership in an identity-conferring group is not so much a euphemism as it is a category mistake. To speak of a harm or a loss is implicitly to make reference to something that can be compensated for. There is at least some imaginable benefit that could make up for a harm. Loss of membership in an identity-conferring group, on the other hand, is an assault on the very person underlying all possible calculations of benefit and cost, rather than being integratable by the person into a full reckoning thereof. The distinction here will be referred to by the terms identity-conferring and identity-neutral.

Fourth, some groups organize their authority structures democratically. Officers are elected by members, or are selected as a result of broad consultation with members, whereas in other groups decisions as to who will make up the governing elite are made by members of the present elite, or are spelled out by some non-democratic rule of succession. Let me refer, rather predictably, to democratic and undemocratic groups.

Finally, I would like to distinguish between groups according to the scope of the authority that those in positions of authority within them claim. Some groups only claim authority over very limited areas in the lives of their members. For example, they require of members that they adhere to Robert's Rules of Order during meetings, that they dress in certain ways during group functions, and that they observe certain rules in activities that relate to the group's mandate. Other groups claim authority over every aspect of people's lives. Religious groups often claim to govern their members' sexual and family lives and to restrict their diets. National groups have historically claimed of their members that in extreme circumstances they be willing to lay down their lives for the nation. This distinction probably marks a continuum rather than a dichotomy: membership in a philatelic association makes fewer claims upon me than does membership in the Boy Scouts of America, which in turn involves the acceptance

of norms across fewer areas of life than does, say Catholicism or Orthodox Judaism. Let me refer to this distinction as one between broad and
narrow groups.

Now clearly, the greatest potential for conflict between group life and
the norms of liberal democracy lies along the fourth and fifth dimensions. There is a *prima facie* conflict between liberal democratic society's
norms and undemocratic groups, and this conflict is heightened when
undemocratic groups are also broad.

The five distinctions I have drawn are conceptually independent. That
is, one can imagine any arrangement of these five distinctions being
instantiated by some group or other (though admittedly some arrangements are more difficult to imagine than others). One can, for example,
imagine people's identities becoming linked in the manner I have
described to issue-specific choice groups. A cause that one has devoted
one's adult life to can come to replace in one's psychic economy those
identity-conferring groups to which one belongs by birth. The only conceptual or near-conceptual exclusion I can see is that one cannot acquire
membership in an issue-specific group by birth. One's parents can defen-
sibly pass on identity in a general group, but they cannot pass on the
particular choices that they have made as to those issues to which they
have decided to devote time and energy.

But for contingent reasons, it would seem that undemocratic and broad
groups also tend to be identity-conferring and general birth-groups. That
is, it happens to be the case that, more often than not, the groups that
pose the most problems for liberal democratic regimes in virtue of the
way in which authority is exercised also happen to be ones that inform
people's identities deeply, and that, rather than being geared towards the
accomplishment of some discrete function, are expressive of who people
take themselves to be. Religious groups are probably paradigmatic here:
they claim authority over wide areas of believers' lives and tend to be
structured hierarchically and undemocratically. And the identities of the
faithful are often quite deeply intertwined with membership in religious
groups, such that loss of membership is experienced by believers as a form
of alienation or loss of self, rather than simply as the loss of a good that
could at least in principle be made up by other goods. But groups structured along cultural or ethnic lines often share both the feature of being
organized politically in ways antithetical to liberal democratic norms,
and that of being most difficult to give up in virtue of their identity-
conferring and general characters. They tend to be groups that provide
us with the canvas against the backdrop of which we lead our lives, rather
than representing an identifiable, and replaceable, element within that
canvas.

I abstain from any psycho-sociological hypothesis of why it is that these properties tend to be found together. I merely want to suggest that they do, and to draw out some consequences of this for the exit rights strategy. The exit rights strategy, espoused as we have seen by autonomists, pluralists and associationists, presupposes that all that is required in order for a group organized around illiberal lines to pass liberal muster is that its members be able to calculate the costs and benefits of continued membership as against the costs and benefits of embarking upon some new membership, and that no obstacle be placed in the path of their being able to act on the result of these calculations. What I am suggesting is that the groups whose inner workings stand in most tension with liberal democratic norms in most cases also happen to be the groups with respect to which people will be least able to view the decision to continue to be a member or not, as resolvable in terms of costs and benefits. To tell a person with (for example) a strong religious identity that the state has done as much as it can do for her by providing her with other possible memberships around which to organize her identity should she decide not to put up with the harsh treatment she is receiving within her community, and by ensuring that no obstacle lies in the way of her accessing these alternatives, is to misunderstand the way in which certain memberships function not as objects of choice, but rather as stable contexts within which the capacity of choice is exercised. It is, in effect, tacitly to equate membership in identity-conferring groups with membership in identity-neutral groups, membership which typically does tend to stand at a distance from people's identities.

Now, as it happens, identity-neutral groups tend also, again for contingent reasons, to be narrow. That is, membership in them typically requires that one subject oneself only to norms having to do with the group's specific remit. The claims of such groups upon their members are therefore usually quite limited. Ensuring exit rights in such cases seems superfluous. Members of such groups are not sufficiently "in" such groups for the need to ensure that they can get "out" to arise.

So in one typical arrangement of the features outlined above, exit rights are inappropriate, a species of category mistake. In another, they represent a kind of overkill. Is the very notion of an exit right thus condemned to being either too much or too little?

I can think of cases in which the judicial enforcement of an exit right might be perfectly appropriate. Broad groups that are identity-conferring for most of their members can continue to claim the membership of individuals who have chosen to quit their membership. They might attempt to subject them to the group's rituals, or to impose sanctions valid within the group upon them. In such rare but important cases, an exit right seems just what is called for. It enforces a choice that an individual has made to exit a group that tends in the typical case to be identity-conferring, and thus non-negotiable, for most of its members.

But exit rights do nothing for the person who feels she has no choice but to continue adhering to a group that treats her badly. Her preference would be to continue to affirm her membership while not having to put up with poor treatment. But proponents of the exit rights strategy are in effect telling her that the most that can be done in a liberal democracy is to help her throw the baby out with the bathwater.[2]

At this point the exit rights theorist's rejoinder is obvious: "Of course we would rather that individuals be able to continue to affirm their identities and that they be treated well by those groups through which they express their identity. But this would involve frequent, massive interventions in the lives of these groups. And the consequences of this would be worse than the ill we would be trying to remedy. It would generate massive mistrust and resentment, as it would be perceived by those at the receiving end as one more way through which the majority lords it over already embattled minorities. Better, in such circumstances, to opt for the *pis aller* of abstention along with a robust guarantee of exit rights."

But this is to assume that the repertoire of the liberal democratic state in dealing with illiberal minorities is limited to the intervention/abstention dichotomy. On this view, either the state steps in and invalidates a group's norms, or it stands idly by and watches as the group imposes illiberal norms. What I want to suggest in the final section of this paper is that the assumption that possible state action is limited in this way is based upon a deeper, underlying assumption that I would like to bring to light, and reject.

III

The assumption shared by those who believe that the palette of policy options available to the liberal state is limited to the abstention/intervention dyad is that the illiberality of a group's norms and practices is an independent variable. Those groups that structure their inner working illiberally do so, on this assumption, because it is in their nature to do so. Illiberality follows, on this view, from the group's sacred texts, or from their ancestral traditions. I will call this the "independence assumption," to refer to the view implicit here that the way in which groups organize

---

[2] This complaint about the exit rights strategy converges with that found in Shachar 2001. See also Okin 2002.

themselves is independent of external considerations, to do with the circumstances that they find themselves in as minorities.

I believe that this independence assumption is mistaken. The ways in which minority groups organize their internal affairs are at least in part strategic responses to the political, legal, social and cultural environments in which they find themselves (Shachar 2001: 37–8). Groups operate in a social "force field" of pressures that might incline them towards illiberality in advance of any policy directly aimed at them. Many forces in contemporary pluralist societies conduce toward what Ayelet Shachar has called "reactive culturalism" (35–7), that is the emphasizing of the most traditional and authoritarian aspects of a culture. I would like to highlight two of them. First, minorities find themselves in a situation of objective numerical threat. They face the assimilative pressures that any small minority faces. The temptation to "be like the others" is one that permanently risks offsetting the hold that a religious or cultural identity has on its members. Call this "the problem of number." The temptation to police identity through incentive, sanction and manipulation is already great simply given the numerical domination of the majority. This kind of policing requires centralized structures of authority, as well as a fairly narrow scope for the creative reinterpretation of a cultural or religious identity.

Beyond the assimilative pressures endemic to any majority/minority relation, minorities often find themselves in a cultural context that they perceive as at best indifferent, and at worst hostile, to their practices and beliefs. Minority/majority relations are often historically related to the uneasy settlement of conflicts and wars. Muslims in France and Britain are not simply people who happen to practice a different faith from that of the majority. They are also erstwhile colonial subjects. They tend to view the culture of the majority not just as different, but rather as the intellectual infrastructure for colonial oppression. To a lesser degree, Jews in largely Christian countries cannot completely ignore the legacy of anti-Semitism that at different historical periods has marked their relations with the majority in almost every country of the Diaspora. Majorities and minorities are therefore rarely unrelated groups that happen to have been juxtaposed on the same territory. Minorities have often suffered at the hands of the majority, and what's more, culture and religion have often been invoked by the majority as justifying different forms of unjust treatment. So regardless of the way in which the state acts towards minorities, there is already something in the very cultural make-up and in the political history of the societies in which the presence of illiberal minorities poses problems that may very well give rise to a defensiveness on the part of the communities. This defensiveness can very well express itself by a withdrawal of minorities from the mainstream, and by a hardening of the cultural lines between groups.[3] Call this the "problem of history."

So in most contexts, public policy-making with respect to the treatment of minorities occurs in a context that is already quite fraught with pressures that conduce to an emphasizing of the lines that separate minority cultures from those of the majority, and that tend to privilege the most conservative, and probably illiberal elements within these cultures.

Now paradoxically, the two main policy directions that have been adopted by modern Western societies in order to address the relation between the state's laws and the norms of minority communities have impacted in strikingly similar ways on the manner in which minority communities have defined themselves. By and large, they have exacerbated rather than moderated the tendency of groups to adopt a hierarchical and illiberal understanding of their own cultures. The first policy direction, that of assimilation, embodied for example in the infamous "White Paper" on aboriginal affairs presented and then withdrawn by the Canadian government in the late 1960s and early 1970s engendered a strong reaction on the part of aboriginal communities that felt that the well-meaning invitation on the part of the Canadian government to accede to full and equal citizenship concealed an insidious design of cultural assimilation. Recent claims for greater autonomy on the part of cultural minorities such as the Basques, the Bretons and the Corsicans in France, similar developments in Spain, as well as the strong reaction of the French Muslim community in what has come to be called "l'affaire du foulard," indicate that the assimilationist strategy almost inevitably engenders a "culturalist reaction," especially when such a model occurs in a society marked by the problem of number and the problem of history.

Paradoxically, however, the apparently more generous policy of granting minority groups broad group rights allowing them to enact and enforce their own norms as against those of the state, creates analogous pressures. Group rights create partial sovereignties within the territory governed by the liberal state, and the granting of such rights is made easier when there is some identifiable agency that responsibility for the

---

[3] Jeff Spinner-Halev is sensitive to the charged political context which often surrounds impositions by the state of the majority's norms, even when the majority's norms are liberal and those of minorities illiberal. But he views this as a concern only in cases in which the state attempts to override a community's internal norms. My point is that this historically charged context poses a problem for inter-group relations even absent the attempt by the state to impose its norms. See Spinner-Halev 2001. For a view according to which group identities are necessarily conflictual, see Hardin 1995.

exercise of a collective right can be transferred *to*. There is thus a natural affinity between the policy of granting group rights and those groups within broader culture that present the most readily legible administrative and hierarchical structure. The policy of conferring group rights creates an incentive for groups which are more loosely structured, and whose lines of demarcation with respect to other groups are less clear, to provide themselves with the kind of "legibility" in the eyes of the state that will make them more suitable candidates for the granting of group rights.[4]

The policy of granting areas of partial sovereignty to groups also creates an incentive for group members and authorities to emphasize their differences from the mainstream culture and from other minority groups. There seems little reason to allow groups to opt out of norms, laws and policies applying more broadly when their cultures resemble that of the (liberal) mainstream, or when aspects of the identities of members of the group present high degrees of hybridity. What, precisely, is being protected, one might ask, when groups become for all intents and purposes indistinguishable from the majority, or when their members' group memberships straddle several groups? The resources and prerogatives that a policy of granting group rights generates thus creates an incentive on the part of group leaders to present an "authentic," "unsullied," "pure culture," one that at the end of the day may never have existed in the past, but one that seems called for by the very idea of a group rights regime.[5] The logic of the groups rights regime therefore paradoxically feeds rather than undercuts the problem of number and the problem of history.

But then is the liberal state before a dead end? If policies of assimilation and policies granting group rights both contribute to the hardening and narrowing of minority cultures' self-understanding and internal mode of organization, are we not at an impasse? Don't accommodation through group rights and assimilation jointly exhaust the relevant policy options?

My suggestion is that once we appreciate the dynamics that tend to create incentives for minority groups to emphasize the more rigid and illiberal aspects of their cultures, we can imagine ways in which the liberal state can attempt to halt the dynamic, rather than intervening in the process once identities have already "congealed." The ideal that the liberal state legitimately pursues is that of creating conditions that might make it less likely that group identities will harden and crystallize around illiberal

---

[4] The concept of "legibility," and the broader idea that the state's policies often require certain simplifications as regards to social reality, is drawn from the work of Scott 1995.

[5] For an interesting analysis of the way in which liberal policies of multiculturalism end up pushing aboriginals towards an impossible ideal of cultural purity in the case of Australian multiculturalism, see Povinelli 2002.

and authoritarian manifestations of any given culture, and that will therefore lessen the number of cases in which individuals have to make tragic,
existentially wrenching choices of forgoing an identity-conferring membership in order to put an end to harsh treatment or continuing to adhere
to a group that does not adequately serve their rights or well-being.
Rather, it hopes to foster conditions that will make members of minority
communities sufficiently secure in their place in the broader societies to
which they belong so as not to feel the pressure to organize their internal affairs according to a rigid and authoritarian understanding of their
traditions.

How might this be done? The general strategy is to find ways to offset
the consequences of what I have called the problems of number and of
history. The particular sketchy suggestions are not meant to be exhaus-
tive. Rather, they are illustrative of the kind of approach that institutional
design aimed at "liberalizing" minority groups might seek to adopt.

Let us begin with the problem of number. The often massive numerical
disadvantage that minority groups find themselves in, gives rise on the
part of their members to the often justified fear of *de facto* assimilation.
That is, of assimilation that, while it is not an explicit policy objective
of the state they find themselves in, happens to be the consequence of
numerical disadvantage and of an insufficient attention on the part of
majority groups, to the ways in which number can marginalize groups,
even in the absence of an overt assimilative intent.

How might a liberal democracy offset the drift towards "reactive culturalism" that the problem of number sets in motion? Here are two suggestions. First, liberal states possessing large cultural, religious or linguistic
majorities should focus to a greater degree than they presently do on ways
in which the institutions, laws, practices and symbols of the state bespeak
the assumption that the state actually "belongs" to the members of the
majority. Members of majorities often do not notice how much the public
sphere is dominated by their values and "shared understandings." They
constitute the unnoticed and taken-for-granted background in which they
lead their lives. But for members of minority groups, reminders, spread
throughout the public sphere of the dominance of the majority groups,
far from going unnoticed, often lead to perception on the part of minorities that they are not truly at home in a public sphere whose practices
and symbols are all those of a different group, and that the only way to
achieve integration in such a context is through assimilation. On the part
of those who are intent upon preserving minority identities, this leads
to the perception of the following stark dichotomy: either we assimilate
and give up all traces of who we formerly were, or we erect strong walls

between ourselves and others, walls that will both prevent our members from leaving, and that will also prevent aspects of the majority culture from seeping in.

A more thoroughgoing commitment to state neutrality in matters religious, ethnic, cultural and linguistic might go a long way in offsetting this dynamic. An example from the area of language policy will illustrate the point.[6] Many societies in the world today are riotously multilingual. Yet it makes sense for reasons of efficiency of communication for states to address themselves to their citizens in some small subset of the total set of languages spoken in the territory. Clearly, communication should occur in the language either of the overall majority or in the languages of regional majorities.

However, many states in their language policies impose restrictions upon the use of non-"official" languages that go well beyond what the imperative of effective communication would in and of itself require. At their most extreme, they will ban schooling in other languages, or make access to them difficult. They will require of the children of immigrants or of members of national minorities not only that they acquire competence in the language of the majority, but that they receive their schooling in that language as well. In myriad ways, such states convey to their citizens the sense that they live in a society that *belongs* to the speakers of the majority language, rather than simply that they live in a society the majority of whose members just *happen* to speak the same language. In France, in Quebec, and in a number of other places around the world, this has poisoned relations between linguistic groups in the manner just described. Were the use of the majority language presented as a matter of efficiency rather than as one of cultural mission, members of linguistic minorities might paradoxically be more inclined to integrate linguistically, having rid themselves of the sense that their only options are complete linguistic assimilation or linguistic separation.

Thus, a greater espousal of the ideal of state neutrality might go some way towards offsetting the problem of number. Another problem bequeathed by the problem of number is, however, more specifically political. Certain forms of democratic decision-making can exacerbate the "tyranny of the majority" by creating *permanent* majorities and minorities. For example, where minorities are territorially dispersed, and where elected officials represent territorially delimited populations, minorities can come to find that they have no way of acquiring political voice. They are relegated to the periphery of the political process, and are thus led to

---

[6] The following few sentences summarize part of the argument in Weinstock 2003.

the adoption of increasingly radical and oppositional stances. A second way in which the problem of number can thus be addressed is through various changes to political institutions. For example, electoral reforms introducing greater proportionality into the election of representatives might counteract this problem in the case of larger territorially dispersed groups. Inclusion on various non-elected consultative bodies might be appropriate for smaller groups. There are any number of ways in which members of minority groups disenfranchised by first-past-the-post systems can be made to feel that they are stakeholders in the political process. Now, this is desirable for reasons of political morality, but the advantage that I want to emphasize here is that inclusion in the political process might offset the pressures that minority groups feel towards reactive culturalism. To the extent that the latter is born at least to some degree from a feeling of powerlessness, acquiring voice within the democratic process can have desirable effects on the way in which a group organizes its internal affairs.

How might states adopt measures to offset the problem of history? Much attention has been devoted, especially, but not exclusively, in the wake of South Africa's Truth and Reconciliation Commission, to institutional mechanisms whereby historical injustices are owned up to by their perpetrators, and forgiveness is granted by erstwhile victims. Such institutions raise thorny questions for political philosophers, to do for example with the conflicts that might arise between the desire to mete out justice for past wrongdoing, and the desire to achieve some degree of reconciliation among previously warring groups. But the point I want to make about institutions such as the TRC, or the Waitangi Tribunal in New Zealand, is that they constitute measures whereby majority groups recognize, openly and explicitly, the legacy of historical injustice and oppression upon which present societies are built. Now talk is cheap, and such mechanisms are unlikely to go very far if not accompanied by a commitment not only to recognize past ills, but also to do justice in the here and now. There is value, however, in the simple fact of institutionalized acknowledgement of fault, and in mechanisms whereby previously oppressed groups can express their grievances, state their claims, or simply tell their stories of pain. Through such acknowledgement, members of minority groups whose minority status is tied in causally to a past of historical injustice are granted what I would call *epistemic standing*. Though they may still suffer the effects of generations of injustice and oppression, something of their story is validated by the majority community. In a sense, acknowledgement of past wrongdoing leads to erstwhile oppressors and victims *living in the same subjective world* with one another. And surely, this is a condition of these groups being able to co-operate and collaborate on equal terms with one another.

So the general strategy of the liberal state in the face of illiberal groups should in my view go beyond the simplistic dichotomy of abstention/intervention. The general strategy it should enact should be to attempt to alter the "force field" within which majority/minority relations constitute themselves, by counteracting two of the most salient features of that field, which I have called the "problem of number" and the "problem of history." There are probably many other relevant features of the context within which relations among groups set themselves up, and many other policies that could be imagined in order to counteract the two problems that I have discussed. I have meant the discussion of this section to be programmatic, to point towards the kinds of policy-making and institutional design that a society might wish to undertake if it wants to maximize the compatibility of group life with liberal values.

Conclusion

In this chapter I have attempted to show that the exit rights strategy is premised upon a misguided view of group membership. I have defended three central claims. First, I have tried to show that it is unsurprising that moderate autonomists and pluralists end up adopting the exit rights strategy that flows most naturally from the associationist framework. These three positions are in fact extensionally equivalent. My second claim has been that the kind of group the internal norms of which tend to diverge the most from liberal democratic values are precisely the ones for which exit rights are not appropriate. The exit rights strategy requires that individuals be able to act on the basis of calculations on the part of the agent of relative costs and benefits of continued membership in groups that might treat the agent badly. But the groups in question are those that membership in, lends itself the least to such calculation, because of the identity-conferring properties that they tend to have. Finally, I have suggested ways in which the liberal state might overcome the simplistic abstention/intervention duality that according to many liberals exhausts the policy repertoire of the state. I have argued that liberals should attend to ways in which the "force field" within which majority/minority relations constitute themselves in many societies incline groups towards illiberality, and enact measures designed to offset these forces.

The question remains however: what should the liberal state do when its attempts at offsetting forces that incline minorities towards illiberality fail? What do we do once we have reduced the amount of illiberality as much as we can? How should those resistant groups (if there are any) that just do seem to be inclined towards illiberality be dealt with?[7]

Let me say two things in response to this question. First, my position is a broadly indirect consequentialist one. I believe that it is an appropriate goal of liberal state policy to minimize the total amount of harsh treatment that individuals receive at the hands of the groups to which they belong. The view developed in this chapter presupposes that this goal will be better served by indirection. Better to set up incentive structures that move people towards wanting to set up their associational life in a manner congruent with liberal democratic values than to intervene directly. But my consequentialism instructs that when such indirect attempts fail, direct intervention might be required.

But note, secondly, that what intervention will be required *for* will not be that all groups come to resemble mini liberal democracies in their internal operations. What is required is that they treat their members well. And there might be some distance between what that requires, and what liberal democracies require. A fair degree of paternalism, some degree of inequality, some focus on tradition rather than on autonomy is undoubtedly compatible with the former requirement, but not with the latter. Clearly, what is needed here is some kind of an account of well-being that might allow us to categorize groups according to their contribution to their members' well-being. Thankfully, the search for such an account lies beyond the bounds of this chapter.

---

[7] I thank Geoff Brahm Levey for having pushed me to address this question.

Part IV

Self-determination

12 Identity and liberal politics: the problem of minorities within minorities

Avigail Eisenberg

Liberal states tolerate some cultural and religious communities even though they adhere to sexist and homophobic values and harmful practices which seem to contradict public laws and values, and to which some of their own members object. Here I explore one factor upon which the tolerance of such values and practices often depends, namely the extent to which the practices or values are seen to be crucial to the identity-related interests of communities and individuals. Arguments for state protection of cultural and religious practices are often advanced by communities on the grounds that the community's identity-related interests and values are at stake and are threatened in the absence of such protection. Moreover, public institutions, such as courts, conventionally attempt to resolve conflicts between cultural and religious communities and their members or between different communities by balancing and assessing the competing identity-related claims at stake. Some of these attempts are objectionable (in the sense that they are unsuccessful or flawed). But objections to them, I want to argue, do not lie with the fact that they were arrived at through the consideration of individual and community identity but rather because courts, or other public institutions, neglect or misread the identity-related interests and values of those involved.

Despite recent concerns about employing the notion of identity in the context of political and legal analysis, the fact remains that identity-related interests and values of individuals and groups are often central to cultural disputes. Moreover, to ignore the identity-related nature of these disputes or to recast identity-related claims so that they are no longer presented in terms of identity offers, at best, an indirect and often inadequate means of resolving such disputes. This is not to suggest that all cultural or religious disputes are about identity. But, whether one is an advocate or opponent of "identity politics," identity matters in many conflicts that

Thanks to Veit Bader, Idil Boran, Suzanne Dovi, Colin Macleod, Margaret Moore and Jeff Spinner-Halev for their comments on this chapter. Also thanks to Anna Drake and Conor Donaldson for their research assistance.

occur within diverse societies. Moreover, the best way to assess whether or not identity is central to a dispute, or to determine whose identity is implicated in a conflict and how, is not to ignore or recast such claims in terms that abstract them from identity-related interests, but rather to develop a framework in which identity-related claims can be advanced and considered in both a public and fair manner. Here I offer the outline of an approach by which contending identity-related claims can be treated fairly in the public sphere.[1]

    This chapter defends two claims. First, to understand the conflicts that involve minorities within minorities in the absence of considering the identity-related interests at stake for those involved, is to neglect a crucial feature of such disputes and to misunderstand what is likely to count as an adequate resolution to such conflicts. A second more ambitious claim is that understanding and weighing the identity-related values and interests at stake in disputes constitute a distinctive approach to the appropriate resolution of many conflicts that involve minority groups. I call this the "difference approach" partly because the aim of the approach is to incorporate a sensitivity towards perspectives that derive from membership in or association with different cultural and religious communities. This approach is not hostile in most respects to liberalism, because liberalism is partly based on accommodating a wide variety of differences and has traditionally regarded the protection of individual and minority dissent from the values, practices and beliefs of the majority as fundamentally important and consequently, a matter to which key rights are attached. The difference approach draws on the resources of this stream of liberalism by suggesting that the ideal of treating like cases alike turns crucially on what we recognize as difference. Fairness and equality demand an awareness of the ways in which different solutions to conflicts have an impact on the practices, values and beliefs by which different groups and individuals have constituted their identities. Approaches that tend to ignore identity, such as approaches that focus only on identifying the putatively inalienable and basic rights at stake in a given conflict, offer, at best, indirect means of understanding and resolving many such conflicts. This is not to argue that a decision to allow or disallow particular community practices should turn only on whether the practices have a damaging impact on someone's identity. Nor is it to neglect the important

---

[1] The public sphere refers to a variety of public contexts in which the consideration of identity might take place. These could include state institutions, such as courts and legislatures, but they could also include non-state forums such as inter- and intra-community associations. The approach is meant to be a fair method for thinking through cultural conflicts that can be appropriately applied in a variety of settings and circumstances.

objections related to using identity as a means to gauge and resolve cultural conflicts. The difference approach is a way of assessing conflicts rather than a framework for organizing politics in general. The argument here is that, despite the challenges associated with publicly scrutinizing identity-related claims, the consideration of identity belongs at the forefront of analyzing many conflicts that involve cultural and religious communities. Decisions which fail to take into account whether and how the different identities of those involved are likely to be affected by one outcome or another, are ones that fail to take into account what is often the central and motivating element of many conflicts and, for this reason, are likely to fail as adequate solutions.

The first part of this chapter examines the dominant approach taken, both in theory and in many understandings of practice, to resolving inter-cultural conflicts that involve minorities within minorities. The dominant approach ignores, or attempts to ignore, identity. In the second part, I describe the difference approach and show how the difference approach works in several legal cases where courts have weighed identity-related claims. I also attempt to answer some of the key objections that arise in relation to the political and legal accommodation of identity, including the public negotiation of seemingly private claims, the risk of misunderstanding a community's identity, and the problem of reifying particular (and often conservative) aspects of group identity in the course of trying to protect the group.

The dominant rights-based approach

In an important sense, there is nothing inherently wrong with rights *per se*. However, a certain rigid conceptualization of rights, common in rights discourse, that understands rights to be inalienable, basic and unalterable claims, which are attached directly to individuals and groups, is problematic. This conceptualization of rights can be detected in what I call the dominant approach. The dominant approach to resolving conflicts that involve minorities within minorities is one that appeals to rights so conceived in the course of expressing and resolving inter-cultural conflict. The first problem with the dominant approach is that often the claims of both sides can be expressed in terms of rights, and therefore, approaches that rely on rights have to make a case for what to do when rights conflict. This problem tends to be posed in a way that suggests that conflicts involving minorities within minorities give rise to stark *dilemmas* between seemingly non-negotiable claims. A dilemma in this context is a conflict between two claims where, taken together, the claims are seemingly irreconcilable and non-negotiable and where each is widely recognized as instantiating important if not fundamental values.[2] Many liberal theorists characterize the conflict between sexual equality and cultural autonomy in terms of a dilemma in this sense. For instance, Susan Okin (1998: 680) has discussed the choices that some women face in terms of *either* enjoying cultural community *or* enjoying sexual equality, both of which she considers important interests. Monique Deveaux describes the struggle by Aboriginal women to advance sexual equality within their communities as "a dilemma of reconciling sex equality rights with collective, cultural rights" (2000a: 81). Martha Nussbaum discusses the problem in terms of a "dilemma" between the rights to sexual equality and the rights to cultural autonomy (1999: 81).[3] And Chandran Kukathas structures the clash between feminism and multiculturalism in terms of a dilemma (2001: 83–98), although one that he aims to solve by favoring cultural autonomy. Even though these theorists resolve the dilemma in different ways, a common thread in their analyses is the idea that communities faced with these conflicts are forced to choose between important and competing claims in such a fashion that vindicating one claim is, in every respect, at odds with accommodating the competing claim.

That cultural rights seem to generate dilemmas for liberals and liberal polities is hardly news. The dominant perspective, which is sometimes expressed in terms of the conflict between collective and individual rights, is a long-standing one in the political debates of those Western states that have recognized the rights of cultural and religious groups to autonomy or special protections. For instance, the Canadian Constitution is often presented as juxtaposing individual rights and collective rights (Morton 1985: 71–84; Magnet 1986); Aboriginal legal scholars have condemned Canada's Charter of Rights and Freedoms because it represents an individualistic rights tradition that is hostile to Aboriginal communities (Turpel 1989–90: 23), which "are based on the paramountcy of collective rights" (*Globe and Mail* (national edition) 24 September 1992: A5); and French Canadians have tended to frame their disdain or support for the Charter in terms of its protection of individual rights, which are more English, as opposed to collective rights, which are more French.[4] Sometimes the paramountcy of individual rights is viewed as a very good thing, as it was by Pierre Elliot Trudeau (1992: 1), who argued against changing the current balance in which "personal, individual rights have

---

[2] See Elster 1989.
[3] Nussbaum abandons this sort of characterization in Nussbaum 2001: especially 187–212.
[4] See Arnopoulos and Clift 1980: 36.

more importance than collective rights." More recently, a key Canadian cabinet minister, Stephane Dion, explained to an American audience at Princeton University that the principal difference between the American Bill of Rights and the Canadian Charter is that the Charter protects "collective rights benefiting notably linguistic minorities and aboriginals." Dion then assured the audience that the "collective rights in the Canadian Charter and in Canadian law in general is delimited by the paramountcy of individual rights, in a way not unlike the practice of your [American] courts" (Dion 2002: 1).

In general, people disagree about how to resolve these dilemmas. Amongst liberal political theorists, both Okin and Nussbaum argue that the right to sexual equality ought to have priority over the right to cultural autonomy, while for Kukathas and Jeff Spinner-Halev (2001: 84–113), cultural autonomy ought to prevail and women ought to exit communities which refuse to change their sexist practices. In the political realm, those engaged in these debates also do not agree about whether individual or collective rights ought to have "paramountcy" or whether the right to sexual equality ought to prevail over cultural autonomy. But these disagreements are largely internal to the dominant approach, which otherwise unites their arguments. According to the dominant approach, rival interests of individuals and groups – of women and their cultural communities – are advanced in terms of incommensurable and fundamental values, which are often best expressed in terms of rights. Once conflicts are framed in terms of a competition between individual and collective rights, or between the right to sexual equality versus the right to cultural autonomy, resolutions appear to turn on choosing between fundamental values, which is what presents the dilemma. Each of those who present the problem in these terms then defends his or her preferred choice. But because no uncontroversial way exists to prioritize values that are represented, as rights are, as normatively basic and incommensurable, none of the resolutions is uncontroversial and, more importantly, all the resolutions entail choosing one fundamental value over the other.

It may seem that fixating on the word "dilemma" or on some idealized and perhaps rarefied understanding of rights diverts our attention from the problem at hand. It may also seem that doing so caricatures the numerous studies of rights conflicts, all of which are richer and more nuanced than my account of them reflects. But I want to argue that the dominant approach pervades political debate and this is a significant problem for two additional reasons.

First, the dominant approach leads us to misunderstand what the courts are doing when they decide cases involving cultural conflict. When the courts are confronted with such conflicts, they will appear to those who adopt the dominant approach to be choosing between "apples and oranges." That is, if the values upon which they adjudicate are convincingly represented as fundamental, their decisions will appear to involve choosing between fundamental values. One predictable consequence of viewing the court's work in this way is that judicial decisions will appear to be arbitrary or based on the personal or cultural biases of the courts (or particular judges) in favor of one set of values or commitments rather than another. For example, when the Supreme Court of Canada favored individual freedom of expression and struck down a law that required only French on commercial signs (*Ford v. Quebec* [1988]), it appeared to those employing the dominant approach to display the Court's bias in favor of English individual rights over French collective rights (Galipeau 1992). Similarly, when a British Columbia court decided that an Aboriginal winter dance, which in this case putatively involved kidnapping and assault, violated the right to security of person (*Thomas v. Norris* [1992]), it was criticized for displaying colonial and Western bias in favor of individualism and against (Aboriginal) collectivism.[5] And when US courts decided to consider cultural or religious beliefs as a mitigating feature in criminal sentencing, they were criticized for a form of cultural overcompensation impelled by an ideology of multiculturalism, which biased their decisions in favor of protecting cultural communities rather than sexual equality.[6]

For the moment, I wish to put aside the question of how these cases ought to be decided and instead highlight the way in which these judicial decisions were understood using the dominant approach. When judicial decisions are understood to implicate courts in choosing between two sets of incommensurable values, values that pose dilemmas, few alternative ways exist to explain the basis upon which courts reach their decisions other than the suggestion that they decide according to their own cultural biases. Notwithstanding the possibility that the court is biased along cultural lines, using the dominant approach implies that, in cases of cultural conflict, judicial decisions which involve a choice between two incommensurable rights-based claims can be resolved on no basis other than the cultural biases or perhaps the political agenda of the courts. Under these circumstances, the need then arises to compensate for the

---

[5] I examine this case at greater length in Eisenberg 1994.
[6] For insightful discussions of the cultural defence, see Song 2002. Also see Volpp 2000. Uma Narayan discusses the anxieties of Westerners which lead them to accept some cultures as radically different from their own in terms of basic values and to suspect themselves of imperialistic attitudes unless they respect non-Western values. See Narayan 1998.

cultural biases of the courts either by requiring that the court uses the biases of another culture to guide its decision, as in some interpretations of why "cultural defences" are accepted by the courts, or by suggesting that only courts internal to communities can render culturally sensitive decisions for cases that arise in those communities.[7]

The second politically significant consequence of the dominant approach is that it leads us to misunderstand the reasons why some people reject liberal-individualist values. The approach suggests that choosing cultural autonomy over individual rights is the result of cultural differences that divide people into those who opt for liberal values and those who favor non-liberal ones. But this "divide," between the liberal and the non-liberal, is partly driven by the choice that the dilemma presents in the first place between *either* liberal rights *or* communal values. If fragile minorities – particularly, communities whose historical and cultural circumstances are shaped by colonialism or by the culturally insensitive application of liberal values – are convinced that they must choose between individual rights and the protection of their cultural community (which is how the dominant perspective presents the problem to them), many will unsurprisingly choose their cultural community. Liberal solutions are rejected by many peoples in the world as inauthentic to building their communities and liberal values are treated as values against which non-liberal communities seek to form their own "authentic" identities. By expressing the choice confronting non-liberal minorities in terms of a dilemma between two sets of values, the dominant approach exacerbates this cultural divide. Moreover, it can distort our understanding of what is at stake in these conflicts and how to resolve them.

In sum, the dominant approach frames conflicts that involve minorities within minorities in terms of conflicting rights claims that generate dilemmas. Three consequences follow from understanding conflicts in this way. First, the approach presents the choice confronting us in terms of

---

[7] It is important here not to conflate arguments based on cultural commensurability and arguments based on self-determination. Aboriginal communities usually favor the development of their own courts and legal systems because these are important components of self-determination or self-government. Here I am suggesting that the dominant approach leads us to understand that the main reason why a minority would need its own court system is to compensate for the cultural biases of the mainstream courts. In this way, the framework supplied by the dominant approach either eschews the question of self-determination or, more problematically, casts self-determination in terms of the problem of cultural biases; that is, a group's claim to self-government seems to turn on whether its culture is sufficiently different from the mainstream. Although I do not pursue this problem here, arguments that reduce the bases for Aboriginal self-determination to cultural difference both misunderstand and diminish the bases upon which claims to self-determination can be and often are justified.

different, fundamental and irreconcilable values where, putatively (given this way of representing the problem), no obvious or uncontroversial priority exists amongst the contending claims. Second, presenting these conflicts as dilemmas potentially leads to misunderstanding how courts decide cases involving cultural conflict. The implication is that courts render their decisions about such "dilemmas" on the basis of their own cultural biases in favor of one set of values over another. And third, the dominant approach exacerbates the cultural divide between mainstream society and those who belong to cultural and religious minorities by framing the choice which minorities, or the minorities within them, confront as one which demands that they choose between their individual rights and their community's values. When the choice is put in these terms, many individuals, no matter how dire their circumstances, will choose the collective rights and cultural autonomy of their own communities over the values held by the community they view as responsible for their cultural oppression.

The difference approach

At some level, the need to sort out competing claims, including those to which rights are attached, is an unavoidable aspect of politics in diverse societies. The question addressed here is not whether we make choices between rights in cases where rights conflict but rather how we make these choices, how we understand the basis upon which we make these choices and whether, in cases that involve cultural minorities, our methods are fair and equitable. I have suggested that the dominant approach constitutes the framework in which rights conflicts are often understood in public debate, and that it leads us to misunderstand the bases upon which rights-based conflicts involving minorities are decided in a manner that both obscures what courts do when they adjudicate such cases and exacerbates the conflict between cultural and religious communities.

There are ways, other than dominant approach, of understanding what happens when rights conflict but none resonates in public debates as strongly as does the dominant approach. One alternative is to translate rights into the purposes that they are meant to serve.[8] Conflicting claims that involve the same rights can then be sorted out on the basis of determining how best to serve the purposes of the right in question. A

---

[8] A purposive approach might inform many different proposals for resolving rights conflicts, including those like that proposed by Cindy Holder (this volume), which distinguishes between basic and derivative rights. Here I consider the purposive approach proposed by Jeremy Waldron.

variant of this approach is proposed by Jeremy Waldron who suggests that rights conflicts are best understood as conflicts amongst the duties that underlie rights and by which they are protected (Waldron 1989). Duties, unlike rights in Waldron's understanding (and mine), are negotiable and subject to compromise. Conflicts are resolved by compromising amongst duties or by choosing duties that do not conflict, rather than choosing one right over another and thereby drawing at least one of the rights into question. In those cases where we cannot find compatible duties, Waldron suggests that we turn to the purpose that a right is meant to serve and assess which duty best fulfills the right's purpose.[9] Waldron's proposal is helpful both in showing how compromise works in the context of a rights-based conflict, and in showing how circumstances shape the protection of rights. But one of its drawbacks is that, in those cases where duties are incompatible, the approach treats as uncontroversial the determination of what purpose a given right is meant to serve.

I want to suggest that one of the purposes that rights serve is to protect individual and group identity-related differences. The difference approach is predicated on the fact that the shape and health of an individual's identity largely depend upon how societal institutions treat differences amongst people and that, in turn, fair treatment is predicated, in part, on whether institutions are sensitive to differences. By "differences" I am referring to the differences amongst people that play a constitutive role in shaping their identities. Differences that are considered central to shaping the identities of people in most societies include culture, religion, language and gender. But many other differences might be added to this list depending on which sorts of values and characteristics have political significance in a particular society. In most ways our identity has little political significance in the sense that societal institutions are indifferent to our identity-related differences, including differences that we might view as crucial to our identities. For instance, that my parents argued about religion when I grew up is a matter to which political and legal institutions are utterly indifferent yet, in my view, is of crucial significance to my identity. However, other identity-related differences

---

[9] Waldron argues that comparing and weighing duties works best in cases of intra-right conflicts, where two instances of the same right seem in conflict. In cases of conflict between two different rights, Waldron cautions that weighing duties might not help because of the priority between the rights. However, in some cases, the duties that conflict will so dramatically differ in terms of their importance to the rights in question that choosing between them is justified. Where right A is more important than right C, it could be the case that fulfilling duty C1, which will have a direct impact on protecting right C, is preferable to fulfilling duty A24 which has an unreliable, indirect and marginal impact on protecting right A.

are politically significant in the sense that they carry with them direct benefits and burdens imposed on individuals and communities by other communities and by societal institutions. In general, differences that have political significance within most liberal societies include ones based on language, gender, sexual orientation, religion, ethnicity, nationality, class and, in some respects, political conviction. The aim of the difference approach is to highlight the political and legal burdens imposed on and benefits enjoyed by those with particular identity-related characteristics and then to provide a means of determining whether these burdens and benefits are fair.

As explained above, the difference approach rejects the assumption that the political and legal struggles between peoples are best viewed as involving the vindication of conflicting, fundamental rights. Nonetheless, the approach recognizes that one important purpose of rights is to protect differences amongst people that play a constitutive role in shaping their identities. Individual rights have historically been helpful in protecting individual difference by ensuring that individuals have freedom of speech, opinion, belief and association, and that they are not subject to legal discrimination because of the beliefs, values and groups through which they have constituted their identity. More recently, collective rights have been defended as means by which group-based characteristics, such as language, culture and some religious practices, can be protected. Within the framework of the difference approach, the recognition of "individual" and "group" rights and differences does not imply that individuals and groups have competing moral or legal standing. The purpose of protecting group or individual difference is to enhance individual well-being and to do so while recognizing that individual well-being is often dependent on the well-being of groups. But individuals and groups are sometimes threatened by different kinds of circumstances and therefore the means by which individual differences are protected might be inadequate to protecting groups. Whether or not rights are useful to protecting either or both individual and group difference depends on factors related to the context and circumstances of a dispute and whether alternatives to rights that also protect difference, such as policies that promote tolerance, institutionalized federalism, treaties and other such means are more appropriate and effective. In any case, within the framework provided by the difference approach, rights, whether individual or collective, are amongst the means by which differences might be protected, but do not, on their own, constitute the object to be protected.

An approach to resolving disputes that involve minorities within minorities, which is predicated on making full use of this notion of difference, requires, first, that those attempting to resolve such conflicts[10] are aware of the ways in which identity-related differences are implicated in political and legal struggles amongst groups and between groups and their members. "Being aware" in this context means considering evidence regarding or assessing claims in relation to the identity-related interests at stake. It also means considering identity-related claims in public debate and possibly accepting such claims as valid reasons to resolve conflicts one way rather than another.

The difference approach asks, first, that we understand the role a practice or value plays in constituting the identities of parties involved in a conflict. In order to do so, the approach solicits the following sorts of questions: What is the role of the tradition or practice in the way that a group defines itself? Is this role or definition in dispute? How disputed is it? To what extent will disallowing the practice alter the group's identity? To what extent will an external court interfering in the internal affairs of a minority community jeopardize that community's ability to define and govern itself? These questions usher into assessments of inter- and intra-cultural disputes the identity-related interests that the dominant approach works to keep out. If conflicts are framed, as they are under the dominant approach, in terms of a competition between fundamental rights, then the degree to which a practice is crucial to a community's identity is entirely beside the point and evidence that speaks to this issue must be considered irrelevant. The dominant approach asks only whether or not the community has a right, or alternatively whether its practices violate a right.

Evidence and argument related to identity-related interests, values and rights are regularly considered by the courts and introduced into public debate. Despite its pervasiveness in one sense, the dominant approach might reflect no more than a rights-based script of how we think conflicts between rights are resolved. The script is a poor reflection of the actual reasoning employed in the course of resolving such conflicts, including (ironically) the implicit reasoning sometimes employed by those who suggest that such conflicts give rise to dilemmas. Consider, for example, how liberal societies resolve the problem of discrimination against women and homosexuals by mainstream churches such as the Catholic Church. No one accepts that religions are free to treat their members (or non-members) in any way they choose. All liberal societies have

---

[10] The question of who can legitimately assess or adjudicate these conflicts is not discussed here. But, as noted above, the difference approach is meant to provide the framework by which any institution or forum, including inter-cultural institutions, courts and forums that employ deliberative democracy, can resolve cultural conflicts.

developed a set of understandings with churches about the types of restrictions that are fair and those that are unfair. These restrictions are then read into what the right to freedom of religion means in Canada, the United States and elsewhere. Liberal societies differ with respect to precisely how they interpret this right. So when Martha Nussbaum suggests that "it would be wrong to require a religious body to ordain open and practicing homosexuals" but not wrong to require that churches hire (or not fire) homosexual gardeners or accountants (Nussbaum 1999: 197), implicit in her argument is a distinction between what is core and peripheral to the character and identity of the Catholic Church that is obvious only to someone who knows a little about its character and history. The determination of the circumstances under which the Church can discriminate on the basis of sexual orientation is shaped, in part, by a judgement about which practices or traditions are central to the Church's identity and which are not. In other words, the matter is not settled on the grounds of what is inherent or obvious about the right to freedom of religion *per se*. Rather, it requires considering and weighing the history, traditions and practices of the Church and then comparing the significance of this practice to the impact such practices have on those who are subjected to discrimination of this sort.

The consideration and weighing of identity-related claims and values shape the jurisprudence developed about cultural and religious "rights," at least in Canada and the United States. Courts regularly consider the identity-related interests and values of communities and individuals in attempting to resolve disputes. This is partly because individuals and communities regularly use legal tools, such as public policy and rights, to defend their disputed practices and values, and then attempt to vindicate their policies or justify their particular interpretation of rights by arguing that these measures are important to protecting crucial aspects of their identities. In relation to court cases, most of which have been extensively discussed elsewhere (and therefore will not be described in detail here), the sort of questions relevant to the difference approach include the following:

- In the case of *Santa Clara Pueblo v. Julia Martinez* [1978], to what extent does the US Supreme Court damage the identity-related interests of the Pueblo by striking down a sexist rule of membership that Pueblo institutions have passed and verified upon reconsideration?
- In the case of *Ford v. AG Quebec* [1988], to what extent does banning English on commercial signs help secure the French language in Montreal?
- In the case of *People of the State of California v. Kong Pheng Moua* [1985] (Song 2002), what is the role of bride-capture amongst the Hmong

people and under what circumstances does it actually resemble sexual assault?

- In the case of *Thomas v. Norris* [1992], what is the role of spirit dancing amongst the Coast Salish Indians? Is it central and integral to their cultural identity or is it an obscure and uncommon ritual?
- In *Reynolds v. United States* [1878], how important is polygamy to the Mormon community and in what ways will banning the practice damage the identity and the interests related to the identity of that community?[11]

The difference approach requires that the contending identity-related claims of those involved in such disputes be compared to and weighed against each other. It requires, for example, an assessment of whether the identity-related interests and values of the contending parties, including fundamental interests to dissent and to enjoy security of person, are undermined or threatened by a group's practices or values. Using the cases mentioned above, the approach requires that the following sorts of questions also be considered:

- What is the impact of sexist rules of membership on the identities of Pueblo women and children who are denied membership by the Pueblo community?
- To what extent does banning English on commercial signs impinge on the identity-related interests of individuals who would otherwise choose English for their signs? Is this a matter that lies at the very core of freedom of speech for Anglophones or are the interests at stake for those individuals less fundamental?
- What are the consequences for the identities of Hmong women in the United States of permitting the Hmong ritual of bride-capture?
- To what extent does the spirit dance, or some aspect of it, violate the identity-related interests of those individuals who are involuntarily initiated into the ritual? Does the dance deny a fundamental interest, such as security of person, or does it impose a relatively mild inconvenience on those who do not want to partake in it?
- In what ways does polygamy either damage the identities of women or otherwise affect the identity-related interests of the broader community?

In all the cases mentioned above, these questions constituted important parts of the evidence presented to the courts and of the courts' deliberation. In most cases, these were not simple questions to answer. But

---

[11] Many additional cases can be added to this list. My point here is that identity-related interests are a common feature of cases involving cultural and religious conflicts and therefore the difference approach is applicable across a large number of cases involving cultural or religious conflict.

the claim here is not that focusing on identity provides an easy way to resolve disputes between minorities and their members. Rather, my claim is that these are the sorts of questions that need to be asked in order to understand what is at stake in these disputes. Courts regularly accept and assess evidence about the centrality and significance of a disputed practice to a community's identity and the impact that practice has on a dissenting individual. They do not always consider such evidence systematically nor do they always interpret the evidence well. On the contrary, sometimes courts misread cultural evidence, engage in cultural misinterpretation and otherwise fail to treat identity-related claims in a fair and systematic manner. One virtue of the difference approach is that it exposes such problems by focusing our attention on how the courts understand, interpret and assess identity-related claims. In contrast, the dominant approach obscures these problems by asking that matters of identity be translated into rights and that court decisions be assessed on the basis of which rights – the right to sexual equality or right to cultural autonomy, individual rights or collective rights – are *really* rights or which rights do the courts tend to favor.

Four problems with using identity

Four immediate problems arise when we contemplate engaging in debate where identity-related claims are permitted and taken seriously: (1) that identity-related claims are not the proper subject of public and political assessment because they are subjective and sometimes based on the truth of religious and metaphysical doctrines; (2) that identity-related claims are self-validating and therefore difficult to challenge even when they appear to be lavish or opportunistic; (3) that groups and individuals use identity as a proxy in power struggles which have little to do with identity; and (4) that an approach which aims at privileging core aspects of community identity will end up having a conservative influence on the development of communities.

With respect to the first problem, Brian Barry (2001a: 253) argues that we cease to engage in moral discourse once claims based on cultural identity are accepted as reasons for or against a course of action because no non-arbitrary and politically legitimate basis exists on which to assess claims about the authenticity of cultural or religious traditions and practices. Authentic identity-related claims are in some sense, as Waldron describes them (2000: 158), "interpersonally and socially non-negotiable" because they are deeply personal and often based on doctrines or beliefs whose authenticity rests with the rationales they have for those who follow or practice them and not with external political or legal institutions. To explain one's attachment to a particular tradition "because it is important to my identity" is to offer an inauthentic explanation of what are often personal and religious reasons for following the tradition. The reason why I *really* follow the traditions I do is because my parents did, or because I believe that God commands me to, or because, according to my holy book, this is a way of being closer to God. These reasons are not the appropriate subjects of public assessment. In contrast, Waldron argues, to justify a tradition on the basis that "it is important to my identity" is to display "a vain and self-preoccupied contempt for the norm itself – by gutting it of *its* reasons, and replacing them as reasons with *my own* need to keep the faith" (2000: 170).

Identity-related beliefs and practices are, without a doubt, deeply personal and subjective in some senses. But to accept this fact does not mean that the only correct way to justify a practice in public debate is to establish the plausibility of the metaphysical or religious doctrine that allegedly really drives the practice. We do not require, for example, that those claiming the right to freedom of religion justify their claim on the basis of the veracity of their religious doctrines. As Jonathan Quong argues (2002: 307–28), "[w]hat would it mean to ask for the religious rationale American Indians have for using peyote in a decision about whether they should be exempted from certain drug laws? There is no standard by which we can assess the 'correctness' of the reasons, and even if we could, it is not clear how or why that should figure in our decision about the exemption." Quong suggests that when individuals and communities seek to justify their practices by claiming that these practices are central to their identity, they are appealing to public standards of fair treatment. They are claiming to have a fundamental interest in following a practice which the public law or the majority's regulations bar them from otherwise pursuing. In this sense, far from diverting debate from moral discourse, such identity claims are a means by which people enter moral and political discourse by subjecting to public scrutiny the claim that something is important to their identity, that it is disadvantaged, or disallowed by public rules and institutions, and that it needs special protection or exemptions from public laws and regulations as a matter of fairness.

A second and similar objection is that identity claims are self-validating in the sense that we have to accept whatever people say is important to their identity because they are, after all, the authors of that identity[12] and

---

[12] To suggest, as I am here, that individuals choose their identity, is not to suggest that they are in control of the resources, context and circumstances on which their choices are based. A similar point is made in most discussion of identity including Sen 1998.

therefore the ones in the best position to assess what is harmful to it.[13] If identity-related claims are treated as self-validating then the worry is that they will be advanced in manipulative ways or to support lavish claims about the normative importance of some aspect of identity. As Veit Bader argues, "identity-claims should not pay" (2001a: 277–99), and allowing them to pay will lead individuals and groups to use identity strategically and opportunistically. So, for example, after a recent vote in Kuwait's parliament to deny, once again, the vote to women, some government officials justified the decision by arguing that Islamic religion and Kuwaiti culture dictate that women cannot vote.[14] Some Kuwaiti women argue that these justifications are false and that the real reason to deny women the vote is because doing so secures the power of an ultra-orthodox clan in Kuwait's government. In this case, identity-related claims are putatively being used opportunistically as a means to secure oligarchic power.

But even if the difference approach motivates parties to frame their interests in terms of identity as a means to ensure that they are heard and taken seriously, this strategy can only pay off if convincing evidence is presented that a crucial aspect of their identity is, in fact, implicated in the dispute, and further that this aspect is, on balance, more crucial to their identity-related interests than is the claim of the other party to the dispute. Moreover, contrary to the claim that identity is self-validating, individuals and groups, whose identity-related values and practices are threatened, conventionally bring evidence before the court that shows how crucial aspects of their identity have been jeopardized by laws, regulations and policies. Self-validation is one strategy that may be employed in such cases. But it is not particularly persuasive in a court of law or in other public forums. The claim that a particular practice is central to the identity of a group can usually be demonstrably established or undermined by historical records, empirical validation, anthropological analysis and other social scientific means. It is important to recognize that some of these means are not without their controversial elements. For instance, anthropologists are acutely aware of the ways in which anthropological evidence used in legal cases about communal identities has been defective and misleading (Asch 1992). Historians have similar methodological disputes (Fortune 1993: 80–101), as do archivists and other social

[13] In this respect, Martha Minow discusses the problem of "victim speak" which, as a form of political discourse, allocates resources partly on the bases of the harm or suffering experienced by groups. One problem with this form of politics, which Minow and others (such as Wendy Brown) have argued characterizes liberal societies today, is that it gives all groups and individuals an incentive to focus on the potential ways in which they have been harmed; these claims proliferate and are difficult to question. See Minow 2002. Also see Brown 1995.

[14] See BBC News 2002; Amnesty International Online 2000.

scientists (McRanor 1997: 64–88). The admissibility of oral history by indigenous peoples as a means to validate their claims is also not free of controversy nor is the issue of what counts as verification of oral history uncontentious (*Delgamuukw v. British Columbia* [1997]). These interesting debates, about what counts as credible and reliable evidence, though not explored here, are significant to the argument I am making; the reason that these are such lively debates is because the veracity of identity-related claims is regularly considered by the courts and considered to be important, if not crucial, in many cases.

Because other means of validation exist, we do not simply accept at face value what individuals or groups tell us is important to them. Rather, the sort of considerations that typically count as contributing to a compelling argument include, for example, that a practice, which is part of a group's identity, has a history; that efforts have been made to retain the practice in light of opposition to it; and that it contributes to the social fabric of a way of life. Similarly, what counts as a compelling reason to limit the practice is not simply because "we don't do that around here" or because "we don't like that others do it." Rather, we argue that certain practices oppress people in the sense that they impair their psychological or physical development, they undermine their self-esteem and render their deliberative capacities on matters crucial to their self next to impossible. One ironic benefit of the difference approach is that it requires that we develop systematic and fair means to identify those cases in which identity-related interests and values are not crucially at stake. The best way to determine whether identity-related claims are used strategically is to investigate what is constitutive of the group's or individual's identity-related differences. Only when claims are not subject to systematic and careful scrutiny is it possible for identity to be used opportunistically.

A related objection to focusing on identity in order to resolve cultural and religious conflicts arises where community practices seem to involve the abuse and mistreatment of some members of the community. In such cases, it seems to contribute little to the resolution of disputes to insist that harmful practices and beliefs are important to a group's identity-related interests even if, in some sense, they can be expressed in these terms. Not all cases involving communities are about identity. Nonetheless, according to the difference approach, identity-related claims ought to be considered, although perhaps not fully accepted, even if they are connected to practices that are harmful because doing so is the means to understand more fully, and to require that groups explain more fully, the role that harmful practices actually play in their cultural or religious identity. Consider, for example, a group of men who are members of the Coast Salish Indians in British Columbia and who set out to protect themselves from being sued for assault, battery, kidnapping and false imprisonment after they initiated a reluctant member of their community into a Salish ritual known as the spirit dance.[15] The evidence they presented to the court showed that, contrary to how they had practiced the initiation ritual, the spirit dance requires that initiators "blow" on the bodies of those initiated, not beat them up. Moreover, it was revealed that, according to custom, initiations can occur on a voluntary or involuntary basis and therefore the restriction imposed by the court, that the community only initiate spirit dancers voluntarily, entailed, in the end, a relatively modest degree of cultural interference.

Similarly, when a Hmong man argued, in a California court, that his sentence for the crime of sexual assault ought to be mitigated because he thought he was engaging in the Hmong ritual of bride-capture, it is unacceptable for the court to be content with superficial evidence about the nature of the ritual and its importance or prevalence in Hmong culture. Perhaps a more comprehensive understanding of the ritual would not alter how we think this particular case ought to be resolved. But a more accurate and thorough examination of the culture would at least clarify what is at stake in the case and whether, by rejecting this putative "cultural defense" we are doing any damage at all to Hmong cultural beliefs and practices. The only way to determine whether rituals, practices or beliefs are used opportunistically and strategically within groups or by individual members is to require that, in cases where conflicts arise, those defending putatively harmful practices fully explain the role that these practices actually play in their cultural or religious identity.

A final objection to the difference approach is that, by privileging identity-related interests that are crucial to a group, the approach is likely to have a conservative influence on the development of a community's identity. Consider, for instance, the political rights of women in Kuwait and imagine a case in which the Kuwaiti parliament brought forward evidence which showed that Kuwaiti culture is indeed built around traditions of male political rule and has historically distinguished itself from other Islamic communities partly on this basis. By privileging identity-related claims, we might end up privileging the argument in favor of male rule because of its connection to the way in which the community has defined itself historically and distinguished itself from other communities. But two considerations must be noted here. First, if by "conservative" what is meant is that decision-making should take seriously the ways in which communities have historically constructed themselves and protected core beliefs and traditions, then the difference approach is conservative. It is

---

[15] I discuss this case at greater length in Eisenberg 1994.

important to remember that, according to the framework supplied by the difference approach, to take these factors seriously is not the same as allowing them to override all other interests at stake in this conflict including the identity-related interests of women in this community. Second, the difference approach takes dissent seriously both in assessing whether or not practices which are defended as core to a community's identity are not, in fact, controversial ones within the community, and in assessing what is at stake for the identities of those who dissent from the community's practice. As I explained above, the difference approach asks that we scrutinize and compare the different identity-related claims of those involved in a dispute. Therefore, a crucial component of the approach is the consideration of the identity-related interests of dissenters. The difference approach requires, for instance, that the identity-related interests of the Kuwaiti community be compared to the identity-related interests of Kuwaiti women. The approach specifically considers the argument that denying voting rights to women in Kuwait threatens their identity-related interests, including capacities and opportunities crucial to their identities, and, moreover, does so in a manner that increases their vulnerability to oppression and abuse. The strength of women's claims to the right to vote in Kuwait rests on showing that denying the vote to them in Kuwait places their identity-related interests at more serious risk than is the risk to the community's identity of extending the franchise. In this way, by taking identity-related claims seriously on both sides of a dispute, the difference approach potentially leads to transformative and radical results.[16]

The general character of resolutions

So far, I have outlined some of the reasons why translating claims into identity-related interests and values is better than the dominant approach as a means to satisfactorily resolving conflicts involving minorities within minorities. The difference approach takes identity-related interests as the common normative currency for the adjudication of claims and, in doing so, avoids, at least in the first instance, analyzing disputes in terms of values that are irreconcilable. I have suggested that often we implicitly rely on our own understanding of the identity-related interests and values at stake in disputes even as we apply rights to resolve conflicts. But unless identity-related claims and values are considered systematically and applied critically, they will easily invite bias and unfairness. In this regard, I have surveyed four objections to using identity and attempted in each case

---

[16] I am grateful to Colin Macleod for pointing this out to me.

to show that the explicit and systematic appraisal of identity-related claims offers the best means to ensure that these claims are understood accurately, that they are treated in an even-handed way, and that they are not advanced opportunistically.

Here I want to suggest that two general tendencies are likely to characterize resolutions in which the difference approach is applied to conflicts that involve minorities within minorities. The first tendency is that, in translating conflicts into contending identity-related claims which can then be weighed and compared to each other, some cases become relatively easy to resolve. There are usually two reasons for this. First, some cases entail practices that place individuals in the way of direct physical harm in ways that so clearly and profoundly damage individual well-being, and thus jeopardize the individual's capacity to shape her identity, that it is hard to imagine how any impact on a group's identity can outweigh these considerations.[17] The second reason is that, in many cases, the importance of a tradition or practice is so questionable to the community that it is difficult for a group to defend the practice in a public setting. For instance, in the commercial sign law case in Quebec, while all parties agreed that protecting French in Quebec, and specifically in Montreal, was an important public policy objective and that requiring French on all signs aided that objective, no party in this case, including the Quebec government (whose law was eventually struck down) could supply convincing evidence to the court which showed that requiring the "no English" rule demonstrably aided that objective. Similarly, in *Thomas v. Norris*, the defense of spirit dancing revealed, not only that the ritual was not being practiced correctly in the case at hand, but that involuntarily initiating individuals into the dance was rare and certainly not a central and integral feature of the tradition.

The second tendency that emerges is that such comparisons tend to favor the claims of individuals over groups, including claims to sexual equality, when these claims conflict with ones based on group difference or identity. This tendency should not be all that surprising. The survival of a group's identity seldom, if ever, depends on its adherence to a single practice. Moreover, the survival of a cultural community does not entail preserving some notion of cultural purity even if some practices and values

---

[17] As discussed above, even in such cases, the consideration of identity-related claims of those who defend harmful practices is still worthwhile in order to understand clearly what is at stake in such cases for these groups. Such investigations might also expose the ways in which conceptions of harm are culturally conditioned and, in some cases, arbitrary. For example, the criminalization of marijuana or peyote in societies where similar intoxicants are legally available may be based on a concept of harm that is suspiciously convenient for mainstream society and importantly inconvenient for Indians who use peyote or Rastafarians who consume marijuana for religious reasons.

can be identified as more central than others to the community's way of defining itself. This is not to say that group claims will always lose in such comparisons. Rather, the point is that a comparison between the impact of discrimination on individual identity and the impact of changing one rule or one tradition on the distinctiveness of the group is unlikely to yield results that favor groups in cases where the identity-related interests of individuals are seriously jeopardized. In my view, this tendency does not draw the difference approach into question. Rather, it clarifies one reason, according to the difference approach, why groups must often yield to the interests of individuals: and the reason is not because my culture favors individual rights over collective ones or even that individual rights are always or automatically more fundamental than group rights to individual well-being. Rather, the reason is because groups rarely have as much at stake in such conflicts as individuals do. According to the difference approach, if it is true that the identity of any group never hangs upon a single practice and that equality and individual rights are crucial to the healthy identities of individuals, then equality and rights *should* never yield to group identity.

But sometimes individual rights ought to yield to the claims of groups and, according to the difference approach, cases of this sort will be ones in which a crucial and constituting feature of a community is jeopardized by a conflicting individual claim. So, if the survival of the French language in Quebec (which is a constitutive feature of French Canadian and Quebec identity) would be clearly enhanced by banning English on commercial signs, then this consideration might be more weighty than the impact of such a policy on the identity-related interests of English-speaking Quebeckers. Similarly, when evidence suggests, as it did in *Martinez*, that interference by the US Supreme Court in the governing decisions of the Pueblo will undermine the legitimacy of Pueblo governing institutions, this consideration might be so significant as to outweigh the threats posed to Pueblo women of rules that discriminate against women who marry outside the community.

To be sure, these conflicts are complicated and difficult to decide. But their complexity rests, not on the inherent nature of rights, but rather on the complexities of cultural understanding and interpretation and on what recognizing difference requires in liberal democratic law and politics. Their complexity is not appropriately sorted out through the dominant approach. Rather, it is best sorted out by examining in the first instance how identity-related claims are implicated in conflicts that involve minorities within minorities. The difference approach provides a way of systematically focusing on identity. It thereby exposes conflicts in which identity-related interests are falsely implicated and provides a common normative currency for resolving conflicts in which identity-related interests are at stake.

In this respect, it is important to realize that the difference approach does not eschew rights. On the contrary, it helps to resolve conflicts that involve contending claims that are each viewed as rights. Rights have been a crucial means by which individual identity is protected, especially the rights that protect individuals when they choose to dissent from their communities' practices. Group identities are protected through a variety of institutional arrangements (e.g. federalism, educational programs, bilingual public services), including so-called collective rights (for example, linguistic rights, the right to self-government, the right to have treaties honored). The difference approach offers a means of sorting out how conflicts between contending rights ought to be resolved by translating these claims into the identity-related interests that rights protect. It thereby engages the very values that individuals and groups sometimes claim are at stake for them in cultural and religious conflicts and also helps to make it clear when these values are not at stake.

13   Internal minorities and indigenous self-determination

Margaret Moore

There has been a fairly persistent pattern of demands by minorities for group-differentiated rights, such as rights to political autonomy, and also sometimes exemptions from laws, at least since the late eighteenth century, when the state began to become more centralized, the rules and practices more standardized and uniform, and the requirements of the state more intrusive on local practices (Hechter 2000). From the 1848 Hungarian Revolution, when Magyars revolted from the Austro-Hungarian Empire to request their own political self-government arrangement, to agitation for "Home Rule" in Ireland in the eighteenth and nineteenth centuries, to various (indigenous) peasant rebellions against state-centered control in the Americas,[1] minorities within the state have sought to wrest power from the central authorities governing them. More recently, there have been various demands by religious and ethnic groups for exemptions from the requirements and rules of the central political authority on religious or cultural grounds, and demands for self-government arrangements for national minorities and indigenous peoples, from Quebec in Canada, the Basque country and Catalonia in Spain, Scotland in the UK, Chechnya in Russia, Chiapas in Mexico, Kashmir in India, and from the Kurds in the south-east of Turkey.

The reasons for these demands are various, but, especially in the case of indigenous peoples, they tend to flow from a sense that the indigenous community constitutes a political community *of its own*, and that their

The author wishes to thank Anna Drake for research assistance, Avigail Eisenberg and Jeff Spinner-Halev for helpful written comments and criticisms, and the participants of the Minorities within Minorities conference held at the University of Nebraska, Lincoln, Nebraska, 4–5 October 2002 for comments, questions and advice. She is also grateful to the Carnegie Corporation for a research grant in support of this project.

[1] Peasant rebellions, such as that led by Emiliano Zapata in the pre-Mexican Revolution period (prior to 1910), were mainly constituted by indigenous peoples and were almost entirely about land reform. However, they have been reinterpreted as early indigenous political activism, especially since the mid-1990s, as is clear with the Zapatista uprising in the state of Chiapas, which is clearly autonomist in aims and views itself as an extension of or faithful in some way to the aims of the earlier Zapata-led rebellion.

aspirations to collectively manage their own affairs and govern themselves are legitimate. Indeed, territorial autonomy arrangements have
been praised as a peaceful, non-paternalistic method of managing ethnic
conflict, in contrast to more coercive, unacceptable methods, such as ethnic cleansing or forced assimilation (McGarry and O'Leary 1993: ch. 1).
Moreover, the exercise of political autonomy converts the groups from
minority to majority status within the political unit that they control and
there are a number of advantages that flow from majority status, which
would improve the position of the minority group, and allow it to pursue
more effectively its own interests.

However, one of the most common criticisms of targeted or group-
differentiated cultural rights to accommodate minority cultural groups
within the state is the fear that minorities will use these rights to oppress or
discriminate against their own minorities.[2] This concern arises in relation
to three kinds of diversity common in the state: cultural diversity, status
or positional diversity, and ideological diversity. In each case, the concern
is that the protection or enforcement of culture will have a homogenizing
influence that will unfairly marginalize or discriminate against people who
occupy positions that are at odds with the dominant or accepted cultural
understanding.

The first kind of diversity within the minority region, or in the area
where the minority exercises authority over its culture, is primarily
directed at people who do not share the same culture, language or religion
as the right-holding cultural group, but who live within regions dominated by the minority who possess the right (and who may now be a
local majority, albeit a minority in the state as a whole). This concern is
raised primarily with respect to territorial self-government arrangements,
such as for the Nisga'a in British Columbia, whose area of jurisdiction
also includes a small white minority who are not members of the Nisga'a
tribe and do not share in its culture (Kesselman 1998: A23). Indeed,
this concern has been raised by some political sociologists and comparative political scientists, from Rogers Brubaker (1998) to Don Horowitz
(1998) and Jack Snyder (2000), with respect to ethno-federalism. The
main problem, it is alleged, with most forms of territorial arrangements to
protect minority cultural groups is that territories are not homogeneous

---

[2] The term "minority" is used imprecisely throughout the chapter. Strictly speaking, the
term "minority" refers to a group's numerical strength in the population as a whole, but in
this chapter the term refers to groups that are marginalized or in some way disadvantaged.
Not all numerical minorities are disadvantaged, and not all disadvantaged groups are
numerical minorities (e.g. women). However, women share many of the same structural
obstacles as are faced by other (disadvantaged) groups in the society, which justifies the
conflation of the term "minority" with the actual position of disadvantage (which is only
sometimes a result of their minority status).

and that minority cultures within the jurisdictional area controlled by the local majority (although perhaps a minority in the state as a whole) will be disadvantaged and marginalized.

Positional or status diversity refers to the fact that members of minority cultures, as in any culture, may occupy different positions within that culture, and that the content of the culture may discriminate in unfair ways against some people within that culture. This concern has been primarily raised by feminist writers who point to the gendered nature of many traditional cultures and the very real possibility that cultural arguments will be used to justify or perpetuate discrimination against women – in the form of unfair divorce, child custody and marriage laws, discriminatory rules concerning the control and division of family property and inheritance, discriminatory laws pertaining to rules of evidence in court, as well as laws controlling women's sexuality (Okin 1999a; Shachar 2001; Spinner-Halev 2001: 84–113; Eisenberg 2003; Deveaux 2000b: 522–39). There are also other social groups, such as homosexuals within the minority culture, who may be marginalized by the rules made by the cultural group and these rules may be protected and enforced under the banner of group-differentiated rights.

Philosophical or ideological diversity is also a source of concern, primarily because of the dynamics of majority–minority relations within the state, and the tendency for the minority group to seek to appear unified, especially vis-à-vis the majority group, in order to gain a better bargaining position. In his article, "Internal Minorities and their Rights," Leslie Green (1995: 256–72) points out that there is a tendency for minority groups in the state to exaggerate the extent of solidarity behind their particular political program, because any dissent from it is likely to be interpreted by the majority group as a sign of weakness, as a sign that compromise is unnecessary, that the elites are not representative of everyone, and so on. This dynamic raises concerns about the effect that cultural rights will have on dissenters within the minority group, who might be silenced or marginalized.

This chapter is concerned with all three types of internal minorities, and specifically with the impact of cultural rights on internal minorities or minorities within the minority group. However, it is not concerned with all kinds of cultural rights, but only with the right to political self-determination or autonomy arrangements within the state, which is often advanced by cultural minorities. Both territorial and non-territorial autonomy arrangements to accommodate minority cultural groups are subject to the problem of internal minorities, and a strong objection to these arrangements is that minorities may use their jurisdictional authority in an oppressive or discriminatory fashion. This chapter takes as its paradigm group that of indigenous people in the Americas and Australasia, who seek to be collectively self-governing. It considers the kinds of arguments that they might advance for that claim, and the implications of the justificatory argument for internal minorities within the group or area in question who have legitimate concerns about the possibility that they will be oppressed or discriminated against by the group. One of the core arguments of this chapter, which is implicit in the methodology employed, is that it is not helpful to address the issues raised by internal minorities simply by articulating liberal principles or the limits of toleration in the abstract. Rather, the appropriate response at least partly depends on the justificatory argument for the political autonomy arrangement in the first place.

This chapter identifies three distinct, albeit related, arguments which are used to justify political autonomy arrangements for culturally distinct groups, which have been employed by, and/or on behalf of, indigenous peoples. These are: (1) cultural incommensurability arguments; (2) respect for identity arguments; and (3) historical/rectificatory justice arguments. These arguments are explored in sections one, two and three, and, in each case, their implications for minority groups within the jurisdictional areas will be considered. The upshot of this discussion is that the first two kinds of arguments are deeply flawed, but the third kind of argument is a very good one, and suggests an internal limit to the extent of power which groups are justified in exercising, and rules out certain kinds of institutional arrangements.

It is implicit in this method of proceeding that the typical way of approaching the issue of internal minorities – as a case of rights conflicts, as when sexual equality rights are in tension with cultural autonomy rights (as in cases pointed to by feminists), or when religious liberty is in tension with cultural deployed to enforce religious uniformity – is only one possible way of looking at the issue, and not the most helpful one (Eisenberg 2003). It is more appropriate to view the issue of political autonomy as a straightforward case of considering who should exercise jurisdictional authority, and that the issue of substantive justice enters into the argument at a later stage, and can be partly addressed by a careful understanding of the issue of jurisdictional authority. This does not resolve the problem fully but it does suggest a clearer way of thinking about the multiple, complex issues involved. It also provides a helpful corrective to some of the dominant approaches to the issue – the identity approach of Eisenberg and the joint governance approach of Shachar, both of which are very useful ways of thinking about how to reconcile the "dilemmas" posed, but both of which are silent on the issue of jurisdictional authority, and indeed view it as unproblematic that white people's courts have authority over how indigenous communities define themselves.[3] This chapter will suggest why that assumption is itself problematic.

Cultural incommensurability arguments

One kind of argument for territorial autonomy to accommodate minority cultural groups rests on the view that cultures are incommensurable and that it is not possible or appropriate for one culture to evaluate the rules and norms of another culture. Incommensurability claims of this kind are often combined with deep moral skepticism about the possibility of arriving at an objective moral judgement. On this view, the fact that cultures are incommensurable means there is no neutral standard by which rival claims or understandings can be assessed or measured, and such a standard is a necessary prerequisite for the evaluation of cultures, and, by extension, the criticism of some cultures and cultural practices as unfair, discriminatory or in some way deeply flawed. Jurisdictional authority or political autonomy for cultural groups is justified because only the group itself is competent to make rules in accordance with its own norms. Any attempt to impose alien values – sexual equality or norms regarding religious toleration, for example – is viewed as cultural imperialism: it is unjustified because it depends on imposing one norm as the right norm on another group, which does not accept that norm; indeed, that norm may be in tension with other values and beliefs accepted within the culture. Since there is no neutral standard to assess these rival claims, it is not appropriate to judge the cultural values of other groups, or to take action against a particular cultural practice based on one's own, local cultural values. To take a concrete case: there is little we should say or do about some culture Y's gender discrimination practices. The value of sexual equality cannot be proven to be superior to rival values, such as the value of stability, family or respect for authority.

---

[3] See here, Shachar 2001: 88–116, especially 116, where she indicates that the state ought to have some form of authority over these groups, and justifies this by arguing that groups with which she is concerned do not seek expansive forms of self-government. This means that her approach may, by her own admission, not apply to indigenous groups, nor indeed to many national minorities. In fact, it raises the potential criticism that her approach really fits the situation of Israel (but not the Palestinians in the occupied territories), but is not really generalizable to many other diverse places. See also Eisenberg 2003, especially her discussion of legal cases (*A. G. Canada v. Lavell*; *Santa Clara Pueblo v. Martinez*), where she never addresses the possibility that the state in question did not have the moral authority to render the decisions. The state-centered nature of Shachar's proposals is discussed in Spinner-Halev (2001: 105).

In his book, *Culture and Equality*, Brian Barry (2001a: 261–6) suggests that *all* cultural rights arguments rely to some extent on cultural relativism, but this seems to me to apply to only some of them: James Tully's argument in *Strange Multiplicity* (1995), which Barry analyzes in the course of making his claim; John Gray's argument for value pluralism (by which he means the uncombinability and incommensurability of values) in *Enlightenment's Wake* (1995: 79); and possibly also weaker versions of the cultural incommensurability argument in Bhikhu Parekh's *Rethinking Multiculturalism* (2000) and Chandran Kukathas's "Are There Any Cultural Rights?" (1992a) respectively. In the case of Tully, it is clear in his central image of a Haida canoe sculpture, which is the motif for the book, that each of the animals – the bear, the raven, the frog – should govern its own life according to its own standards, that the goods of one type of animal are not necessarily goods for another, and it is therefore inappropriate for the bear clan to claim superiority over the other creatures (Tully 1995: 202–5). When this idea is extended, by analogy, to cultural groups, it suggests that each cultural group should make decisions over its own members, but no other group is entitled to make decisions or impose values on others, because the goods and values are internal to each culture. Parekh's argument does not go so far, since he does deploy some basic norms of human well-being to rule out certain kinds of harmful practices as unacceptable (such as the immolation of widows on their husbands' funeral pyres),[4] but in his critique of the Western tradition he repeatedly warns about the dangers attached to cultural imperialism, and emphasizes the point that cultural diversity is a good analogous to the way that botanical or zoological diversity is a good (Parekh 2000: 114–41).

The incommensurability argument is vulnerable to a number of different objections, which I argue are decisive. The ostensible relationship between plurality of values, radical cultural relativism and jurisdictional control over one's own culture is quite tenuous, and each element of the link can be pressed on. First, it does not follow from the idea that cultural values are sometimes incommensurable and that a full-scale ranking scheme for different values is not possible, that radical moral skepticism is in order. As Judith Shklar (1990) has argued persuasively, it might not be possible to delineate fully all the values of the good life, or to agree on what justice consists in, much less to rank these diverse values and goods, but it might be possible to identify what is morally evil: to recognize that

---

[4] This argument is made in Parekh 2000: 114–141. However, it is clear at the end of this chapter that this does not mean that we can deduce the superiority or priority of certain values, especially when different cultures prioritize the values differently. This point is made in the context of the debate over East Asian values.

unnecessary death, human suffering and cruelty, degradation, humiliation and physical harm are evils that any moral system should recognize and prohibit.

If this is right, then it is, after all, possible to identify some cultures as more valuable (in the sense of contributing more to human well-being) than others, particularly if one culture justifies or permits gross cruelty towards some of its members or towards outsiders, and/or justifies the violation of their physical integrity or harm to them. This suggests that the incommensurability and uncombinability (in one life or one culture) of cultural values should not be used to defend practices that marginalize, exclude, degrade or harm people. No doubt, the fact that this judgement is not susceptible to a complete prioritizing, and that there are questions about what constitutes harm or degradation, means that this cannot constitute a complete theory: but, at the same time, it means that moral relativism is inappropriate, because some cultural practices may be unacceptable in terms of a basic minimum of human functioning.

This insight tends to be confirmed when we try to address concrete cases where value judgements might appropriately enter into the culture-based claims to group-differentiated rights. For example, we might make moral judgements about the kinds of practices that groups or cultures have developed with respect to outsiders. Many theorists who appeal to the incommensurability of cultures do not do this: they tend to treat cultures as if they are bounded entities and multicultural societies as if they are composed of distinct, relatively bounded communities and cultures. In fact, multicultural societies may be characterized not only by multiple communities but also by individuals who move between communities, thereby suggesting a fluidity and hybridity that is at odds with the assumption of multiple bounded communities. Also, cultural communities are not exclusive and bounded in the sense that they govern only their own members: they also impact on members of other cultural communities. Sometimes, cultural communities seek to express and celebrate their distinctiveness and culture in ways that alienate members of other groups, and in this way jeopardize the conditions for peaceful coexistence. It would seem to follow from a recognition of the non-hierarchical nature of cultures that we should at least endorse a norm that rules out privileging particular groups; and that implicit in this idea is a commitment to principles that rule out practices that degrade or humiliate other groups in the society. This suggests that radical cultural and moral relativism does not necessarily follow from the recognition of multiple cultural values and the problems in ranking such values. The normative principle implicit here is that all cultural communities should be able to express their culture and distinctiveness without threat to the achievement of equal status and the conditions of equal respect for other cultural communities. This follows because there is no basis on which to privilege any particular culture, since there is, according to this argument, no neutral scale according to which cultures can be evaluated.[5] Therefore, any cultural practice that disrespects or humiliates another culture is unacceptable.

Further, the fact that there might be members of the cultural groups themselves that are rendered vulnerable by cultural rights or there might be dissenting voices within the group, who do not share the same ideological or philosophical perspective, suggests that it is wrong to assume, as this argument does, that cultural groups are homogeneous or possess a coherent or unified world-view. Cultural groups are diverse and heterogeneous; they are often driven by elites; and their core traditions and values are subject to radically different interpretations. The issue raised by the cultural incommensurability argument – whether one culture should evaluate another – is not the only issue: there are also important questions about who represents the culture, and how the culture becomes interpreted, legitimated and enforced.

This insight presses on the link between moral relativism and the claim that the group should have jurisdictional authority to protect and enforce cultural norms. This link is tenuous indeed, especially once we see that rights are enforced at the expense of, or in the face of, opposition of some minority members themselves. The fact that there is no single scale by which all values can be evaluated and prioritized certainly does not mean that the dominant or majority or elite understanding of the culture is the "right" one: indeed, since there is no "right" or "wrong" here, the internal minority's understanding of what is required by a culture is equally valid (or equally invalid). The only way to make the move from cultural relativism to jurisdictional authority to protect cultures is to focus on the issue of whether outsiders should exercise authority over cultural groups: but it certainly does not follow that the group should be able to enforce a certain cultural understanding over its own members. There is no justification, internal to this argument, for the group to enforce a certain understanding of the culture on its members.

---

[5] For a similar argument, and a discussion in the context of Northern Ireland, see Shane O'Neill 2000. O'Neill argues that, when these principles are applied to the parading controversy in Northern Ireland, they yield determinate results. He discusses Protestant marchers' insistence on their historic right to parade from their church at Drumcree through the largely nationalist area of the Garvaghy Road, celebrating the supremacy and victories of Britishness and Protestantism over Irishness and Catholicism. In O'Neill's view, this practice clearly degrades and humiliates the other main cultural community (Irish Catholics) in the society.

Respect for identity arguments

Another kind of argument to justify collective self-government arrangements for cultural minorities, which is common in the literature on group-differentiated cultural rights, begins by arguing that people have an interest in having their identity respected, and moves from recognition of this interest to justify jurisdictional control or authority over the collective conditions of their existence. At the heart of this type of argument is the claim that there is value in having one's culture and one's practices recognized, or having the culture and identity with which one identifies (one's collective identity) publicly affirmed. This argument is clearly expressed by Taylor (1992) and Tamir (1993: 42–8). Taylor identifies the desire for public recognition as central to the modern quest for authenticity and an integral part of the right to collective self-determination or political self-expression. Tamir similarly argues that individuals have a strong (and legitimate) interest in expressing their culture collectively – through participating in the social, cultural and political life of their community. There is one strand of Kymlicka's argument which also suggests reliance on such an interest: he points to the impossibility of abandoning all practices that favor particular cultures and so assumes as an empirical starting point that people have a strong, and reasonable, preference that their culture is the one that is publicly expressed in decisions about internal boundaries, jurisdictions, policies regarding language, public holidays and the symbols of the state (Kymlicka 1995: 107). Kymlicka's view that this preference is a reasonable one could arguably be interpreted as claiming that this is a legitimate interest, which can serve as the basis of a right.

Considerations connected to this legitimate interest in the expression of one's culture and identity are invoked to suggest that the public sphere should affirm the culture and identities that people have. This type of argument is superior to the previous one, because it does try to demonstrate, empirically and normatively, the kind of interest involved in cultural recognition. Once we accept Kymlicka's point that the public sphere will have some cultural biases, then the next question is whether people have a legitimate interest in ensuring that the public sphere will have a character or public culture of a certain kind. This tendency to prefer that the public culture of the state is one that they can identify with is easily explained in terms of the structural disadvantages that attach to minority status. Being a member of a *majority* cultural group has distinct advantages in a society that must reflect and express some culture: he or she will not have to be fluent in a second language in order to access third-tier education, not have to be familiar with two cultural codes and sets of symbols, not have to worry about the consequences of discrimination, or the unintended biases of rules made for the cultural majority. Further, it seems that there are non-instrumental participatory and identification interests in seeing the culture and identity extended into the public sphere. These interests are collective in the sense that they flow from membership in a social group, where collective enjoyment and collective production of the good is part of what constitutes the interest.

However, grounding jurisdictional authority in a cultural group based on the interest that people have in expressing their culture publicly is problematic, especially when we focus on internal minorities. This is so whether they are cultural minorities, dissenters or members of vulnerable groups within the cultural community. The problem with moving straight from considerations of identity to the idea that the public sphere should affirm the cultures and identities that people have is apparent when we consider the identities that are not publicly affirmed in this arrangement – the internal minorities.

The appeal to identity is problematic because, as many have pointed out (Barry 2001a: 63–109; Laitin 1990: 3–35; Moore 2001: 5–21), identity-formation is not a constant sum game where the acquisition of a new identity necessarily occurs at the expense of the original one, but may be entirely compatible with various ethnic/regional/sexual identities. This capacity for additive identities is related to the capacity to learn and use more than one language, acquire new cultural habits, and transform many aspects of the self. This is often illustrated by the example of hyphenated Americans, but it can apply to many different sorts of identities: one can have an identity as both gay and American, woman and native, Basque and Spanish, Muslim and British. Not all identities are of this kind – there are some national identities, for example, which preclude any kind of nested characteristics, because they were initially formed in opposition to one another[6] – but in many cases it is possible to have multiple nested affiliations and identities, which are of varying salience depending on the social context.

In the case of women in a culture where women are regarded as inferior, political autonomy is likely to result in a situation where only one aspect of a minority woman's identity is affirmed, at the expense of other parts. As Ayelet Shachar (2001: 37–44) and Avigail Eisenberg (2003) have emphasized, it puts minority women in the impossible position of having to choose between two integral aspects of their identity, or, to be more precise, of having one part of their identity affirmed, respected and recognized publicly, while another part of their identity – their identity as women – is subject to inferior, harmful or discriminatory treatment,

---

[6] One thinks of the French and German national identities as of this type.

and thereby disrespected. In the context of a culturally plural society, any attempt by minority women to challenge this discriminatory treatment by their own elites is likely to be perceived by their cultural community as "siding" with the majority, as breaking down the solidarity and unity that the minority group seeks to project in its relations with the overall majority in the state (cf. Eisenberg 2003).

This issue also arises with adherents of minority religious faiths in the context of the self-government of a particular cultural group. The best-known example in the political theory literature of this type of problem involved members of the Pueblo community in the south-western United States who no longer practiced the traditional Pueblo religion but who had converted to Protestantism (cf. Svensson 1979: 421–39, at 438–9; Kymlicka 1989a: 196–8). They were subject to discriminatory treatment in the form of denial of resources.[7] For the Pueblo Protestants, like the woman in the sexist culture, they could only enjoy their constitutionally protected rights (as American citizens) to the free exercise of religion by giving up their Pueblo Indian status. Many analyses conceive of this case as a straightforward example of an individual right (religious liberty, equal treatment norms) conflicting with a collective right (right to collective self-government of the Pueblo people). However, the identity-based justificatory argument for conferring self-government on the Pueblo examined here reveals an additional problem, namely, that it is not clear that membership in a religious community is qualitatively different, in terms of the collective rights that attach, or should attach, to it than membership in a cultural community (which, on this argument, is a ground of a right to be collectively self-governing). Membership in many different minority groups – including religious communities – may be bound up with significant collective interests, where the value of the group membership (in the religious community) is part of the ground of the right. There is no reason, internal to this argument, for thinking that only national or cultural minorities have collective interests of this kind, and therefore no basis for adjudicating between rival collective rights when they conflict.

The identity-based argument is also vulnerable to objections concerning rival cultural communities that do not share in the public culture of the right-holding minority. In this case, it is not one aspect of their identity that is affirmed at the expense of other parts of their identity: rather,

---

[7] They were also ostracized. However, as Brian Barry correctly argues (2001a: 164 and following), no one has a right to the associative goods intrinsic to the association. For example, in the case of minorities in discriminatory associations (such as homosexuals in the Mormon Church), there is the possibility of exit and there are no additional costs of exit other than the loss of the association itself. In the Pueblo case, the charge involved discrimination against converts to Protestantism in the form of denial of housing benefits.

the point here seems to be the logical one that, if minority cultural groups have rights, based on their interests in protecting and promoting their culture and identity, then it must be the case that internal cultural minorities have rights. They are all minorities, but they have different majorities to deal with. This contradiction is especially acute in the case of cultural groups inside a territorial region, governed by the local majority, because there the analogy seems to be strongest.

The problem with the identity argument to justify political autonomy for cultural groups is that it is vulnerable in two ways: it fails to explain what exactly is special about cultural identities rather than other kinds of identities (sexual orientation, gender, religious identities), which could arguably be described as sub-cultural. It is in equal, perhaps even more, difficulty when faced with the exactly analogous situation of a cultural group, X, living within the minority region, Y, where the public extension of group Y's culture and identity is at the expense of cultural group X. If this is right, the argument only works well in the unrealistic situation of having a homogeneous territorially concentrated group, all of whom aspire to promote the same culture, and have the same understanding of the culture, and there are no social identities that are marginalized by the culture.

Historical injustice and rectificatory justice arguments

The third justificatory argument for self-government for indigenous peoples does not proceed directly from either claims about the hierarchies (or lack thereof) of culture, or from claims about the nature of identity. Rather, the argument proceeds by evaluating the conditions in which groups might be said to have the moral authority to have jurisdiction over their own lives and the conditions of their collective existence.

One problem with most arguments about minorities within minorities is that they tend to begin from the question about whether and what decisions we (as liberal democrats) should make concerning illiberal groups. This may be the wrong way to think about the issue. It presupposes that non-indigenous people already have the moral entitlement to make decisions about the lives of indigenous peoples. Both Eisenberg's and Shachar's approaches, for example, assume that white people's courts have the moral entitlement to make decisions over indigenous people, although in Shachar's account, the jurisdiction is shared with the group in question, and in Eisenberg's account, the courts in such cases, she argues, must consider the identity-based merits of the rival claims being advanced. In both cases, the idea that the majority society has jurisdictional authority is treated as relatively unproblematic. The argument

examined here, by contrast, does not assume this: it takes as its starting point an examination of the conditions in which groups should have
jurisdictional authority (self-government) to run their own affairs, and
then considers, separately, the substantive justice of the exercise of that
jurisdictional authority and institutional mechanisms to improve it.

There are two ways of looking at the issue of the state's jurisdictional
authority over indigenous peoples: positive and negative.[8] The positive
argument for collective self-determination invokes considerations of the
kind put forward by Mill in relation to the liberty principle without further
appeal to rectificatory justice considerations. Mill argued in *On Liberty*
(1993: 80) that each individual is most interested in his or her own well-
being and so should be entrusted with rights to protect him or her from
interference in making decisions over his or her own life. Margalit and
Raz, in their argument justifying political self-government for groups
within the state, have extended this argument to groups: just as the individual person is in the best position to decide how to arrange his or her
life, so members of a group are best placed to judge the interests of the
group. This may not be a conclusive argument but it does offer good reasons for a presumption in favor of collective autonomy or self-government
as a means to address group disadvantage.[9]

Of course, whether a group is able to make decisions in its best interests
will depend upon the nature of group decision-making. In fact, unless
the decision-makers represent, and are accountable to, the whole group,
it is a mistake to say that self-government is really government by the
group. In order for the Millian argument to work, we must assume that
the decision-makers are representative of the group and that there are
institutional mechanisms to ensure their representative and accountable
nature.

The Millian argument, that groups are in the best position to make
decisions over their own affairs, is not a direct cultural or identity-based

---

[8] Most of this discussion of jurisdictional authority is also found, in somewhat different
form, in Moore 2003.
[9] Of course, this line of argument does not address the difficult questions relating to the
extent of jurisdictional authority, or territory, that such groups should have. To see this
problem, consider the disanalogies between J. S. Mill's argument for individual liberty
and the justification for group autonomy. If Mill's distinction between self- and other-
regarding behavior in individuals is problematic, this is doubly so for groups which
aspire to self-government over (diverse) territory. In the latter case, the "self" that is
self-governing comprises two elements: (1) attachment to a group or membership in the
group; and (2) attachment to territory or land. To the extent that government is over a
territorial jurisdiction, it is inclusive of all peoples resident in that territory and so may
not necessarily correspond to group membership. This is not a decisive criticism of this
line of argument, but it does suggest that there are crucial ambiguities at the heart of the
extension of the Millian insight to groups.

argument, but it does incorporate these considerations indirectly. The issue of cultural difference is indirectly invoked, because one reason why indigenous peoples are in the best position to make decisions over their own lives, and the institutional structure that they live in, is that they understand the meanings and values internal to their culture, and that non-indigenous peoples, operating within a different cultural framework, make mistakes, even while being well-meaning, because they do not share indigenous people's cultural understandings and values. The issue of divergent identities is also an indirect consideration because the argument that indigenous peoples should be collectively self-governing presupposes that they share an identity as indigenous peoples and that this identity has a political dimension. However, the basis of the jurisdictional authority is not the cultural difference *per se* nor the identities that people hold.

The negative, and more contextual, argument concerning appropriate jurisdictional authority involves a historical analysis of the relationship between indigenous and non-indigenous people. The starting point in this analysis is that indigenous people were once self-governing communities, who governed themselves according to their own practices, and that the conquering and colonizing regime often did not treat their claims fairly.[10] The process by which indigenous peoples were colonized and dispossessed involved stripping them of the institutions of self-government that they enjoyed prior to colonization, and silencing and excluding them. Just as the history of imperial powers' relations with the non-white societies that they ruled was done without the involvement of the colonized peoples, so, in the Americas and Australia and New Zealand, the process of settlement and state-creation proceeded without the consent of the indigenous peoples who lived there. The fact that indigenous peoples were entirely marginalized from the processes of state-creation raises the question of the basis for the state's authority over indigenous peoples.[11] If the exercise of legitimate authority is based on the principles of democratic will and the sovereignty of the people, then the current

---

[10] Allen Buchanan (2003: ch. 9) identifies a number of different grounds for recognizing indigenous self-government. The remedial rights argument that he identifies corresponds to the rights that arise as a result of the injustice suffered by indigenous peoples, and rectificatory justice considerations justify the resurrection of some form of political self-rule which indigenous peoples were denied. This corresponds roughly to my discussion of jurisdictional authority.

[11] In his book, *Politics in the Vernacular* (2001: 122), Will Kymlicka identifies the historic differences in the relationship to early state-formation as one of the key differences between indigenous peoples and minority nationalists. He argues that national minorities were losers, but players, in the process of European state-formation, while indigenous people were entirely outside that process. This chapter develops that argument to highlight the parallel between the process of colonization and indigenous settlement.

state does not exercise legitimate authority over them.[12] If indigenous peoples were entitled, through the same normative principle, to exercise collective self-government in the past, then how, normatively, has this right been extinguished?[13] It is counter-intuitive to suppose that the continued subordination and unfair treatment of indigenous peoples has left them also with fewer (moral) rights, and no longer entitled to collective self-government.

Moreover, the states in which indigenous peoples have been incorporated have manifestly failed to work in the best interests of indigenous peoples. This point is often illustrated through an analogy with imperial forms of authority over societies in Africa and Asia, and the relations between indigenous peoples and white elites in the Americas, Australia and New Zealand. The tutelary relationship implicit in the relations between indigenous and non-indigenous peoples can properly be seen as a localized version of a global phenomenon in which European powers such as Britain, France, Portugal, the Netherlands (and, before 1918, Germany) controlled non-white peoples everywhere (Cairns 2000: 17). These European empires extended throughout Asia and Africa, and operated on the premise that European civilization was superior to other cultural forms and practices; that power was merited in some way – a result of the Darwinian competition in which the fittest tend to rule; and skin color was highly correlated with power, and, by extension, civilization and progress.[14]

---

[12] Of course, the notion of popular sovereignty typically carries with it the idea that it is *all* the people who are the source of the government's legitimacy. However, this is problematic in societies that are deeply divided in the sense that the laws, policies and institutions typically reflect the culture and understanding of only one group (the non-indigenous community) on the territory, and where the subordinated group (indigenous people) has been marginalized from the process of state-creation, and whose minority status renders them vulnerable if they are included simply as equal undifferentiated individuals.

[13] This is related to, though distinct from, the international law account of historic sovereignty. On that account, the loss of sovereignty of the three Baltic republics and their forcible incorporation into the USSR in 1940–1 meant that the sovereignty of these areas could be revived in international law and their place in the world community of states could be restored to them. There are some parallels with the situation of indigenous peoples, but it is not necessary to engage in such retrospective invalidation (with its enormous implications) or to suppose that the self-governing indigenous communities were "sovereign" in the sense that we use the word today. It is only necessary to note that most indigenous peoples have an account or a memory of an earlier era of political independence and the basis on which this independence was lost was often illegal, and also morally suspect. For a discussion of the relationship between the international law account and the normative account, see Kingsbury (2001: 69–100, at 100).

[14] The point is made in Cairns (2000: 14–56). However, curiously, he does not connect that historical story at all with the solutions that he proposes in the bulk of the book.

The European imperial relationship with their subject peoples was mirrored in the relationship between white settlers – extensions of the empire, fragments of European civilization – and indigenous peoples in the Americas and Australia and New Zealand. The assumption that indigenous peoples were culturally backward and their assimilation into white society was both in their interests and an inevitable result of the Darwinian competition among cultures, permeated almost all the policies made by white settler majorities over indigenous peoples. It is fundamental to the colonial nature of the relationship between the white social majority and indigenous people because it meant that indigenous peoples were not included in the discussions that led to the founding of the state in which they were incorporated. Indeed, in almost every respect, and every policy decision, indigenous peoples were described as wards and treated like children. As John A. Macdonald, Founding Father of Canada and its first prime minister, claimed in 1887: "The great aim of our civilization has been to do away with the tribal system and assimilate the Indian people in all respects with the inhabitants of the Dominion, as speedily as they are fit for the change" (Cairns 2000: 57). The consequences of the policies based on the related assumptions of the cultural inferiority of indigenous peoples and the merits of assimilationist policies have been disastrous. Inuit communities in Northern Canada were forcibly removed from their homes and relocated thousands of miles away at the recommendation of distant bureaucrats who claimed to want to more efficiently direct services to scattered indigenous communities, but also as a method to establish sovereignty over the High Arctic by populating parts of it (Royal Commission on Aboriginal Peoples 1994: 71–7, 15–132). Indigenous children in Canada and Australia were forcibly removed from their families and sent to live with non-indigenous families or in non-indigenous residential schools, where they were sometimes physically and sexually abused and, even when they were not, they were stripped of their indigenous culture and forbidden to speak their language (Armitage 1995: 236–7, 106–13). The old culture was forgotten – because not taught – and the new white culture was perceived as foreign or alien, and inconsistent with native identity. This was not surprising: it is hard to adopt the culture and identity of the group that engaged in large-scale theft and sometimes murder of your forefathers and foremothers. The result, of course, was that indigenous children were left with very few cultural resources, having been deprived of one culture and unable to adopt another. In short, white monopoly on policy over indigenous peoples, based on the assumption of white superiority and indigenous inferiority, has led to a legacy of failed programs. For indigenous peoples, it has meant social and economic depression and marginalization, high rates of alcoholism, suicide and of incarceration, as well as cultural anomie and despair on the part of a whole generation.

There is little doubt that the economic marginalization of indigenous peoples in the Americas and Australasia is directly (causally) related to the dispossession and injustice that they experienced at the hands of the non-indigenous-controlled state.[15] In many cases, indigenous people lack legal entitlement to land and resources because their claims and their holdings were not recognized by the conquering regime, which forcibly incorporated them. There is a long history of broken promises in the relationship between indigenous and non-indigenous peoples: the American government has unilaterally abrogated certain treaties with Indian tribes (Franks 2000: 227); the New Zealand treaty of Waitangi signed by Maori chiefs and British colonists was declared a "simple nullity" in 1877 (although its status has very recently been reinterpreted) (Maaka and Fleras 2000: 89–109); the language and land rights guaranteed to the Métis under the Manitoba Act of 1870 were rescinded by white anglophone settlers, once they became a majority. From 1834 to the 1920s, under the Bureau of Indian Affairs, Indian peoples in the United States were gradually dispossessed of their territory and confined to reserves of land (Prucha 1981: 27–34). Under the Dawes Act (or General Allotment Act), passed by the United States Congress in 1887, tribal lands were broken up, and allotted to individual Indians, while "surplus" land was sold to white settlers. By 1934, some 2.75 million hectares, more than 60 percent of the remaining Indian land base, had been taken from indigenous peoples (Cornell 1998: 42). Since the disadvantaged status of indigenous peoples is a direct result of the actions of non-indigenous societies and of the state in which indigenous peoples are incorporated, dominant groups not only have a collective responsibility to dismantle the institutions and processes that marginalize native peoples and address the inequality that they experience, but the basis for legitimate governance of indigenous people is brought into question (Williams 1998: ch. 6).

There is, moreover, another normative argument implicit in the analogy between indigenous peoples and other colonized peoples in

---

[15] Of course, the memory of oppression may be more vivid for its victims than for members of the dominant society, and the meaning of the oppression may also be different. This is because the experience of oppression helps to mobilize the victimized group, but is not a defining experience for the dominant group, and is often not conceptualized as a group-based action at all. In addition, there are often competing historiographies, and reliance on these sorts of arguments is, in some cases, very problematic. However, in the case of indigenous peoples, there are objective sources of evidence – law, documents, as well as narratives that can be corroborated – that the group had been oppressed, stolen from, discriminated against, and this can be causally related to the group's current experience of poverty and marginalization.

Africa and Asia. The colonization and subordination of indigenous peoples in Australia, New Zealand and the Americas involved the same assumptions of cultural inferiority, strongly correlated with race, that underlay European imperialism, and the related view of European entitlement to mastery over the world. The process differed mainly because, in Africa and Asia, the European population was frequently very tiny, and political control could be returned to the people who had been deprived of it simply through a process of making these territories independent. In Australia, New Zealand and the Americas, the settlement of Europeans was more complete, and the decimation of the original population more serious. These historical differences suggest two related points. The first is that, if decolonization was right – if the process of stripping Europeans of their imperial control over non-white societies was morally right – then indigenous self-government must also be morally right. Indigenous peoples should control the conditions of their existence through the exercise of political self-government, just as the peoples of Africa and Asia have had their capacity for political agency restored to them through the process of decolonization.[16] However – and this is the second point – because of the numerical strength of the non-indigenous population, and the interdependent nature of the indigenous and non-indigenous communities in Australasia and the Americas, self-government cannot take the same form as with decolonization. The argument for self-government in both cases still has normative force, but the remedy must be different, because the context is different. The specific challenge for indigenous peoples is to develop models of the kind of self-determination that it makes sense for them to pursue. In almost all cases, indigenous peoples have been concerned to argue for limited forms of self-government within the state, which typically involves maximal jurisdictional authority, consistent with numbers, but also with some increased representation at the center.[17]

[16] The formulation does not clarify whether self-determination of particular groups within areas of decolonization could be morally justified. For an argument concerning the limited contexts in which this might be the best (optimal) overall result, see Moore (2001: ch. 7).

[17] In Mexico, this basic formula is embodied in the San Andres Accord of 1996, which outlines a structure aimed at creating a multiethnic nation in Mexico that encompasses differences, permits decisions in the decentralized tradition of the Mayas, and ensures both broader political representation of indigenous people and fair representation within the justice system. The text of the Accord is found at: www.usip.org/library/pa/chiapas/agreement_960216.html as of 3 January 2002. In Canada, the 1996 Royal Commission on Aboriginal Peoples, which interviewed hundreds of Aboriginal peoples in many different communities, proposed a model of treaty federalism, which is similar to the San Andres Accord in that it recognizes the interdependence of non-indigenous and indigenous communities through endorsing both shared rule and self-rule. It recognizes the previously self-governing nature of indigenous

What does this justificatory argument suggest for how to approach the question of minorities within minorities? What principles relevant to internal minorities are embedded in this argument for a right to collective self-determination?

This issue is often framed in terms of whether indigenous peoples in Canada, the United States and so on should be subject to the United States or Canadian Supreme Court, especially with respect to the claims of their own people regarding the infringement of their rights. However, this way of looking at it muddies the issue.

The rectificatory justice argument suggests why indigenous peoples are justified in being self-governing in their own communities, and so on a par with all other legitimate political authorities. The issue of the internal treatment of the political authority's own citizens arises with respect to any political jurisdiction, which legitimately exercises power in the sense that they are recognized political actors, and so sovereign over their own territory, and in a position to deny their own people basic civil liberties and human rights. Indeed, there is at least one morally important difference between indigenous peoples and sovereign states that treat some of their members badly: the right to exit exists in the former but not in the latter.[18] Women can leave indigenous tribes for the larger state without getting permission from anyone or getting a visa. But leaving an oppressive state is much harder. While the right to exit (for indigenous peoples) may be difficult to exercise, its existence is important and represents an option for vulnerable minorities within indigenous communities. By contrast, minorities in sovereign states, who are oppressed by the central government, may be prevented from leaving and may not have anywhere to go. This is obviously unsatisfactory, at least from the point of view of anyone concerned about human rights violations, and has led many to argue for the need to move beyond the Westphalian political sovereignty model, and develop and institutionalize general principles at the inter-state level and neutral mechanisms to adjudicate violations (Buchanan 2003). This more long-term approach to the problem of internal repression of internal minorities would address the concerns of indigenous peoples to be treated as legitimate political actors in their own right, and is entirely consistent with the rectificatory justice argument for self-determination discussed here.

communities through emphasizing the voluntary nature of the federal project. Unfortunately, the San Andres Accord in Mexico was not implemented by the government and the proposals of the Royal Commission in Canada were not acted upon by the federal government.

[18] I owe this point to Jeff Spinner-Halev. On the issue of rights of exit and gender justice in cultural communities, see Susan Moller Okin 2002.

This is because, unlike the culture-based argument canvassed earlier, this argument does not *identify* indigenous people with a particular culture or way of life. It suggests a much more flexible approach to the adoption of values and norms in different legal and political jurisdictions. The problem with traditional culture-based conceptions of indigenous peoples is that they tend to define indigenous people in purely traditional terms and indeed suggest that self-government should be conferred on indigenous people to the extent that they adhere to traditional ways and maintain their old culture. This fails to recognize the dynamic and adaptable nature of both culture and identity. As Will Kymlicka (2001: 130) has argued, it means cultural and political isolation, not cultural and political self-determination. A further problem with the culture-based approach is that it not only justifies the group in the exercise of self-government, but also in maintaining certain cultural norms and practices, some of which might deny the essential equality and humanity of some of the members. The historical argument concerning rectificatory justice and the basis of state authority canvassed here operates with a more dynamic and fluid understanding of indigenous peoples, who construct their culture over time. Insofar as this is not a static traditional cultural argument, but an argument for collective self-rule, it follows that, while indigenous communities should have the jurisdictional authority to ensure by democratic means the extension of their culture in the public sphere (through teaching their own language, history and culture), they are not *defined* by their distinct culture or tradition. Further, this argument does not imply anything about the type of culture adopted in communities that have an indigenous identity. Presumably, some communities will seek to preserve some indigenous ways, to teach their language and history. However, the precise kind of accommodation that they may seek with the larger state and majority culture will be up to them to decide. The arguments put forward here explain only why indigenous people are justified in exercising self-rule in accordance with their aspirations and their historic status as self-governing people, but are also consistent with debate within the community about the meaning of their culture and the precise weight accorded to the diverse values they endorse, and the way they are institutionalized.[19]

One of the reasons why the usual way of approaching this issue – in terms of whether indigenous people's self-government should be subject

---

[19] This suggests a point that space does not permit me to elaborate on here, but which is important to understanding the dynamics of internal minorities. This is that non-territorial forms of autonomy (over schools, or cultural forums and so on) often lead to a more static conception of the culture and are less liberal than territorial forms, which do not identify the group with a specific culture, but merely empower them through ensuring that they have the jurisdictional capacity to be collectively self-governing.

to limitation by liberal rules and rights, guaranteed by a bill or charter of rights – is inappropriate is because indigenous people quite rightly do not trust the non-indigenous-dominated legal system and judiciary. This was, after all, one of the main institutional means by which they were dispossessed and disadvantaged in the past, as the courts frequently failed to recognize their claims and their holdings. They do not trust the domestic court systems (of Australia, Canada, the United States and so on), and so question the jurisdictional authority of such a court in making decisions over their affairs. This means that any institutional mechanism for protecting the internal minorities will have to be acceptable to indigenous peoples and should avoid the colonial implications of a system in which non-indigenous peoples stand in a hierarchical authority relationship to indigenous people and make judgements about the legitimacy of their policies and practices.

If liberal democrats are serious about protecting human rights – about ensuring that the individual human rights of individual indigenous and non-indigenous peoples are recognized and supported – they must be prepared to accept a general limitation on all exercises of political power, not just that indigenous political authority should be limited by a white-controlled domestic (American/Australian/Canadian) judiciary. They will have to be willing to accept the same principles limiting political power that indigenous peoples accept, and the jurisdiction of a neutral (international) legal body to determine violations of these principles, which can be appealed to by both non-indigenous and indigenous peoples, the composition of which is subject to the agreement or consent of both.

Finally, the emphasis on the group that should be collectively self-governing carries with it assumptions about the accountable and representative nature of indigenous people's leadership. As mentioned earlier, this argument only works if the leadership is in fact accountable and representative. Clearly, self-rule of a people can be jeopardized not only by the imposition of alien cultures and rules, but also by local self-interested elites, who use their authority to preserve and maintain their power base. Mobutu Sese Seko's Congo, which was completely subordinated to its ruler, and treated as his own personal fiefdom, is an extreme case of government which had become completely personalized. Problems of corruption and the exclusion and marginalization of elements of the community can also arise in smaller communities. This problem is particularly pertinent in the case of indigenous self-government because indigenous communities are typically economically disadvantaged and meaningful self-government must be accompanied by redistribution from the non-indigenous population. This raises the problem of accountability insofar as the people who provide the economic resources do not receive the services, which can lead to a dynamic where the leadership of the indigenous community has an incentive to maximize the extraction of resources, but not necessarily to pursue policies aimed at more efficiently providing services to their community. It also obfuscates the lines of responsibility and so makes unfair, nepotistic policies and allocation of resources more likely.[20] Following from the idea that indigenous peoples are entitled to be self-governing and make decisions over their own lives, this system needs to be reformed. What is needed is direct redistribution to indigenous people, while at the same time conferring on indigenous governments the jurisdictional capacity to tax back what is needed to provide services to their communities, and democratic control by indigenous peoples themselves over the governance of their communities.[21]

Conclusion

In this chapter, I have examined three different arguments for a right to political self-government and applied these arguments to the context of indigenous peoples. I have argued that the third type of argument (the historical/rectificatory justice argument) is the strongest one, and that it suggests that the issue of the substantive justice meted out to internal minorities should be regarded in exactly the same way, and addressed by the same mechanisms, as human rights violations at the international level. This is not intended to trivialize the problem of internal minorities, but rather to stress the pervasiveness of the problem, and the need to strengthen international surveillance and enforcement of a minimum standard of human decency and treatment. Indeed, liberal democratic societies that accommodate their indigenous minorities through territorial autonomy arrangements should not be as concerned about the issue of human rights violations and abuses by those governments as violations by sovereign states, because one morally significant difference between

[20] The financial structure on Canadian reserves, for example, whereby wealth is distributed to chiefs and the band council, reproduces the authority and structure of the paternalist Department of Indian Affairs, which controlled indigenous people and treated them as children. This diagnosis is found in Boldt 1993: 140. It is repeated in Flanagan 2000: 94–111, but in Flanagan's book, it is put forward, not as an argument for needed reform, but as an argument against indigenous self-government.
[21] One criticism of this proposal, which will probably be put forward by those people who operate with a static cultural conception, is that this hampers indigenous people in the exercise of self-determination by requiring them to meet externally imposed standards – in this case, to be fully democratic. There is, however, a difference between specific externally imposed moral principles, and democracy. Democracy simply requires that the elites are responsive to, and accountable to, their own people. The principles are designed to ensure that indigenous people are able to effectively exercise self-rule, and have the capacity to make decisions over their own lives.

the two institutional arrangements is that at least the indigenous person has the option to leave the indigenous community, to become part of the larger, non-indigenous society. This is not complete freedom of exit, since that option may not always be attractive, but it is an option which is not always available when the abuser is the state itself. In the latter case, the abusive state may prevent its people from leaving and other states in the international community may have very restrictive immigration and refugee policies or practices.

In addition, this chapter has argued that the notion of collective self-rule has implications for the kind of institutional structure that is justified. Specifically, it implies a form of democracy that ensures that elites are accountable and responsible to their community: they are not guardians of a particular identity or culture, but exercise authority consistent with the aims, desires and legitimate goals of the community.

14   Self-determination as a basic human right: the Draft UN Declaration on the Rights of Indigenous Peoples

Cindy Holder

Introduction

Conventional wisdom suggests that promoting self-determination for peoples and protecting the human rights of individuals are competing priorities. By this is meant that securing individuals in their human rights requires limits on the rights of their peoples, and vice versa. In contrast, the Draft UN Declaration on the Rights of Indigenous Peoples (the Draft Declaration) treats the two as not only mutually supporting but mutually necessary. In the Draft Declaration, the right of peoples to self-determination is more than a principle that constrains states in their behavior towards other states and territories "outre-mer"; it also constrains states *within* their domestic realm. This view of self-determination reflects the experience of many indigenous groups, for whom refusal to respect the integrity of their group and failure to respect the integrity of their persons have gone hand in hand.

In this chapter, I give the basic outline of the Draft Declaration's treatment of self-determination. I argue that this view of self-determination is right: self-determination is a human right and this human right is the same right that underpins the rights of states. Treating an interest of peoples like self-determination as a constitutive element of human dignity raises practical worries about the stability of the international system, and philosophical worries about potential conflicts between individuals and peoples. But it also casts state sovereignty itself in a different light. This new light has interesting consequences both for international law and for philosophical debates about minorities within minorities. In particular, it allows one to think about questions about internal minorities as ultimately questions about legitimacy and representation.

Self-determination in the Draft Declaration

The Draft Declaration consolidates, clarifies and elaborates international norms regarding the rights of indigenous peoples. It is a standard-setting instrument: a statement of basic principles that an international organization (in this case, the United Nations) has agreed should guide states (or other actors) in their development of national legislation and their interpretation of their international obligations. Standard-setting instruments are important interpretive tools in international law, and they may contribute to the development of treaties or serve as evidence of an emergent norm of customary law. The archetypal standard-setting instrument is the UN's Universal Declaration of Human Rights. Other such instruments include the UN Declaration on the Rights of Persons Belonging to National or Ethnic, Religious or Linguistic Minorities (Declaration on Minorities), Standard Minimum Rules for the Treatment of Prisoners, and declarations from regional bodies such as the Organization of American States (OAS), the European Commission on Human Rights, or the Organization of African Unity (Toman 1999). The Draft Declaration is currently under consideration by a working group of the UN's Commission on Human Rights, whose aim is to produce a version of the text that has sufficient support among UN member states to be adopted as a resolution. The working group is primarily made up of representatives of states; it hears statements from representatives of indigenous peoples, non-governmental organizations, and inter-governmental organizations as well as from governments.

The rights set out in the Draft Declaration can be grouped under three distinct categories. The first grouping (articles 9, 13, 14 and 16) focuses on language, religious or spiritual expression, and history or heritage. These articles establish a right to *develop* and *interpret* a way of life that is distinctively one's own, both as an individual and as a group.[1] A second group of articles (10, 12, 17 and 24–6) sets out rights of access to and control over land, physical resources and intellectual tools. These articles focus on the material underpinnings of life. They establish a right to *support* and *effect* a way of living that is distinctively one's own.[2] A

---

[1] Article 9 sets out the right of persons to belong to an indigenous community in accordance with its traditions and customs. Article 13 names rights to spiritual and religious traditions, customs and ceremonies; to religious and cultural sites; to the use and control of ceremonial objects; and to the repatriation of human remains. Article 14 states that indigenous peoples have a right to their histories, languages, oral traditions, philosophies, writing systems and literatures, and to designate and retain their own names for communities, places and persons. Article 16 sets out a right to have their cultures, traditions, histories and aspirations appropriately reflected in education and public information.

[2] Article 12 states that peoples have the right to maintain, protect and develop manifestations of their cultures, such as archeological and historical sites, artefacts, designs, ceremonies, technologies and visual and performing arts and literature; and the right to restitution of cultural, intellectual, religious and spiritual property taken without their free and informed consent or in violation of their laws, traditions and customs. Article 17 lists the right of peoples to their own media in their own languages. Article 24 includes

third set of articles (15, 29, 33–34) sets out rights to control the development and maintenance of institutions, rules of membership, and the terms on which a community interacts with other communities. These articles focus on the institutional underpinnings of life, and in particular on the link between institutions of governance and cultural expression and development both for individuals and for groups. They establish a right to support and effect a *way of interacting* with other people (both intimates and strangers) that is of one's own choosing, both as an individual and as part of a group: in effect, a right of persons and of communities to some form of self-government.[3]

Each of these categories includes rights of both peoples and persons. For example, article 42 describes the rights set out in the Draft Declaration as "the minimum standard for the survival, dignity and well-being of the indigenous *peoples* of the world" (emphasis added). Article 7 describes indigenous peoples as having "the collective and individual right not to be subjected to ethnocide and cultural genocide." Article 8 ascribes "the collective and individual right to maintain and develop their distinct identities and characteristics including the right to identify themselves as indigenous and to be recognized as such." In fact, the document often seems to go out of its way to identify rights as *both* collective and individual. This is in part to make it unambiguous that the subjects of the rights it names are not just persons belonging to indigenous groups but also the groups themselves.[4]

In itself, naming groups as well as individuals as bearers of human rights is not a radical departure from existing international practice. It articulates in a principled way an idea that has been influencing the development of international norms for quite some time (Anaya 1993: 131–64,

---

the right to protection of vital medicinal plants, animals and minerals as part of the right to traditional medicines and health practices. Articles 10, 25 and 26 link rights to not be forcibly removed from their lands, territories, waters and resources, to rights of people to maintain and strengthen their spiritual and material relationship with these, and to own, develop, control and use them in accordance with their own laws, traditions and customs, land-tenure systems and institutions.

[3] Article 15 states that indigenous peoples have the right to establish and control their own institutions and system of education. Article 29 sets out a right to full ownership, control and protection of cultural and intellectual property. Article 32 sets out the right of indigenous peoples to determine citizenship in accordance with their customs and traditions. Article 33 names a right to promote, develop and maintain institutional structures and distinctive juridical customs, traditions, procedures and practices. Article 34 states that indigenous peoples have a collective right to determine the responsibilities of individuals to their communities.

[4] Many human rights documents use the locution "persons belonging to" rather than "peoples". This has the advantage of avoiding the contentious word "peoples" and so making it easier to gain the support of certain states. Of course the reason the "persons belonging to" locution more easily gains support is that it leaves it ambiguous whether, in fact, groups as such may make claims of the states that host them.

1996: ch. 3). It is true that the Draft Declaration is distinctive (at least among United Nations instruments) in offering the possibility that complaints may be filed on behalf of groups as such. As it stands, most of the international forums in which violations of human rights may be pursued as a breach of legal obligation only accept complaints on behalf of individual persons, either severally or in groups. However, this does not arise from the nature of the rights such forums consider, but rather from the specific mechanisms for processing complaints that the various human rights treaties have set up.[5] So although explicitly naming peoples as the subjects of human rights is somewhat of a departure from the wording of many human rights documents, it is nonetheless consistent with existing international norms and practice; and it can certainly be incorporated into the international bill of human rights without doing violence to its underlying framework.

However, the Draft Declaration goes beyond merely incorporating groups into international human rights discourse. Its interpretive framework presents certain rights of peoples (such as the rights to culture and to self-determination) as not just claims that must be respected as a *matter* of human right, but as fundamental or basic rights in themselves. With respect to self-determination, the document's interpretation implies that the (now widely accepted) norm that states must refrain from attempts to assimilate, submerge or otherwise manipulate the organization, culture and development of "insular minorities" (communities within their borders who are culturally, religiously or linguistically distinct) (Hannum 1990: chs. 3, 4; Lerner 1991; Casesse 1995: ch. 5) establishes a right of such communities to determine for themselves the terms on which they associate with the government that hosts them. The Draft Declaration suggests that states may not interfere with insular minorities because self-determination itself is a basic human right.

Basic rights, derivative rights and particular claims

Treating self-determination as a basic human right implies three things: that it is a right of all peoples, as such; that it imposes constraints on states'

---

[5] For example, the HRC (the monitoring body for the ICCPR) and CERD (the monitoring body for the International Convention on the Elimination of All Forms of Racial Discrimination) only accept complaints on behalf of individual persons, either severally or in groups. However, the amendment of the European Convention on the Protection of Human Rights and Fundamental Freedoms to allow individuals and groups to bring complaints before the Court, and the Additional Protocol to the European Charter Providing for a System of Collective Complaints show that, as a pragmatic matter, complaints from groups can be brought within the mandate of instruments for the oversight and enforcement of human rights treaties if there is a will to do so.

behavior that they must respect as a *matter* of human right (i.e. that they must conform to insofar as they respect human rights at all); and that the interest that underwrites a people's right to self-determination is one of a special or basic set, whose moral status is such that they may not be traded off against interests not also within that special set.

Basic human rights generate claims regardless of their having instrumental value in securing or realizing other rights. *Derivative* or *non-fundamental* rights generate claims because they contribute to or are preconditions for securing or realizing basic rights. What a person can claim as a matter of human right may include things which, taken on their own (i.e. apart from the contribution they make to other rights), are not fundamental to securing human dignity.

For example, the right to due process is usually treated as a basic right: it is treated as important in and of itself, regardless of its contribution to protecting or promoting other rights like the right to free expression. Consequently, it is enough to show that a state has not provided me with due process to show that it has violated my human rights. In contrast, the right to an interpreter during legal proceedings is usually treated as a derivative right: it is treated as a right one has because of its contribution to the right to due process. So if a state can show that in a particular set of circumstances providing me with an interpreter was not necessary for me to enjoy due process, it will have shown that in fact it has not violated my human rights in the circumstances (even though, in most cases, refusal to provide an interpreter is rights-violating).

Both of these (the basic right to due process and the derivative right to an interpreter) can further be distinguished from *particular claims* to which those rights give rise, such as the ability to choose for oneself the interpreter that one uses. Particular claims name specific institutional arrangements, ranges of services and/or performances that persons (or peoples) must be able to command or enjoy for one to judge that the state in which they live is in fact observing the constraints on its behavior that respect for human rights requires. For example, in an institutional context that does not offer imprisoned persons parole before the end of their full sentence, the right to non-discrimination on the basis of race could not give rise to particular claims to parole. In an institutional context that grants parole to some persons before the end of their full sentence it may well be that the human right to non-discrimination requires that certain applicants be approved as a matter of human right. In other words, the right to non-discrimination on the basis of race may give rise to particular claims in the latter context where it would not do so in the former.

So basic rights are the constitutive elements of a special set of rights: rights that in themselves justify constraints on state behavior. These elements may in turn ground other (derivative) rights.[6] The basic set names capacities, interests or activities which are of such universal and fundamental importance to human beings as such, that securing people in the enjoyment of these as *rights* should be adopted as an end in itself. Achieving this purpose – securing people in their development or enjoyment of capacities, interests or activities vital to them – may, as a matter of contingent fact, require one to protect and promote interests, capacities and activities that are not of vital importance taken on their own, but as a matter of fact are necessary to protect and promote elements of the basic set. Both elements of the basic set (basic rights) and activities, capacities and interests that are important contributions thereto (derivative rights) give rise to particular claims. These claims must be recognized as a matter of universal human right, even though they arise because of specific features of a social, historical or institutional context.[7]

Distinguishing between basic rights, derivative rights and particular claims is important for at least two reasons. First, it distinguishes between the *grounds* on which a particular claim is argued and the state of affairs that a claim is intended *most immediately* to secure in a way that helps clarify what is actually at issue in disagreements about whether specific policies or actions violate one's human rights. For example, the entitlement of all citizens to vote according to their consciences most immediately

---

[6] In this, the notion of a basic or fundamental right is similar to Joseph Raz's concept of a core right: a right that can ground duties and is not itself grounded in another right. See Raz 1986: 168–9.

[7] This distinction can be seen in practice in the differing positions adopted by the justices of the European Court of Human Rights in the case of *Buckley v. United Kingdom*. The complainant in that case was a gypsy woman who had been denied permission to park her caravan on a piece of property which she owned on the grounds that using her land in this way "would detract from the rural and open quality of the landscape, contrary to the aim of the local development plan." The complainant argued that her rights to respect for private life, family and home, and the right to enjoy all Covenant rights without discrimination under the European Convention for the Protection of Human Rights and Fundamental Freedoms, had been violated. The European Court's assessment of the complaint was divided. The majority opinion (six of nine) found that there had been no violation on the grounds that the decision as to whether the complainant's interests in parking her caravan on her property could be traded off against the municipality's interests in controlling local development lay within the authority of the national government in question to decide. Each of the dissenting opinions rejected this. They took the complainant's Covenant rights to be fundamental or basic constraints on the kinds of trade-off between interests that state parties may make, and so argued that reviewing the appropriateness of the trade-offs that internally determined norms permit is precisely what the Court in its supervisory capacity is supposed to do. A difference in various judges' understanding of what kind of constraint the rights set out in the Covenant represent – derivative or fundamental – led to very different conclusions regarding the scope of freedom in their decision-making that states are allowed. *Case of Buckley v. United Kingdom*, European Court of Human Rights Reference Number 00000664, Reports of the European Court of Human Rights 1996(IV), 23/1995/529/615, 25 September 1996.

secures persons' capacity to establish and maintain a democracy. The *grounds* on which individuals claim this entitlement as a human right is not a right to vote; it is a right to political participation (or perhaps a derivative right to democracy). It may turn out that there is disagreement about whether voting is, in fact, necessary to secure persons in their right to political participation. Distinguishing between political participation as the grounds for particular claims, and voting as the particular claim that the right to political participation (allegedly) establishes clarifies the conceptual relationship that is supposed to obtain between a person's human right to political participation and prohibitions on voting.

Second, the distinction between basic rights, derivative rights and particular claims separates out the specific actions, policies and/or provisions that respect for human rights requires a state (or other actor) to undertake or refrain from undertaking, and the general and abstract form in which the rights themselves are couched. For example, the right to due process may ground a particular claim for Cree persons to have the manner in which they interact with judges or other officers of the court left out of deliberations about credibility or sentencing. But this is not to say that the right to culturally sensitive legal institutions is a *basic* right, nor that the only way to ensure that Canada's legal institutions are sensitive to cultural differences between Cree persons and Anglo-Saxon persons who appear before a criminal court is to bar judges from considering *anyone's* manner of interacting with court officers. Rather, there is an abstract universal right to due process, respect for which requires (among other things) that one limit as much as possible the likelihood that a person will fail to receive a fair hearing (be it as defendant or as victim) because an officer of the court misreads his or her body language. This establishes a derivative right to culturally sensitive legal proceedings, which (depending on the context) may in turn establish a particular claim for a Cree person to have his or her interactions with officers of the court treated differently than is usually the case.

Self-determination as a basic right

Obviously the rights that the Draft Declaration lists are supposed to be read as constraints that states must respect as a *matter* of human right. But this does not necessarily mean that each clause within the document names a right that is basic in and of itself. There are several arguments in favor of indigenous self-government in the contemporary literature on group rights that appeal not to a general right of peoples to self-determination but rather to the specific circumstances in which indigenous peoples find themselves in many parts of the world. For example,

Allen Buchanan argues that the strongest case for according collective rights to indigenous peoples is "that they are needed as special protections for the distinctive interests of indigenous peoples and other minorities – typically as a result of historical injustices perpetrated against them (1993: 104). Will Kymlicka similarly defends indigenous rights to cultural and political protection as a response to unequal circumstances (1989a: ch. 9). On these (derivative) justifications, the right of self-determination has an (historically contingent) empirical relationship to securing the dignity of indigenous persons, and *that* is why it is appropriate to talk about a right of indigenous peoples to self-determination that must be respected as a matter of human right. There is no basic right to self-determination. At best there is a derivative right; more probably there is only a particular claim.

The Draft Declaration treats self-determination of peoples as a *basic* right. Failing to respect the right of self-determination is explicitly included with rights that are usually taken to be fundamental such as the right to life, to physical integrity and to freedom of conscience. Denying or obstructing an indigenous group's self-determination is treated as wronging the members of that group directly, over and above any wrong done to them by such action's undermining of other of their rights (Anaya 1996: chs. 3, 4). In this it offers an argument for indigenous self-determination that applies *in addition* to arguments based in indigenous peoples' legal rights to have their treaties honored, but that does *not* rely on the special circumstances in which indigenous persons and peoples find themselves in many parts of the world. In the Draft Declaration self-determination is a right that indigenous peoples have as peoples, regardless of the circumstances in which they find themselves, and not only a special right that they have as subjects of past injustice.

There the Draft Declaration's view reflects a more realistic conception of the role of group autonomy in securing human dignity, even though the derivative view is more common. In the words of Rosemarie Kuptana of the Inuit Tapisariat of Canada, "Our humanity has a collective expression, and to deny us recognition as a people is to deny us recognition as equal members of the human family" (Moss 1995: 70). Human lives are lived in concert with other people, and not just in separation from them. This is true not only symbolically but materially as well. People live their lives in *groups* as well as individually. This implies that some of the decisions they make will be decisions about aspects of life that they share with specific others and about features of themselves that tie others to them.

Further, individual human beings require continuous investments of time, energy and resources to bring them to maturity, and even healthy, strong adults continue to require significant physical as well as mental contributions from other people to maintain themselves and flourish. How social and political systems distribute the burdens of those investments, ensure (or fail to ensure) that such burdens are borne and organize the delivery of contributions from others has a huge impact on individuals' day-to-day lives.

This suggests that self-determination is an essential condition for indigenous persons to live dignified lives because it is an essential condition for groups of persons whose lives are closely integrated to determine for themselves what their collective life means and what future course it should take. Indigenous persons, *like everyone else*, have an interest in determining the circumstances under which their lives unfold, and this *includes* an interest in determining for themselves the significance and terms of their relationships with one another, with the state that hosts them, and with the people and way of life that have gone before them.

An example may help to bring home this point. Suppose I own and live in a condominium that is part of a larger complex. Decisions about the schedule and terms of work on the building, use of facilities, exterior decoration and so on will have a significant effect on the way members of my family organize our time, resources and joint activities, and on the way I as an individual organize my time, resources and activities. My ability to make decisions in my own life will consequently be importantly affected by my ability to influence decisions about the life of the condominium complex. In fact, the potential for such decisions to make my life easier or more difficult, better or worse, is one of the reasons that such decision-making is usually at least partly democratic or co-operative within such complexes.

Now imagine that some branch of government were to try to take decision-making about the building's administration and upkeep out of my and my fellow condominium-owners' hands and put it instead into the hands of government officials (a "Ministry of Condominium Affairs"). Most of us would say that they ought to have a very good reason, grounded in the need to protect persons within the complex or outside of it from a serious harm. And if the government did not have a compelling reason, if there is no reason to think that government officials are better qualified to guard against the harm in question, or if it looked as though the take-over was going to be more than temporary, most would agree that both I and the complex ownership as a whole had a legitimate grounds for complaint.

Of course, membership in an indigenous community and ownership of a condominium are importantly different. One might say that I have chosen to live in a condominium rather than a separate house; and so that I have (at least implicitly) agreed to the vulnerability to actions and decision-making by others that such a living arrangement entails. A condominium owner can sell up and move if she finds the situation undesirable. And really, at the end of the day, it is just an apartment.

In contrast, individuals do not choose to be born into an indigenous community; and membership in such a community is not a severable good that one may sell on the open market. The lives of persons within an indigenous community are often closely integrated and inter-dependent in a way that the lives of persons who own units within a condominium complex usually are not. It is rare for a person who owns a condominium to find herself discriminated against because of such ownership. Governments seldom see the mere existence of condominium complexes as a barrier to national projects or unity. And those who own condominiums often have considerable economic and political resources at their disposal in battles over resources, land and other goods that they control but others want.

Yet these differences seem to make communal decision-making more important for persons in indigenous communities than for communities such as my condominium complex. Most of my claims to independence from government interference in decisions about my condominium complex arise from interests in being able to secure and enjoy important items of personal property; but the common life of an indigenous community often includes much more than property. In an indigenous community, decisions about communal organization and administration often affect a person's ability to maintain family ties, to develop intimate relationships, to express and develop views of her own about her life and her surroundings, to learn and practice a livelihood, and more. This is the core of the case for treating indigenous peoples' right to self-determination as a basic human right. Self-determination is a group's right to make decisions *together* and *for themselves* about the conditions and terms that govern shared aspects of life. The more extensive and integrated a group of persons' common life, the greater the scope of activities, institutions and conditions of life for which their capacity to deliberate as a group becomes part of what it is for each of them to live life on their own terms.

Establishing self-determination as a basic right is also significant for pragmatic reasons. First, by obviating the need to go looking for empirical arguments establishing that the violation of self-determination violates other rights, and by making it possible for self-determination to figure as a grounding right for particular claims and for derivative rights such as the right to land,[8] it shortens the chain of argument for a large range

---

[8] Many would argue that right to land is itself a basic right. In the case of indigenous people, the grounding of a right to land is overdetermined: it may be grounded through the right to culture, the right to due process or the right to non-discrimination.

of complaints. In effect, it reduces the scope for those resisting a human rights claim to use empirical indeterminacy as an excuse to continue their course of action, and makes the relationship between problematic state action and respect for human dignity starker.[9]

Second, the symbolism of redescribing indigenous peoples' right to self-determination as a derivative right or a (mere) particular claim is deeply problematic. Historically there is a pattern of treating indigenous rights as exceptions, different in scope or kind from the rights of persons as such. The effect of this is usually to exempt states and other actors from (otherwise universal) obligations when their actions regard an indigenous person or group (Barsh 1983; Williams 1990; Anaya 1996: ch. 1). Historically, describing indigenous rights as exceptional or special has had the practical effect of making them less constraining.

One might worry that these pragmatic arguments miss the point of derivative justifications. One might reply, for example, that describing self-determination as at most a derivative right is not intended to make them less threatening to *states*, only less threatening to individuals, and in particular to individuals within a group. In this regard, it is important to note two things.

First, it is illusory to think that one can weaken a right's importance vis-à-vis the rights of other individuals without this having an effect on the extent to which it constrains states. These days it is rare for a state to argue that they may violate a human right "just because." States rather argue that they must act as they do, even if that *seems* to violate a right because their obligation to protect the rights of other segments of their citizenry requires it. In *Buckley v. United Kingdom*, for example, the state party successfully argued that the decision to interfere with a gypsy complainant's right to culture (by forbidding her to park a caravan on her land) ought to be left to the state's discretion because it involved a trade-off between comparable interests (the complainant's interest in culture and the interest of local residents in an unobstructed view of the countryside). Deflating or otherwise qualifying group rights widens the scope

---

[9] For example, in *Lansmann v. Finland* a group of Saami reindeer breeders argued that the Finnish government violated the right to culture outlined in Article 27 of the International Covenant on Civil and Political Obligations (the ICCPR) by granting logging concessions in areas that reindeer normally use for winter grazing. The decision went against the complainants because the Committee found that the evidence did not permit them to conclude that the logging concessions constituted a pressing threat to the Saami's ability to herd reindeer. The Finnish government has taken this to indicate that it need not change its policies with respect to logging in the area. Had the Saami been able to appeal to a right of self-determination, their claim to a say in the distribution of logging concessions would have been easier to establish empirically. *Lansman v. Finland*, Communication No. 511/1992 and *Lansman et al v. Finland*, Communication No. 671/1995, UN Doc. CCPR/C/58/D/671/1995 (1996).

for this kind of argument, and in so doing it widens the scope for state interference in minority decision-making.

The real argument on behalf of derivative justifications is not that reducing self-determination to a derivative right does not strengthen states' hand with respect to minorities. The real argument is that as a general rule the protection that individuals within the group gain from such a strengthening is worth it. This is the crux of the choice that theories of minority rights confront when they turn to questions about minorities within minorities: at the end of the day, ought one to lay one's bets with the strengthening of states or the strengthening of groups when looking out for individuals' human rights? In suggesting that self-determination is one of the human rights whose promotion must be taken into account, the Draft Declaration makes it much less obvious that the costs of widening states' scope for interference are acceptable. Below, I will give some reasons for thinking that this is a good thing in two respects: it encourages one to rethink the role of groups in a dignified human life, and it demands that states themselves justify their authority in these terms. For now, it is enough to note that one important difference between basic and derivative views is the willingness to lay one's human rights bets with political authorities other than a state.

Second, whether intended or not, describing indigenous peoples' right to self-determination as less than a general or universal principle has the rhetorical effect of making it appear less important. This is particularly so when the rights that the group would otherwise wield are left in the hands of a state. After all, even though the right to self-determination of peoples that underwrites states' rights to territorial integrity and non-interference is not presented as a human right, that right is treated as one of the basic norms that makes the existing international legal regime possible and worth preserving. So insisting that indigenous self-determination is different in kind from the sort that grounds states' rights does more than simply bolster states' powers to protect minorities within a minority; it establishes states' rights as, if not more fundamental, then at the very least *less threatening* to individuals than those of other groups (Falk 1992).

Self-determination as a right of all peoples

The United States, Argentina and Brazil, among others, have repeatedly objected to including a people's right to self-determination in the Draft Declaration on the grounds that indigenous peoples are not peoples under international law and ought not to be given the power to break up states (which power the phrase "right to self-determination" is argued to confer). Some of those objecting have argued that the phrase "self-determination" should be excised from the document entirely. Others have suggested that it be explicitly distinguished from the general right of peoples to self-determination by attaching a disclaimer to the effect that nothing said about self-determination in the document should be interpreted as meaning that indigenous peoples have a general right of self-determination under international law.

The heart of these objections is that the Draft Declaration's use of the terms "people" and "self-determination" is confused. "Peoples" (the argument goes) ought to be limited to two types of group: *nation states* and *populations within colonially governed territories*. The right of peoples to self-determination reflects the nature of the type of group to which it belongs: it is a right of independent statehood, grounded in facts about what makes for a state and how best a system in which states exist may promote peace and stability between them (Shaw 1997: 181–2).

On this view, treating self-determination as a *human* right errs on two counts: it ascribes a right to all peoples that ought properly to be restricted to a select few; and it fails to distinguish between the kinds of principles that establish rights for individual persons and the kind of principles that establish rights for groups.[10]

Read in this way, the objections of state parties such as the United States and Brazil reflect assumptions about group rights that are also widespread in the philosophical literature on minority rights: that the kind of rights a group may claim depends primarily on the *type* or *kind* it represents; and that one cannot use the same arguments to justify rights for groups that one uses to justify rights for individuals.

For example, in *Multicultural Citizenship* Will Kymlicka (1995) distinguishes between national minorities, ethnic minorities and immigrant groups, arguing that the rights that such groupings may claim of a liberal state as a matter of justice vary according to the type they represent, and this move has become common in the literature (Margalit and Raz 1990; Tamir 1993; Kymlicka 1995.) Kymlicka's distinction is based on (purported) differences in the role different types of group play in organizing individuals' options and experiences; such differences are argued to make for different impacts on individuals' capacity for autonomy and it is because of this that the rights that can be generated by membership are argued to vary. Other theorists have typologized groups on slightly

---

[10] In fact, this reflects both a very conservative view of the international legal conventions governing the terms "peoples" and "self-determination" and a very generous view of the political and legal regimes governing indigenous communities in most parts of the world. For example, it is not at all clear, given the legal and administrative regimes that govern indigenous peoples in Canada, the United States, New Zealand and Australia, that restricting the term "peoples" to populations within a colonized or occupied territory would rule out treating indigenous groups as peoples.

different grounds. For example, James Nickel (1997) sorts groups according to their pragmatic capacity to wield rights; and Leslie Green (1994) sorts them according to the likelihood that promoting them will also promote autonomy. In each of these accounts, groups must *qualify* for rights: they must exhibit specific properties that mark out groups that are potential rights-wielders from those that are not. As with objectors like the United States, then, many theorists of minority rights would likely reject the Draft Declaration's statement of peoples' rights to self-determination as unacceptably vague. Before figuring out whether indigenous peoples may claim a right of self-determination, one must first figure out what *kind* of group an indigenous people is: one must identify what it is to be an indigenous people. Only then can one determine whether such groups are even candidates for rights, let alone whether in the particular case, the potentiality for rights-wielding is actual. On most views, it is only by figuring out what makes something *count* as a people as such that one can figure out whether they have rights and in what those rights consist.

Many theorists of minority rights further argue that at any rate arguments purporting to establish rights for groups as such cannot avail themselves of the same range of justifications that are open to arguments that establish rights for individuals. For it is argued that groups as such may acquire rights only derivatively, in virtue of their instrumental contribution to (more important) individualistic rights. In particular, the interests of groups as such are usually rejected as proper grounds for human rights. Even when groups as such are of a type that may wield rights, it is often argued that their rights must always (except, perhaps, in extreme or special circumstances) give way when they come into conflict with the rights of an individual internal to them (Buchanan 1993; Kymlicka 1995; Jones 1999). Like conservative interpretations of international law, then, many discussions of minority rights argue that questions about the moral entitlements of individuals ought to be treated separately from questions about the entitlements of groups.[11]

These concerns about the Draft Declaration's treatment of self-determination are important. Yet to fully appreciate the nature of the disagreement between the Draft Declaration and its critics, one must pay closer attention to what the document is actually doing. Conservative approaches to international law suggest that the Draft Declaration is problematic because of its broadened conception of peoples and its multiplication of potential candidates for statehood. But in fact, the document's use of the terms "peoples" and "self-determination" is not as big

---

[11] But whereas most minority rights theorists would argue that the moral claims of individuals must be treated first so that it may serve as a foundation for one's consideration of the legal entitlements of collectivities, most conservative interpretations of international law would reverse that priority.

a departure from existing international practice as its critics suggest.[12] The Draft Declaration's real innovation is that it shifts the basis on which states themselves claim political authority in the international sphere. Its motivation for this shift is instructive for theories of minority rights.

The Draft Declaration suggests that indigenous peoples, national, ethnic, and linguistic minorities and other sub-state groupings have independent status under international law and that this is so for the same reasons that states have their status: because it is a constitutive element of showing respect for the individuals that comprise them. In this, the real worry that the Draft Declaration seems to raise is not that its conception of peoples and self-determination is *confused* but rather that its conception is *impractical*. Figuring out who peoples are does not seem to be a problem so much as figuring out how the system can be stable with so many of them claiming rights to decide for themselves the rules and political institutions that apply.

However, a doomsday scenario of widespread instability as existing political systems are broken up by a plethora of indigenous mini-states is not plausible.[13] International tribunals and organizations have historically taken a very conservative approach to attempts to dismember a pre-existing state, in part out of respect for the principles of territorial integrity and collective security;[14] and many of the representatives of indigenous

[12] For example, the increasing importance of international human rights law has established individual persons as subjects of international law in addition to states. And regardless of whether they count as colonized populations, there is a widespread international legal practice of describing indigenous groupings as "peoples." On this see Brownlie 1998: ch. XXV; Shaw 1997: 182–4.

[13] Of course, to say that a right to self-determination *need* not imply a right to set up an independent state does not mean that self-determination *does* not imply such a right. It might turn out that the realities of negotiating with a modern state are such that it must be in principle possible for a group to claim a state of its own for that group to successfully negotiate any measure of autonomy. If this is true, then the (basic) right of self-determination will imply a (derivative) right to set up an independent state. Or it might turn out that the specific circumstances and history of most indigenous groups is such that having the option of establishing an independent state is necessary for indigenous groups to successfully negotiate any measure of autonomy. In this case the basic right of self-determination will imply that most indigenous peoples have a particular claim to an independent state. There is also a third possibility: that the right to an independent state is implied by something apart from or in addition to the right to self-determination, such as the right to equality before the law.

[14] For example, the United Nations 1970 Declaration on Friendly Relations seems to rule out an unconditional right to unilateral secession See United Nations, Declaration on the Principles of International Law Concerning Friendly Relations and Cooperation among States in Accordance with the Charter of the United Nations, General Assembly resolution 2625, 24 October 1970. Its implications for indigenous self-determination are discussed in Anaya 1996 ch. 3. For an interesting discussion of the right to unilateral secession see *Reference re Secession of Quebec* [1998] 184 S.C.R. 217.

peoples have stated over and over again that they do not plan to demand an independent state (Report of the Working Group established in accordance with Commission on Human Rights resolution 1995/32, 3 March 1995, UN Doc E/CN.4/1997/102(1996); 15 December 1997, UN Doc E/CN. 4/1998/106; 20 January 1999,UN Doc E/CN/1999/82, Pritchard 2001 at IV: A). In this they generally bear out Ian Brownlie's observation that, in practice, claiming a right of self-determination is not necessarily a first step to secession or statehood (Brownlie 1992).

In fact, most states already exhibit overlapping jurisdictions and multiple sites of governance that are not mutually exclusive and in whose dealings with one another no one party may claim the final say. Moreover, international human rights norms already compel states to answer to someone outside their borders for behavior and policy within it. In short, self-determining indigenous peoples do not *create* an international system in which states comprise multiple and overlapping levels of governance; such a system already exists.

However, as it stands, the internal messiness of the international system's units (states) tends to be glossed over or ignored in discussions of the operation and foundations of international legal principles (Kingsbury 1992). So the Draft Declaration does imply an important change: that the international system should explicitly recognize that political authority within a state may be multiply located, and not necessarily organized in hierarchical tiers, each subsuming the level below it. It treats states' internal messiness as not only normal but also desirable insofar as it seeks to protect one source of that messiness (indigenous self-determination).

This is where the document's real innovation lies. In equating self-determination with setting up an independent state, conservative approaches to international law make self-determination seem like something that only a select number of groups may have by *reducing* it to the bundle of rights traditionally associated with independent statehood. Political autonomy *within* or *in concert with* an existing state suggests something much more radical, however: it suggests that governing authorities may have substantial positive obligations to a group of persons within their jurisdiction without the compensation of exclusive authority over the individuals that group contains.

In both treating self-determination as a human right and insisting that it is the same right that appears elsewhere in the international legal canon, the Draft Declaration grounds the legal standing of *states* as well as that of sub-state groupings in considerations of human dignity. The Draft Declaration's inclusion of self-determination in the list of basic rights provides indigenous groups more scope for limiting the behavior of states in part by recognizing the importance of participation in an indigenous people. But it also, and perhaps more significantly, provides greater scope by *deflating* the rights that states themselves may claim.

Self-determination as a human right

The Draft Declaration also offers an alternative conception of the role of the interests of collectivities in securing human dignity. Its conception of the relationship between individuals and groups makes it plausible to think that certain interests of groups as such are important enough to ground basic rights. This is the significance of the document treating self-determination of peoples as a *human* right and as a right that is of basic and not only derivative importance.

In naming self-determination as a human right the Draft Declaration firmly fixes the interests of indigenous *peoples* as well as those of persons as the grounding of basic rights. In this, it elevates the interests of groups as such in a way that makes many political theorists and philosophers uncomfortable. There is a widespread worry that properly speaking a human right ought not to be grounded in the interests of groups *per se*, only in those of individual persons (even if such persons may sometimes have to use the fiction of a group to effectively claim their rights). After all, the whole point of human rights is supposed to be to protect individuals against predatory behavior. And people have again and again shown themselves most likely to behave predatorily when acting in and on behalf of groups.

There are two separate concerns here. One is that if the commitment to human rights means anything, it must mean that there are limits on the actions and decisions that institutions and institutional actors may pursue.[15] Allowing the interests of groups as such to ground human rights seems to commit one to treating collective actors as inviolable and entitled to the same independence of judgement with respect to their sub-parts that is usually accorded to individual persons. Grounding rights in groups' interests seems straightforwardly to conflict with respecting the individuals that make them up.

This concern can be defused by recognizing the difference between groups (irreducibly collective subjects) and the entities or persons acting on a group's behalf. That a human rights document's language recognizes collective subjects is not to say that the document implies that the specific organizations and institutional actors who will in many cases wield the

---

[15] This is particularly apparent in the way rights-based approaches are often characterized by contrasting them with utilitarian or communitarian views. See for example Donnelly 1985, especially ch. 4; Howard 1995.

rights of those subjects cannot be understood as proxies. It is possible to deny that *particular actors* may wield a right on a group's behalf without denying that there is a right to be wielded. This, in effect, was the reasoning behind denying membership of international organizations to South Africa during the latter years of apartheid. The massive and consistent violation of human rights within the state, in combination with its exclusion of the majority of the population from a say in the workings of government were taken to make it so implausible that those who claimed to speak on behalf of South Africa's population actually did so that it was incompatible with a commitment to the principle of self-determination to accredit members of the South African government as legitimately representing South Africa (Casesse 1995: ch. 5).

So just as an individual person and the legal actor that claims to speak on her behalf may not be the same, so a collective subject and the organization that may legitimately claim to speak on its behalf may be different. Being able to claim that one speaks on behalf of a group requires that one demonstrate that the right kind of relationship obtains between the actor or institutions that claim to express the group's decisions and the actual persons who make up the group. So in the same way that the state may fail to be a legitimate spokesperson for members of a minority because its internal structures disempower or marginalize them, so the minority must have structures that allow the participation of each member and each member must participate in a way that leaves room for and facilitates the participation of everyone else, at the risk of losing their legitimacy. The question of whether there are interests that persons have in concert with others (as part of a collective subject) that are of sufficient importance to establish rights that have an internal as well as external dimension, and the question of whether and under what circumstance one may legitimately interfere with the internally directed choices of those who act on behalf of a group are distinct.[16]

---

[16] James Nickel (1997) has argued that groups which do not exhibit both the capacity to form goals, deliberate, choose, intend, act and carry out evaluations of action (what he calls "effective agency"), and a clear identity are fatally deficient as right holders. However, Nickel explicitly rejects the suggestion that no actual group could meet these criteria and points out several ways in which groups which at the present time fail to exhibit effective agency and clear identity can develop these later on. Thus that some groups may fail to be plausible candidates for the bearing of group rights in no way undermines the plausibility of claims by others. Moreover, his reasons for accepting the thesis that groups failing to exhibit effective agency and clear identity are fatally deficient draws heavily on problems which arise were such a group to attempt to *exercise* any rights attributed to it. So Nickel's argument would not exclude a group from *basic* rights without the further claim that one may not distinguish between having and exercising a right with groups in the way that is regularly done in cases of persons incapacitated by age, unconsciousness or mental incompetence. In contrast, Allen Buchanan (1993)

The heart of the issue is a different worry: that the interests persons have as part of a collective subject – as part and only as part of a group – are just not sufficiently important to establish human rights on their own account. After all, rights imply constraints not just on institutional actors like states but on other individuals. The worry is that imposing constraints on individual persons – especially individuals within the group – requires much more to be at stake than the interests that individuals typically have as part of a group can muster.

Yet it is possible to conceive of interests persons have as part of a group that can justify imposing constraints on a group's own members without reducing these to individualistic ones and without ignoring potential dissent or divergence by an internal minority. Consider, for example, cases of communal ownership of land, or cultural resources. In such cases, recognizing a right of the group as an irreducible collective, to make decisions about land use, or to determine when rituals may be performed, or how symbols and techniques may be used, involves placing constraints on the behavior of individuals within a group as well as outside of it. The group's right to determine land use may mean that I am not permitted to plant potatoes in my back yard, even though I desperately want to. The reasons that my fellow group members give me for restricting the use of potato growing may not make sense to me. Or they may make sense as a general prohibition, but not (I believe) in this particular instance. Unless the group's right can be conceived as legitimately placing restriction on persons within the group as well as those outside of it, my fellow group members will have difficulty preventing me from ignoring their proscription. But intuitively, it seems that my reasons for wanting the capacity to ignore that proscription on potato growing matter a lot to whether I ought in fact to be able to get away with doing so. If my reasons for wanting to ignore the proscription do not reflect a very important interest, capacity or activity of mine, it seems hard to justify curtailing the capacity of my fellow group members to pursue an activity that is very important to each of them (deciding in common how land we all own is to be used).

This example illustrates how the ability to make communal decisions about an aspect of life *and to make those decisions stick* can be very important to individuals. Recognizing this possibility – that who has a say in decisions that affect communal organization and resources can have identifiable effects on the material options open to a person – points up a crucial assumption about group integrity that underwrites the worry about

---

has argued that not only can one distinguish between having and exercising rights with groups, but that such a distinction is necessary if one is to make sense of group rights at all (see Buchanan 1993; Nickel 1997).

group interests outlined above: that their impact on a person's day-to-day life is simply not as tangible or specific as the impact of individualistic interests.

In fact, however, interests one has as part of a collective subject can have as important an impact as interests one has on one's own. For example, one of the reasons that self-determination of peoples is so important to indigenous groups is that the state and status of a people is reflected in the lives of its members in very specific and tangible ways. Some of the most destructive effects of governmental violations of the rights of indigenous persons are the devastation of the community's infrastructure and demographic base, which undermines their ability to effectively organize the day-to-day conduct of their communal life (Report on the Situation of Human Rights in Brazil 1996: ch. VI; Report on the Situation of Human Rights in Ecuador 1996: ch. IX; Report on the Situation of Human Rights in Colombia 1999: ch. X at F). In addition, there is considerable evidence that a particular group's social status and its overlap in membership with other groups can make a difference to how easy it is for members to engage in social reform or political activity and to the likelihood that such engagements will succeed (Eschen, Kirk and Pinard 1971; Tilly 1987; Jenkins 1983; Navarro 1989).

Moreover, many of the harms that people experience are directed toward them by *outsiders* who have power at their disposal, and perceive a group with whom they are associated as hateful, threatening or inconvenient, and those outsiders have sufficient power at their disposal to make life problematic for the group.[17] In such a context, intra-group dependencies (and the vulnerabilities that accompany them) are often intensified, and liability to predation from fellow group members may be perceived as the lesser of two evils or the price of protection from the risks of a hostile social environment (Narayan 2002). These harms are not psychological, they are physical, economic or political; and the primary source of the problem does not lie in the beliefs or sense of self of members of the minority, it lies in the beliefs and *actions* of those who identify with the nation or people of the state.

In particular, many harms result from persons in a dominant group failing or refusing to believe that members of a minority *have* interests of their own, separate from those of the dominant group, or are *capable* of identifying or pursuing interests without dominant tutelage. The wrongs

---

[17] For example, Marilyn Frye (1983) and Catharine MacKinnon (1989)(among others) have pointed out that social and political structures often use physical features of individuals, such as their sex role, to mark them out for oppression (i.e. diminishing, exploitative or immobilizing treatment). See Frye 1983: ch. 3; MacKinnon 1989.

in such cases are not vague or difficult to trace; and the structures, identity or activities of the targeted individual's people are only incidentally involved in an explanation of the problem.

This is why the Draft Declaration's treatment of self-determination is so important for the document's primary goal: discouraging the abuse to which indigenous persons in many parts of the world are currently subject. Over and over again, one of the first steps in denying that indigenous persons have rights at all has been to deny that persons who are indigenous are capable of making decisions for themselves. Hostility to self-determination for indigenous peoples and violations of rights to physical security, political participation, equality before the law and other basic rights of indigenous persons tend, as an empirical matter, to go hand in hand.[18] It is hard to imagine a state that consistently respects the rights of all the individuals within its borders without respecting the rights of the peoples of which those persons are members. Justifications for oppression of persons in collections usually mirror justifications for their oppression as individuals.[19]

Conclusion

Self-determination secures a group in its capacity to determine *as a group* the terms and circumstances under which the common life of those within it will unfold. Decisions about the terms on which individuals may enter and exit a community, the responsibilities they incur by continued participation, the uses to which they may put cultural artefacts and culturally significant resources have effects for everyone within a community and not just those to whom those decisions are applied in a specific instance. Consequently, it is misleading to describe what is at issue in peoples' rights like self-determination as whether one ought to protect groups

---

[18] For example, in Canada and the United States, policies regarding the removal of indigenous children to residential schools and non-indigenous adoptive families (which in themselves constituted violations of a number of human rights) were *driven* by a desire to end the existence of independently functioning indigenous communities. Similarly, the motivation for attempts by many state legislatures in the United States to eliminate Indian gaming by rewriting state gambling laws is a desire to curb the independent political and economic power that some of the communities which operate gaming facilities have been able to develop, and to divert some of the economic revenue that such communities generate into state coffers for the benefit of non-indigenous citizens.

[19] This is in large part why treaty-monitoring bodies such as the CERD, the HRC and the Inter-American Commission regularly demand that state parties include information on the status and treatment of communities as well as individuals in their periodic reports on the implementation of their treaty obligations and why organizations such as the ILO, UNESCO and the OAS in the Protocol of San Salvador include collectivities as well as individual persons as potential victims of human rights violations.

from the power of the majority at the price of allowing them to constrain their own members.

What is really at issue in discussions of self-determination is when a state's preventing a group from making decisions independently or interfering with their capacity to make their decisions stick constitutes a violation of the human rights of the individuals involved in that decision-making. This suggests a slightly different framing of the issue of minorities within minorities than the standard group-versus-individual: under what circumstances does the impact of a person's actions on his fellow group members justify giving them a say in how that person conducts himself? A central issue in constructing institutions that embody one's answers to these questions is what kind of role one assigns to states versus other political authorities.

As a human rights document, the Draft Declaration is stronger for including self-determination on the list of basic rights. Reading the human right of indigenous peoples to self-determination as a particular case of the general principle in international law that all peoples have the right to self-determination suggests that the legal norms that govern states' obligations to one another and the legal norms that govern states' obligations to persons as such should be read as mutually informing one another: that the norms that govern behavior towards persons are neither completely separate from the norms that govern relations between peoples, nor completely reducible to them. This is not a new suggestion. (Right to self-determination: General recom. XXI: 1996; Vienna Declaration and Programme of Action: 1993 at 20.) But the wording of many human rights documents makes the connection between peoples and persons easy to ignore. The Draft Declaration names peoples explicitly as the subjects of human rights, and treats self-determination as one of the basic rights.

Perhaps the most important innovation of the document is its framing of the role of group interests in securing human dignity. The Draft Declaration departs from the assumption that living parts of their lives in common ties persons together in patterns of inter-dependence and shared vulnerability that have to be recognized in accounts of their human rights. Peoples' rights of self-determination need not be conceived as competitors with human rights once this is recognized. Rights of self-determination put the rights of states in their proper perspective: as rights which may themselves be justified in terms of the human rights of those within their jurisdiction.

Part V

Democracy

15   Associative democracy and minorities within minorities

Veit Bader

That policies of multiculturalism are confronted with a serious dilemma is not really contested. Structural and cultural inequalities between majorities and minorities may require a fair amount of autonomy for minorities. However, structural and cultural inequalities within minorities require the protection of individuals and vulnerable minorities (women, minors, homosexuals, dissidents) against their organizations and leaders. These inequalities may be strengthened by multicultural policies. Roughly, one can distinguish between three different approaches: (i) a radical "absolutist free exercise," "deference" or "unavoidable costs" approach; (ii) a radically secularist and individualist "re-universalizing citizenship" approach; and (iii) a "liberal democratic accommodationist" approach.

(i) Complete deference to the *nomos* (customs, ecclesiastical law), decision-making and authority of ethno-religious groups is defended by two radically different, theoretical and political positions. Radical libertarians like Kukathas (1998) defend complete deference to the *nomos* of religious groups, far-reaching autonomy and absence of any state intervention or scrutiny. These radical libertarians assume free, informed consent by adults and that entry into groups, associations and organizations should be as free as exit.

Traditionalist or conservative communitarians (as well as conservative religious leaders and fundamentalist religious politicians) defend absolutist deference and autonomy in a completely opposite way. "Our" illiberal and anti-democratic religion does not value "individual autonomy" and "free choice" at all, or not in the same way as radically individualist, modern liberals do.

(ii) Universalist egalitarian liberals took a long time to recognize the particularity of all cultures and that cultural inequalities pose an important normative problem (Kymlicka 1995). Currently, however, "re-universalizing citizenship" is becoming increasingly prominent among liberal universalists, including feminists, and among republicans and deliberative democrats, as a reaction to undifferentiated theories of cultural group rights and to undifferentiated policies of "identity" and multiculturalism. Unreconstructed individualists try to avoid the "apparent dilemma for the modern liberal regime"

> If the government defers to the wishes of the religious group, a vulnerable group of individuals will lose basic rights; if the government commits itself to respecting equal human rights of all individuals, it will stand accused of indifference to the liberty of conscience. (Nussbaum 1997: 98; see also 2001: 14, 168, 187)

Brian Barry (2001a), a self-declared defender of egalitarian liberal universalism, claims that "culture is the problem, not the solution." Many feminists also insist on a rigorously individualistic, secularist interpretation of human rights and in particular, religious freedom. They fiercely attack group rights and any associational or collective autonomy for (organized) religions. They proscribe separate codes or systems of religious law and insist on a uniform civil code, as all individualist liberals do. Such strictly individualist, secularist and context-insensitive universalism favors radical policies of state-imposed and state-controlled liberal democratic congruency.

Both of these first two positions (absolute accommodationism and external interventionism) deny that a serious dilemma exists and that one has to balance conflicting claims. Although opposed to each other in most respects, these two positions share three crucial assumptions (Shachar 2001). First, they tend to reproduce a mythical image of culture as static, isolated, homogeneous and uncontested, either with an apologetic or a critical intent. Second, both solve the dilemma of multicultural accommodation by declaring it non-existent. They either neglect injustice inside minorities or they neglect cultural inequalities between majorities and minorities. Only structural inequalities are seen as unjust. Cultural inequalities do not enter the cognitive and normative frame of authors like Barry at all. Third, in practical terms, both confront vulnerable individuals and minorities within minorities, with a simplistic, tragic choice: "your culture or your rights" (Shachar 2001: 90).

For conceptual, theoretical and practical reasons, both positions are also counter-productive (Robbins 1987: 148; Rosenblum 1998: 79, 2000c: 166). The first position reduces the requirement of an even minimally understood, compatibility with human rights and a "priority for liberal democracy" practically to zero. The second tries to impose "thick" notions of liberal autonomy and democracy in a self-contradictory way, on all associations. It requires "liberal and democratic congruency" all the way down (Galston 2002: 9).

(iii) A more attractive third approach is "liberal democratic accommodationism." This third approach accepts the need to balance individual autonomy and individual freedoms with associational freedoms, with multilayered, collective autonomy, and with other human rights. As I see it, those who adopt this third approach share three important insights. First, there is a real dilemma to be addressed, yet the nature of this dilemma may be contested. Some authors try to show that the dilemma should not be seen as a conflict of moral principles, e.g. as "competing equality claims" (Phillips, this volume: 118ff., 122), or a "rights conflict" (Moore, this volume: 274). Instead, these authors express concerns that are more pragmatic. Political conflicts about interests, power, positions, or identity as they claim, allow for easier negotiations, practical deliberations, compromise and contextual ways of resolution (Deveaux, this volume; Eisenberg, this volume). These authors accept that they may be confronted with hard strategic dilemmas (Phillips, this volume). This attempt to redefine the tension or to harmonize conflicting rights (Holder, this volume: 294) may be laudable and productive, as not all cases are hard cases. We should not be trapped by strategies of reactive ethnicization or culturalization which sometimes present pure, homogeneous, essentialist, static, uncontested cultures in conflict.

Other authors, however, insist that at least sometimes, we cannot reduce all tensions to strategic dilemmas or soft cases. We have to deal with conflicting moral principles and rights and also with conflicting, incompatible (though not incommensurable) cultural practices (Mahajan, this volume: 98; Okin, this volume). As a convinced moral pluralist, I accept that conflicts of moral principles and rights are the normal stuff of liberal morality and of practical judgement even in the absence of any deep cultural diversity. These conflicts – e.g. between individual and associational autonomy – are more serious if they are overdetermined by more or less deeply conflicting predominant cultural practices.

A second insight is that minorities that explicitly accept the principles and practices of liberal democracy, not only politically but internally, are not the problem. Instead, the problem rests with deeply illiberal and anti-democratic minorities like "anti-modern," "totalistic" "conservative" religions of either the isolationist/ "retiring" variety (Spinner-Halev 2000; Swaine, this volume), or of the more aggressive, "ambitious" and politically fundamentalist variety. The third shared insight is that there are "no easy answers" (Okin, this volume) that are applicable to all minorities within minorities in all contexts.

Within this broad range of agreement, liberal accommodationists seriously and reasonably disagree about the interpretation and balancing of appropriate principles, about adequate institutions and policies. The varieties of liberal accommodationism range from moderate civil libertarians (Rosenblum), liberal democrats, liberal communitarians (Selznick 1992: 288) and communitarian liberals (Etzioni 1996: 191), structural accommodationists (Glendon and Yanes 1991; McConnell 1992), associative democrats and other democratic institutional pluralists like Galston (2002: 10, 36f.) and Shachar (2001). My own approach has two characteristics. First, it is a moderately anti-perfectionist, justice-based approach (Carens 2000), and not a perfectionist or conservationist one. Secondly, it is a contextualized approach to morality, opting for an institutional turn in political theory (Bader and Engelen 2003e; Bader and Saharso 2004). Minorities within minorities problems cannot be resolved in a universal and context-independent way (Okin, this volume: 72, 73; Moore, this volume: 274; Phillips, this volume: 125, 127). History matters, contexts matter, institutions matter, and policies and issues matter.

The central substantive claim I want to make plausible in this chapter, is that institutionally pluralist arrangements provide more promising options for the incorporation of all kinds of cultural minorities, compared with monistic arrangements (see Bader 2003d; on religious minorities, see Bader 2003a, 2003b, 2003c). Institutionally pluralist arrangements are "power-sharing" systems requiring a conceptual break with absolute, unlimited and undivided sovereignty, jurisdiction, and property and a theoretical break with monistic, unitarian or majoritarian strategies. Such "power sharing" systems are defined by two core aspects. First, the existing pluralism of minorities must be integrated into the political process. The ways and means of minority representations are extremely variable. Second, minorities, their associations and organizations, must have a fair amount of *de facto* autonomy or self-determination.

My more specific claim is that associative democracy (AD) provides better institutional options for resolving inevitable conflicts between individual and collective autonomy (Hirst 1994; Vertovec 1999; Bader 2001b). AD is the most open and flexible version of democratic institutional pluralism. It provides better resolutions than the alternative approaches to minority within minority problems.

In the first section I state these claims. In the second section I try to substantiate and elaborate them in comparison with other "joint governance" approaches.

Why does AD provide a better institutional setting than its main rivals?

Like other "joint governance approaches," AD shares three important assumptions developed in the tradition of institutional pluralism. First, as already indicated, it presupposes notions of differentiated, delegated and limited autonomy, jurisdiction and sovereignty. Second, it is critical of the individualist social ontology of traditional liberalism or "the individual–state–market framework" (Glendon and Yanes 1991: 546f.). AD theorists fully recognize "the criss-crossing networks of associations and relationships that constitute the warp and woof of civil society." Third, it presupposes a fully-fledged moral and legal recognition of the importance of associational autonomy in general, and of associational freedoms of religion in particular.

Institutional pluralism, however, was originally illiberal and anti-democratic. The most vivid defenders of church autonomy can be found in the Catholic tradition. In contrast, AD is a modern, flexible, mod-erately libertarian version of democratic institutional pluralism. Its core proposition is that as many social activities as possible should be devolved to self-governing voluntary associations. It fully takes account of the fact of reasonable pluralism and argues that different contents and styles of the provision of public services go along with the different versions of the good life. Services should be public and publicly funded, open to all, but not controlled by the state. Associations should be free to compete with one another for members and for the provision of services. Members would bring public funds with them according to a common per capita formula, with a voucher system, which can and should be assessed to cor-rect for serious inequalities. Thus, under AD, instead of one welfare state, there would be as many welfare institutions as citizens wish to organize. Each of these welfare institutions would cater to the different ways of life of individuals and groups, but also be based on common entitlements. Such organizations would be democratically self-governing. Some would be highly participatory while others would not be. All members of these organizations would have the basic right to elect the governing council and, periodically, would have the option to exit if dissatisfied.

AD supplements, but does not replace, representative political democ-racy. Associations have to play an important role in setting public stan-dards and scrutinizing services. They should be involved in a flexible way, in the political process (see Hirst 1994; Bader 2001a).

My claim is that AD provides a better institutional setting and bet-ter policy options than its main rivals do, in order to protect vulnerable minorities against majorities and, at the same time, to resolve problems related to minorities within minorities. As for the main rivals: libertarian-ism is unattractive (i) because of its heroic and implausible assumptions about freely consenting adults (it fully trusts upon free entry and free exit neglecting external control/interference and voice), and (ii) because of its deep inegalitarianism. Political liberalism is unattractive (i) because of its exclusionist public reason assumptions (see Bader 1999; 2003b: 4f.; Bader and Saharso 2004; Weinstock, this volume, Deveaux, this volume), and (ii) because it restricts such a narrowly conceived "reasonable" pluralism to the private sphere or to civil society, and, for fear of factions arising, tries to prevent any overspill into political society and the state. (Neo-) republicanism is unattractive (i) because its distrust of institutional pluralism is even more pronounced than in political liberalism. Republicans may or may not defend federalist arrangements, but they try to prevent private associations or organizations (except, ambiguously, political parties) from playing any public or political role; (ii) they claim that liberal and democratic congruency all the way down (except of course, in "private business") would solve problems of minorities within minorities. Deliberative democracy has recently acknowledged the consequences of deep and enduring moral disagreement. It has softened the exclusionist versions of public reason requirements (see Deveaux, this volume; Tully, forthcoming) but (i) is still institutionally underdeveloped (e.g. in addressing the pressing problem of how to correct serious background inequalities and their consequences for public deliberation); and (ii) it still cannot resist the temptation that "democracy is the answer," even in the more considered versions (e.g. Fung and Wright 2001; Williams 2000; Deveaux, this volume). The costs of imposing democracy on undemocratic minorities are downplayed, even when accepting some illiberal outcomes of fair negotiations and deliberations.

AD is attractive for minorities mainly for three reasons (more fully developed in Bader 2001b). First, like libertarianism and those versions of political liberalism which respect associational autonomy in civil society, AD guarantees fair amounts of *associational autonomy* in matters crucial to minorities. Second, it provides for flexible rights and opportunities of representation in the political process which are vehemently criticized by libertarians, republicans and political liberals. The focus of traditional debates about minority representation, with national minorities, and indigenous peoples as exemplary cases, has been the political process where that process is narrowly understood as decision-making, implementation and adjudication in the state, i.e. as "voice" (e.g. guaranteed seats in legislative chambers) and as political "muscle" (power sharing in executive and judicial bodies). However, decision-making also involves issue definition, information and the elaboration of decision-making alternatives. In all these regards, according to AD, ethno-religious minorities may claim a legitimate role. Their representative organizations should be given specific information rights and corresponding information duties by state agencies ("ear"). They should be given rights and opportunities to participate in public forums and hearings to correct majority bias in relation to issue definition. They can be included in advisory councils on specific issues or in specific fields (advisory and consultation rights and duties: "listen to voice"), and they can be included in standard-setting and supervisory bodies.

Third, by providing such opportunities, AD empowers minorities and minority organizations and helps to correct majority bias hiding behind neutrality and the benign neglect of differences. As we all should know, actual religious freedoms for minorities, particularly for indigenous people (see Sheleff 2000: ch. 13) have to be continuously fought for. Their guarantee should not be left to law and supreme courts, let alone to political majoritarianism (McConnell 1992: 693, 721f., 728, 734; Monsma and Soper 1997: 200, 209f.). Public and political pressure by (organized) religions, which have rights guaranteed by freedoms of political communication but are threatened by liberal political philosophical attempts to purify public reason, helps to remind "benevolent" religious majorities (including judges) of discriminatory practices. Some form of political or formal recognition of (organized) religions provides them with important additional political and legal resources. These resources are needed in order to achieve more freedom from "intrusive interference" by actual states and organized majority religions, and in order to achieve more relationally neutral interpretations and applications of presumed neutral rights and regulations. States may be helped to be more relationally neutral instead of simply assuming (like Weinstock and Mahajan) liberal states to be neutral.

Although this may all be true, in strengthening minority organizations and leaders, does AD not, like illiberal and anti-democratic varieties and rigid, corporatist modern varieties of institutional pluralism, contribute to make women, children, homosexuals etc. more vulnerable? Are they not made more vulnerable than they inevitably are, even in liberal states trying to follow policies of liberal and democratic congruency all the way down? Why is AD attractive for minorities within minorities? Here I briefly state four main reasons which are elaborated in the next section.

The first reason is that AD acknowledges that differences amongst minorities make a difference for appropriate institutions and policies. It makes a difference whether predominant minority practices conflict with the core of modern criminal law, with modern marriage and divorce law or with non-discrimination and equal opportunity in labor law. Instead of favoring only one policy repertoire exclusively, e.g. external control and intervention (like classical liberals and republicans); or internal voice (like deliberative democrats); or voluntarism and leave them alone (like libertarians), AD prefers a minority-, context- and issue-specific mix of policies. Second, AD proposes ways and means to enlarge moderate voluntarism trying to create more actual freedoms of entry and exit. Third, AD provides opportunities for voice for minorities within minorities, although it does not "bet on this horse" alone and recognizes serious structural dilemmas. Fourth, AD is designed to cope with problems of multilevel polities and shifts in governance. Therefore, it provides better opportunities to balance legitimate claims to individual, parental and associational autonomy, with legitimate but morally minimalist claims of external control by states, international organizations and NGOs.

The claims explained

"There is no point in pluralizing the state only to create totalitarianist potentialities and authoritarian practices at the level of associations" (Hirst 1994: 68).

Minimal moral constraints: minorities, issues and policy mix

Minorities: For a contextualized theory of morality, it is obvious that differences between minorities make a difference. First, however one exactly likes to draw the boundaries, it is a commonly shared intuition that indigenous peoples should be treated differently from national minorities, immigrant minorities and religious minorities. The minorities-within-minorities dilemma is concerned only with illiberal and undemocratic minorities. It is important to state right at the outset that many recent national, immigrant and religious minorities are not much different from majorities in democratic constitutional states. Many indigenous peoples have been democratic although not liberal, long before conquering majorities became democratic.

Second, regarding illiberal and undemocratic minorities, three different types seem to require different treatment by liberal democratic polities. These types include (i) isolationist, "retiring," internally "decent" and externally peaceful religious minorities, not asking for public money and political representation and just wanting to be left alone (paradigm cases: Amish, Hutterites); (ii) "ambitious," totalistic but peaceful, conservative or "neo-fundamentalist" religious minorities, asking for public money and striving for public presence or even political hegemony (paradigm cases: minority Catholic or Orthodox Churches, neo-fundamentalist Protestants, neo-fundamentalist Muslims); (iii) modern, illiberal and anti-democratic religious fundamentalists using all means including violence to impose their totalistic, reactively purified religious regime (paradigm cases: Islamicists and some Protestant fundamentalists).

In all three cases, as in all other cases, liberal democratic polities have to intervene if and to the degree that minorities seriously harm their own minorities in their most basic needs (as discussed below). Isolationist religious minorities, however, do not harm non-members and do not pose a threat to internal social and political stability, minimally understood.

They also do not threaten external peace and do not ask for public money or other positive privileges. If these three types of arguments, which legitimize external interference and stronger scrutiny, are absent, there are few good reasons for liberals not to leave them alone if they desire it (discussed below in relation to minors within minorities).

The rights of ambitious, totalistic but peaceful conservative religions to go public and propagate an illiberal and authoritarian *Heilsstaat*, are guaranteed by the freedoms of political communication and restricted by the same contested rules that hold for all others (e.g. libel, clear and present danger, etc.). However, if they vie for and accept public money, either directly (subsidies) or indirectly (tax exemptions), liberal democratic polities have a special mandate to investigate. Polities would have a greater regulatory mandate over these institutions, according to the assumptions of public trust theory (Robbins 1987) shared by AD.

Violent religious fundamentalists not only blatantly violate the basic needs of their members and of others if they are able to, they also threaten social and political stability and peace. Even the most minimalist interpretations of no-harm principles and a "priority for liberal democracy," require extremely close public scrutiny and, if prudent, prohibition and prosecution within the confines of the rule of law.

Issues: Predominant cultural practices of illiberal and undemocratic minorities however internally contested, may conflict in numerous ways with a broad and extensive list of human rights of vulnerable minorities. These rights include the right to life, bodily integrity, non-discrimination, due process, property and civil capacity, nationality, political participation, health care, education, employment, social security, marriage and so on (Nussbaum 1997, 2000, 2001 for women). Contrary to conservative leaders and "absolutist Free Exercise" lawyers, associational religious freedom must be constrained by individual religious freedom and other human rights of members. This intuitively plausible argument, however, is often misused (depending on the length of the list and the interpretation of the respective rights), in order to impose "thick," perfectionist liberal morality upon everybody. This occurs under the guise of universalism and overrides any meaningful associational autonomy with strong policies of liberal and democratic congruency all the way down. For many reasons that cannot be discussed here, it seems wise, then, to focus on minimalist but strong moral and legal constraints. The longer the list of needs, interests, rights and capabilities, the greater is the danger of cultural imperialism that is incompatible with reasonable pluralism internally and globally. The chances of reaching agreement or even consensus are much higher if one focuses on serious injustice, serious inequalities and serious misrecognition, "malfare," instead of developing ideal theories, of justice, equality and recognition. Threshold or satisfying theories, instead of maximizing theories, also increase the chances to implement and control a moral and legal minimum. My focus is, then, on cases in which predominant practices conflict with basic needs or rights of vulnerable minorities in three legal areas and which seem to require different responses from liberal democratic polities. These three areas involve conflicts between the *nomos* (customs, group laws) and (i) the core of modern criminal law; (ii) the core of modern private personal law; and (iii) minimal requirements of non-discrimination and equal opportunity in labor law.

Group *nomos* vs. modern criminal law: Practices of slavery, caste, bondage, or of an unequal civil and political status for ascriptive minorities, are incompatible with the most minimalist interpretation of modern freedom and equality. Practices like *Sati*, domestic violence, stranger-rape, marital rape, sexual abuse, genital mutilation, honor killing and forced collective suicide are surely incompatible with the most minimalist interpretations of basic rights to life and bodily integrity.[1] Group autonomy should not be allowed to legitimize these practices. Public opinion and liberal democratic polities must try to convince minorities to change these practices, and jurisdictions must prosecute and punish perpetrators.

Given the broad agreement about the necessity of external intervention in this regard, three sobering remarks seem appropriate. First, even basic rights like bodily integrity are interpreted and applied in divergent ways in deeply different cultural traditions. For example, are certain forms of corporal punishment regularly applied by Indian tribes in Columbia to be understood as torture (Hoekema 2001: 170–2; Shachar 2001: 160–5 for sentencing; Sheleff 2000: ch. 14, "cultural defense")? Are all forms of female circumcision to be understood and prosecuted as genital mutilation (as infibulation or pharonic circumcision certainly is)? Is the removal of the tip of the clitoris a harmless version of piercing (Sheleff 2000: 354–74)? Second, most criminal codes are rife with ethno-religious particularism, hardly required by a relationally universal morality or permissible in a truly culturally diverse society. Legal proscriptions of homosexuality in general or homosexual partnerships/marriages in particular, are a clear case in point. The same is true, in my view, with regard to the hypocritical proscription of all varieties of polygamy.[2] Third, modern Western

---

[1] See Moore, this volume: 292; Mahajan, this volume: 98; Levy 2000: 17.

[2] See *Reynolds v. US*. See the excellent, general treatment by Sheleff 2000: 330–53. Deveaux (this volume), while accepting polygamy as an outcome of negotiations and deliberations, still thinks it is an inevitably illiberal outcome.

Christian societies and cultures have been and still are deeply marked by the discrimination and exclusion of "races," women, homosexuals and other religions. There is no reason for the self-congratulatory stance and the double standards so often characterizing these discussions. For example, domestic violence is certainly not confined to Jewish, Muslim or Hindu traditions, but is a human stain in Christian and secular families as well (Okin 1998).

Group *nomos* vs. modern marriage and divorce law: Civil marriage and divorce law are based on the two moral principles of "equality between the spouses" and "free consent" (free entry vs. marriage under duress, and *favor divortii*). Protestant and particularly Catholic churches have been strongly opposed to both for centuries. However, conflicts in liberal democratic polities today between religious family law and modern family law, mainly involve Hindu, Muslim (see Mahajan, this volume; Phillips, this volume) and Jewish family law (Shachar 2001; Reitman, this volume). These conflicts are routinely dealt with and practically resolved by inter-national private law (see, for the Netherlands, Rutten 1988; d'Oliveira 1995).

Most feminists are, in principle, in favor of a uniform, civil code in order to overcome the unequal position of women, but some defend limited versions of legal pluralism for strategic reasons.[3] Shachar defends associ-ational autonomy for religions in general, in a much more principled way, even tending to lose sight of inequalities between majorities and minori-ties (see Spinner-Halev 2001: 93). Like AD, she makes use of concepts and practices of limited, overlapping jurisdictions. She proposes to dele-gate jurisdiction about the "demarcating functions" of family law (crucial for the internal reproduction of the *nomos* of the group, control of mem-bership in particular) to "inside courts" of religious groups while reserv-ing jurisdiction about property matters (the "distributive functions" of family and divorce law) to state courts. Her "intersectionist" or "trans-formative joint governance approach" permits input "from two legal sys-tems – a group's essential traditions and the state's laws – to resolve a single dispute" (1998a: 299 for the *Martinez* case). Compared to con-flicts with the core of criminal law, in these cases interference from the

---

[3] Nussbaum argued like a "secular humanist feminist" (2000: 174–87) herself in 1997: religious liberty as an "individualistic concept" (125), all group rights rejected (126–31), legal pluralism declined as "medieval idea" (124). In 2000 she allows for some legal pluralism in personal law, particularly in cases of minority religions (212–15 for Mus-lims in India) but still virtually neglects associational religious freedoms (188–92, 226). Phillips (this volume) and Mahajan (this volume) clearly focus on strategic dilemmas of minority religions. Reitman (this volume) gives clear priority to sex equality and proposes accommodation for purely strategic reasons.

outside can be much more limited and the space for legitimate group autonomy can be much broader, without neglecting the basic rights of women.[4]

Associational autonomy vs. non-discrimination and equal opportunities: Predominant practices of illiberal and undemocratic minorities (and majorities!) often conflict with principles of non-discrimination and equal opportunity. Racist, sexist and genderist discrimination and exclusion are now widely perceived as morally wrong and proscribed by law. However, it is also widely accepted that ascriptive exclusion and discrimination – however morally wrong – have to be legally tolerated in some cases, depending on the goals of associations (broadly understood) and the degree of voluntariness of membership. "Miscegenation laws" should be banned (Hollinger 2002) but ethno-racial and religious self-segregation in "close interpersonal relations such as love, family, friendship, and primary group attachments" (Warren 2001: 129) is legally allowed. Intimate relationships should be treated differently from private clubs, pubs and discos, churches and church-related non-profit organizations, profit-organizations, political parties, neighborhoods and public spaces. A certain shield of intimacy seems necessary and morally legitimate, but its unavoidable side-effect is the legal protection of ascriptive exclusions. Protection of intimacy has been traditionally guaranteed by protection of "the private sphere" against state intervention, hiding structural power asymmetries within private families, associations and capitalist corporations from view. Criticism of this standard ideology of privacy, however, does not resolve the tensions between the need to legally protect familial and associational autonomy, and the discriminatory and exclusionary effects of such protections.

Consider the legal disputes about church autonomy in the USA as an example. In property disputes the general reluctance of the Supreme Court to interfere in the private sphere has resulted in unconditional deference to ecclesiastical law, decision procedures and practices as interpreted by church authority. This rule of non-interference could not be upheld in cases of tax exemption and subsidies for churches and church-related institutions, which do not live up to anti-discrimination rules in labor and employment, minimal standards in education, health and social service, or to rules of financial accountability. However, even

---

[4] If minority law, however, tries to make use of state enforcement in order to compensate for its weak status (see Reitman, this volume, for Jewish law in England) then, as in cases of accepting public money, the pressures by liberal democratic polities on minorities to introduce more equality in religious marriage and divorce laws are much more legitimate.

critics of such an unconditional extension of the shield of privacy[5] and a generalized non-application of anti-discrimination laws to religious organizations have accepted that meaningful associational autonomy for religions implies the legal toleration of ascriptive exclusion and discrimination by religious core organizations (in matters directly connected with core beliefs and practices). Sexist and genderist discrimination is still part of the predominant understanding of Catholicism and Islam, and the exclusion of Blacks is claimed to be central to some racist Protestant churches in the United States. To the degree that this is so, ascriptive exclusion can be legally defended because "control over membership" is crucial to the viability of the organization.

> Compelled association *is* a threat to the viability of groups whose liberty is grounded in voluntary association and fellowship. Religious liberty means individuals are not forced to join or prevented from leaving groups; *Dade* introduces a third element – freedom from compelled association. The ruling compelling a church school to admit unwelcome members is the very definition of loss of self-government. (Rosenblum 1998: 98)

Ascriptive discrimination inside religious organizations, if directly and not just accidentally connected with core beliefs and practices, can also be defended in a similar way. If the Catholic Church, according to its own established decision-making procedures and authorities, rejects the possibility of female priesthood, the state should not legally impose non-discrimination legislation upon the Church, even if feminist Catholics would ask for such legal action. If churches, following their established procedures would not allow women or homosexuals as members, or would excommunicate them if they "come out" – as they have done and still do with dissenters – the state cannot legally forbid this practice without overruling and completely eroding associational autonomy. Church-related organizations such as denominational schools may require from their core personnel and teachers that they adhere to, or at least not oppose, the religious core and that they do not "come out" as gays or lesbians. In these cases, the state should not legally impose non-discrimination or "equal opportunity in employment" acts. However, the shield of protection for associational autonomy does not, and should not, automatically cover the selection of students, administrative personnel or janitors (Rosenblum 2000b: 174–9).

---

[5] Pfeffer 1987; Kelley 1987; Robbins 1987; Rosenblum 1998: 79–94; Spinner-Halev 2000: ch. 7. The relevant cases are: *EEOC v. Southwest Baptist Theol. Seminar; Bob Jones University v. United States; Goldsboro Christian Schools v. Amos.*

To argue that the state should refrain from legal intervention in core organizations and activities does not imply that the state or public opinion should not interfere in other ways (public criticism, campaigns etc.). Nor does it imply that the state should not interfere by other means, such as refusing to grant tax exemptions or subsidies, making exit options less costly, and stimulating the voice of dissenters. The state can listen to dissenters and give them some say in all cases in which church authorities ask for public help, public money or other privileges. Guaranteeing meaningful associational autonomy does not exempt religions from public criticism and scrutiny. The further the distance from religious core organizations and core activities, the weaker the shield of "Free Exercise" should work, the more legitimate is the legal imposition of non-discrimination and equal opportunity legislation, and the more demanding the standards and procedures of public scrutiny may become. Here, the claims of the public trust theory and of AD are fully in line (Hirst 1994).

To sum up, AD combines different policy repertoires which include leaving minorities alone as much as possible and making use of external legal intervention only to protect the basic needs and rights of individuals and vulnerable minorities inside minorities. Policy repertoires also include applying stricter standards of public scrutiny and external control in cases when minorities ask for legal support, subsidies or other privileges from the state. The choice of appropriate policies depends upon the type of minority, the issue-specific conflicts of predominant practices with liberal morality and law, the specific goals of associations, and the degree of voluntariness and vulnerability of minorities.

AD, moderate voluntarism, and free entry and exit

Radical libertarians assume free and informed consent by adults to enter groups/associations and free exit rights, neglecting actual degrees of freedom of consent and actual exit options. Associative democracy as a moderately libertarian approach can avoid these fictions of voluntariness, which may be harmless only in ideal worlds and still rescue the attractive features of libertarianism. AD does not only stipulate free entry and exit, but tries to achieve higher actual degrees of freedom. It takes differences in the degrees of voluntariness between minorities and amongst minorities within minorities into account. Children are obviously the most vulnerable category because their freedom of entry is zero, they are the main objects of inter-generational transmission lacking agency, and they are captive targets incapable of exit (Reich, this volume).

Entry into and remaining within minority (and majority) groups is only rarely the result of free and voluntary decisions, as it sometimes is with religious associations (conversion and anabaptism), gender and linguistic groups (e.g. "coming out," switching gender or linguistic identities). Most people, however, are either born into or raised in communities. This "involuntary" membership may be a constitutive element for their cultural practices and self-definitions (Eisenberg 1995: 20, 24, 171, 177–83; Warren 2001: 96–109; Weinstock, this volume: 234). People will remain members because they are accustomed to being a part of the group. Membership becomes "non-voluntary" only if exit is legally proscribed or is socially either impossible or extremely harsh. Still entry and exit are matters of degree, and it is obvious that exit is easier to facilitate.

What, if anything, can AD do to make entry more free? Two features of associative democracy may help to soften the harshness of this destiny. First, in regarding minors, they should not be treated as the property of their parents or of their group. Parents and other guardians have to behave as trustees or social stewards of their children (Hirst 1994: 202; Shapiro 1999: 68–84). No single agent or group should assume total authority over the lives of children. AD provides better opportunities to balance the interests of the different relevant stakeholders such as children, parents, minorities, states, international agencies (like the ILO), and NGOs. AD recognizes, on the one hand, the interests of parents and minorities to transmit religious and cultural ways of life to the next generation. These interests are met through the guarantees of parental religious freedoms. And it recognizes, on the other hand, the basic needs and rights of minors. Minors may have to be protected against parents, minorities (and majorities!) and external agents. AD criticizes both absolutist parental and group freedoms defended by conservative religions (*Mozert v. Hawkins County Board of Education* [versus any "exposure"], and *Wisconsin v. Yoder*), and absolutist state paternalism overriding parental and group interests.[6]

Accepting overlapping authorities, in this as in any other case, provides opportunities for fair and sensible negotiations and deliberations. It also increases sensitivity to the fact that morally permissible solutions (e.g. with regard to different forms and degrees of external scrutiny and intervention) may look differently depending on types of minorities, on the one hand, and different societal contexts, welfare regimes and policy

[6] The consequences of taking children out of native, tribal and isolationist families and groups are far more serious than in other ethno-religious minority cases, making outplacement a morally and prudentially nearly impossible option, in my view. I also think that an inter-culturally defensible concept of a basic interest of children developing into an autonomous adult (Reich, this volume; Shapiro 1999: 72, 85–8) should be even more minimalist in order to prevent the imposition of still fairly "thick" liberalism or republicanism.

traditions, on the other hand. Even bracketing minorities, the balance in Sweden (fairly extensive external supervision and intervention by state-agencies) is very different from that in the USA.

Second, regarding both adults and maturing youngsters, who are gaining agency individually and collectively, the pluralization of membership stimulated by AD not only promises to increase actual exit options but also promises to considerably increase the range of freer entry into a whole variety of associations.

Most people agree that guaranteeing full *exit* rights is a necessary but not a sufficient condition for providing and strengthening actual exit options. Compared with entry, it is generally much easier to develop policies stimulating higher degrees of free exit. This is the main reason why Rosenblum (1998: 101, 103), Galston (2002: 55f., 62, 122f.) and Hirst focus on freedom of exit. The achievable degrees of freedom of entry will inevitably be lower than those of exit. Actual exit, however, is difficult. Exit from indigenous peoples and from totalistic religions is very restricted. First, this is because exit costs are extremely high (Warren 2001: 99–103) as they involve more than "identity" costs (e.g. the loss of constitutive parts of individual identity for which no ready-made or real alternatives are available, given an individual's psychological make-up) and "social" costs (e.g. social ostracism and the loss of social relationships and networks). Exit costs may also include high material costs, loss of care and shelter, loss of social and physical security (if social ostracism is combined with disinheritance, loss of employment and social security provided by community-specific institutions).[7] Second, exit is difficult because it requires "knowledge, capacity, psychological, and fitness conditions" (Galston 2002: 123). As a general rule it is plausible in my view that the moral requirement for public scrutiny and external protection of vulnerable minorities increases the lower their actual exit chances are (most obvious for minors), or, vice versa, the higher the degrees of free exit, the less need for overriding associational autonomy and the less demanding the standards.

Three features of associative democracy may help to reduce exit costs and thus increase actual exit options. First, the proposal of a universal, individualized basic income for all residents (Hirst 1994: 179–84), if implemented, guarantees that basic needs of subsistence and social security are satisfied in a way which is far less bureaucratic and intrusive than statist welfare arrangements. It also may help to address not only

---

[7] It may even be legitimate for certain minorities to make exit very costly in cases of common property of land (many native people) or more generally (e.g. Hutterites). Even then it is possible to work out options safeguarding high degrees of communal autonomy without completely sacrificing individual exit options, as Spinner-Halev (2000: 77f.) has convincingly shown.

extreme poverty of minorities within minorities and particularly of children (rightly highlighted by Reich, this volume: Shapiro 1999: 105–6), but also the poverty of minorities more generally.

Second, open access to a whole variety of public, semi-public, and private service providers (education, health and other varieties of care, etc.) by means of a weighted voucher system, creates opportunities for minorities to run their own services in a more egalitarian way. But such access also increases exit options for individuals into public associations and opens avenues for dissenting minorities within minorities to set up their own services.

Third, the whole institutional design of associative democracy, its specific policies and its public propagation, intentionally and explicitly serve to pluralize membership (Rosenblum 1998) and to prevent unwelcome lock-in effects. All of this works indirectly to heighten the degree of voluntary entry and exit. As in Rosenblum's work, AD promotes the "moral uses of pluralism" (real exit options, overlapping and cross-cutting membership in many associations), but not in a direct way by trying to impose "autonomy," "choice" and "free exit" on all minorities. First, AD distinguishes processes of (unintended and intended) cultural change from policies, pointing out that living in modern societies and making use of a modern legal system inevitably have an impact on indigenous peoples and on conservative religions (Rosenblum 1998: 103–8; Swaine 2001: 318; Tomasi 2001: 43f.) whether this is intended or not. Even the most isolationist minorities are unable to shield their children completely from any exposure to the surrounding society and cultures. Second, by intentionally making the surrounding society and cultures more open, plural and flexible, AD even makes these "tragic choices" (see Bader 1999: 616) for all isolationist minorities more pressing.

AD and voice

Giving voice to minorities within minorities is the preferred option of republicans, (empowering) deliberative democrats (Fung and Wright 2001) and feminists (Okin, this volume: 72ff.; Deveaux, this volume: 343, 348–9; Moore, this volume: 283; Phillips, this volume). In my view, AD is more skeptical for two reasons. First, state-imposed policies of democratic congruency are incompatible with meaningful notions of associational autonomy. AD, like Rosenblum's civic libertarianism, resists this democratic temptation. Deveaux acknowledges an

important conundrum. There is no doubt that requiring democratic decision-making procedures for setting the status of disputed social practices and arrangements, and where necessary, reforming them, will trigger social changes within traditional communities. (Deveaux, this volume: 361)

She also recognizes the "tension between respect for group autonomy and the norm of democratic legitimacy" (Deveaux this volume: 362), but tends to downplay the costs of overriding collective autonomy.

Second, high degrees of free exit and of voice may not be equally possible. As in Hirst's version, AD increasingly privileges exit over voice for three reasons. First, voice is much more demanding and, as a tendency, elitist. Exit is less demanding because voting by one's feet is open to all, if actual exit options are available. Second, the assertion that easy exit increases the voluntarism of staying and thereby breeding loyalty seems theoretically and empirically sound. Third, but more dubious, is the widely shared hope that free exit contributes to voice.

To make a complex story (Hirschman 1970; Warren 2001: 103–9) simple, this hope seems not very plausible for two reasons. First, free exit does not stimulate the need to participate because instead of raising your voice, you can leave. Free exit may only weakly contribute to the motivation to participate because freely staying increases loyalty to the association or organization, but pre-existing high degrees of loyalty seem to be much stronger sources of motivation to participate. High degrees of loyalty, however, result from being treated with respect and concern (not necessarily with "equal" respect and concern, but with some decency), and from opportunities to exercise voice. Yet, the latter is absent in undemocratic minority organizations. Second, the threat to exit, as a means of communication in strategies to increase the chances for voice inside organizations, requires high degrees of loyalty and a credible, organized and massive threat (making leaders vulnerable or threatening the existence of the organization). It requires resources and a high degree of strategic arts.

These arguments, if plausible, show a structural dilemma for all approaches that try to ameliorate the position of vulnerable minorities inside minorities by way of giving them more voice. Voice (internal democracy) is most important and urgent in cases in which exit is impossible or extremely costly, such as cases of illiberal and anti-democratic groups and organizations in which the voices of vulnerable minorities (e.g. of feminist Catholics) that seek the liberalization and democratization of their respective cultures or religions, are silenced or cases in which oppositional leaders are threatened with excommunication or actually excommunicated. It would be foolish to claim that AD has a ready-made answer to this dilemma. This particularly severe irony makes it all the more understandable why AD focuses on exit.

However, in all other cases, in which less isolationist minorities accept public money and other privileges, or want to be represented in the political process, AD provides many more opportunities for institutionalized voice compared to rival democratic theories. And finally, it also explicitly requires that the relevant stakeholders, including minorities within minorities, be included in negotiations and deliberations. Compared with traditional religious or linguistic pillarization (e.g. in the Netherlands and Belgium respectively), and with neo-corporatist settings, the relevant stakeholders cannot only be the entrenched, conservative organizations and leaders of minorities. In all these cases, AD and modest versions of deliberative democracy join hands.[8] Democratic government should, in my view, impose minimal requirements of even-handed representation in order to prevent illegitimate exclusions. To the degree that this can actually be achieved, the standard objections against democratic institutional pluralism and AD, namely they favor only the most purist conservative organizations and privilege the "worst" radical leaders, are pointless.

The problem to be addressed by all approaches, not only by AD, is the following: Given serious structural power-asymmetries between majorities and minorities, how can minorities prevent reactive essentialism – the purification of cultures or religions – and the silencing of dissenting voices without being prey to the strategies of divide and rule often successfully used by majorities (and "their" state)? This is, indeed, a structural, strategic dilemma for all minorities. In my view, it cannot be resolved by "strategic essentialism."

Conclusion

The most promising institutional approaches to deal with our problem are varieties of liberal, democratic institutional pluralism all of which can be seen as "joint governance approaches" (Shachar 2001: ch. 5; Swaine 2001, 2003a, and this volume; Sheleff 2000; Holder, this volume; Moore, this volume). Space prevents a full discussion of their differences.[9] All

---

[8] See Deveaux, this volume: 353–60 for negotiations, consultations and hearings in the "Harmonization of the Common Law and the Indigenous Law" sponsored by the South African Law Commission. In comparing experiences of Parsi, Christian and Muslim personal law reform in India, Mahajan has shown that voice is not always necessary (the Parsi case), that it has to be organized (this volume: 109f., the Christian case) and that the status of minority community members as citizens has to be secure (the case of the failure of attempts to make Muslim personal laws more just for women).

[9] Compared with Shachar's "transformational accommodation" (2001: 118–26) approach which is supposed to avoid the disadvantages of the other joint governance approaches (federal, temporal, consensual and contingent accommodation), my approach looks – *prima facie* – similar to the contingent accommodation model in which "the state yields jurisdictional autonomy to *nomoi* groups in certain well-defined legal arenas, but only so long as their exercise of this autonomy meets certain minimal state-defined standards. If a group fails to meet these minimal standards, the state may intervene in the group's

of these proposals are skillfully, institutionally underdetermined, general models. They all need careful crafting and sensitive application, and this is what contextualized morality is all about.

The main research task ahead is to show what AD, "transformational accommodation" or "semi-sovereignty" require in specific countries, and with regard to specific minorities and minorities within minorities. Yet it seems fair to say that none of the available approaches of broadly speaking, liberal democratic accommodationism can adequately solve the hard dilemma of how to protect vulnerable minorities within illiberal, anti-democratic and isolationist minorities. Here, it is most difficult to find morally defensible balances between individual, associational or group autonomy and external interference. In principle, my approach is not so much different from that of Shachar, Swaine, Spinner-Halev, Moore or Holder.[10] What we can and should do is guarantee basic needs and rights, increase real exit options, and try to strengthen the voice of insider

affairs" (Shachar 2001: 109). I place this minimally required state intervention, however, within the framework of AD, and this enables me to resolve the main difficulties mentioned by Shachar: (i) Who defines the minimal standards? How are they defined, interpreted and applied? (Shachar 2001: 115f.). AD provides for excellent ways and means to challenge majority bias hiding as "modern" or "neutral." (ii) Intervention "requires a complex regulatory regime" (Shachar 2001: 110, inspections of actual performance and compliance). AD combines self-regulation and self-scrutiny with public scrutiny and gives associations an important role not only in standard setting but also in control-regimes. (iii) Given the power asymmetries "it is hard to see how this (analytically attractive) model of mutual 'mirror-image policing' can be applied in practice" (Shachar 2001: 112). AD exactly tries to redress these power asymmetries (and does so much more effectively than Shachar's preferred "transformational accommodation" model). (iv) It "relegates individual group members to a more passive position" (whistleblowers) (Shachar 2001: 113). AD not only provides important exit options for minorities within minorities, it also enables organized voice inside religious associations. (v) The most crucial interests of "at-risk group members" would not be "maximized." In my view, the combination of actual voluntarism, real exit options and critical public scrutiny does a lot to protect vulnerable minorities. Shachar's transformational accommodation encounters difficulties in explaining why traditionalist leaders should not choose to ostracize, exclude or excommunicate critical voices inside (Shachar 2001: 124f., also see 139, 143), and it shares the problem with associative democracy of how to respond to the trade-off between (threat of) exit and voice.

[10] See Swaine 2001: 328f.: exit requirements, educational and human rights requirements, zones of legal autonomy discriminating between civil matters, criminal areas, etc. Jeff Spinner-Halev's treatment of conservative religions within the confines of citizenship also stresses exit rights and options (2000: 57, 63, 70ff.); no physical harm to members (torture of girls); basic health care; no marriage before the age of consent; and educational requirements. But his interpretation of his first principle of "non-intervention" is clearly much weaker than Swaine's semi-sovereignty or my defense of associational autonomy. And his care for "support for healthy mainstream liberal society" (Spinner-Halev 2000: 205) allows for fairly anti-accommodationist sweeping generalizations (see also 208ff.). Kymlicka's interpretation of minimal autonomy is also much thicker than mine (2002: 228–44). Clearly, the range of "minimal requirements of liberal-democracy" is large and contested (see Moore, this volume: 282ff., Holder, this volume).

minorities by means which do not override associational autonomy. For the rest, we can hope that the fact that minorities (are forced to) live in and have to cope with modern societies will do some work in the long run. Requiring less (e.g. by granting full sovereignty) would sacrifice vulnerable minorities; and requiring more would impose specific liberal ways of life and sacrifice meaningful free exercise and associational autonomy.

16   A deliberative approach to conflicts of culture

Monique Deveaux

Liberal political theorists have recently argued liberal democratic states may jeopardize the principle of formal sex equality if they attempt to meet the demands of non-liberal or traditional cultural groups for greater recognition and powers of self-governance.[1] This is not only a political claim, but rather includes a moral argument about which social practices liberal principles can permit and which it must proscribe. Brian Barry (2001a), Will Kymlicka (1995: chs. 3 and 5, 1999), and Susan Moller Okin (1999a, b) insist that cultural practices and arrangements that discriminate against women are morally indefensible from the standpoint of a liberalism committed to norms of autonomy and equality.[2] Martha Nussbaum has employed her Aristotelian-inflected liberalism to argue that citizens' capabilities for human functioning are undercut by customs common in traditional societies, such as arranged marriage and polygyny (1999; 2000: 94, 109, 230, ch. 4). The broad political approach to non-liberal cultural practices favored by these thinkers is one that endorses liberal but not necessarily democratic principles and procedures, for states are said to determine the permissibility of minority cultural practices by gauging their compatibility with liberal, individual rights or particular capacities.

Against this liberal view, I argue that the best way to resolve tensions between traditional cultural practices and liberal principles in socially plural, democratic states is to defend and strengthen deliberation and decision-making practices that reflect a radical principle of democratic legitimacy. Such an approach to mediating disputes about the value and

---

[1] By "non-liberal" I refer to traditional groups adhering to practices that reflect and reinforce conservative cultural (often religious) norms, roles and world-views. The main sense in which the customs of traditional groups are non-liberal, for present purposes, is that they stipulate social hierarchies and strict sex-role differentiation.

[2] As Okin notes, Kymlicka's earlier work left ambiguous whether inequalities in the private and domestic spheres are included in Kymlicka's account of unjust internal restrictions. Kymlicka has since said (1999: 32) that he considers "the domestic oppressions that Okin discusses to be paradigmatic examples of the sorts of 'internal restrictions' that liberals must oppose."

status of cultural practices will require that women members of cultural groups have a direct say in these matters, through the expansion of sites of democratic contestation and the inclusion of women in formal decision-making processes. To accomplish this greater enfranchisement, we will need to pay close attention to the cultural barriers women face in public and private life. But equally, we will need to attend to the numerous ways in which girls and women can and do contest and revise cultural practices and arrangements in their everyday lives. To illustrate the feasibility of a deliberative approach for resolving cultural conflicts, I discuss the recent reform of customary marriage in South Africa later in the chapter.

Reconceiving democratic activity and the basis of legitimacy

The deliberative democratic approach to mediating conflicts of culture developed here begins with a claim about the requirements of democratic legitimacy in plural, liberal societies. Insofar as liberal states fail to centrally include cultural group members in deliberations about the future status and possible reform of their community's customs and arrangements, they ignore the demands of democratic legitimacy. In suspending this norm and assuming that fair decisions about cultural practices do not require (or indeed may preclude) the meaningful inclusion of cultural group members, juridical liberal approaches may contribute to outcomes that are ill-conceived as well as undemocratic. Policies for the reform of cultural practices that are derived from the application of liberal principles or constitutional norms risk misconstruing the actual or *lived* form of these practices. As such, they may generate proposals which, if implemented, might leave untouched or even worsen the many forms of oppression faced by vulnerable members of cultural groups, such as women. Where no attempt has been made to include cultural communities in conceiving of relevant and plausible reforms of contested practices, new legislation may hold out the promise of formal equality in a context in which deep social and cultural inequalities persist. Not only is the necessary information base for appropriate and beneficial reforms overlooked, but their successful implementation is seriously impaired: reforms that require cultural transformations at different levels are usually unsuccessful in the absence of community involvement, both because they lack legitimacy and because the necessary grassroots structures for implementation are lacking. By contrast, when cultural communities have a central role in re-evaluating their own customs together with state bodies and civil society groups, the legitimacy of the ensuing proposals – for retaining, eliminating or reforming practices – is underscored and their practicability greatly increased.

In the context of socially plural, liberal democratic states, justice requires that we deepen our democratic practices and foster greater inclusion of minority citizens in political deliberation and decision-making processes. Crucially, however, this is not just a matter of including diverse citizens in existing political institutions, but rather requires that we expand our understanding of democratic political activity and proliferate the spaces for such activity. Democratic activity is not exhausted by formal political processes; it is also reflected in acts of cultural subversion and reinvention, and dissent and resistance in a range of social settings. Inchoate democratic activity can be identified in the homes, schools and places of worship and religious training of traditional communities; in social practices around marriage, birth and the initiation of young people into adulthood; and in the provision of grassroots community and social services. These important forms of democratic expression are rendered invisible by oversimple distinctions drawn between social and family life and public, political life. We can counter this invisibility by asking how work and social activities and arrangements function as spaces of cultural resistance and transformation.

With an expanded view of the scope of democratic activity also comes an expanded view of the *basis* for democratic legitimacy. It is against the backdrop of these expanded conceptions of democratic activity and democratic legitimacy that I propose we adopt a deliberative democratic approach to evaluating and reforming traditional cultural group practices which conflict with the liberal constitutional state's commitment to sex equality. Deliberative democracy theory, suitably revised, offers a robust, egalitarian model of power-sharing in political deliberation and decision-making. It can also provide a political framework for the democratic and respectful resolution of both inter- and intra-cultural conflicts in socially plural, liberal democratic states. Other democratic theorists have made similar claims. James Tully, for example, envisions a model of inter-cultural dialogue – inspired by such liberal and discourse ethical principles of consent, equal regard and mutual recognition – in which participants can build common political constitutions from the background of their divergent cultural and political traditions (1995: 183–4). Seyla Benhabib contends that a "deliberative democratic approach to multicultural politics" places individuals at the center of "processes of cultural communication, contestation, and resignifiation . . . within civil society" and so can capture the complexity and contestability of cultural identities in ways that the liberal, juridical model cannot (2002: 71). But while I share Tully's and Benhabib's belief in the importance of a deliberative democratic approach to the justice claims of cultural minorities, my aim is to develop a less idealized model of deliberation that takes *interests and needs* as its focus, rather than the normative and identity-based claims of cultural group members.

My central claims are as follows. First, by fostering (formal and informal) democratic and politically inclusive forums for deliberating about the concrete implications and purposes of contested cultural practices, as well as the needs and interests of cultural members, we express a substantive commitment to the norm of democratic legitimacy and respect for cultural pluralism. Second, a deliberative framework for resolving conflicts of culture can help to successfully engage and amplify existing criticisms of particular practices and arrangements by supporting their safe public articulation both within the community and in the larger society, and also by expanding the scope of democratic activity and contestation. And third, practical dialogue and deliberative decision-making which include cultural group members and state and civil society representatives can produce democratically legitimate – though not necessarily liberal – solutions to cultural disputes that both protect and empower vulnerable group members, such as women.

Problems with deliberative democracy as usual

Disagreements about cultural roles, arrangements and practices within minority communities in liberal democratic states share several features. First, they reflect considerable *intra-cultural* conflict over the interpretation, meaning and legitimacy of particular customs or forms of customs:[3] communities themselves disagree about the purpose and proper form of a set of practices. Second, these disputes tend to share a strategic or political character in the sense that they are primarily about interests, benefits and power, rather than ethical disagreements. The recognition that disputes about cultural conflicts are often intra-cultural and primarily political in character gives us a preliminary glimpse into why a *deliberative* approach to resolving such disputes might be preferable to either a liberal approach or an idealized discourse-ethical model of deliberation. If disputes about the status of cultural practices and arrangements are primarily internal and reflect struggles over decision-making authority and power, then a democratic process specifically designed to engage the views of all stakeholders should help to focus debate on what is really at stake, as well

---

[3] Bronstein (1998: 390) has also argued that disputes within customary law are primarily matters of "intra cultural conflicts between internal women and other members of the group."

as to enfranchise and empower many of those previously excluded from political decisions. I shall outline such a process shortly.

This brief characterization of cultural conflicts, however, also generates at least two objections to the adequacy and fit of idealized deliberative democratic frameworks for addressing political conflicts in diverse societies. These are the challenge from pluralism and the problem of covert power and interests. Below, I discuss these objections and the deliberative models of politics that are most vulnerable to them. Subsequently, I try to show why an *amended* model of public deliberation – one that is pragmatic (not idealized), pluralist, and which emphasizes strategies of negotiation and compromise – holds out the most promise for democratic and legitimate resolutions to many cultural conflicts.

The challenge from pluralism

Critics of deliberative democracy theory have issued a range of objections to formal, idealized forums of deliberation. These criticisms center on the following issues and questions: Who is to participate in deliberation? Who is included, silenced, and who speaks for whom? What norms are presupposed by the deliberative scheme, and are these genuinely shared norms or do they result in exclusion? How is deliberation conducted – who does it privilege, and who does it disadvantage? What kind of outcome is desired? If thick consensus, whose views does this stifle? These objections take on particular salience in contexts of social diversity. In connection with the first two problems, Iris Young criticizes the assumption that particular representatives can speak for whole communities or social groups in democratic politics (2000: 121–2). James Bohman concurs that although idealized versions of deliberative democracy require "the inclusion of everyone affected by a decision", failure to account for the effect of social inequalities on civic participation and political inclusion can render the norm of inclusion ineffectual (Bohman 2000: 16–18). Potential participants can also be excluded from deliberation, or else silenced within a deliberative setting, through the introduction of onerous normative constraints on the form and content of deliberative communication. The insistence that participants adhere to norms of reasonableness and/or rationality by giving "public" reasons – reasons that are morally universalizable and so accessible to public reason – can render deliberative designs inhospitable to some citizens. Particularly where norms of rationality and reasonableness are stipulated as *criteria for inclusion* in public deliberation, they can have a tremendously exclusionary effect, as John Dryzek (2000: 58) and others have observed (Bohman 1997). Cultural minorities whose traditions of communication and standards of justification are at odds with these norms, including some religious minorities, risk having their particular styles or forms of deliberative communication discredited or disqualified (Young 2000: 75).

In addition to their potentially exclusionary effect, models of public deliberation that stipulate norms of reasonableness and moral universalizability often *presuppose* agreement upon what kinds of arguments and procedures are fair and reasonable. If agreement about fair procedures is merely assumed, then the outcomes of deliberation will be equally contested. But norms of reasonableness and universalizability can be rejected as conditions for participation in public dialogue; deliberation must have more "expansive conditions of entry" if it is to help mediate conflicts arising in plural societies (Knight and Johnson 1997: 287). Similarly, deliberative models of politics that emphasize normative and reasoned public discourse have been roundly criticized for stipulating that deliberation should result in moral consensus, for this assumes a greater degree of overlap and agreement among citizens than is warranted in a socially plural society. To forge moral consensus from citizens' divergent convictions, needs and interests typically requires an appeal to a conception of the *public good* that may deny the scope and significance of citizens' differences.

The requirements of consensus and shared rational grounds appear to be losing support among a number of deliberative democracy proponents, some of whom now agree that moral consensus is not a sensible goal for public deliberation in socially diverse societies (Bellamy 1999: 110; Dryzek 2000: 47–8; Ferejohn 2000: 79–80). We do not necessarily need to abandon *agreement* as a broad goal of discourse, for as Dryzek points out, "reasoned agreement" is not the same as consensus, which requires agreement on "the exact normative grounds for choice" (Dryzek 2000: 47). A pluralized conception of public reason, wherein participants can agree to a particular course of public action for different reasons, makes it possible for interlocutors to acknowledge and address each other's differences in political deliberation without jeopardizing the prospect of agreement (Bohman 2000: 83, ch. 2). Even Habermas has recently acknowledged that conditions of deep social pluralism in liberal democratic states make it difficult to discover "generalizable interests" or to reach agreement on issues with normative content, and so now accords more importance to bargaining and compromise as strategies in deliberation (Habermas 1996: 165–6). These signs of a shift away from strictly ideal and rational models of deliberation reflect the conviction of many deliberative democrats, which I share, namely that we need to move towards more practical and strategic models of conflict resolution.

The problem of covert power and interests

A further reason to worry that deliberative democracy theory is ill-equipped to help mediate conflicts of culture is that norms of reasonableness and universalizability *can have a distorting effect on the actual issues and conflicts at stake in politics*. When public deliberation is conceived primarily as reasoned argumentation about policies and norms that reflect citizens' *normative* differences, the practical interests and motivations of participants tend to recede from view. In disputes over the meaning and status of cultural practices, it can be counter-productive to insist that participants convey their views in normative terms or frame their arguments in terms of public reasons. As the intra-cultural nature of these conflicts suggests, they are often much more about concrete interests and the distribution of power in communities than they are about normative differences.[4] If so, then attempts to resolve disagreements about cultural practices that focus on the evaluation of normative claims and beliefs may fail to get to the heart of disputes.

To suggest that we demote the normative dimension of deliberation in this way – at least where intra-cultural conflicts are concerned – may seem a strange proposal. Much more so than rival liberal models of politics, deliberative democracy endorses explicitly moral reasoned discussion between rational, uncoerced and equal participants as a means of resolving disagreement and conflict. It is this conviction in the normative basis of politics that, as Bohman notes (2000: 5), links together diverse models of deliberative democracy: "they all reject the reduction of politics and decision making to instrumental and strategic rationality". Through deliberation, participants are expected not simply to communicate their beliefs, but more importantly, to reflect upon and transform these in dialogue with others (Dryzek 2000: 30). Obtaining this level of ideal argumentation, however, requires normative constraints of reasonableness and publicity that may produce unjust exclusions in political life. Moreover, to construct a model of political deliberation that privileges normative reason-giving and universalizability is to invite individuals and groups to present their interest-based concerns in terms of cultural identity claims. Arguments that appeal to cultural identity have increasing purchase in liberal constitutional democracies committed to policies of cultural pluralism; by contrast, the desire to maintain one's own status or the status of one's sub-group within the wider community, to shore up one's position of power vis-à-vis others, or an interest in one's own

---

[4] For an example of a view stressing normative differences, see the "difference-based approach" advanced recently by Eisenberg (2003).

financial gain, do not make for good reasons in deliberation. Defenders of idealized models of deliberative democracy often argue that these kinds of motives cannot count as valid justification for policies. However, attempts to neutralize unjust motives and pernicious interests by excluding certain kinds of reasons *a priori* from public discourse – as illustrated by the deliberative approach advocated by Amy Gutmann and Dennis Thompson (1996) – may simply push these underground. An idealized model of deliberation that either denies the force of participants' interests and relative power in determining outcomes, or else rules out certain kinds of reasons in advance in the hope that these will not impact deliberation, may succeed in only reinforcing the advantages enjoyed by powerful participants in deliberation.

If I am right that struggles over the meaning and validity of contested cultural traditions in liberal states are centrally about the concrete interests of group members and the distribution of power and decision-making authority in these communities, then arguably any sound procedure for mediating cultural conflicts ought to recognize this. What this means practically is that reason-giving in deliberation ought not to privilege, or be restricted to, normative kinds of justification, but rather should foreground practical concerns and discussion about the concrete consequences of particular practices. This focus on negotiation and compromise within public deliberation need not exclude reasoned, moral argumentation entirely. Rather, what is aimed for is a more *transparent* political process in which cultural group members can present some of their concerns about particular practices and arrangements, and these concerns and interests – and the normative justifications that may or may not attach – are then subject to critical scrutiny and evaluation in democratic processes of deliberation and negotiation. Political deliberation about contested practices should aim to provide an accurate description of the *lived form* of contested cultural practices (for this is often precisely what is in dispute) as well as some account of what the concrete, practical interests of diverse participants are, and finally, should aim to generate negotiated political compromises.

An amended model of political deliberation: negotiation and compromise

If a deliberative framework for resolving mainly intra-cultural conflicts about traditional customs is to take seriously the principle of democratic legitimacy, the inclusion of diverse voices from traditional communities is essential. Democratic legitimacy is not secured by merely soliciting the views of established leaders in communities, but rather, requires that a plurality of group members be included in deliberation. As Spinner-Halev (2001: 108) has recently argued in connection with the issue of personal laws, this requires that the liberal state cede much of its power of interpretation to cultural or religious communities "and insist that these laws be established by democratically accountable representatives, not just the traditional male religious leaders."[5] Deliberative democratic procedures can provide spaces for these voices, as well as help to amplify existing criticisms of particular practices and arrangements within communities by supporting their safe public articulation. The establishment of forums and neighborhood panels by some local government authorities in areas of Britain with a high density of racial, religious and cultural minorities is an example of how local decision-making structures might be transformed so as to facilitate greater community input and even self-governance (Stewart 1996: 51). It may also be possible, as Ayelet Shachar proposes (2001: 132), to "empower at-risk group members" by allocating formal legal jurisdiction over certain cultural practices and arrangements to some social groups, provided that democratic processes of decision-making are observed.[6]

The inclusion in deliberation of a diverse range of group members – both those rejecting change and those seeking reform – is therefore not a gloss on, or afterthought to, legislated reforms but instead a critical part of the process of democratic conflict resolution. For cultural conflicts involving cultural communities that are reasonably democratic in their internal structure, group members could well constitute the majority of participants to deliberation. Yet the traditional cultural groups under discussion are ones that are often marked by dramatic inequalities of power and in which issues of authority and governance are precisely at issue. Consequently, unlike those who argue essentially for group autonomy over cultural practices and arrangements, I contend that decision-making about contested cultural practices should often bring to the table representatives from legal reform and women's groups, as well as scholars and government policy-makers. In part this move is in recognition of the permeable boundaries of different cultural communities of citizens in plural, liberal states, and of the common constitutional norms that bind these citizens. But the inclusion of these activists and representatives – some of them also members of the cultural group in question – can also serve as

---

[5] Okin also makes this point (1999b).

[6] My argument for a deliberative approach to resolving cultural conflicts is largely compatible with Shachar's (2001) proposal for a system of "joint governance" that aspires to "transformative accommodation" of non-liberal communities. However, whereas I focus on the public deliberations that might produce reforms, Shachar tries to develop legal and jurisdictional power-sharing strategies for socially plural, democratic states.

much-needed political pressure on the reform process as well as providing solidarity and support for cultural dissenters.

Participants in the proposed deliberative process initially use the framework of discussion and consultation as a means of gaining a clearer picture of social customs and practices, and to negotiate the different interests and needs at stake. The democratic tools of negotiation, bargaining and compromise emerge here as crucial alternatives to deliberative democracy's traditional focus on reasoned, normative argumentation. By making it possible for participants in deliberation to give frank and concrete reasons in support of particular customs and proposals for or against change with a view to securing a political compromise, it becomes easier to expose unjust reasons and to foreground the abuses that certain practices perpetuate. By framing the process of conflict resolution in terms of debate about the concrete purposes, benefits and disadvantages of cultural traditions, it becomes difficult fully to camouflage the strategic concerns and interests at work. These interests, whether articulated by those who hold them or identified by critics, are then subject to critical evaluation in policy debates about the proposed reform of customs, and are reflected in the ensuing political compromise. Such a deliberative approach would still encourage debate and decision-making about norms and the social practices that they help to shape, and indeed, good normative reasons will remain more persuasive in public deliberation than will those interest-based reasons that fail to speak to the needs of other citizens. However, practical and interest-based reasons would no longer be shunned, but rather be subject to evaluation and discussed as possible grounds for concessions and compromises.

Previously, proponents of deliberative democracy have suggested that negotiation, bargaining and compromise are to be used in public deliberation only when conditions of social pluralism preclude common premises and consensual outcomes. For Habermas, it is only when normative discussion is not feasible or collapses as a result of incommensurable moral differences that bargaining and compromise become readily acceptable processes of decision-making (1996: 165–6). By contrast, I argue that these are sometimes the best methods to adopt in resolving disputes about the validity or future status of a contested cultural practice. Negotiation, bargaining and compromise lend themselves better to discussion and decision-making that openly *acknowledge* participants' strategic interests without necessarily privileging or catering to those interests. As my discussion of the reform of African customary marriage law in South Africa will show, it is precisely in negotiation-style debate that the validity of participants' interests can be assessed: those who simply seek to maintain control over vulnerable members of their community, for instance,

will be hard pressed to disguise this motive or to find a legitimate justification for it that cannot be revealed as cynical window-dressing. A
model of deliberation that foregrounds negotiation and compromise can
also more readily accommodate citizens' diverse perspectives and styles
of discursive participation than can idealized models of reasoned public
discourse.

How can this explicitly political model of deliberation avoid merely
shoring up the advantages of the powerful? It is not the case that bargaining somehow suspends all norms of respect and reciprocity among participants to a dialogue. Quite the contrary: procedures can and should be
implemented which prevent any one participant or faction from dominat-
ing deliberation or its outcome. Specifically, negotiation and bargaining
as strategies in political deliberation are subject to the norm of democratic
legitimacy, as discussed earlier. But in addition to this, I contend that the
process of political deliberation ought to be bound by three further normative principles: *non-domination, political equality* and *revisability*. I do not
claim that these norms are deliberatively conceived, nor do I suggest that
they should be open to negotiation. Rather, I argue that they are justified as deliberative constraints because of their central role in supporting
democratic legitimacy precisely in settings where cultural and political
authority is contested and subordination is widespread.

Non-domination (or non-coercion) may seem a very minimal constraint
but is nonetheless an important background condition for democratic
political dialogue. In disputes over the validity of cultural customs and
arrangements in liberal democratic states, there is always the danger that
traditional leaders or elites of cultural groups will seek to silence dissenters
through pressure tactics or more overt forms of oppression. Even where
intra-cultural disputes are not at issue, non-domination in deliberation
can be an important principle to stipulate. Bohman, for instance, uses a
version of this, the "non-tyranny constraint" – drawing on the work of
James Fishkin – as a way of preventing concentration and abuse of power
in deliberation generally (Bohman 2000: 35).

The principle of *political equality* is more controversial both because it
is ambiguous in content and may potentially constrain decision-making
more directly than the mere principle of non-domination. Following
Bohman, I take political equality in the context of deliberative democracy to mean the presence of real opportunities for all citizens to participate in debate and decision-making. This means not only ensuring
that such opportunities are available, but also trying to prevent "extra-
political or endogenous forms of influence, such as power, wealth, and
pre-existing social inequalities" from impacting deliberation and its outcomes (Bohman 2000: 36). Who can participate in deliberation – as

Joshua Cohen has observed (1997: 74) – ought not to be determined by their access to power and resources. We can and should use the ideal of political equality to shape discussion and decision-making procedures, by ensuring wherever possible that participants have equal access to formal political deliberation and also that their contributions *count* – for example, by balancing interests in negotiations and employing equal voting procedures.

Political equality as applied to deliberation about cultural conflicts is a still more complex matter, especially if we take this principle, as I do, to require substantive equality of opportunity (for participation) and equality of influence in political deliberation.[7] Who can participate in political life is, for many, culturally determined. Often it is precisely the role and status of certain sub-groups that is at issue – for example, whether women ought to have a political voice. Moreover, who counts as a member of what cultural group is not always clear: sometimes membership is contested as a way of denying the justice claims of minorities within the group. Even if agreement about membership and roles is reached, the difficulty of ensuring that marginalized segments of communities are fully included is enormous. In addition to insisting on guidelines for fair and representative inclusion in formal political consultations, the political enfranchisement of marginalized and vulnerable members of communities can be fostered through the deliberate *expansion* of informal sites of social and political debate and contestation. State funding for social and community services, local media sources with a broadly democratic outlook, and community groups that foster debate about the changing face of cultural practices, are a few examples of ways in which the liberal state can directly facilitate the expansion of spaces of democratic activity.

The third principle that I propose ought to shape political deliberation about cultural conflicts is that of *revisability*. By this I mean that decisions and compromises, once reached, may be revisited at a later point when there are good grounds to do so. The prospect of revisability may make it easier to reach compromises in the first place, for participants and groups understand that if and when they need to redress problems or settlements it will be possible to do so. But the main advantage of an assumption of revisability in the context of deliberation about cultural conflicts, however, is that it acknowledges the gradual character of real change and the ways in which a range of processes *outside* of legislation – processes of a social, cultural and economic nature – contribute to the

---

[7] Knight and Johnson (1997) use the term "equal opportunity of political influence" to capture these criteria, which they suggest implies both procedural and substantive dimensions of political equality.

transformation of customs and cultural arrangements. A revisable deliberative process for evaluating particular customs and initiating reforms
can be sensitive to the way in which cultures are constantly changing, in
response to the needs and preferences of individuals within the culture as
well as local, national and global processes of change. Internal criticism
of practices and arrangements by group members are often the impetus
for their reform, and by allowing policy decisions about customs to be
revisited we remain open to this input.

The revisability condition implies a further constraint mentioned
briefly at the outset of this article. This is in fact also a constraint on
what counts as a just outcome of political deliberation: just as outcomes are
not legitimate if they systematically exclude sections of the community
seeking to be heard, they are not legitimate or tenable if they undercut the ability of citizens to deliberate on these or other issues in the
future, if and when policies are revisited. This Kantian-style constraint
(Onora O'Neill 2000) would be violated, then, by a policy that prohibits
all women in a particular society or community from voicing their views
in public or from voting. The ban on female political participation would
in any case also violate the constraints of democratic legitimacy, political
equality and, probably, non-coercion, but skeptics might ask, what of a
situation where women appear to endorse or at least not to protest such
a rule? My response to this is that it is difficult if not impossible to imagine a scenario whereby such a policy could be *democratically arrived at*,
under conditions of non-coercion and non-intimidation. Wherever customs and cultural arrangements subordinate women and harm them in
tangible ways, there are signs of resistance, faint as these may be in some
circumstances. Acts of cultural subversion and resistance are not always
easy to recognize, especially as they often occur in informal settings, such
as in the home and in social rituals and customs.

The constraints that I propose should shape political deliberation about
contested cultural practices and arrangements in plural, liberal democratic societies are designed to accord maximum support to the principle
of democratic legitimacy. Participants in deliberation debate the meaning, relevance and future status of contested social practices and try to
reach negotiated political compromises, not merely in formal political
institutions but in forums sponsored by local community and cultural
associations, media resources, and more spontaneous public responses to
incidents in the community. Those involved in deliberations speak from
their partial, situated perspectives, with their beliefs and interests intact,
though these may of course change. The inclusion of the perspectives
of diverse members of cultural and religious communities contributes
to a more accurate picture of *actual* social customs and their problems

and benefits; this more representative account of *lived cultural practices* is needed to determine which reforms might render customs more empowering for vulnerable members of the group, including women.

Deliberation, on this account, is bound by minimal norms, and ultimately aims to secure democratic political solutions, emphasizing concessions for contending parties.[8] Rather than a zero-sum game, the dialogue aims for imperfect, negotiated compromises.[9] In many cases, deliberation about the development of cultural practices would be linked to processes of legislative reform, through public hearings and community consultations and the like, and therefore subject to certain procedural and even constitutional norms. The example of the reform of customary marriage laws in South Africa, discussed below, is one such illustration. However, what is proposed here is by no means politics as usual: the strong emphasis placed on democratic legitimacy, and the relative minimalism of the principles to serve as procedural constraints, leaves the outcome of deliberation in many ways undetermined.[10]

Sex equality and the reform of customary marriage in South Africa

To understand how a deliberative democratic approach to conflicts of culture might work in practice, it is useful to consider a specific case. In late 1998, the South African legislature passed into law the Customary Marriages Act, for the first time granting traditional or customary African marriage equal status with civil (usually Christian) marriage. That the Act recognizes and sets out national guidelines and laws governing customary marriage for the *first* time is surprising given that at least half of the country's 80 percent black majority marries under some form of customary arrangement. Finally put into force in November 2000, the Act was the culmination of deliberative and consultative hearings held to solicit views about the practice of customary marriage and to draft proposals for its reform. It is for this reason an instructive example for

---

[8] Bellamy (1999) also advocates a politics of negotiation and compromise for democratic societies.

[9] Shachar makes a similar claim in support of her joint governance proposal: state and cultural group officials, she writes, "are . . . forced to abandon their perfectionist and maximalist jurisdictional aspirations, which are so often the source of conflict" (2001: 143).

[10] My argument presupposes that deliberation about contested cultural practices takes place against the background of a liberal democratic state that protects fundamental rights and freedoms, and which prohibits harm or other cruel treatment through criminal laws. These protections go hand in hand with a deliberative democratic approach to conflict resolution and policy development; without them, this discussion would look very different.

exploring how deliberative solutions to cultural conflicts might work in practice. The impetus for the Act was the need to bring some of the more discriminatory traditional customs associated with customary marriage in line with the state's 1996 Constitution, widely considered to be the most liberal and progressive in the world. The founding provisions of the Constitution declare that South Africa is committed to principles of "non-racialism and non-sexism," and the Bill of Rights it contains sets out extensive protection for individual rights as well as an equality clause prohibiting discrimination on practically every possible ground.[11] At the same time, the Constitution also recognizes the validity of African customary law and the system of traditional leadership associated with it.

As could be expected, constitutional protections of the right to culture and the right to sex equality have been seen to clash in practices governing marriage, divorce and family law (including inheritance) in black South African communities. Traditional southern African cultures, such as those of the Zulu, Xhosa and Sotho peoples, are patriarchal and patrilineal. Under the system of customary law that most black South Africans adhere to in their family affairs, women were until recently accorded the legal status of a minor – unable to inherit land, enter into contracts, or indeed to initiate their own divorces. At the heart of the official code of customary law lies the institution of primogeniture, whereby, in the absence of a male heir, the nearest senior male relative in an extended family inherits the property and the responsibilities of his deceased male kin. Women married under customary law are first under their fathers' realm of authority and subsequently that of their husbands (or nearest senior male relative) for the duration of their lives. Payment for the bride – known as bride-wealth, or *lobolo*, traditionally paid in cattle but nowadays more commonly in cash – passes from the prospective groom to the father of the bride (or a male guardian in the event of his death) and without it, marriages are deemed invalid. If a woman subsequently seeks to leave her marriage, the bride's family is expected to return the *lobolo* to the groom or the groom's family – a requirement widely blamed for keeping women, fearful of impoverishing not only herself but her family, trapped in abusive marriages. Finally, custody of children is automatically awarded to fathers (or the father's family) under customary law, as required by the principle of primogeniture. These customs, rightly seen by many as harmful to women's interests, are in keeping with the "official

---

[11] The South African Constitution states that neither the state nor individuals may "unfairly discriminate directly or indirectly against anyone on one or more grounds, including race, gender, sex, pregnancy, marital status, ethnic or social origin, colour, sexual orientation, age, disability, religion, conscience, belief, culture, language, and birth."

code of customary law" which was recorded by colonial administrators in the nineteenth and twentieth centuries.[12]

The potential for friction between customary law provisions and the equality clause in the Bill of Rights made it crucial to eliminate any ambiguity in the relationship between these two, but instead political disagreement about the issue plagued the constitutional process. In the CODESA (Convention for a Democratic South Africa) talks leading up to the drafting of the 1993 Interim Constitution, traditional leaders sought to ensure that customary law would not be limited by the provisions of the Bill of Rights. Later, in talks surrounding the drafting of the final 1996 Constitution, African chiefs urged that the Bill of Rights be interpreted as applying only vertically between the state and individuals, and not horizontally between private citizens, in a bid to drastically restrict the Bill's scope. By contrast, feminist activists wanted to ensure that the equality clause in the Bill of Rights would trump the authority of customary law, as well as applying to relations between private individuals.[13] In the end, a political compromise was struck. The final 1996 Constitution recognizes and protects customary law and the right to culture to the extent that these are consistent with the rights guaranteed in the Bill of Rights.[14] Yet like all new Constitutions, this one merely provides broad legal guidelines for facing future legal dilemmas; it is not a blueprint for social and political change. As a result, the relationship between customary law and sex equality in South Africa remains to some extent indeterminate and fraught with political uncertainty.

The Constitution, still very much in its infancy, has seen some legal challenges that do not bode well for gender equity. In *Mthembu v Letsela*

---

[12] Not surprisingly, this official code reflected a particularly patriarchal interpretation of local customs. Traditional African leaders were also later wooed by apartheid administrators, who in turn underwrote the chiefs' power and authority in return for guarantees of loyalty. The "official code of customary law" was later to facilitate the establishment of distinct tribal "homelands" for blacks, the hallmark of the apartheid ideology of the "separate development" of the races. The patriarchal interpretation of customary law suited some tribal leaders very well; many local headmen and chiefs clung tenaciously to their positions of authority under apartheid. See Bennett 1999.

[13] The Women's National Coalition, an ad hoc alliance of women's groups, applied direct political pressure to the negotiations. Less seasoned political activists were also involved: famously, women from the Rural Women's Movement traveled up to Johannesburg from the Eastern Cape to lobby the CODESA talks in favor of sex equality protections. Interview with Gertrude Fester, Commissioner for the Western Cape, Commission on Gender Equality, at Bloubergstrand, Western Cape Province, 16 January 2002.

[14] The Constitution also states that in interpreting the provisions of the Bill of Rights, the courts should consider relevant international treaties, an important inclusion in light of the fact that South Africa has signed and ratified the Convention on the Elimination of All Forms of Discrimination Against Women, which specifically calls for the reform of cultural traditions that perpetuate sex discrimination against women.

and Another [1997], the Supreme Court of Appeal heard a challenge from a widow married under customary law who wanted to have her only child, a daughter, declared the sole heir to her husband's estate, contrary to the rules of primogeniture. The judge ruled against her, reasoning that customary law did not represent an instance of *unfair* discrimination as the system of primogeniture provides for the maintenance of the deceased's widow and her children.[15] Aside from the *Mthembu* decision and a few others like it is the fact that actual practices and arrangements in African communities have not magically altered in accordance with the constitutional recognition of sex equality. Customary law continues to permit discrimination against women on many fronts: by denying them inheritance and oftentimes leaving them destitute after divorce or upon the death of their spouse.

It is no surprise, then, that in 1998, as part of a long-term project on the Harmonization of the Common Law and the Indigenous Law, the South African Law Commission sponsored a series of consultations and hearings on the reform of customary marriage. These meetings included a cross-section of the community, including representatives of legal reform groups and women's associations; chiefs from the Congress of Traditional Leaders of South Africa (CONTRALESA); and scholars of constitutional law and customary law. Representatives from CONTRALESA, in keeping with their position during constitutional negotiations, argued that the government should simply recognize marriage under customary law as it is currently practiced, including those aspects that subordinate women. A customary law specialist, Likhapa Mbatha, reported that in meetings she attended, traditional leaders kept hiding behind the word "culture" when making their case against proposed reforms, and steadfastly resisted suggestions that women should enjoy greater decision-making roles in African society.[16] Contrarily, women's equality and legal reform advocates voiced their opposition to women's status as minors under customary law, and to the systems of primogeniture more generally. Proponents of more radical reform advocated the institution of a single civil marriage code that would protect the rights of all women, irrespective of their race, culture or religion. Interestingly, this option was unpopular with many involved in the consultations, and generated little support.[17]

---

[15] As Fishbayn (1999: 163–5) notes, the customary duty to support widows and their children has diminished *in practice* in Southern Africa in recent years, due to urbanization, migrant labor and the dramatic rise in HIV and AIDS.

[16] Interview with Likhapa Mbatha of the Centre for Applied Legal Studies (CALS) at the University of the Witswaatersrand (Johannesburg) 25 January 2002.

[17] Cathy Albertyn, director of CALS, reports that her organization recommended a single, civil marriage process which could have ceremonial aspects if the participants so

By including participants who represent different interests in African communities – traditional leaders, customary law scholars, rural women's advocates, etc. – as well as concerned members of legal reform and women's groups, the Commission made it possible for a range of views on the merits and disadvantages of different aspects of traditions surrounding customary marriage to be heard. This deliberative process also ensured that no single, canonical (and likely false) account of customary marriage was taken at face value. Instead, discussion focused on marriage under the actual or "living" customary law and the changing gender roles and practices that it reflects. Mbatha and others pointed out in the Law Commission meetings that women's roles have in fact already changed in African communities, and that chiefs misrepresent reality by conjuring up romantic ideals of separate spheres and men's leadership. For example, Likhapa noted that under the "living" customary law, women negotiate and receive *lobolo* and often act on behalf of their sons and daughters in negotiating the precise terms of marriages. Another widespread but false belief pointed to in the course of discussions was the notion that wives have no economic responsibilities in marriage and that they are provided for both by their husbands and by their husbands' families if they are widowed (Himonga 1998: 298; Fishbayn 1999: 165).

The broad representation of participants in deliberations about the future of customary marriage made possible not only a more accurate description of the specific practices surrounding this institution, but a manifestly political style of debate. Indeed, the process of deliberation initiated by the Law Commission can best be characterized as putting into motion a politics of negotiation and compromise in which the focus was on practical interests, prospective policies and their potential consequences. This frankness accounts for the easy exposure of some of the more pernicious interests and motivations on the table, particularly those of the chiefs who were concerned that their own positions of power might be endangered if they were no longer permitted to adjudicate matters of divorce, custody and inheritance in their local traditional courts. The openness and political tone of deliberations also accounts for the relative ease with which compromises were ultimately reached regarding specific reforms and policies.

As in the debate on the status of customary law in constitutional negotiations, a political compromise was struck in the debate on customary marriage. On the side of reform, women's contractual and proprietary

---

desired, but that this proposal was seen by many as a demotion of customary marriage and customary law more generally, and so was rejected. Interview, 24 January 2002, Johannesburg.

capacities are now fully affirmed and wives have (formally) equal status. Both spouses are deemed to be married in community of property[18] as the default arrangement, consistent with the wide popularity of the principle of shared or joint property among black South African women (Govender 2000: 26–8).[19] Women are now entitled to initiate divorce proceedings, and married parents have equal guardianship and custody rights with respect to their children. On the issue of family law jurisdiction, it was decided that in future only family courts may handle divorce, maintenance and custody matters, taking this power away from local chiefs (but not their right to try to mediate relationship disputes). Equally, the Law Commission deliberations yielded a number of concessions for traditional leaders. Chiefs were relieved that *lobolo* is still recognized, although it is no longer required to prove a marriage's validity. Initially the Law Commission thought *lobolo* might be eliminated on the grounds that it is offensive to women's dignity, but the widespread support for the custom voiced in consultations made this all but impossible.[20] An important reform of the practice, however, now leaves it open to either parent to assume the role of negotiating and receiving bride-wealth. Another custom that the Commission originally expected to be abolished is that of polygyny, or the practice of a man taking more than one wife. Most participants in deliberations felt this would be a mistake, both because the practice is deemed by many to be an important (though diminishing) variation of customary marriage and because merely abolishing it in law would be ineffectual, leaving women in polygynous marriages essentially unprotected. An agreement was eventually reached whereby polygyny will continue to be permitted, but a man intending to marry another wife must have a written contract with his wife that protects her financial interests and establishes an equitable distribution of his assets in the event of divorce or his death.

The explicitly political nature of the consultation process surrounding the recognition and reform of customary marriage in South Africa rendered power relationships and interests more visible, and at least on some level, more open to contestation. Reforms that might not have been

[18] The community of property reform was viewed as especially important by women's legal reform groups, which view women's financial destitution (as the result of desertion and divorce) as the gravest problem facing rural black women. Interview with Coriaan de Villiers of the Women's Legal Centre, Cape Town, 18 January 2002.

[19] In a study of attitudes of women in the Western Cape and Eastern Cape Provinces, 82% of women supported joint ownership and control of property in monogamous marriages (Govender 2000: 26–8).

[20] As Govender (2000) notes, "abolishing it would merely have meant passing a law which would be consistently disregarded"; her study found that women overwhelmingly (85%) support the custom of *lobolo*.

thought necessary were proposed, and other reforms were dismissed or amended as a response to political pressures. The relative openness of the political process made clear just what the most forceful complaints were. In particular, the denial of women's proprietary and contractual capacities was seen as the most odious aspect of customary law, and proposals to eliminate these were not especially contested.[21] Similarly, it was only through consultation and deliberation that the Law Commission was able to discover which practices were widely thought to be valuable and worth keeping.

This example illustrates that a deliberative approach to resolving disputes about contested cultural practices, one that emphasizes inclusive debate and decision-making and which uses strategies of negotiation and compromise, can produce fair and equitable solutions. The outcome of deliberations – the draft proposals that became the Customary Marriage Act – did not please all of the participants. Traditional leaders would have much preferred to retain their role in adjudicating divorce and custody disputes, largely because of the power that it represents. Some women's groups, including the government-initiated Commission for Gender Equality (CGE), were unhappy with the retention of polygyny (CGE 1998: 7).[22] But the compromises that the hearings eventually produced were nonetheless seen by most as reflecting a fair and legitimate outcome of deliberation and negotiation. To sustain this legitimacy, it will be important to follow up the new legislation with government spending on programs needed to implement the reforms.[23]

Finally, this case also shows that deliberation may yield outcomes with *non-liberal* features – in this case, the preservation of African customs of polygyny and bride-wealth payment – that are consistent with norms of political equality and democratic legitimacy. The revisability of the outcome of deliberations – through future amendments to the Act – will help to ensure that any unjust or unfeasible aspects of the new laws that come to light can be revisited and changed. For instance, one problematic aspect of the new Act is that it has only very limited applicability to customary marriages entered into before the Act came into effect. In part this provision reflects the difficulty of amending marriage contracts retrospectively, but it also signaled a concession to traditional leaders.

---

[21] Likhapa Mbatha (personal communication). Also, Govender (2000: 27) found that a mere 2% of married women supported the principle of primogeniture.
[22] The Commission for Gender Equality (CGE), in a brief addressing the Recognition of Customary Marriages Bill, describes the practice of polygyny as "discriminatory."
[23] In particular, local magistrates need to be trained to apply the new laws, and it must be made easier for rural women to register their customary marriages. Interview with Johanna Kehler, director, National Association of Democratic Lawyers, Cape Town, 18 January 2002.

Already there are calls from women's equality groups and legal reform groups to reform this aspect of the Act, and it is likely that new legislation will need to be brought in to ensure greater equity for those whose customary marriages predate the Act. Similarly, at some point the new laws governing polygyny may well need to be changed to reflect changing attitudes and practices in black South African communities.

Conclusion: a conundrum?

I have argued that a deliberative approach to resolving disputes about the status of contested practices meets the demands of democratic legitimacy and demonstrates respect for the diverse cultural and religious commitments and attachments of citizens. Three important objections to the deliberative democratic approach to conflicts of culture are, however, sure to be raised.

One objection points to the open-ended and possibly illiberal nature of the political outcomes of this approach. My response to this concern is to reiterate the importance of taking seriously the principle of democratic legitimacy. The deliberative democratic model of conflict resolution sketched here insists on radically democratic and inclusive processes of discussion and decision-making; as such, it cannot guarantee that deliberation about cultural conflicts will issue in liberal outcomes. The open-endedness of outcomes is consistent with the centrality accorded the principles of pluralism and democratic legitimacy by my approach. Democratic legitimacy of course requires that people agree to the norms and laws that they are to be bound by, but the liberal view sketched at the outset suggests that dilemmas of justice involving non-liberal cultural groups can be determined in the abstract, without the central participation of community members. This may ensure that liberal policies follow from deliberation, however ineffectual they may be in practice; but it cannot deliver democratically legitimate solutions. Similarly, the extensive normative constraints that some democratic theorists propose to impose on deliberation, are in large part meant to ensure that results are just by measurable liberal standards, but these constraints may not be consistent with the demands of democratic pluralism.

A second objection is that the deliberative approach I defend rests on a conception of political legitimacy paradoxically at odds with the canonical views of certain traditional groups whose cultural practices are in question, particularly conservative religious communities. In requiring groups to democratize their own internal political processes and permit dissenting members to have a role in decision-making, do we not fail to respect their collective political practices and self-understandings? While acknowledging the tension, this objection wrongly supposes that the ideal of democratic legitimacy is strictly a liberal conception – that it has no purchase at all within non-liberal cultures, not even among vulnerable and exploited members. It further assumes that democratic activity is neither permissible nor evident within traditional cultures in liberal states. Those who argue against – or simply fail to see justification for – the application of the norm of democratic legitimacy in disputes involving traditional cultural and religious communities may of course remain unpersuaded by this defense of the principle of democratic legitimacy. Those who completely reject the principle's validity with respect to non-liberal cultural groups may fail to see the extent to which *internal dissent* is nearly always present in such communities within liberal democratic states, even if it is actively suppressed by traditionalists. Non-liberal social groups may be marked by deeply hierarchical relationships which may make it difficult to recognize signs of resistance or democratic activity.

A third, related worry points to the possible effects on traditional communities of the requirement that deliberations about the status of contested cultural practices be broadly inclusive and raises an important conundrum. There is no doubt that requiring democratic decision-making procedures for settling the status of disputed social practices and arrangements, and where necessary, reforming them, will trigger social changes within traditional communities. As Bohman observes, "the cost of interaction in the public sphere may well be the loss of some cultural forms of authority. The self-interpretations of such cultures and their traditions will be thrown open beyond their authorized interpreters to a wider set of participants, even to non-members with whom they engage in dialogue" (2000: 146). The requirement that groups adopt changes that will permit the democratic inclusion of their own members in formal spaces of democratic activity may indeed be onerous in some cases. But as I have argued, disputes about the status of customs of traditional cultures in liberal societies frequently arise as a result of dissent *within* cultural communities, and include challenges directed against prevailing decision-making structures. Since such democratic contestation often occurs outside formal political spaces, it is easily overlooked and the conflict described, falsely, as a clash of core values held by the liberal state and traditional or illiberal cultures (Okin 1999a; 2002). Those who insist that the liberal state oppresses non-liberal groups in requiring them to open up or democratize their internal decision-making procedures often overlook or downplay the role of dissenting members within the community in bringing the issue of contested customs to the fore.

Notwithstanding this tension between respect for cultural group autonomy and the norm of democratic legitimacy, a political process that aims to facilitate deliberation among members of cultural communities, representatives of groups in civil society, and state officials is potentially more democratic and equitable than the alternatives. Within the context of liberal democratic states, demonstrating respect for cultural communities does not require that any or all practices, however much in tension with democratic norms, be accommodated. Equal respect is better demonstrated by requiring the meaningful inclusion of group members in the process of evaluating, defending and proposing changes to their communities' cultural practices. By putting members of cultural communities at the center of debates and decision-making processes about the future of their cultural practices, we express formal respect and equal regard for them as citizens and as members of groups – surely a moral requirement of plural, liberal states. A deliberative democratic approach to cultural conflicts does not contrive to guarantee liberal outcomes, nor does it promise that deliberative outcomes will always be the most fair or just from the point of view of all concerned. But the procedures for evaluating and, if necessary, reforming, contested cultural customs sketched here are democratic and practically grounded. As such, they can generate proposals that are both democratically legitimate and politically viable in their reflection of cultural practices and communities in flux.

References

Abramson, Paul. 1983. *Political Attitudes in America: Formation and Change.* San Francisco: W. H. Freeman.

Abu-Laban, Yasmeen. 2002. "Liberalism, Multiculturalism and the Problem of Essentialism." *Citizenship Studies* 6 (4): 459–82.

ADL Fact-Finding Report – Armed and Dangerous: Militias Take Aim at the Federal Government. 1994. New York: ADL Publications.

ADL Fact-Finding Report – The Other Face of Farrakhan: A Hate-Filled Prelude to the Million Man March. 1995. New York: ADL Publications.

Agnes, Flavia. 1999. *Law and Gender Equality.* New Delhi: Oxford University Press.

Agnes, Flavia and Veena Gowda. 2000. *Church, State and Women: Christian Marriage Bill.* Bombay: Majlis.

Ahmed, Anees. 2001. "Reforms within the Spirit of Islam." Paper presented at The Second Lawyers Collective, Women's Rights Initiative Colloquium on Justice for Gender, Empowerment through Law, Gender Justice and Personal Laws: A Constitutional Perspective. India Habitat Center, New Delhi, 14–16 December.

Al-Hibri, Azizah. 1999. "Is Western Patriarchal Feminism Good for Third World/Minority Women?" In *Is Multiculturalism Bad for Women?* Joshua Cohen, Matthew Howard and Martha C. Nussbaum eds. Princeton, NJ: Princeton University Press.

Altman, Andrew. 2003. "Religion, Taxes, and Sex Discrimination: Where do Liberal Principles Lead?" Unpublished manuscript.

Amnesty International Online. 2000. *Kuwait: Women Win Right to Challenge Discriminatory Electoral Law,* 2 June. http://web.amnesty.org/ai.nsf/Index/MDE170032000? OpenDocument&of=COUNTRIES%5.

Anaya, James S. 1993. "A Contemporary Definition of the International Norm of Self-Determination." *Transnational Law and Contemporary Problems* 3: 131–64.

— 1996. *Indigenous Peoples in International Law.* Oxford: Oxford University Press.

An-Na'im, Abdullahi. 1999. "Promises We Should All Keep in Common Cause." In *Is Multiculturalism Bad for Women?* Joshua Cohen, Matthew Howard and Martha C. Nussbaum eds. Princeton, NJ: Princeton University Press.

Armitage, A. 1995. *Comparing the Policy of Aboriginal Assimilation: Australia, Canada and New Zealand.* Vancouver: UBC Press.

Arneson, R. and I. Shapiro. 1996. "Democratic Autonomy and Religious Freedom: A Critique of *Wisconsin v. Yoder.*" In *Political Order: NOMOS XXXVIII.* I. Shapiro and R. Hardin eds. New York: New York University Press.

Arnopoulos, Sheila McLeod and Dominique Clift. 1980. *The English Fact in Quebec.* Montreal and Kingston: McGill-Queen's University Press.

Asch, Michael. 1992. "Errors in Delgamuukw: An Anthropological Perspective." In *Aboriginal Title in British Columbia: Delgamuukw v. the Queen.* Frank Cassidy ed. Vancouver and Montreal: Oolichan Books.

Audi, Robert. 1989. "The Separation of Church and State and the Obligations of Citizenship." *Philosophy and Public Affairs* 18: 259–96.

— 1997. "Liberal Democracy and the Place of Religion in Politics." In *Religion in the Public Square: The Place of Religious Convictions in Public Debate.* Robert Audi and and Nicholas Wolterstorff eds. London: Rowman & Littlefield.

— 2000. *Religious Commitment and Secular Reason.* Cambridge: Cambridge University Press.

Aull Davies, Charlotte. 1996. "Nationalism: Discourse and Practice." In *Practising Feminism: Identity, Difference, Power.* Nickie Charles and Felicia Hughes-Freeland eds. London: Routledge.

Avineri, Shlomo and Avner De-Shalit eds. 1992. *Communitarianism and Individualism.* Oxford: Oxford University Press.

Bachrach, Peter and Morton S. Baratz. 1962. "Two Faces of Power." *American Political Science Review* 56: 947–52.

— 1963. "Decisions and Nondecisions: An Analytical Framework." *American Political Science Review* 57: 632–42.

Bader, Veit M. 1997. "The Cultural Conditions of Trans-national Citizenship." *Political Theory* 25 (6): 771–813.

— 1998. "Egalitarian Multiculturalism." In *Blurred Boundaries.* R. Bauboeck and J. Rundell eds. Ashgate: Aldershot.

— 1999. "Religious Pluralism, Secularism or Priority for Democracy?" *Political Theory* 27 (5): 597–633.

— 2001a. "Introduction." In *Associative Democracy – The Real Third Way.* Paul Hirst and Veit Bader eds. London, Portland: Frank Cass.

— 2001b. "Associative Democracy and the Incorporation of Ethnic and National Minorities." In *Associative Democracy – The Real Third Way.* Paul Hirst and Veit Bader eds. London, Portland: Frank Cass.

— 2002. "Defending Differentiated Policies of Multiculturalism." Paper presented at the Conference on Ideas and Politics for Our Times, University of Minho, Braga, Portugal, 17 May.

— 2003a. "Religious Diversity and Democratic Institutional Pluralism." *Political Theory,* 31 (2): 265–94.

— 2003b. "Introduction: Taking Religious Pluralism Seriously." *Ethical Theory and Moral Practice,* 6: 3–22.

— 2003c. "Religions and States." *Ethical Theory and Moral Practice* 6: 55–91.

— 2003d. "Democratic Institutional Pluralism and Cultural Diversity." In *The Social Construction of Diversity.* D. Juteau and C. Harzig eds. New York, Oxford: Berghahn.

Bader, Veit M. and E. Engelen. 2003e. "Taking Pluralism Seriously: Arguing for an Institutional Turn in Political Philosophy." *Philosophy and Social Criticism* 29: 375–406.

Bader, Veit M. and S. Saharso. 2004. "Contextualized Morality and Ethno-religious Diversity: Introduction." *Ethical Theory and Moral Practice.*

Barry, Brian M. 2001a. *Culture & Equality: An Egalitarian Critique of Multiculturalism.* Cambridge, Mass.: Harvard University Press.

— 2001b. "The Muddles of Multiculturalism." *New Left Review* 8: 49–71.

— 2002. "Second Thoughts – and Some First Thoughts Revisited." In *Multiculturalism Reconsidered: Culture and Equality and its Critics.* Paul Kelly ed. Cambridge: Polity Press.

Barsh, R. 1983. "Indigenous North America and Contemporary International Law." *Oregon Law Review* 62 (1): 73–125.

BBC News. 2002. *Kuwaiti Women in Voting Rights Protest,* 17 Feb. http://news.bbc.co.uk/1/hi/world/middle_east/543408.stm.

Becher v. Becher 245 AD 2d 408; 667 NYS 2d (NY App Div 1997).

Bellamy, Richard. 1999. *Liberalism and Pluralism.* London and New York: Routledge.

Benhabib, Seyla. 1999. "Sexual Difference and Collective Identities: The New Global Constellation." *Signs* 24: 335–62.

— 2002. *The Claims of Culture: Equality and Diversity in the Global Era.* Princeton, NJ: Princeton University Press.

Bennett, T. W. 1999. *Human Rights and African Customary Law.* Cape Town: Juta & Co.

Berlin, Isaiah. 1969. *Four Essays on Liberty.* London: Oxford University Press.

Board of Education of Kiryas Joel School District v. Grumet 114 S.Ct. 2481 (1994).

Bohman, James. 1997. "Deliberative Democracy and Effective Social Freedom: Capabilities, Resources, and Opportunities." In *Deliberative Democracy: Essays on Reason and Politics.* James Bohman and W. Rehg eds. Cambridge and London: MIT Press.

— 2000. *Public Deliberation: Pluralism, Complexity, and Democracy.* Cambridge, MA: MIT Press.

Bohman, James and W. Rehg, eds. 1997. *Deliberative Democracy: Essays on Reason and Politics.* Cambridge and London: MIT Press.

Boldt, Menno. 1993. *Surviving as Indians: The Challenge of Self-Government.* Toronto: University of Toronto Press.

Bronstein, Victoria. 1998. "Reconceptualizing the Customary Law Debate in South Africa." *South African Journal on Human Rights* 14: 388–410.

Brown, Wendy. 1995. *States of Injury: Power and Freedom in Late Modernity.* Princeton, NJ: Princeton University Press.

Brownlie, Ian. 1992. "Rights of Peoples in International Law." In *The Rights of Peoples.* James Crawford ed. Oxford: Clarendon Press.

— 1998. *Principles of Public International Law.* 5th edition. Oxford: Oxford University Press.

Broyde, Michael. 1997. "The New York Get Law: An Exchange." *Tradition* 31: 27.

Brubaker, Rogers. 1998. "Myths and Misconceptions in the Study of Nationalism." In *National Self-Determination and Secession*, Margaret Moore ed. Oxford: Oxford University Press.

Buchanan, Allen. 1993. "The Role of Collective Rights in the Theory of Indigenous Peoples' Rights." *Transnational Law & Contemporary Problems* 3 (1): 89–108.

— 1997. "Theories of Secession." *Philosophy and Public Affairs* 26 (1): 31–61.

— 2003. *Justice, Legitimacy and Self-determination*. Oxford: Oxford University Press.

Buckley v. United Kingdom, European Court of Human Rights Reference Number 00000664, Reports of the European Court of Human Rights 1996(IV), 23/1995/529/615, 25 September 1996, especially at B.14 (1), E.2 (74–84).

Bullock, Katherine. 2002. *Rethinking Muslim Women and the Veil: Challenging Historical and Modern Stereotypes*. Herndon, VA: International Institute of Islamic Thought.

Cairns, Alan. 2000. *Citizens Plus: Aboriginal Peoples and the Canadian State*. Vancouver: UBC Press.

Callan, Eamonn. 1997. *Creating Citizens: Political Education and Liberal Democracy*. New York: Clarendon Press.

Callister, S., J. Long and L. Zaitz. 1985. "On the Road Again." *The Oregonian*, 30 December.

Carens, Joseph H. 2000. *Culture, Citizenship and Community: A Contextual Exploration of Justice as Evenhandedness*. Oxford: Oxford University Press.

Carens, Joseph H. and Melissa S. Williams. 1998. "Islam, Immigration, and Group Recognition." *Citizenship Studies* 2 (3): 475–500.

Carroll, Lucy. 1997. "Muslim Women and Islamic Divorce in England." *Journal of Muslim Minority Affairs* 17: 97–115.

Carter, Stephen L. 1993. *The Culture of Disbelief: How American Law and Politics Trivialize Religious Devotion*. New York: Basic Books.

— 1998. *The Dissent of the Governed: A Meditation on Law, Religion, and Loyalty*. Cambridge, MA: Harvard University Press.

— 2000. *God's Name in Vain: The Wrongs and Rights of Religion in Politics*. New York: Basic Books.

Casesse, Antonio. 1995. *Self-Determination of Peoples: A Legal Reappraisal*. Cambridge: Cambridge University Press.

CERD, Right to Self-determination: General Recom. XXI, Adopted 15 March 1996 (48th session), contained in UN Doc. A/51/18; World Conference on Human Rights, Vienna, Declaration and Programme of Action, Vienna, 14–25 June 1993, UN Doc. A/CONF.157/24 (Part I) at 20 (1993), section 2.

Chambers, Simone. 1998. "Contract or Conversation?: Theoretical Lessons from the Canadian Constitutional Crisis." *Politics and Society* 26 (1): 143–79.

Chang, Ruth, ed. 1997. *Incommensurability, Incomparability, and Practical Reason*. Cambridge, MA: Harvard University Press.

Chatterjee, Jyotsana. 2001. "Changes in Christian Personal Laws." Paper presented at The Second Lawyers Collective, Women's Rights Initiative Colloquium on Justice for Gender, Empowerment through Law, Gender Justice and Personal Laws: A Constitutional Perspective. India Habitat Centre, New Delhi, 14–16 December.

Chatterjee, Partha. 1994. "Secularism and Tolerance." *Economic and Political Weekly*, 9 July: 1768–77.

Chiu, Diana C. 1994. "The Cultural Defense: Beyond Exclusion, Assimilation, and Guilty Liberalism." *Pacific Basin Law Journal* 8: 80–90.

Citrin, Jack and Donald Green. 1986. "Presidential Leadership and Trust in Government." *British Journal of Political Science* 16: 431–53.

City of Richmond v. J. A. Croson Co., 488 US 469, 505 (1989).

Cohen, Cathy J. 1999. *The Boundaries of Blackness: AIDS and the Breakdown of Black Politics*. Chicago: Chicago University Press.

Cohen, Joshua. 1997. "Deliberation and Democratic Legitimacy." In *Deliberative Democracy: Essays on Reason and Politcs*. James Bohman and W. Rehg eds. Cambridge and London: MIT Press.

Cohen, Joshua, Matthew Howard and Martha C. Nussbaum, eds. 1999. *Is Multiculturalism Bad for Women?* Princeton, NJ: Princeton University Press.

Coleman, Doriane Lambelet. 1996. "Individualizing Justice through Multiculturalism: The Liberal's Dilemma." *Columbia Law Review* 95: 1093–1166.

Commission for Gender Equality (CGE). 1998. *Submission to the Justice Portfolio Committee*. South Africa.

Connolly, William. 2000. "Secularism, Partisanship and the Ambiguity of Justice." In *Political Theory and Partisan Politics*. E. Portis, A. Gundersen and R. Shively eds. Albany: SUNY Press.

Cornell, Stephen. 1998. *The Return of the Native: American Indian Political Resurgence*. New York: Oxford University Press.

Cowan, Sam. 2000. "Sanity or Profanity?" *Jewish Chronicle*. London, 16 June: 33.

Crawford, James, ed. 1992. *The Rights of Peoples*. Oxford: Clarendon Press.

Dahl, Robert A. 1956. *Preface to Democratic Theory*. Chicago: Chicago University Press.

DeCaro, Louis A., Jr. 1998. *Malcolm and the Cross: The Nation of Islam, Malcolm X, and Christianity*. New York: New York University Press.

Delgamuukw v. British Columbia [1997] 2 S.C.R. 1010.

Deveaux, Monique. 2000a. *Cultural Pluralism and Dilemmas of Justice*. Ithaca and London: Cornell University Press.

— 2000b. "Conflicting Equalities? Cultural Groups and Sex Equality." *Political Studies* 48: 522–38.

Devlin, Patrick. 1965. *The Enforcement of Morals*. Oxford: Oxford University Press.

Diamond, Sara. 1998. *Not by Politics Alone: The Enduring Influence of the Christian Right*. New York: Guildford Press.

Dion, Stephane. 2002. "The Canadian Charter of Rights and Freedoms: The Balance between Individual and Collective Rights." Canadian Studies lecture, Woodrow Wilson School, Princeton University, Princeton, New Jersey, 1 April.

d'Oliveira, Hans U. Jessurun. 1995. "Le droit international prive Néerlandais et les relations Maroc-Pays-Bas." *Cahiers des Droits Maghrebins* 1: 137–66.

Donnelly, Jack. 1985. *The Concept of Human Rights*. New York: St. Martin's Press.

Draft United Nations Declaration on the Rights of Indigenous Peoples. UN Doc. E/CN.4/Sub.2/1194/56.

Dryzek, John. 2000. *Deliberative Democracy and Beyond: Liberals, Critics, Contestations*. Oxford: Oxford University Press.

Dunfield, Alison. 2002. "US Backs Away from Border Brouhaha." *Globe and Mail*, 31 October.

Dworkin, Ronald. 1977. *Taking Rights Seriously*. Cambridge, Mass.: Harvard University Press.

— 1994. *Life's Dominion: An Argument about Abortion, Euthanasia, and Individual Freedom*. New York: Vintage Books.

Eisenberg, Avigail. 1994. "The Politics of Individual and Group Difference in Canadian Jurisprudence." *Canadian Journal of Political Science* 27 (1): 3–21.

— 1995. *Reconstructing Political Pluralism*. Albany: State University of New York Press.

— 2003. "Diversity and Equality: Three Approaches to Cultural and Sexual Difference." *Journal of Political Philosophy* 11 (1): 41–64.

Eisgruber, Christopher L. 1994. "Political Unity and the Powers of Government." *UCLA Law Review* 41: 1297–1336.

— 1996. "The Constitutional Value of Assimilation." *Columbia Law Review* 96: 87–103.

— 2001. *Constitutional Self-government*. Cambridge, Mass.: Harvard University Press.

Elster, Jon. 1989. *Solomonic Judgements: Studies in the Limitations of Rationality*. New York: Cambridge University Press.

Employment Division of Oregon v. Smith, 494 US 872 (1990).

Englander, David. 1994. *A Documentary History of Jewish Immigrants in Britain, 1840–1920*. Leicester, UK: Leicester University Press.

Epstein, Mendel. 1989. *A Woman's Guide to the Get Process*. Israel: Private Press.

Eschen, Donald Von, Jerome Kirk and Maurice Pinard. 1971. "The Organization Substructure of Disorderly Politics." *Social Forces* 49 (4): 529–44.

Etzioni, Amitai. 1996. *The New Golden Rule*. New York: Basic Books.

Falk, Richard. 1992. "The Rights of Peoples (in Particular Indigenous Peoples)." In *The Rights of Peoples*. James Crawford ed. Oxford: Clarendon Press.

Feinberg, Joel. 1985. *Offense to Others*. Oxford: Oxford University Press.

Feldman, Jan L. 2003. *Lubavitchers as Citizens: A Paradox of Liberal Democracy*. Ithaca: Cornell University Press.

Ferejohn, John. 2000. "Instituting Deliberative Democracy." In *Designing Democratic Institutions: NOMOS XLII*. I. Shapiro and S. Macedo eds. New York: New York University Press.

Finnis, John. 1980. *Natural Law and Natural Rights*. Oxford: Oxford University Press.

Fish, Stanley. 1999. *The Trouble with Principle*. Cambridge, Mass.: Harvard University Press.

Fishbayn, Lisa. 1999. "Litigating the Right to Culture: Family Law in the New South Africa." *International Journal of Law, Policy and the Family* 13: 147–73.

Flanagan, Tom. 2000. *First Nations? Second Thoughts*. Montreal & Kingston: McGill-Queen's University Press.

Ford v. Quebec (A.G.), [1988] 2 S.C.R. 712–89.

Fortune, Joel L. 1993. "Construing Delgamuukw: Legal Arguments, Historical Argumentation, and the Philosophy of History." *University of Toronto Faculty of Law Review* 51 (1): 80–101.

Franks, C. E. S. 2000. "Indian Policy: Canada and the United States Compared." In *Aboriginal Rights and Self-Government.* Curtis Cook and Juan Lindau eds. Montreal & Kingston: McGill-Queen's University Press.

Friedman, Marilyn. 2003. *Autonomy, Gender, Politics.* Oxford: Oxford University Press.

Frye, Marilyn. 1983. *The Politics of Reality: Essays in Feminist Theory.* New York: Crossing Press.

Fung, Archon and Erik Wright. 2001. "Deepening Democracy: Innovations in Empowered Participatory Governance." *Politics and Society* 29 (1): 5–41.

Galipeau, Claude Jean. 1992. "National Minorities, Rights and Signs: The Supreme Court and Language Legislation in Quebec." In *Democracy with Justice.* Alain G. Gagnon and A. Brian Tanguay eds. Ottawa: Carleton University Press.

Galston, William A. 1995. "Two Concepts of Liberalism." *Ethics* 105: 516–34.

— 2002. *Liberal Pluralism: The Implications of Value Pluralism for Political Theory and Practice.* Cambridge: Cambridge University Press.

Gates, Henry Louis, Jr. 1998. "The Charmer." In *The Farrakhan Factor: African-American Writers on Leadership, Nationhood, and Minister Louis Farrakhan.* Amy Alexander ed. New York: Grove Press.

Gaus, Gerald F. 1990. *Value and Justification: The Foundations of Liberal Theory.* Cambridge: Cambridge University Press.

— 1996. *Justificatory Liberalism.* New York: Oxford University Press.

George, Robert P. 1994. *Making Men Moral.* Oxford: Oxford University Press.

— ed. 1996. *Natural Law, Liberalism, and Morality.* Oxford: Oxford University Press.

George, Robert P. and Christopher Wolfe, eds. 2000. *Natural Law and Public Reason.* Washington: Georgetown University Press.

Gill, Emily R. 2001. *Becoming Free: Autonomy and Diversity in the Liberal Polity.* Lawrence, Kansas: University Press of Kansas.

Glazer, Nathan. 1978. *Affirmative Discrimination: Ethnic Inequality and Public Policy.* New York: Basic Books.

— 1981. "The United States." In *Protection of Ethnic Minorities: Comparative Perspectives.* Robert G. Wirsing ed. New York: Pergamon Press.

— 1983. *Ethnic Dilemmas.* Cambridge, Mass.: Harvard University Press.

— 1997. *We Are All Multiculturalists Now.* Cambridge, Mass.: Harvard University Press.

Glendon, Mary A. and R. F. Yanes 1991. "Structural Free Exercise." *Michigan Law Review* 90 (3): 477–550.

Goldshtain, Timna and Hadar Kleinman. 2000. *Sister Wife (Ahotishar).* Los Angeles: Seventh Art Releasing.

Goodkin, Judy and Judith Citron. 1994. *Women in the Jewish Community: Review and Recommendations.* London: Da Costa Books.

Goodstein, Laurie. 2002. "Conservative Churches Grew Fastest in 1990's, Report Says." *New York Times,* 18 September: 22.

Govender, Prakashnee. 2000. *The Status of Women Married in Terms of African Customary Law: A Study of Women's Experiences in the Eastern Cape and Western Cape Provinces [Research Report No. 13]*. Cape Town, South Africa: National Association of Democratic Lawyers.

Graham, Jessica. 2000. "Hasidic Wife Fights Back: Sues Rabbis who Branded Her Crazy." *New York Post*, 16 February: 7 and 27.

Gray, John. 1994. *Post-Liberalism: Studies in Political Thought*. New York: Routledge.

— 1995. *Enlightenment's Wake: Politics and Culture at the Close of the Modern Age*. London: Routledge.

— 1998. "Where Pluralists and Liberals Part Company." *International Journal of Philosophical Studies* 6: 17–36.

— 2000. *Two Faces of Liberalism*. New York: New York University Press.

Green, Leslie. 1994. "Internal Minorities and their Rights." In *Group Rights*. Judith Baker ed. Toronto: University of Toronto Press.

— 1995. "Internal Minorities and their Rights." In *The Rights of Minority Cultures*. Will Kymlicka ed. Oxford: Oxford University Press: 256–72.

Greenawalt, Kent. 1995. *Private Consciences and Public Reasons*. Oxford: Oxford University Press.

Greenberg, Blu. 1981. *On Women and Judaism: A View from Tradition*. Philadelphia: Jewish Publication Society.

Griffin, James. 1986. *Well-Being: Its Meaning, Measure, and Moral Importance*. Oxford: Clarendon Press.

Gutmann, Amy. 1987. *Democratic Education*. Princeton, NJ: Princeton University Press.

— ed. 1992. *Multiculturalism and "the Politics of Recognition": An Essay by Charles Taylor*. Princeton, NJ: Princeton University Press.

— ed. 1994. *Multiculturalism: Examining the Politics of Recognition*. Princeton, NJ: Princeton University Press.

— 1995. "Civic Education and Social Diversity." *Ethics* 105: 557–79.

— 1996. "Challenges of Multiculturalism in Democratic Education." In *Public Education in a Multicultural Society: Policy, Theory, Critique*. Robert K. Fullinwinder ed. New York: Cambridge University Press: 156–79.

Gutmann, Amy and Dennis Thompson. 1996. *Democracy and Disagreement*. Cambridge, Mass.: Harvard University Press.

— 2000. "The Moral Foundations of Truth Commissions." In *Truth v. Justice: The Morality of Truth Commissions*. Robert I. Rotberg and Dennis Thompson eds. Oxford: Princeton University Press.

Habermas, Jürgen. 1996. *Between Facts and Norms*. Trans. W. Regh. Cambridge, Mass.: MIT Press.

Halperin-Kaddari, Ruth. 2000. "Women, Religion and Multiculturalism in Israel." *UCLA Journal of International Law and Foreign Affairs* 5: 339–66.

Hameed, Syeda. 2000. *Voice of the Voiceless: The Status of Muslim Women in India*. New Delhi: National Commission for Women.

Hampshire, Stuart. 2000. *Justice is Conflict*. Princeton, NJ: Princeton University Press.

Hannum, Hurst. 1990. *Autonomy, Sovereignty and Self-Determination*. Philadelphia: University of Pennsylvania Press.

Hardin, Russell. 1995. *One for All: The Logic of Group Conflict*. Princeton, NJ: Princeton University Press.

Hart, H. L. A. 1963. *Law, Liberty, and Morality*. Oxford: Oxford University Press.

Hechter, Michael. 2000. *Containing Nationalism*. Oxford: Oxford University Press.

Herr, Ranjoo. 2004. "A Third World Feminist Defense of Multiculturalism." *Social Theory and Practice* 30: 73–103.

Himonga, Himonga. 1998. "Law and Gender in Southern Africa: Human Rights and Family Law." In *The Changing Family: International Perspectives*. J. Eekelaar and T. Nhlapo eds. Oxford: Hart Publications.

Hirschberg, Peter. 1998. "Figures Show Couples Ignoring Rabbinate." *The Jerusalem Report*, 17 August: 9.

Hirschman, Albert. 1970. *Exit, Voice, and Loyalty: Responses to Decline in Firms, Organizations, and States*. Cambridge, Mass.: Harvard University Press.

Hirst, Paul. 1994. *Associative Democracy*. Cambridge: Polity Press.

Hirst, Paul and V. Bader, eds. 2001. *Associative Democracy – The Real Third Way*. London, Portland: Frank Cass.

Hobbes, Thomas. [1651] 1991. *Leviathan*. Richard Tuck ed. Cambridge: Cambridge University Press. 2nd edn. 1996.

— [1662] 1680. *Considerations upon the Reputation, Loyalty, Manners, & Religions, of Thomas Hobbes of Malmesbury*. London: William Crooke.

— [1679] 1963. *Behemoth: The History of the Causes of the Civil Wars of England*. William Molesworth ed. New York: Burt Franklin.

Hoekema, André. 2001. "Reflexive Governance and Indigenous Self-rule: Lessons in Associative Democracy?" In *Associative Democracy – The Real Third Way*. Paul Hirst and Veit Bader eds. London, Portland: Frank Cass.

Hofer v. Hofer [1970] SCR 958.

Hollinger, David. 2002. "Miscegenation." Lecture in Ethno-religious Cultures, Identities and Political Philosophy, Amsterdam, 4 July.

Horowitz, Don. 1998. "Self-Determination: Politics, Philosophy and Law." In *National Self-Determination and Secession*. Margaret Moore ed. Oxford: Oxford University Press.

Howard, Rhoda. 1995. *Human Rights and the Search for Community*. Boulder, CO: Westview Press.

Inter-American Commission. 1996a. *Report on the Situation of Human Rights in Brazil*.

Inter-American Commission. 1996b. *Report on the Situation of Human Rights in Ecuador*

Inter-American Commission. 1999. *Report on the Situation of Human Rights in Colombia*.

Ivison, Duncan. 2002. *Postcolonial Liberalism*. Cambridge: Cambridge University Press.

Ivison, Duncan, Paul Patton and Will Sanders, eds. 2000. *Political Theory and the Rights of Indigenous Peoples*. Cambridge: Cambridge University Press.

Jacob, Walter. 2001. "Reform Judaism and Divorce: American Reform Responsa." In *Gender Issues in Jewish Law: Essays and Responsa*. Walter Jacob and Moshe Zemer eds. New York: Berghahn.

Janzen, William. 1990. *Limits of Liberty: The Experiences of Mennonite, Hutterite, and Doukhobour Communities in Canada*. Toronto: University of Toronto Press.

Jenkins, Craig J. 1983. "Resource Mobilization Theory and the Study of Social Movements." *Annual Review of Sociology* 9: 527–53.

Jones, Peter. 1999. "Human Rights, Group Rights and Peoples' Rights." *Human Rights Quarterly*. 21 February 1: 80–107.

Josephus. 1976. *Against Apion*. Trans. H. St. J. Thackeray. Cambridge, Mass.: Harvard University Press.

Kelley, Dean M. 1987. "The Supreme Court Redefines Tax Exemption." In *Church-State Relations*. Thomas Robbins and Roland Robertson eds. New Brunswick, NJ: Transaction Inc.

Kesselman, Jon. 1998. "Civil Rights under the Nisga'a: The Experience from Musqueam." *The Vancouver Sun*, 14 August: A23.

Kim, Nancy S. 1997. "The Cultural Defence and the Problems of Cultural Pre-emption: A Framework for Analysis." *New Mexico Law Review* 27: 101–39.

King, Martin Luther, Jr. 1963. *Why We Can't Wait*. New York: New American Library.

Kingsbury, Benedict. 1992. "Claims by Non-state Groups in International Law." *Cornell International Law Journal* 25: 482–513.

— 2001. "Reconciling Five Competing Conceptual Structures of Indigenous Peoples: Claims in International and Comparative Law." In *Peoples' Rights*. Philip Alston ed. Oxford: Oxford University Press.

Kishwar, Madhu. 1986. "Pro-women or Anti-Muslim? The Shahbano Controversy." *Manushi* 32: 4–13.

Knight, Jack and James Johnson. 1997. "What Sort of Political Equality does Deliberative Democracy Require?" In *Deliberative Democracy: Essays on Reason and Politics*. James Bohman and W. Rehg eds. Cambridge and London: MIT Press.

Korematsu v. United States, 323 US 214 (1944).

Kukathas, Chandran. 1992a. "Are There Any Cultural Rights?" *Political Theory* 20: 105–30.

— 1992b. "Cultural Rights Again: A Rejoinder." *Political Theory* 20 (4): 674–80.

— 1997. "Cultural Toleration." In *Ethnicity and Group Rights: Nomos XXXIX*. Ian Shapiro and Will Kymlicka eds. New York: New York University Press.

— 1998. "Liberalism and Multiculturalism: The Politics of Indifference." *Political Theory* 26: 686–99.

— 2001. "Is Feminism Bad for Multiculturalism?" *Public Affairs Quarterly* 5 (2): 83–98.

— 2002. "The Life of Brian, or Now for Something Completely Difference-Blind." In *Multiculturalism Reconsidered: Culture and Equality and its Critics*. Paul Kelly ed. Cambridge: Polity.

— 2003. *The Liberal Archipelago: A Theory of Diversity and Freedom*. Oxford: Oxford University Press.

Kymlicka, Will. 1989a. *Liberalism, Community and Culture*. Oxford: Oxford University Press.

— 1989b. "Liberal Individualism and Liberal Neutrality." *Ethics* 99: 883–905.

— 1992. "Two Models of Pluralism and Tolerance." *Analyse & Kritik* 13: 33–56.

— 1995. *Multicultural Citizenship: A Liberal Theory of Minority Rights*. Oxford: Oxford University Press.

— 1999. "Liberal Complacencies." In *Is Multiculturalism Bad for Women?* Joshua Cohen, Mathew Howard and Martha Nussbaum eds. Princeton NJ: Princeton University Press.

— 2001. *Politics in the Vernacular: Nationalism, Multiculturalism and Citizenship*. Oxford: Oxford University Press.

— 2002. *Contemporary Political Philosophy*. Oxford: Oxford University Press.

Kymlicka, Will and Wayne Norman, eds. 2000. *Citizenship in Diverse Societies*. Oxford: Oxford University Press.

Kymlicka, Will and A. Patten, eds. 2003. *Language Rights and Political Theory*. Oxford, New York: Oxford University Press.

LaFramboise, T., H. L. K. Coleman and J. Gerton. 1993. "Psychological Impact of Biculturalism: Evidence and Theory." *Psychological Bulletin* 114 (3): 395–412.

Laitin, David D. 1990. *Identity in Formation. The Russian-Speaking Populations in the Near Abroad*. Ithaca and London: Cornell University Press. 2nd edn. 1998.

— 1999. "Identity Choice Under Conditions of Uncertainty." In *Competition and Cooperation: Conversations with Nobelists about Economics and Political Science*. James E. Alt, Margaret Levi and Elinor Ostrom eds. New York: Russell Sage.

Lansman v. Finland, Communication No. 511/1992 and *Lansman et al. v. Finland*, Communication No. 671/1995, UN Doc. CCPR/C/58/D/671/1995 (1996).

Laponce, Jean. 1984. *Langue et Territoire*. Quebec: Presses Universitaires de Laval.

— 1993. "The Case for Ethnic Federalism in Multilingual Societies: Canada's Regional Imperative." *Regional Politics and Policy* 1: 23–43.

Larmore, Charles. 1987. *Patterns of Moral Complexity*. New York: Cambridge University Press.

— 1990. "Political Liberalism." *Political Theory* 18: 339–60.

— 1996. *The Morals of Modernity*. New York: Cambridge University Press.

Lee, Martha F. 1996. *The Nation of Islam: An American Millenarian Movement*. Syracuse, NY: Syracuse University Press.

Lee, Ronald. 2001. "The Rom-Vlach Gypsies and the Kris-Romani." In *Gypsy Law: Romani Legal Traditions and Culture*. Walter O. Weyrich ed. Berkeley: California University Press.

Lerner, Natan. 1991. *Group Rights and Discrimination in International Law*. Dordrecht: Martin Nijhoff Publishers.

Levey, Geoffrey Brahm. 1997. "Equality, Autonomy, and Cultural Rights." *Political Theory* 25 (2): 215–48.

Levinson, Meira. 1999. *The Demands of Liberal Education*. New York: Oxford University Press.

— 2003. "Minority Participation and Civic Education in Deliberative Democracies." In *Forms of Justice: Critical Perspectives on David Miller's Political Philosophy*. A. De-Shalit and D. A. Bell eds. Lanham, MD: Rowman and Littlefield.

Levy, Jacob. 2000. *The Multiculturalism of Fear*. Oxford: Oxford University Press.

Lieb, Michael. 1998. *Children of Ezekiel*. Durham, NC: Duke University Press.

Locke, John. [1689] 1955. *A Letter Concerning Toleration*. Patrick Romanell ed. Indianapolis: Bobbs-Merrill.

— [1689] *A Letter Concerning Toleration*. London: Awnsham Churchill.

— [1689] 1983. *A Letter Concerning Toleration*. Indianapolis: Hackett.

— [1695] 1999. *The Reasonableness of Christianity: As Delivered in the Scriptures*. John C. Higgins-Biddle ed. Oxford: Clarendon Press.

Lord Scarman. 1987. "Toleration and the Law." In *On Toleration*. Susan Mendus and David Edwards eds. Oxford: Oxford University Press.

Lukes, Steven. 1974. *Power: A Radical View*. New York: Macmillan.

— 1989. "Making Sense of Moral Conflict." In *Liberalism and the Moral Life*. Nancy L. Rosenblum ed. Cambridge, Mass.: Harvard University Press.

Maaka, Roger and Augie Fleras. 2000. "Engaging with Indigeneity: Tino Rangatiratanga in Aotearoa." In *Political Theory and the Rights of Indigenous Peoples*. Duncan Ivison, Paul Patton and Will Sanders eds. Cambridge: Cambridge University Press.

Macedo, Stephen. 1990. *Liberal Virtues: Citizenship, Virtue, and Community in Liberal Constitutionalism*. Oxford: Clarendon Press.

— 1995a. "Liberal Civic Education and Religious Fundamentalism: The Case of God vs. John Rawls." *Ethics* 105: 468–96.

— 1995b. "Homosexuality and the Conservative Mind." *Georgetown Law Review* 84: 261–300.

— 2000. *Diversity and Distrust: Civic Education in a Multicultural Democracy*. Cambridge, Mass.: Harvard University Press.

MacIntyre, Alasdair. 1984. *After Virtue*. 2nd edn. Notre Dame: University of Notre Dame Press.

MacKinnon, Catharine. 1989. *Towards a Feminist Theory of the State*. Cambridge, Mass.: Harvard University Press.

Magnet, J. E. 1986. "Collective Rights, Cultural Autonomy and the Canadian State." *McGill Law Journal* 32: 170–86.

Mahajan, Gurpreet. 1998. *Identities and Rights: Aspects of Liberal Democracy in India*. New Delhi: Oxford University Press.

Mahmood, Tahir. 1995. *Statute-law Relating to Muslims in India: A Study in Constitutional and Islamic Perspectives*. New Delhi: Institute of Objective Studies.

Malinowitz, Chaim. 1994. "The New York State Get Bill and its Halachic Ramifications." *Journal of Halacha and Contemporary Problems* 27 (5): 5–25.

Manuto, Ron. 1992. "The Life and Death of Rajneeshpuram and the Still Lingering Dilemma of the Religious Clauses of the First Amendment." *Free Speech Yearbook* 30: 26–39.

Margalit, Avishai and Moshe Halbertal. 1994. "Liberalism and the Right to Culture." *Social Research* 61 (3): 491–510.

Margalit, Avishai and Joseph Raz. 1990. "National Self-Determination." *Journal of Philosophy* 87: 439–61.

Mason, Andrew. 2000. *Community, Solidarity and Belonging: Levels of Community and their Normative Significance*. Cambridge: Cambridge University Press.

McConnell, Michael. 1992. "Accommodation of Religion." *George Washington Law Review* 60 (3): 685–742.

— 2001. "Old Liberalism, New Liberalism, and People of Faith." In *Christian Perspectives on Legal Thought*. Michael W. McConnell, Robert F. Cochran, Jr. and Angela C. Carmella eds. New Haven: Yale University Press.

McDonald, Michael. 1991. "Should Communities Have Rights? Reflections on Liberal Individualism." *Journal of Law and Jurisprudence* 4 (2): 217–37.

McGarry, John and Brendan O'Leary. 1993. *The Politics of Ethnic Conflict Regulation*. London: Routledge.

McLaren, John and Harold Coward, eds. 1999. *Religious Conscience, the State, and the Law*. Albany: SUNY Press.

McRanor, Shauna. 1997. "Maintaining the Reliability of Aboriginal Oral Records and their Material Manifestations: Implications for Archival Practice." *Archivaria* 43: 64–88.

Mendus, Susan. 1987. "Introduction." In *On Toleration*. Susan Mendus and David Edwards eds. Oxford: Clarendon Press.

— 1989. *Toleration and the Limits of Liberalism*. Basingstoke: Macmillan.

Mendus, Susan and David Edwards, eds. 1987. *On Toleration*. Oxford: Oxford University Press.

Menski, Werner. 1999. "South Asian Women in Britain, Family Integrity and the Primary Purpose Rule." In *Ethnicity, Gender and Social Change*. Rohit Barot, Harriet Bradley and Steve Fenton eds. Basingstoke: Macmillan and New York: St. Martin's Press.

Michel, Lou and Dan Herbeck. 2001. *American Terrorist: Timothy McVeigh and the Oklahoma City Bombing*. New York: Regan Books.

Mill, John Stuart. [1859] 1991. *On Liberty and Other Essays*. John Gray ed. Oxford: Oxford University Press.

— 1993. "On Liberty." In *On Liberty, Utilitarianism, On Representative Government*. London: J. M. Dent.

Minow, Martha. 2002. *Breaking the Cycles of Hatred: Memory, Law and Repair*. Princeton, NJ: Princeton University Press.

Mizrahi, Giti. 1992. *A Review of the Effectiveness of the Get Provision of the Divorce Act*. Department of Justice, Canada.

Modood, Tariq, Richard Berthoud et al. 1997. *Ethnic Minorities in Britain: Diversity and Disadvantage. Fourth National Survey of Ethnic Minorities*. London: Policy Studies Institute.

Moghissi, Haideh. 1999. "Away from Home: Iranian Women, Displacement, Cultural Resistance and Change." *Journal of Comparative Family Studies* 30: 207–17.

Monsma, Stephen and Christopher Soper. 1997. *The Challenge of Pluralism: Church and State in Five Democracies*. Lanham, New York: Rowman & Littlefield.

Montagu, Rachel. 2001. *Marriage*. Available from http://www.reformjudaism.org.uk/rsgbartman/publish/article_38.shtml.

Moore, Margaret. 2001. *The Ethics of Nationalism*. Oxford: Oxford University Press.

— 2003. "An Historical Argument for Indigenous Self-Determination." In *Secession and Self-Determination: NOMOS XLV*. Allen Buchanan and Stephen Macedo eds. New York: New York University Press, 151–205.

Morgan, Edmund. 1966. *The Puritan Family: Religion and Domestic Relations in Seventeenth-Century New England*. New York: Harper & Row.

Morgan, Kathryn. 1991. "Women and the Knife: Cosmetic Surgery and the Colonization of Women's Bodies." *Hypatia* 6 (3): 25–53.

Morton, F. L. 1985. "Group Rights versus Individual Rights in the Charter: The Special Cases of Natives and the Québécois." In *Minorities and the Canadian State*. Neil Nevitte and Alan Kornberg eds. Oakville: Mosaic Press.

Moss, Wendy. 1995. "Inuit Perspectives on Treaty Rights and Governance." *Aboriginal Self-Government: Legal and Constitutional Issues, Royal Commission on Aboriginal Peoples*. Ottawa: Canada Communications Group.

Mozert v. Hawkins County Board of Education 827 F. 2d 1058 (1987).

Mthembu v. Letsela and Another [1997] S. Africa.

Mulhall, Stephen and Adam Swift. 1996. *Liberals and Communitarians*. 2nd edn. Oxford: Blackwell.

Muslim Women's (Protection of Rights on Divorce) Act. 1986. India.

Narayan, Uma. 1998. "Essence of Culture and a Sense of History: A Feminist Critique of Cultural Essentialism." *Hypatia* 13 (2): 86–106.

— 2000. "Undoing the 'Package Picture' of Cultures." *Signs* 25 (4): 1083–6.

— 2002. "Minds of their Own: Choices, Autonomy, Cultural Practices and Other Women." In *A Mind of One's Own: Feminist Essays on Reason and Objectivity*. 2nd edn. L. Antony and C. Witt eds. Boulder: Westview Press.

Nation of Islam. 1991. *The Secret Relationship Between Blacks and Jews, Vol. I*. Chicago: Historical Research Department.

Navarro, Marysa. 1989. "The Personal is Political: Las Madres de Plaza de Mayo." In *Power and Popular Protest*. Susan Eckstein ed. Berkeley: California University Press.

Newey, Glen. 1999. *Virtue, Reason, and Toleration*. Edinburgh: Edinburgh University Press.

Nickel, James. 1997. "Group Agency and Group Rights." In *Ethnicity and Group Rights: Nomos XXXIX*. I. Shapiro and W. Kymlicka eds. New York: New York University Press.

Nimer, Mohamed. 2001. *The Status of Muslim Civil Rights in the United States: 2001*. Washington, DC: Council on American-Islamic Relations. Available at http://www.cairnet.org/civilrights/2001_Civil_Rights_Report.pdf

Norris, Pippa. 1999. "Conclusions: The Growth of Critical Citizens and its Consequences." In *Critical Citizens: Global Support for Democratic Governance*. Pippa Norris ed. Oxford: Oxford University Press.

Nussbaum, Martha C. 1997. "Religion and Women's Rights." In *Religion and Contemporary Liberalism*. P. Weithman ed. Notre Dame: University of Notre Dame Press.

— 1999. *Sex and Social Justice*. Oxford: Oxford University Press.

— 2000. "Religion and Women's Equality: The Case of India." In *Obligations of Citizenship and Demands of Faith: Religious Accommodation in Pluralist Democracies*. Nancy Rosenblum ed. Princeton, NJ: Princeton University Press.

— 2001. *Women and Human Development: The Capabilities Approach*. Cambridge: Cambridge University Press.

O'Neill, Onora. 2000. *Bounds of Justice*. Cambridge: Cambridge University Press.

O'Neill, Shane. 2000. "Cultural Freedom and the Right of Self-expression: Contentious Parades in Northern Ireland." Paper presented at IPSA XVIII World Congress Meeting, Quebec City, August.

Okin, Susan Moller. 1989. *Justice, Gender, and the Family*. New York: Basic Books.

—— 1997. "Is Multiculturalism Bad for Women? When Minority Cultures Win Group Rights, Women Lose Out." *Boston Review* 22: 2–28.

—— 1998. "Feminism and Multiculturalism: Some Tensions." *Ethics* 108 (4): 661–84.

—— 1999a. "Is Multiculturalism Bad for Women?" In *Is Multiculturalism Bad for Women?* Joshua Cohen, Matthew Howard and Martha C. Nussbaum eds. Princeton, NJ: Princeton University Press.

—— 1999b. "Response." In *Is Multiculturalism Bad for Women?* Joshua Cohen, Matthew Howard and Martha C. Nussbaum eds. Princeton, NJ: Princeton University Press.

—— 2002. "Mistresses of their Own Destiny: Group Rights, Gender, and Realistic Rights of Exit." *Ethics* 112 (2): 205–30.

—— Forthcoming. "Is Multiculturalism Bad for Women? Continuing the Conversation." In *Feminism, Multiculturalism and Group Rights*. Deen Chatterjee ed. Oxford: Oxford University Press.

Oldfield, Duane Murray. 1996. *The Right and the Righteous: The Christian Right Confronts the Republican Party*. New York: Rowman & Littlefield.

Olsen, Laurie. 1997. *Made in America: Immigrant Students in Our Public Schools*. New York: New Press.

Parekh, Bhikhu. 1994. "Cultural Diversity and Liberal Democracy." In *Defining and Measuring Democracy*. David Beetham ed. London: Sage Publications.

—— 2000. *Rethinking Multiculturalism: Cultural Diversity and Political Theory*. Cambridge, Mass.: Harvard University Press.

Parry, Geraint, George Moyser and Neil Day. 1992. *Political Participation and Democracy in Britain*. Cambridge: Cambridge University Press.

Pateman, Carole. 1998. *The Sexual Contract*. Cambridge: Polity Press.

Pathak, Zakia and Rajeswari Sunder Rajan. 1989. "Shahbano." *Signs* 14 (3): 558–82.

Patten, Alan. 2001. "Political Theory and Language Policy." *Political Theory* 29 (5): 691–715.

—— 2003a. "Liberal Neutrality and Language Policy." *Philosophy and Public Affairs* 31 (4): 356–86.

—— 2003b. "What Kind of Bilingualism?" In *Language Rights and Political Theory*. Will Kymlicka and Alan Patten eds. Oxford: Oxford University Press.

Patten, Alan and Will Kymlicka. 2003. "Introduction: Language Rights and Political Theory: Contexts, Issues and Approaches." In *Language Rights and Political Theory*. Will Kymlicka and Alan Patten eds. Oxford: Oxford University Press.

PBS.org. *Six Billion and Beyond, Italy: Women's Status*. 2003. Available at http://www.pbs.org/sixbillion/italy/it-status.html.

People v. Chen (Supreme Court, NY County, 2 Dec. 1988).

Perez, Nahshon. 2002. "Should Multiculturalists Oppress the Oppressed?" *Critical Review of International Social and Political Philosophy* 5 (3): 51–79.

Pfeffer, Leo. 1987. "Religious Exemptions." In *Church–State Relations*. Thomas Robbins and Roland Robertson eds. New Brunswick: Transaction Inc.

Phillips, Anne.1995. "Democracy and Difference: Some Problems for Feminist Theory." In *The Rights of Minority Cultures*. W. Kymlicka ed. Oxford: Oxford University Press.

— 2002. "Multiculturalism, Universalism and the Claims of Democracy." In *Gender Justice Development and Rights*. Maxine Molyneux and Shahra Razavi eds. Oxford: Oxford University Press.

— 2003. "When Culture Means Gender: Issues of Cultural Defence in the English Courts." *Modern Law Review* 66: 510–31.

Phillips, Anne and Dustin, Moira. 2004. "UK Initiatives on Forced Marriage: Regulation, Dialogue and Exit." *Political Studies* 52: 531–51.

Pipes, Daniel. 2003. "The Enemy Within." *New York Post*, 4 Jan. Available at http://www.danielpipes.org/article/1009.

Ponting, J. and R. Gibbons eds. 1980. *Out of Irrelevance: A Socio-political Introduction to Indian Affairs in Canada*. Toronto: Butterworths.

Posner, Richard. 1992. *Sex and Reason*. Cambridge, Mass.: Harvard University Press.

Povinelli, Elizabeth. 2002. *The Cunning of Recognition: Indigenous Alterities and the Making of Australian Multiculturalism*. Durham: Duke University Press.

Pritchard, Sara. 2001. *Setting International Standards: An Analysis of the United Nations Declaration on the Rights of Indigenous Peoples and the First Six Sessions of the Commission on Human Rights Working Group*. 3rd edn (2001) at IV.A, "Indigenous Perspectives," http://arena.org.nz/unindigp.htm.

Prucha, Francis Paul. 1981. *Indian Policy in the United States: An Historical Essay*. Lincoln: University of Nebraska Press.

Putnam, Robert D. ed. 2002. *Democracies in Flux: The Evolution of Social Capital in Contemporary Society*. New York: Oxford University Press.

Quong, Jonathan. 2002. "Are Identity Claims Bad for Deliberative Democracy?" *Contemporary Political Theory* 1 (3): 307–28.

Raday, Frances. 1996. "Religion, Multiculturalism and Equality: The Israeli Case." *Israel Yearbook on Human Rights* 25: 193–241.

Rawls, John. 1993. *Political Liberalism*. New York: Columbia University Press.

— 1996. *Political Liberalism*. Paperback edition. New York: Columbia University Press.

— 1999a. *The Law of Peoples*. Cambridge, Mass.: Harvard University Press.

— 1999b. "The Idea of Public Reason Revisited." In *Collected Papers*. Samuel Freeman ed. Cambridge, Mass.: Harvard University Press.

Raz, Joseph. 1986. *The Morality of Freedom*. Oxford: Clarendon Press.

— 1988. "Autonomy, Toleration, and the Harm Principle." In *Justifying Toleration*. Susan Mendus and David Edwards eds. Cambridge: Cambridge University Press.

— 1994. *Ethics in the Public Domain: Essays in the Morality of Law and Politics*. Oxford: Clarendon Press.

Raz, Joseph and Avishai Margalit. 1994. "National Self-Determination." In Joseph Raz, *Ethics in the Public Domain: Essays in the Morality of Law and Politics*. Oxford: Clarendon Press.

Razack, Sherene. 1994. "What is to be Gained from Looking at White People in the Eye? Culture, Race, and Gender in Cases of Sexual Violence." *Signs* 19: 894–923.

Reed, Ralph. 1996. *Active Faith: How Christians are Changing the Soul of American Politics*. New York: Free Press.

Reference re Secession of Quebec [1998] 2 SCR 217.

Reich, Rob. 2002. *Bridging Liberalism and Multiculturalism in American Education*. Chicago: Chicago University Press.

Reitman, Oonagh. Forthcoming. "Multiculturalism and Feminism: Shifting Perspectives." *Ethnicities*.

Report of the Working Group Established in Accordance with Commission on Human Rights Resolution 1995/32, 1995.

Reynolds v. United States 98 US 145 (1878).

Robbins, Thomas. 1987. "Church–State Tensions and Marginal Movements." In *Church–State Relations*. Thomas Robbins and Roland Robertson eds. New Brunswick: Transaction Inc.

Rosenblum, Nancy L. 1985. "The Rule of Law in Residential Associations." *Harvard Law Review* 99: 472 490.

— 1998. *Membership and Morals: The Personal Uses of Pluralism in America*. Princeton: Princeton University Press.

— ed. 2000a. *Obligations of Citizenship and Demands of Faith*. Princeton, NJ: Princeton University Press.

— 2000b. "Introduction: Pluralism, Integralism, and Political Theories of Religious Accommodation." In *Obligations of Citizenship and Demands of Faith*. Nancy Rosenblum ed. Princeton, NJ: Princeton University Press.

— 2000c. "*Amos*: Religious Automony and the Moral Uses of Pluralism." In *Obligations of Citizenship and Demands of Faith*. Nancy Rosenblum ed. Princeton, NJ: Princeton University Press.

— 2003. "Institutionalizing Religion: Religious Parties and Political Identity in Contemporary Democracies." *Ethical Theory and Moral Practice* 6: 23–54.

Royal Commission on Aboriginal Peoples. 1994. *The High Arctic Relocation. A Report on the 1953–55 Relocation*. Ottawa: Ministry of Supply and Services.

Runnymede Trust. 1997. *Islamophobia: A Challenge for Us All*. London: Runnymede Trust.

Rutten, Susan. 1988. *Moslims in de Nederlandse Rechtspraak*. Kampen: Kok.

Saharso, Sawitri. 2000. "Female Autonomy and Cultural Imperative: Two Hearts Beating Together." In *Citizenship in Diverse Societies*. Will Kymlicka and Wayne Norman eds. Oxford: Oxford University Press.

Samad, Yunas and John Eade. 2002. *Community Perceptions of Forced Marriage*. UK: Foreign and Commonwealth Office. Available at www.fco.gov.uk.

Samuels, Alex. 1981. "Legal Recognition and Protection of Minority Customs in a Plural Society in England." *Anglo-American Law Review* 10 (4): 241–56.

Sandel, Michael. 1990. "Freedom of Conscience or Freedom of Choice?" In *Articles of Faith, Articles of Peace*. James Hunter and Os Guinness eds. Washington DC: Brookings Institute.

— 1996. *Democracy's Discontent: America in Search of a Public Philosophy*. Cambridge, Mass.: Harvard University Press.

Sanders, Jaime M. W. 1985. "Religious Community as a City: The Oregon Constitutional Puzzle of *State of Oregon v. City of Rajneeshpuram*." *Willamette Law Review* 21: 707–65.

Sanders, Lynn. 1997. "Against Deliberation." *Political Theory* 25 (3): 347–76.

Santa Clara Pueblo v. Julia Martinez 56 Ed 2nd 106 (1978).

Scanlon, T. M. 1996. "The Difficulty of Tolerance." In *Toleration: An Elusive Virtue*. David Heyd ed. Princeton, NJ: Princeton University Press.

Schaefer, Axel R. 1999. "Evangelicalism, Social Reform and the US Welfare State, 1970–1996." In *Religious and Secular Reform in America: Ideas, Beliefs, and Social Change*. David K. Adams and Cornelis A. van Minnen eds. New York: New York University Press: 249–73.

Schemo, Jean. 2003. "Electronic Tracking System Monitors Foreign Students." *New York Times*, 17 Feb.: A11.

Schlesinger, M. Jr. 1992. *The Disuniting of America*. New York: Norton.

Schmool, Marlena and Stephen Miller. 1994. *Women in the Jewish Community: Survey Report*. London: Da Costa Books.

Schwartz, Alan M., ed. 1996. *Danger: Extremism – The Major Vehicles and Voices on America's Far Right Fringe*. New York: ADL Publications.

Scott, James. 1995. "State Simplifications: Nature, Space and People." *Journal of Political Philosophy*, 3: 1–42.

Selznick, Phillip. 1992. *The Moral Commonwealth*. California: California University Press.

Sen, Amartya. 1998. *Reason before Identity*. The Romanes Lecture. Oxford: Oxford University Press.

Shachar, Ayelet. 1998a. "Group Identity and Women's Rights in Family Law: The Perils of Multicultural Accommodation." *Journal of Political Philosophy* 6: 285–305.

— 1998b. "Reshaping the Multicultural Model: Group Accommodation and Individual Rights." *Windsor Review of Legal and Social Issues* 8: 83–111.

— 1999. "The Paradox of Multicultural Vulnerability: Identity Groups, the State and Individual Rights." In *Multicultural Questions*. Christian Joppke and Steven Lukes eds. Oxford: Oxford University Press.

— 2000a. "On Citizenship and Multicultural Vulnerability." *Political Theory* 28 (1): 64–89.

— 2000b. "The Puzzle of Interlocking Power Hierarchies: Sharing the Pieces of Jurisdictional Authority." *Harvard Civil Rights–Civil Liberties Law Review* 35: 385–426.

— 2000c. "Should Church and State be Joined at the Altar?" In *Citizenship in Diverse Societies*. Will Kymlicka and Wayne Norman eds. Oxford: Oxford University Press.

— 2001. *Multicultural Jurisdictions: Cultural Differences and Women's Rights*. Cambridge: Cambridge University Press.

Shah-Kazemi, Sonia Nûrîn. 2001. *Untying the Knot: Muslim Women, Divorce and the Shariah*. London: Nuffield Foundation.

Shapiro, Ian. 1999. *Democratic Justice*. New Haven and London: Yale University Press.

Shaw, Malcolm. 1997. *International Law*. 4th edn. Cambridge: Cambridge University Press.

Sheleff, Leon. 2000. *The Future of Tradition: Customary Law, Common Law and Legal Pluralism*. London, Portland: Frank Cass.

Shenhav, Sharon. 1998. "A View from Israel." In International Council of Jewish Women, *Halachic Solutions to the Problems of Agunot*. Proceedings of a meeting held in London, 13 November. London: ICJW.

Shklar, Judith N. 1989. "The Liberalism of Fear." In *Liberalism and the Moral Life*. Nancy Rosenblum ed. Cambridge, Mass.: Harvard University Press.

— 1990. *The Faces of Injustices*. New Haven: Yale University Press.

— 1998a. "Obligation, Loyalty, Exile." In *Political Thought and Political Thinkers*. Stanley Hoffman ed. Chicago: Chicago University Press.

— 1998b. "The Bonds of Exile." In *Political Thought and Political Thinkers*. Stanley Hoffman ed. Chicago: Chicago University Press.

— 1998c. "The Liberalism of Fear." In *Political Thought and Political Thinkers*. Stanley Hoffman ed. Chicago: Chicago University Press.

Siame, Chisanga N. 2000. "Two Concepts of Liberty Through African Eyes." *Journal of Political Philosophy* 8 (1): 53–67.

Skorupski, John. 1999. "Irrealist Cognitivism." *Ratio* 12: 436–59.

Snyder, Jack. 2000. *Voting and Violence: Democratization and Nationalist Conflict*. New York: W. W. Norton & Co.

Song, Sarah. 2002. "Majority Norms and Minority Practices: Reexamining the Cultural Defense in American Criminal Law." Paper presented at the Meetings of the American Political Science Association, Boston, Mass.: August.

Southall Black Sisters. 2001. *Forced Marriage: An Abuse of Human Rights. One Year After "A Choice by Right."* London: Southall Black Sisters.

Special Marriage Act No. 43 of 1954, Parliament in the Fifth Year of the Republic of India.

Spinner, Jeff. 1994. *The Boundaries of Citizenship: Race, Ethnicity and Nationality in the Liberal State*. Baltimore: Johns Hopkins University Press.

Spinner-Halev, Jeff. 2000. *Surviving Diversity: Religion and Democratic Citizenship*. Baltimore: John Hopkins University Press.

— 2001. "Feminism, Multiculturalism, Oppression, and the State." *Ethics* 112 (1): 84–113.

Spinner-Halev, Jeff and Elizabeth Theiss-Morse. 2003. "National Identity and Self-esteem." *Perspectives on Politics* 1 (3): 515–32.

Stewart, John. 1996. "Democracy and Local Government." In *Reinventing Democracy*. P. Hirst and S. Khilnani eds. Oxford: Blackwell.

Sullivan, Andrew. 1995. *Virtually Normal: An Argument about Homosexuality*. New York: Vintage Books.

— 1998. *Love Undetectable*. New York: Knopf.

Sunder Rajan, Rajeswari. 2003. *The Scandal of the State: Women, Law and Citizenship in Postcolonial India*. Durham, NC: Duke University Press.

Sunstein, Cass. 1999. "Should Sex Equality Law Apply to Religious Institutions?" In *Is Multiculturalism Bad for Women?* Joshua Cohen, Matthew Howard and Martha C. Nussbaum eds. Princeton, NJ: Princeton University Press.

Svensson, Frances. 1979. "Liberal Democracy and Group Rights: The Legacy of Individualism and its Impact on American Indian Tribes." *Political Studies*, 27: 421–39.

Swaine, Lucas. 1999. "Theocratic Community and the Liberty of Conscience." Unpublished manuscript.

— 2001. "How Ought Liberal Democracies to Treat Theocratic Communities?" *Ethics* 111: 302–43.

— 2003a. "Institutions of Conscience: Politics and Principle in a World of Religious Pluralism." *Ethical Theory and Moral Practice* 6 (1): 93–118.

— 2003b. "Religious Pluralism and the Liberty of Conscience." In *Pluralism without Relativism: Remembering Sir Isaiah Berlin*. João Carlos Espada, Marc F. Plattner and Adam Wolfson eds. Lanham, MD: Lexington Books.

Syrtash, John Tibor. 1992. *Religion and Culture in Canadian Family Law*. Toronto: Butterworths.

Tamir, Yael. 1993. *Liberal Nationalism*. Princeton, NJ: Princeton University Press.

— 1996. "Hands off Clitoridectomy." *Boston Review* 21 (3): 21–2.

— 2000. "Remember the Amalek: Religious Hate Speech." In *Obligations of Citizenship and Demands of Faith*. Nancy Rosenblum ed. Princeton, NJ: Princeton University Press.

Taylor, Charles. 1992. "The Politics of Recognition." In *Multiculturalism and "The Politics of Recognition": An Essay by Charles Taylor*. Amy Gutmann ed. Princeton, NJ: Princeton University Press.

— 1994. "The Politics of Recognition." In *Multiculturalism: Examining the Politics of Recogntion*. Amy Gutmann ed. Princeton, NJ: Princeton University Press.

Teixeira, Ruy. 1992. *The Disappearing American Voter*. Washington DC: Brookings Institution.

Thomas v. Norris, [1992] 2 *Canadian Native Law Reporter* BCSC, 139–63.

Tilly, Charles. 1987. *From Mobilization to Revolution*. New York: Random House.

Toman, Jiri. 1999. "Quasi-legal Standards and Guidelines for Protecting Human Rights." In *Guide to International Human Rights Practice*, 3rd edn. Hurst Hannum ed. New York: Transnational Publishers.

Tomasi, John. 2001. *Liberalism Beyond Justice*. Princeton, NJ: Princeton University Press.

Trudeau, Pierre Elliot. 1992. *Trudeau: A Mess that Deserves a Big NO*. Toronto: Robert Davies Publishing.

Tully, James. 1995. *Strange Multiciplicity: Constitutionalism in an Age of Diversity*. Cambridge: Cambridge University Press.

— Forthcoming. "Exclusion and Assimilation." In *Political Exclusion and Domination: NOMOS XLVI*. Melissa Williams and Stephen Macedo eds. New York: New York University Press.

Turpel, Mary Ellen. 1989–90. "Aboriginal Peoples and the Canadian Charter: Interpretive Monopolies, Cultural Differences." *Canadian Human Rights Yearbook* 6: 3–45.

United Nations, 1970. *Declaration on the Principles of International Law Concerning Friendly Relations and Cooperation among States in Accordance with the Charter of the United Nations, General Assembly resolution 2625,* 24 Oct.

Utter, Glenn H. and John W. Storey. 1995. *The Religious Right.* Santa Barbara: ABC-CLIO.

Van Parijs, Philippe. 2000. "Must Europe be Belgian? On Democratic Citizenship in Multilingual Polities." In *The Demands of Citizenship.* Iain Hampsher-Monk and Catriona McKinnon eds. London: Continuum.

Verba, Sidney, Kay Lehman Schlozman and Henry E. Brady. 1995. *Voice and Equality: Civic Voluntarism in American Politics.* Cambridge, Mass.: Harvard University Press.

Vertovec, Steven. 1999. "Minority Organizations, Networks and Public Policies." *Journal of Ethnic and Migration Studies* 25 (1): 21–42.

Volpp, Leti. 1994. "(M)isidentifying Culture: Asian Women and the 'Cultural Defense'." *Harvard Women's Law Journal* 17: 57–101.

— 2000. "Blaming Culture for Bad Behaviour." *Yale Journal of Law and the Humanities,* 12: 89–116.

Waldron, Jeremy. 1989. "Rights in Conflict." *Ethics* 99: 503–19.

— 1992. "Minority Cultures and the Cosmopolitan Alternative." *University of Michigan Journal of Law Reform* 25 (3): 751–93.

— 1996. "Multiculturalism and Mélange." In *Public Education in a Multicultural Society.* Robert K. Fullinwider ed. Cambridge: Cambridge University Press: 90–118.

— 2000. "Cultural Identity and Civic Responsibility." In *Citizenship in Diverse Societies.* Will Kymlicka and Wayne Norman eds. Oxford: Oxford University Press.

— 2003. "Teaching Multicultural Right." In *Citizenship and Education in Liberal-Democratic Societies.* Kevin McDonough and Walter Feinberg eds. Oxford: Oxford University Press: 21–55.

Walzer, Michael. 1983. *Spheres of Justice: A Defense of Pluralism and Equality.* Oxford: Blackwell.

— 1994. "Comment." In *Multiculturalism: Examining the Politics of Recognition.* Amy Gutmann ed. Princeton, NJ: Princeton University Press.

— 1997. *On Toleration.* New Haven: Yale University Press.

Warren, Mark. 2001. *Democracy and Association.* Princeton, NJ: Princeton University Press.

Weinstock, Daniel. 2003. "The Antimony of Language Policy." In *Language Rights and Political Theory.* Will Kymlicka and Alan Patten eds. Oxford: Oxford University Press.

Williams, Bernard. 1977. *Moral Luck.* Cambridge: Cambridge University Press.

Williams, Melissa. 1995. "Justice Toward Groups: Political not Juridical." *Political Theory* 23 (1): 67–91.

— 1998. *Voice, Trust and Memory. Marginalized Groups and the Failings of Liberal Representation.* Princeton, NJ: Princeton University Press.

— 2000. "The Uneasy Alliance of Group Representation and Deliberative Democracy." In *Citizenship in Diverse Societies*. Will Kymlicka and Wayne Norman eds. Oxford: Oxford University Press.

Williams, Robert. 1990. *The American Indian in Western Legal Thought*. New York: Oxford University Press.

Wisconsin v. Yoder 406 US 205 (1972).

Working Group on Forced Marriage. 2000. *A Choice by Right*. London: Home Office Communications Directorate.

Young, Iris Marion. 1990. *Justice and the Politics of Difference*. Princeton, NJ: Princeton University Press.

— 2000. *Inclusion and Democracy*. Oxford: Oxford University Press.

Yuval-Davis, Nira. 1992. "Fundamentalism, Multiculturalism and Women in Britain." In *"Race", Culture and Difference*. James Donald and Ali Rattansi eds. London: Sage.

— 1997. *Gender and Nation*. London: Sage.

Zornberg, Lisa. 1995. "Beyond the Constitution: Is the New York Get Legislation Good Law?" *Pace Law Review* 15: 703–84.

Index

Aborginal peoples. *See* Indigenous peoples
accommodation
  cultural/religious 7–8, 27, 37, 38–40,
    95
  dilemmas of 7, 27, 67, 95–6, 210
  linguistic 135–6, 137
  transformative 174–5, 189, 196–8,
    203
  also see multicultural accommodation
acculturation 335
activism, political 19, 49, 117, 118, 133
African American 168
Amish 34, 44, 46, 48
Arab Israelis 212
Arar, Maher 23 n5
assimilation 210, 239, 240, 242, 286
  cultural 91, 92
  linguistic 135, 137
associations
  autonomy of 324, 329, 330–2
  voluntary 10, 100, 159, 302, 323
authority
  coercive 159–60, 170
  group 235–6
  jurisdictional 274, 275, 280
  parental 333
  state 161
autonomy 25–6, 31, 35, 301, 314
  group 59, 121, 223, 240–1, 274
  individual 10–12, 34, 75–7, 79, 100–2,
    158, 161, 162, 165, 171, 211, 214,
    217, 218, 223–4, 228–9, 231
  also see self-governance
  political 309
  territorial 272, 292
  also see women

Bader, Veit 264
balkanization 33, 34, 210, 308
Barry, Brian 115, 120, 168, 175–6, 262,
  276, 320, 340
Benhabib, Seyla 342

Bohman, James 344, 346, 350, 361
Branch Davidians 48
Britain 118, 129
Brownlie, Ian 309
Buchanan, Allen 284 n10, 301
Buckley v. United Kingdom 299 n7,
  304

Callan, Eamonn 6
Canadian Constitution 252
Carens, Joseph 96, 98 n1, 98–9
Catalonia 139
Catholics 87, 164, 166–7, 175, 178, 186,
  259, 331
Chatterjee, Jyotsana 111
children 26, 34, 78, 120, 159, 161, 177,
  209–11, 216, 219, 223, 224–5, 286–7,
  332, 333, 333 n6
citizenship
  norms of 168, 180–1, 215, 225
  rights of 30–1, 33, 73, 319
Cohen, Joshua 351
colonialism 239, 255, 284
communities
  and hierarchy 236
  cultural 277
  gay/lesbian 184–6
  nature of 303, 312–13
  patriarchal 81, 83–5, 167, 192, 354
communitarians 319, 321
compromise 80, 116, 349–50, 357–8,
  359
consensus 345
consent 76–8, 232, 319, 332–3
constitutionalism 97–8
context 88, 125, 153–4, 239
  political 128, 133
context of choice 141–5, 146, 218, *also see*
  language and social mobility
contextual approaches 322
  historical 116, 117
cosmopolitanism 221

385